by Alan Brosnan and Duke Henry
with Bob Taubert

The stories of two former Kiwi SAS men in their continuing world-wide careers of adventure.

TO MARK,
PLEASURE WORKING WITH A MOTIVATED PROFESSIONAL.

"WHO DARES WINS"

Alan

NOV 13, 2003

Soldiering On
by Alan Brosnan and Duke Henry, with Bob Taubert

The stories of two former Kiwi SAS men in their continuing world-wide careers of adventure.

Published by TEES, Southaven, Mississippi
First printing, January 2003
ISBN 0-9626925-4-9

PRINTED IN THE UNITED STATES OF AMERICA

Cover photo, Harry and Julie Sargent

Contact
TEES USA
P.O. Box 1345
Southaven MS 38671
USA
1-800-950-8337
662-781-9423 (outside USA)
teestrng@bellsouth.net
http://www.tees-training.com

TEES Brazil
Caixa Postal 17709 — CEP 80.310-990
Curibita - PR - Brazil
55 41 269-1676
tees@netpar.com.br
http://www.teesbrazil.com.br

Contents

This book is dedicated —

To our wives, TeAo and Elaine — two incredible women who, along with our children, have shared this fractured lifestyle with us for so many years.

and

To our fellow SAS operators — the old and the bold, past and present, and the ones who haven't started yet. Good luck to all of you.

Introduction

Duke and Alan at Ruatoria's number one watering hole – Duke's own Blue Boar Tavern – Ruatoria, New Zealand, Christmas Day, 2001

What you have in your hands are two biographies in one book that relates the distinguished lives of two men who have dedicated themselves to fighting terrorism and injustice world wide, while at the same time making a respectable living pursuing their often risky vocations. Both men are quite appropriate for the New Millennium where "security" has become the new mantra for industrialized societies. Powerful nations now feel impotent as their cultures, freedoms, and laws are being used as weapons against them. As a result of this contemporary fanaticism, once more hard men and women have stepped to the front to shield their countries against this proliferating threat.

These two warriors are among the elite fraternity of contemporary specialist trainers that the world's operators seek out to develop their martial skills so that they may perform competently in this violent arena. Operators as well as trainers, our two brothers-in-arms continue to hone their own skills and increase their knowledge so that they can pass on contemporary, cutting-edge information to their charges.

This book does not only reveal the excitement and adventure they experienced as members of the New Zealand's Special Air Service and as current operators on police SWAT and private security teams, but in many ways is also a training manual for those who aspire to get into the "grand game" and test themselves in the cauldron of conflict.

Join us while slugging it out with the enemy in the jungles of South Vietnam, taking down drug pads in America's deep South, responding to violent and bloody prison riots in Brazil, and rubbing elbows with the rich and famous. Confront indigenous tribes on the warpath and remnants of the Taliban and other Islamic terrorists that have turned countries into shooting galleries. Take an intimate look into the Maori culture and life in New Zealand and its rural environs, where men are still men. In short, join Alan and Duke on their eclectic journey through lives filled with challenges and where they eagerly marched to the sound of the guns, wherever they could find the action.

— Bob Taubert

Lonely Days and Lonely Nights

Duke's Story

Growing up in Hawkes Bay, Taranaki, and Early Military Career 1949-1968

My name is Duke Henry. I was born in New Zealand in 1949. There was nothing about my background that predicted the direction my life would take in my later years. My dad was a quiet and unassuming little guy. He had served, as the majority of his generation did, in the Second World War. He was an airman in the Royal New Zealand Air Force (RNZAF), and after his initial training in Edmonton, Canada he returned to Guadalcanal, where he remained on active duty until the war ended. During this period, my Mum also became a member of the military by joining the newly formed Women's Army Corp as a signaller. Mum was always in style and impeccably dressed. The drab and ill-fitting issue Army uniforms really compromised her dress standards, because among the ladies they were hardly considered fashionable garments. Signaller June Yvonne Pope, in her own way, was a pioneer for women's equality among men in the armed forces. Even to this day, she still looks back upon that era with fond memories.

Duke with his mother, June, and brother, Neil – also a member of the SAS.

With New Zealand's long history of participating in just wars around the globe and my own family's commitment to patriotic causes, it was inevitable that I would serve my country in some manner and for me, it was through the military. I joined the army to escape the tedium of the normal middle class New Zealander's lifestyle. I was completely unaware of what the military had to offer but the chance to go to Vietnam and fight in a war irresistible to an 18 year old youth of the time.

My parents divorced when I was three and my Dad received custody of my elder brother Paul and I as part of the settlement. In turn, he moved back in with his mother and so we in turn came under Nan's protective wing and care. We did not miss out on much since Doris, my Grandmother, spoiled us rotten. Alex Henry, my Grandfather, also contributed by being a good and generous provider.

Somewhere along the line Dad remarried and we moved from heaven to hell. We relocated on a block of land in rural Havelock North. Dad was working for James Wattie's Canneries in the nearby city of Hastings. As a shift electrician, Dad would go to work early and come home late. This left my older brother and I to milk the house cow, feed the calf, the chickens, and complete other daily farm chores. Our new stepmother tried her best to instill her own brand of discipline, but unfortunately for her we had our own ideas. Paul wised up pretty quickly and conjured up these slick deals so he could stay in Hastings with Nan (Doris) and Pop. At one point, he even claimed to have an interest in learning the bagpipes just so he could be excused from having to do farm work. I swore at the tender age of seven that pulling cows tits and feeding calves was not for me. Our free time was further eroded when our new baby sister arrived. If that wasn't enough, my workload increased to include mowing lawns with the dreaded push mower, hanging numerous loads of washing, cutting firewood, slashing thistle and blackberry thickets, hauling the trash, and numerous other menial tasks. One afternoon, I broke and decided that enough was enough. I had only reached the age of reason, but I took direct action.

With Dad's old 12 gage double-barrelled shotgun loaded with a couple of rounds of buckshot, I took aim, and without too much hesitation, slapped one of the triggers. The round ignited and the barrel belched flame and smoke.The washing line, complete with baby's nappies and clothespin basket, was totally destroyed. As my awareness increased, I discovered that there was severe collateral damage in the form of two innocent roosters lying dead within the beaten (kill) zone. After this damaging display of juvenile frustration, I panicked big time, put the shotgun away, and hid in the woods until evening. I was scared to death and anxiously awaited the storm to burst when my parents got home. Amazingly, to this day they have never mentioned a word about the clothesline massacre in my presence.

After shirking his barnyard duties for all those years, Paul, at the age of sixteen, joined the Farm Cadet Corp. For the next five years he worked as a farm hand, which included stints on Canadian and European farms overseas. I never could figure my big brother out.

A walleyed, twenty-year-old stallion called Snowy and a black cocker spaniel named Whiskey were my best and only friends at that time. I was extremely shy, and coupled with the scruffy, overly large and hand-me-down clothes that I was obligated to wear, that caused me to develop a huge defensive chip on the shoulder. As a result, I presented a difficult challenge to my stepmother and schoolteachers. My lack of confidence certainly interfered with my advancement at school, and for me those early days are best forgotten. Nothing good came out of any of that troublesome period other than a burning desire to prove that I was better than others had perceived me to be.

At age eight, in an effort to acquire friends at school I fell into the trap that many kids are tempted with — "borrowing" money. My intentions were simple. I stole money from Dad's hideaway stash to spend among my schoolmates in an effort to purchase popularity. Not being the brightest burglar, I went for the big stuff and the next morning I hit the only shop in the village that sold mince pies and donuts with a one-pound note. With all my new found mates chomping on donuts and clutching three-penny bags of aniseed balls I went back to school quite chuffed and proud of myself. My newfound popularity lasted all of two hours. That sonofabitch shopkeeper who had accepted all my money promptly dobbed me in to the headmaster for possessing such a large amount of cash. A pound in those days was significant money, considering that with overtime, my dad collected only twenty pounds per week. In addition, a few of my classmates had stolen some pocket knives from the same store. This happened the same day as my shopping spree. While sitting outside the headmaster's office awaiting my fate, the local police sergeant arrived and after he was finished, it seemed that I had been charged with every crime committed within a ten mile radius within the last several years. As a young delinquent with very little experience, I quickly arrived at the conclusion that crime does not pay. In short order, I became the kid never to invite home. To my Havelock North schoolmates who let "Tramp" take the rap for their thievery, thanks guys, I owe you one.

In 1963 we moved from Hawkes Bay to the Taranaki Province. This was fortunate since my parents' relatives resided here. Several generations of the Williamson's, Penniall's, Henry's, Pope's, and Kidd's have all lived since the late 1890's under the mantle of Mt. Taranaki. My mother had remarried and was also living in New Plymouth, the Province's main city. At age fourteen, I left my Dad and moved in with my Mother. The chip on my shoulder was now larger than ever and I was definitely a troubled teenager. I suffered from low self-esteem, was a non-achiever at school, and I was totally dissatisfied with the life style I was leading. My future was anything but promising. Poor old Mum didn't deserve the anger and hostility that I bought with me and I was definitely on the brink of becoming an adolescent criminal. However, my fate was reversed when my younger Brother Neil joined the Army as a sixteen-year old Cadet Soldier.

When Neil returned home on his first leave, he was wearing the biggest and shiniest boots I had ever seen, and an ego to match. Along with one of his clubbie mates, Gibbo Gibson, he stormed into the house in full regalia and accompanying bravado. Granddad just about swallowed his false teeth. He was highly indignant that these two young pups would dare come inside the house with their spit-polished boots and headdress on, full of bullshit and bluster. Even then barely nine stone (125 lbs.) dripping wet and with only three months into his first year, Neil was totally convinced that one day he would become the regimental sergeant major of an infantry battalion.

He wasn't far wrong, and amongst several other notable achievements he was, at one stage, in the 1980's, the youngest warrant officer first class (WO1) in the N.Z. Infantry Corp.

Neil's military move was the final kick in the guts for me. I was determined to get into the armed forces. I had just turned 18 and was still living with my Mum and not enjoying it at all. The Vietnam conflict was underway and New Zealand was committed along with Australia, to increasing our military presence in the theatre. At the time I was working in a menswear shop and although I detested it, I had to make a living. However, one of the perks included the latest and trendy clothes. My work mates, Evan Mason and Jim King and I knocked around together. The Friday night parties were plentiful and the young women were starting to take the bait. Unfortunately for me, it still wasn't enough.

Earle Pope, my Grandfather, finally retired, sold his dairy farm in Ngaire and moved in with my Mum. I happened to be named after him and at times he could be a cantankerous old sod. With World Wars One and Two and the Great Depression, things had been extremely tough in his day. His wife had died many years earlier, so he relied on my Mum to do all his domestic chores, while he ruled the house. We sure had our moments and at the end of the day he continually scoffed at my intentions of joining the Army and going to Vietnam. However, without his constant cynicism I would probably never have had the balls to join up. Maybe this is nature's way of forcing the young to establish their independence. In later years I realised that Granddad was a fiercely loyal New Zealander and tremendously proud of three of his grandsons for serving in the countries Infantry Battalions. In 1968 though, Granddad and my needless confrontations seemed almost endless.

At the Army recruiting office in New Plymouth, I started the process by taking the required mental tests, with twenty other wannabes. To my surprise, I passed and after the Medical Board I was cleared to sign up. In those days, if you were eighteen you still required your parent's consent for overseas postings. Once again, my Mum became the stumbling block so I shot across and got Dad to sign the papers. I guess in retrospect he would have been secretly chuffed that two of his boys were doing the right thing. At that stage, Vietnam was not the controversial subject that it was about to become in the very near future. I looked around the recruiting office at Paul Bracegirdle and two other guys that were getting train tickets and meal vouchers. I don't know what happened to the majority of the other lads, but we were off to Waiouru and the great unknown. As we headed to the station, Granddad's kind and loving words were still ringing in my ears, "You'll be back. You won't be able to handle the kicks up the arse. Ill give you five minutes and you'll drop your bundle." Once again, Earle Pope's namesake proved him wrong, but only just.

Among all soldiers that have served in this country, the Waioru Military Camp has an infamous reputation. Both domestic and foreign troops that have experienced its harsh climate and the savage terrain that surrounds it also possess few fond memories of this shit hole. It is inconceivable to Kiwis, who truly believe that they live in God's country, that such a place can exist on paradise's soil. Most people don't even know it exists and I can see why. It was then New Zealand's only military garrison town and if you were not serving in the military and posted to it, you kept the hell away from the place. To many Kiwi's, Wellington is the backside of New Zealand. If that's true, then Waiouru is two hundred miles up it.

The train always arrived early in the morning and recruits were often required to walk the two miles to the camp's main gate. This gave us a little more time to do some soul searching and I could tell that some of the lads were struggling with their decisions, perhaps made in anger, or impulsively, as they dropped further and further to the rear.

Once in military harness, we suffered the normal threats and abuse that confront all young recruits on their march to becoming useful soldiers in the Army. Along with Mana Fong, Bill Keach, Kara Edwards, Titty Harris, Gomer Hughes, and Julie Tohirere, we negotiated icy parade grounds, forced marches over snow covered tussock hill country, and the dreaded hill country runs over Totem Mountain and other such craggy features. We fought tooth and nail in the barracks with the opposing sections over the use of the industrial floor polishers, washing machines and drying room space. We polished toilet bowls and scrubbed brass fittings on fire hydrants. Dust, spider webs, or wrinkles on drum tight bedrolls and blankets were punishable offences, and dirty laundry or lack of uniformity was almost considered treasonable. If summoned to the orderly room for some offense, you had to prove your innocence, which was always difficult. Prior to being marched in to the commanding officer (CO), the company sergeant major (CSM) would stand behind you and give some gentle advice, "You will not question the charging officer! You will reply to any questions with a *Yes Sir, No Sir,* or *I accept your punishment, Sir.* Do you fucking understand!" Orderly room front ups were usually over in minutes and it wasn't until I got a bit of time in that I realised that the officers appreciated a good yarn and appreciated inventiveness. In the end, you learned a lot about private soldier's rights, it was quite simple on basic training you didn't have any.

Going through an orderly room ordeal takes a little getting used to. The officer handling the charge report sat behind a desk while you were raced into the office by the CSM. You were required to stand at attention in front of the officer. With the CSM screaming commands at the back of your head from point blank range it's damn near impossible to stand without exhibiting at least a slight tremor of visceral fear. A mistake in protocol could result in the offender being marched out for the first offense and immediately marched back in for a new charge.

It's all-good stuff they say, but at the time most of us were focused on one thing and that was Vietnam. It was our *raison de'tre* and the combat arms elements were desperately trying to build up sufficient numbers for our recent commitment to the South East Asian theatre. Basic courses were being started every five weeks and running back-to-back. Every man jack of us that volunteered during that period did so knowing full well that he was going to serve in South Vietnam. As far as I was concerned, it was bloody brilliant.

The competition was fierce and if you failed any module you would be "back-squadded" to repeat the program. I had met some hard men in my young life, but nothing I couldn't handle, or so I thought. The junior non-commissioned officers (NCO) running the recruit courses destroyed that misconception in seconds. They had total control and power over our miserable lives. It didn't stop there; everyone in Waiouru Command seemed to have some control over our very spartan existence.

At the end of the first week's training, our first camp command parade, was a total disaster. It had to be a set up, because everyone who outranked us tore us new ass holes over our disastrous performance.

The whole garrison was on parade and the regimental sergeant majors (RSM) and CSM's were screaming and yelling commands. For us virgins, it was pure chaos. We rigidly stood in three ranks at attention, eyeballs glued to the front. We did not know how to move our toes in our boots or slowly relax the body muscles to prevent fainting. Cold sweat appeared on every brow as we tried to anticipate the next verbal barrage of commands. Any mistake was unthinkable and would incur incredible verbal abuse and possibly a dreaded charge report. Every now and then the clatter of a rifle followed by the thump of a body could be heard hitting the icy parade ground as blood drained from the brain and pooled in the feet. This was occurring before the commandant had started inspecting the troops. Eventually he appeared in front of our platoon with the RSM and several other barracudas cruising along in his wake. He stood ramrod straight in front of our Platoon Marker, gave him a menacing stare, and promptly charged him with some misdemeanour. In rapid-fire fashion, he moved to the next man and charged him as well. Things were not looking good for us. Exasperated, he spun about on his heel and blasted our young platoon commander. The commandant was livid and in no uncertain terms told our officer that the platoon's dress and turn out was totally unacceptable and to put the whole platoon on a charge report.

Totally shaken by this set back, the situation was made much worse when we received unsolicited but further attention from the RSM, the CSM, and the extremely pissed off platoon sergeants, respectively. When the platoon sergeant had given us his verbal reefing we doubled back to the barracks, but that was not the end of it. The junior NCOs waded in while we were braced in front of our bed spaces.

The entire platoon received a full week's confinement to barracks (CB). This meant that we were confined to the camp perimeter. We were not allowed to use any of the camp's leisure facilities and we had a stringent parade format to meet. This punishment was administered by the camp's RSM. For the next seven days we responded to the bugle and from six in the morning until eleven at night we paraded at the orderly sergeant's (OS) hut. This was in addition to our required daily routine of training, so we became pretty knackered in short order.

The parades varied, but they all involved considerable harassment and stress. They included squad runs in full field service marching order, rifle webbing and pack. The distances and speeds were at the discretion of the person in charge and heaven help you if the Orderly Sergeant turned out to be a physical training instructor or someone wearing Special Air Service (SAS) wings.

Pack drill on the parade ground was every bit as demanding as any physical training session. You are marched out to the center of the parade ground and the Ord. Sgt. starts bellowing drill commands. All drill was conducted in double quick time and if you fucked up it meant more charges or more time on the drill field.

Military change parades are a unique form of torture. Since we were issued numerous items of military dress, which were carefully ironed and pressed and conveniently hanging uniformly in our wardrobes, the Ord. Sgt. would nominate a form of dress and you would double back to the barracks and reappear wearing that uniform in the stipulated time. Failure to meet the timings or failing an inspection would incur additional charges, resulting in more confinement.

Two regular infantry force battalions composed our active duty combat infantry forces. One was based at the Burnham Military Camp, Christchurch and the other in Terendak Military Camp, Malaysia. Upon completion of our Basic All Arms course we enjoyed a short leave break. We returned and then began our ten-week Corps Training with the N.Z. based battalion.

By now we had built up a platoon and section identity that would provide the nucleus of our rifle company in South Vietnam. Corps training was simply that, a helter skelter paced training module over a three-month period in section, platoon, company, and battalion infantry tactics. We cross-trained as machine gunners, lead and cover scouts, signallers, and all the other related tricks of the trade that are necessary for survival. We patrolled the craggy peaks and hill country of Tekapo, in section and company formations. Once this was deemed sufficient we became familiar with the close country and jungle tactics that had been designed and perfected by Kiwi infantryman in the Malaysian and Borneo campaigns. We stripped, assembled, and fired all the weapons systems in use by our forces. Every infanteer carried the reliable 7.62 x 51 MM NATO FN Self-Loading Rifle (SLR), eight 20-round magazines, and spare bandoleers of ammo. Platoon commanders, platoon sergeants, section commanders, and signallers were all armed with U.S. 5.56 x 45 MM M-16 rifles instead of pistols.

In 1968, winter warfare gear was extremely basic. We had small WWII canvas 08 packs that were totally unsuitable for the task, two woollen blankets and a canvas poncho. This was wrapped around your blankets and lashed as a bedroll to your pack. Sometime during this period the army began to issue sleeping bags. The small, lightweight half tents, or shelter halves, were worth their weight in gold and were the only relevant and functional luxury we had. On our belt order we carried a butt pack, two water bottles, canteen cup, utility pouches, two magazine pouches, and a bayonet frog for the SLR bayonet.

New Zealanders did not wear helmets in Vietnam and preferred the floppy bush hat. Its irregular shape and profile was far more suitable for jungle operations than the steel pot mandated for U.S. forces. We wore drill-green, cotton uniforms with ankle boots and gaiters. WWII era woollen jerseys, leather jerkins, woollen caps comforter, and a set of rough textured woollen long johns completed our issue. It was damn difficult to carry all this kit dry, but when it got wet, forget it. No one complained, because nothing better was available and, democratically, everyone suffered in the bush. During winter training, most days and nights were spent totally soaked to the skin and we would lie on the snow covered ground, shivering and gibbering in platoon ambush positions while wrapped up in our sodden blankets. Nothing remained dry in our canvas packs, so we sucked it up and prayed for daylight so we could get moving again.

Tapa Dickson became our new Platoon Sergeant and he unknowingly became one of my first mentors. He was a short, nuggety Maori in his mid 30's, extremely soft spoken and was more than a match for any of his young soldiers. Furthermore, he was a former member of the NZSAS and was held in awe by us because of the unit's mysterious reputation. He never had to raise his voice, but issued quiet verbal commands augmented with a piercing stare. Not that he gave a rat's arse, but the boys developed a deep affection for him as well. His ability to mix it up with the boys on a lost weekend and fall out of the back of an RL Bedford truck unscathed reinforced his status with us. He was a classic example of the SNCO of those days. Sergeant Dickson always led by example and always from the front.

In those early days, questioning anything was sinful and punishments were liberally handed out to the complainers. A bang to the eye, or rap on the skull from the Section Commander, or the Platoon Sergeant's left or right hooks were usually all that was required. We never considered this to be bullying or sadistic and realized that its purpose was to get us to react quickly and efficiently to situations that required it. We were training for war and within a year we would be actively involved in a confrontation that was proving to be somewhat difficult for the Americans and their allies. For the first six months of our Basic recruit and Corps training we lived in eight and twelve man rooms and privacy did not exist. This is not a cost-effective move, but is designed to further develop unit bonding and cohesiveness.

At the conclusion of our corps training, we deployed to Fiji for a company exercise. As always, the training was intense, but most importantly the heat and humidity was a great conditioner for the conditions we were going to be subjected to in South East Asia. Fiji and particularly its people are a wonderful experience. As an eighteen-year old serviceman it was like going to another world and in many respects it was. Little did I realize at this juncture that I would be forming lengthy relationships with their outstanding soldiers and friendly islanders. Fijians are a truly wonderful race of warriors and they are a tremendously strong and physically imposing people. I have soldiered and worked with many Fijian servicemen over the last 30 years and I cannot speak of them highly enough. They are an integral part of N.Z.'s military's history and have served in the Commonwealth's forces since WWII.

As our training progressed, some of my mates had slipped by the wayside and had been reassigned. Others had been medically downgraded or held back for retraining. Only one was required to take a rare early discharge because of a mental breakdown. Initial enlistments were for three, five, and eight years and you were locked in to the day, hour, and minute.

We arrived in Malaysia at the height of the 1969 riots. The killings that occurred between the Chinese and Malays were horrific. This racial war was inconsequential to most of us, although Mana Fong and Charlie Lee, both Maori with Chinese ancestry, may have felt otherwise. Our only, but major, problem was getting laid within the curfew timings. The "Hong Kong Bibles" (old style, hand-written porn booklets) had been circulating through the barracks and we all wanted some of that fabled Asian pussy. The plane's wheels were barely on the tarmac in Singapore and we were anticipating our introduction to the "Knock Shops" and bar girls of the infamous Terendak Strip and Malacca City. As I stepped off the aircraft, I didn't know that at the time, but Cyrano's bar was about to become my new home for the next six months.

The infamous "Kiwi Flying Nines" promptly loaded us into their Bedford's for our "express" road trip to Terendak Military Camp. Road rules in Malaya and Singapore were quite simple and in fact, there was only one — the biggest vehicles have all rights of way. Our driver thoroughly embraced these road regs, and somewhere just beyond Johore Baru he gave us a graphic demonstration.

Up ahead of us, a local villager on a pushbike laden with a small haystack of cut grass was struggling to climb the hill. The speed and turbulence generated by the narrowly missing convoy of Bedford trucks caused him some concern for his precarious load as he wobbled awkwardly along. Totally pissed off, he made the big mistake of screaming some Chinese obscenities and shaking his fist at the convoy. The Flying Nine Transport Platoon had this drill down pat and upon coming abreast of the blaspheming cyclist we slowed down. The driver nodded to his co-driver, and like a speed brake, he swung open his door. Fortunately, the large bundle of grass absorbed most of the impact but it was enough to catapult the protesting cyclist into the rubber trees and beyond.

Malaysia cab drivers were suicidal and they passed everything in front of them at any speed. Blind corners, and like Dave Marshall's practice, stop signs were completely ignored. They incessantly honked their horns. They leaned on them when they wanted to pass, they activated the honk when they wanted another car to do something and I swear they talked to each other by bleeps. In N.Z., blowing your horn at somebody usually indicated extreme displeasure and acts of road rage against the offender were common. They were also extremely thrifty, and while going down hill they took advantage of gravity and turned off engine and lights to theoretically save power and fuel. I became convinced that these guys must have been the offspring resulting from the union between local women and Japanese Kamikaze pilots during their WWII occupation of Malaya.

Terendak was one of the best camps I have ever been stationed at. In 1969, the British Garrison's Camp was also home to Australian, New Zealand, Gurhka, and Malaysian military units. It was extremely well policed and controlled. For a young soldier it provided us with almost every amenity. Low cost beer was available at the beachfront serviceman's clubs and we couldn't be happier.

As lowly private soldiers we were barely one step above the company's native boot boys and about two steps above the Dhobi Wallahs that were employed to hand wash all military equipment and clothing for a small monthly fee. This inexpensive system of labor eliminated all the tedious, time wasting duties of washing, ironing, and starching uniforms.

This also gave us almost unlimited free time and we made the most of it. At the end of the day's activities and particularly after payday, we would rocket off to Terendak's notorious bars and brothels and get rat-assed drunk. The next morning, I would fall out of bed, shit, shave, and shower and then slip into the immaculate uniform of the day and front up. On days when funds were low, we would loiter around the camp's clubs trying to bludge drinks off each other and generally agonize over the probability that another trooper with a fatter wallet was slipping one into your favourite bar girl during your absence.

As I matured in the military, the training began to become more easily assimilated. The drills that had been hammered into us over the last six months were now second nature skills. Nevertheless, we still retained our new-boy-on-the-block status and were commonly called "Milk Bottles," because of our pale extremities and the fact that we remained untested as newly minted rifle company members. Many of the NCOs were veterans of Malaya, Borneo, and Vietnam and proudly wore their campaign ribbons on their chests. On parade, our naked uniforms stood out like illuminated highway signs and we felt that we were not yet worthy enough to be in the presence of the beribboned command.

In Malaya, we acquired a new platoon commander and platoon sergeant. Young Stan Kidd was not the typical Kiwi lieutenant. He was gregarious, fairly loud, and, at times, boisterous in his demeanor. He was popular, had our interests at heart, and because he was a "Clean Skin" like the rest of us, we didn't give him much opportunity to demonstrate his potential. However, Sergeant Dave Heywood was an entirely different kettle of fish. At first glance he appeared to be a fairly ordinary looking guy with goofy ears and a funny, nasal voice. He didn't openly exhibit the menacing glare or hint of malice that Sergeant Dickson did. As we soon found out, we were in for a big surprise. There was no doubt that Lieutenant Kidd was the boss, but his authority was dramatically reinforced by his new platoon sergeant. Sergeant Heywood literally ran us into the deck at every conceivable opportunity. He was a fitness fool years before it became fashionable. It was only when he stripped down for physical training that we could see the little fucker was deceivingly well built and he could run, jump, and fight with the best of them. He swore like his life depended on it. "Awww riiight you fucken cunts," was his favorite opening statement. Surprisingly, when away from the military environment he was a quietly spoken and humble gentleman. The icing on the cake for the 2 Platoon, was, of course, the SAS winged dagger sewn onto his dress uniform. Dave was one of the best and he became a good friend and mentor in the years to come.

The most hated members of the Terendak establishment were the Garrison Military Police (GMP) that was composed mostly of British "Red Caps," with a smattering of Aussie and Kiwi provosts to augment their ranks. They were bastards to a man, and along with the good old Aussies, they were the Kiwi infantryman's favorite sparring partners. Even though we were traditional rivals, the ANZAC spirit never wavered in Malaysia and many a Kiwi and Aussie joined forces to do battle on the sports field, bars, and back alleys against our Scotch, Irish, and British brethren. We had our priorities all squared away in those days, and both on and off the sports field competition among commonwealth forces was fierce. No outsider dared to trespass into another battalion's drinking den unless he was prepared to go twelve rounds. The GMP's controlled the "gates to freedom" that led to the delights awaiting us on the Terendak strip and in the bars in Malacca. But we Kiwi's controlled the rest, or so we thought.

The Kiwi battalion lines were pretty substantial. Parade grounds, barrack quarters, officer and SNCO's messing facilities and an excellent selection of rugby fields. To further keep us in line we had our own Battalion and Regimental Police (RP) entities. Assisting were the Orderly Officer, orderly sergeant and a quarter guard of JNCO's and privates. This involved a twenty-four-hour assignment and one that we all detested. We were so tightly scrutinized that with all this martial force arrayed against us; it was pretty damn easy to get locked up in the cells. These people all reported to the RSM. He was God and nothing moved without his knowledge or permission.

RSM Brighouse was a tough old boy, and in his starched British military issue uniform he looked like a green version of Sesame Street's "Big Bird." However, his skinny and wiry body and knobbly knees gave no indication of this old boy's potential. RSM Brighouse had served in the original NZSAS and was not a man to fuck with. He had acquired a speech impediment and it was amusing to hear him bark, "Shettle down Sholdiers," while on battalion parade. Speech impediment or not, he had us firmly under control and many a man spent a night in the cells because the RSM felt that his drill while on the parade ground wasn't up to speed.

One off-pay weekend as we were moping around the club playing darts and drinking cans of detestable Anchor and Tiger beer, Dave W. came up with one of his remarkable revelations. He bet anybody in the bar that he could run around the six rugby fields in some incredibly fast time. We all took the bait and pooled our meager resources to purchase the prize, a carton of Tiger beer. Because of our incredible generosity, we decided to compromise with Dave and started sampling the prize before it had been won. There was no way Dave could achieve this feat and he knew it. Even when faced with the impossible, Dave was no quitter and drank on until his alcohol level reached his required standard for maximum performance. He confidently belched, stood up, stripped off all his clothes and with a quick nod to the time keeper took off. Initially, he didn't do too badly. He galloped past the RP hut at a fairly respectable clip, but, unfortunately, in doing so, he picked up a couple of running companions, Corporals Harry Jellick and Paul Sciascia, both wearing RP uniforms and spit polished boots, fell in behind this obviously fleeing and perverted felon. Down the main road he sprinted and the RP's had no prayer of catching naked Dave because their starched uniforms and parade boots heavily encumbered them. I don't know who vectored on whom, but Dave's bare ass closed rapidly with two young, female British dependants walking along the footpath from the opposite direction. His bizarre appearance rendered them speechless. They couldn't believe what they were seeing, but they couldn't or wouldn't avert their eyes. This proved to be Dave's undoing. As he passed the ladies, all Sergeant Heywood's fitness training suddenly turned to jelly. This gave Harry and Paul enough of a pause to nail him and they all ended up in a sweaty tangle of arms, legs, and a solitary set of hairy bollocks.

He spent the night in the guardhouse with a blanket as his only companion, nursing a few bruises and a raging hang over. He lost the bet, but it was an example of the outrageous behavior and fun we engaged in to break up the monotony of garrison life. There was no television or other such electronic entertainment readily available on base and in those days, it was all hands on and self-generated fun. Dave was quite a character, and along with Gannet Mullins, Scrubber Ryalls, and Bill Keach, they made our time in Terendak anything but tedious.

Terendak camp was self-contained, and support groups, such as a helicopter squadron, were also tenants on the base. Lush jungle and rubber plantations completely surrounded the place, making it an ideal training facility for jungle operations.

On a typical day, we would parade as a company in the morning, take our anti-malaria tablets and account for all hands. We would either move to the numerous weapons ranges, or head for the jungle areas to perfect our bush skills. Everything we needed was conveniently located and could be accessed by foot. One aspect of the indispensable training that had been developed by the Battalion Training Wing were the presentations given by the rifle company that had just returned from a year in Vietnam of their actual contacts and incidents they had experienced. The would be dressed in authentic uniforms and weapons and often in the very position or role they had during the original contact, Sgt. Sam Christie and his boys would walk and talk us through the re-enactments. We were totally engrossed and well aware that men had died and military reputations were won and lost in bringing these lessons home to us. We would then move off in section, platoon or company formations into the neighbouring ulu and, under their supervision, practice and perfect the skills and techniques they brought to us.

Weapons skills were also paramount to our survival. We were required to qualify with the previously mentioned SLR, the General Purpose Machine Gun, WWII British Bren Gun, now chambered for 7.62 X 51 NATO, M79 40 MM grenade launcher and the light weight, but lethal, M-16 rifle. I preferred the heavier SLR, because it was capable at any range and the heavy bullet bucked the bush better than the 5.56. However, within its optimum operational range, the M-16 was devastating on soft tissue. For us peons the weapon selection was not a choice and other than the Command element and Signallers we all had an SLR as personal weapon.

All facets of training were included. Weapons stoppages, malfunctions, immediate action drills, known distance, close country, and jungle lane shoots were only part of the lexicon of combat. It was sinful to fail any of this instruction and your penance could well mean your trip to Vietnam would be delayed up to six months until you achieved acceptable levels of performance. Punishment for habitual failures could be severe and having a negligent discharge with a weapon would cost the miscreant 21 days in the cells automatically.

Lieutenant Kidd got the word and he was called up as a replacement officer for Vietnam. Understandably, he was pretty pleased by this, but we were bloody envious. As a farewell gesture, Stan wanted a beach BBQ with his boys. He was the boss and, more importantly, he was fronting up for the food and drink, so we all enthusiastically supported the idea. Dave Heywood sorted out the details and we ended up on a beautiful Malaysian beach miles from civilization, drinking Anchor beer and generally getting rat assed drunk. Stan was doing his best to entertain the group with his guitar. For some obscure, alcohol driven reason, several of the boys had dug a six-foot deep "grave" in the sand earlier in the morning. I am not sure if it was Stan's choice of music or song or the content of his farewell speech, but suddenly the gravediggers rioted and our fair leader ended up head-first in the hole with his guitar. Sergeant Dave took serious exception to this and restored order and respect for Stan by quickly distributing a few uppercuts and left hooks among the crew until we all settled down. Our leader's dignity was restored but the party was over. Lieutenant Kidd departed for his destiny and within the week we had a replacement officer.

[Six months later, while serving with Victor 4 Company in SVN, Lieutenant Stan Kidd was killed in action. This incident occurred only weeks before the conclusion of his tour of duty.]

Lieutenant Bobby Upton was a damn big bastard and looked like a fucken front row prop for the All Blacks rugby team. Standing in front of us with his hands on his hips, we privately wished that good old Stan Kidd were there instead. Bobby gave us a stirring talk and we all quickly realised that times had indeed changed. Later on, we found out that Bob's father had been a Warrant Officer in the infantry and his family had a tradition of military service.

Whiskey 3 Company was sent up to the Cameron Highlands of Malaysia, where the altitude was higher and the climate considerably cooler, for a week of health and recreation. I think it was for a training wind-down, but it also provided us with a welcome opportunity to operate without being bathed in sweat. It was a sound medical decision and many of us managed to heal and get rid of numerous lurgies that the tropics can inflict on you.

Somehow Sergeant Dave didn't get the message and the change in scenery was merely an opportunity to charge up and down more bloody big hills. Within the first week, we came to hate the road around the golf course with a vengeance.

Back in Terendak, the training continued without letup. One of the quarterly requirements was the ten-mile, Battle Efficiency Test (BFT). In Terendak the BFT were administered by the PTI's and they were conducted in the general camp area. We would front up early before the dreaded sun came out and pound along the red clay back roads until we ended up at the six-foot wall, rope climb, and long jump. On this particular morning, Ben Tenamu, with most of the platoon and I, fronted up reeking of alcohol and suffering from megaton hangovers. For some reason, Sergeant Dave was not the least sympathetic and after a vicious ass chewing, we (buuurp) got underway. We ran as a platoon and that was the end of the story. No one dared fall out with Sergeant Dave hovering over us.

We commenced our Tactical Approach to the Battlefield (TAB) by mixing the pace with run, walk, run segments until it was over. Unfortunately, our stocky Platoon Commander had only been in-country for a couple of weeks or had not had sufficient time to acclimatise. After several miles, he was in a bad way and started to buckle. Ben and I latched onto him and under a glare of disapproval from Sergeant Dave, we assisted our boss to the finish line — albeit at a walking pace and an hour behind the main body. It was in the traditional Western military spirit of leave no one behind that motivated us and it was a great, but painful way to sober up.

Our Malaya Jungle training had reached its conclusion, and most of the guys had made the grade. We were confident that we were prepared mentally and physically for the real thing.

During this period of preparation, Sergeant Dave decided to get married, and for some mysterious reason, Peaches Brown, Rex Ryan, and I were invited to the Chinese wedding reception. Dave's new wife, Susan, and her in-laws were Chinese and from Kuala Lumpur. We sat down and tried our best to behave during the celebration and Dave, uncharacteristically, was smiling and in a friendly and relaxed mood. Although we had spent six raucous months in Asia and had considerable bar and brothel experience, we were completely ignorant of the lifestyle and customs of the majority of the Malaysian and Chinese citizenry. As the myriad assortment of food arrived we heaped our plates with these delicacies, but ate carefully and like gentlemen under Dave's approving gaze. Little did we realize that a Chinese wedding meal consisted of up to twelve courses and by about the fourth, I was busting. As I looked around the festive setting, I noticed that my friends weren't far behind. This was my first and last Chinese wedding.

Weeks later, we sent our advance party to Vietnam to prepare for the arrival of the main body. Our platoon representative was Private Rex "Charley West" Ryan. He was a miniature Dave Heywood, incredibly fit, an excellent boxer, almost complete teetotaller, and top soldier. He was from the Deep South of New Zealand and a typical Bluff Islander of Maori and European extraction. Rex was a couple of years older than most of us, but with his quick wit and likeable stories he became a great mate and loyal friend. Unfortunately, every few months or so, with the help of copious cans of Anchor beer, his alter ego, "Charlie West," would emerge. On the eve of his farewell, we all went on the town, and in short order Charlie was in fine form and going strong. Through the haze of time, I still recall the hilarious commotion Charlie created at "Maylees" house of ill repute when he tried to drag a water buffalo by its nose ring and rope into the building. The next morning, Sergeant Dave had to make a pilgrimage to the holding cells to collect his young protégé. It was all hushed up, but we all knew that Charlie West had also punched out a few of the British military police in the process and, still belligerent, cold cocked a couple more when they let him out of the cells. This boy was ready for Vietnam and Charlie became our platoon hero, and even if some of the night's events may have been exaggerated with time, the legend of Charlie West continued to grow.

A couple of weeks later, we departed Terendak and the general feeling was one of immense relief and satisfaction. I couldn't wait to get to SVN.

Like all Kiwi rifle companies that preceded us, Whiskey 3, unlike U.S. forces, deployed to Vietnam as a complete unit. This system, over the centuries of commonwealth combat, has proven to be successful in maintaining unit cohesiveness and identity. The training we received was as good as you could get and our discipline in the field was unquestionable. Typically, we were not too responsible back in garrison, and like Private soldiers in other armies, required a big stick and short leash.

Major Evan Torrance, our Company Commander, was an extremely popular leader and respected by his company. His ability to handle men was a particular skill that he appeared to possess in abundance.

Captain Jim Brown was his Second in Command (2IC), as an ex-ranker (Mustang), he was well aware of the tricks and angles all young soldiers try from time to time.

Bill Blair, Bobby Upton, and Circles Fisher were our three Platoon Commanders.

Pinky Macintosh, our CSM, wore the dreaded SAS badge and was one of the unit's original members. Sergeant's Denny King, Dave Hayward, and Joe Yandall ably supported him. They were all well qualified to lead this new band of Kiwi brothers.

The night before we left we celebrated with the rest of the battalion and for some, we knew it would be a final farewell. Poor old Bill Keach, roommate and good friend since our basic recruits course, had a bit of a scuffle with another soldier and stuffed his leg by falling in a storm drain and, consequently, missed the next day's flight.

[Bill continued with his streak of bad luck and after only weeks in-country, while serving with Victor 4, he was wounded in a heavy contact and sent home. Sadly, he drowned in a boating mishap shortly after his repatriation to New Zealand.]

For us, the Vietnam Experience was about to begin; I couldn't get there quick enough.

A Southerner By Birth

Alan's Story

My Youth and Early Military Experiences

It was January 1977 and quite warm. I was sweating puddles and I wasn't sure if it was the weather, or because I had never flown before. I was seventeen years old and I was about to take my first plane trip, which in fact, was also my first "overseas" journey. I was flying from Dunedin, my hometown, which is situated in the southern part of the South Island of New Zealand, to Waiouru, the Army's central North Island recruit training depot. I landed in Wellington, the country's capital, and there to meet me was an enlisted Army driver who was probably a private, but to a wide-eyed bumpkin who had never been away from home before he may as well have been a general. He was dressed in a smart looking uniform and I imagined that I would be an exact replica in a couple of days as I proudly stood in front of the barrack room's full length mirror prior to fronting up on my first parade as a soldier. However, from there it was off to the train station where I was herded, along with all the other recruits, mostly from the "mainland," onto the Northerner Express train for the overnight journey to Waiouru.

The train was an old smoker and it belched, sneezed, rattled, bumped, and groaned under the weight of its animate and inanimate cargo. In spite of our fatigue, anxiety and the lurching tons of steel prevented most of us from getting any shut-eye. Slowly raising one eyelid, I noticed that it was 0030 hours when the grizzled old conductor came through the carriage and began kicking us all in the guts. I guess he had performed this duty thousands of times before. He sure looked like a salty old war dog that had been through it himself, maybe thirty-eight years ago on his way to North Africa.

As I landed on the station platform, I rubbed the fragmented sleep from my eyes and I slowly became aware of the other twenty or so recruits looking around as nervously as I was. All of a sudden, lightning and thunder struck the station in the form of, "Get your fucking asses over here at the double." It was a God-awful scream that came from my left and I was too afraid to look. "At the double"! What the hell does that mean, I asked myself as if there were two of me? I quickly figured it out as nineteen other young dickheads flew past me at a high rate of knots. Oh shit! There to meet us was the biggest, blackest, and nastiest looking Maori I had ever seen in my life. In actuality, he was only the third one that I had ever seen, so that made it all the more frightening. Fierce warriors, the warlike Maoris are predominately from the northern parts of our country. God knows why, but I guessed it has something to do with the snow down south. We had one Maori guy at our school, and my first girlfriend was also a Maori, so I was not a complete alien to this race of martial people.

Standing in front of us was our "Oh-Lord," Platoon Sergeant Rolly Horopapara, a highly decorated veteran of the Vietnam War. He could not have been more that five feet, eight inches in height, but he completely offset this modest stature with his massive chest and biceps that bulged and strained to get at you from his highly starched green shirt that told me in no uncertain terms, "Don't fuck with this dude." We were literally blown into formation by his commands and I could visibly discern shaking bodies among the wankers in the first ranks. "Ten hut!" This might as well as been Swahili, because Military lingo was a foreign language to most of us. Sergeant Horopapara, obviously disgusted, threw his clipboard down and bellowed, "Shit birds, attention means look straight ahead, lock your fucking heels together, and put your fucking finger tips along the fucking seams of your fucking trousers. Do you understand? OK! Let's try it again ladies! Ten hut! Damn it! Ten hut means attention! Do you read me? It looks like this! Do this! OK! Right turn! Forward march!" With veins popping out of his massive neck, Sergeant Horoparpara turned beet red and remained that way until we were all safely aboard the military bus that would transport us to his special kingdom where he and others like him were gods. As an aside, Sergeant Horopapara's "recruit manner" may remind some of you Yanks of your first day at Parris Island, or San Diego recruit depots. New Zealand and the United States Marine Corps have a close and very affectionate relationship that stems form WWII. The Marines used New Zealand as a staging area for the Pacific campaign and a number of those that had survived, returned, married and settled down here. As a result, some of the Marine Corp's Es Sprit rubbed off on our military.

My older brother Mike had joined the army two weeks before I did and it was several more long weeks before I was able to make contact with him again, even though his recruit barracks were right next door to mine. It was quite frustrating, because I could see him marching around and frequently spotted him from a distance in the chow hall. I really missed him like I never imagined I would, because even though I have never experienced homesickness, I longed for the day we could sit down and swap stories. It was no big deal when I saw Mike off at the airport, but I did notice that it was weighing heavily on my Mum, and I knew that she was worrying about me leaving in two weeks time. A quiet woman, it was pretty traumatic to lose two of her four kids so suddenly. My younger brother Garry followed suit a few years later. After doing a couple of years as a soldier, Garry became an officer in the New Zealand Army, and as a Major graduated from the United States Army's Command and General Staff College. As an infantry officer, Garry has risen to the rank of Lieutenant Colonel. I have followed his career with great interest and I am extremely proud of what he has achieved. He is currently serving as the commander of the New Zealand contingent as part of the United Nations Force in the Sinai. The same goes for Mike. After completing his initial enlistment he decided that Army life wasn't for him. He went on to become one of Dunedin's best and most respected publicans. His business partner was Lance Pearson, a former New Zealand cricket player of considerable fame. As a result of this partnership, Mike became part owner of several pubs and clubs throughout the province of Otago. As the second eldest of four siblings, I was born 13 months after him. He and I remained extremely close until after basic training, when we went our separate ways.

Dunedin, my birthplace is a small city of approximately 120,000 inhabitants, which lies on the east coast of the South Island. The city is most noted for its great university, our national social lubricant, Speights beer, and our famous Otago rugby team. By age four, there isn't a boy in New Zealand that doesn't strap on his first pair of rugby boots and I was no different. Being involved with our national sport was all part of growing up anywhere in New Zealand. There wasn't a Saturday for the next 25 years that I wasn't involved in the game in one capacity or another.

As Catholic kids, we ran the gantlet of Nuns and Brothers together. Like a family fire team, we played sports, socialized, chased girls, fought, and protected each other. In those days, the Catholic schools were co-ed up till the age of 11. After that, we were segregated from each other and it was agonizing. The only time we mixed was during the annual folk dancing outing! No wonder we Catholic boys were such bad little bastards. My primary school (grades 1-5) years were spent at St. Francis Xavier, literally getting whipped into shape by the Nuns. Intermediate grades 6-7 were spent at St. Edmunds, where I got my first taste of behavior modification from Brother Sullivan and his team of heavy-handed brethren. Under the tutelage of these men, I also acquired, almost as a matter of survival, the martial discipline of boxing. The school was fortunate to have had obtained the services of Vince Rowe, a legendary boxing trainer from Dunedin, and his extremely able assistant, Bruce Bond. The personal need to obtain a self-defense skill arose for one simple reason — Mike and I were getting our

My parents, Ray and Alice, with (from left) – Garry, myself, and Michael – Dunedin, New Zealand, 1964

asses whipped every day on the way home from school. After we were dropped off at the bus stop, our normal route home was via 365 steps that led down to our street. Unfortunately, this was also a primary route home for many of the kids who went to Kaikouri Valley High School. These guys were older and bigger than us and did not have a lot of good feelings for anyone who supported the Pope. Once we reached the top of the steps, we saw one of two things. Either the steps were empty, which meant that we ran like fuck down them to get to the house, or sitting there smoking was a bunch of local dickheads waiting for fools like us to run the gauntlet. If the latter situation was the case, we either charged right in and took the pain or we could turn around and add an extra 30 minutes to our walk by taking the alternate route. As scared as we were, turning tail wasn't the manly thing to do, so down we went. It was always better if Mike and I were together, because he was the biggest and always went first. While they were working him over, I would usually try to make a hasty and cowardly exit.

However, as my confidence and my boxing skills grew, this was about to change for the better. Now most of my weekends during the winter, were spent travelling around the Province fighting. As a result of this hardening process I actually looked forward to my trips home from school, because the "worm" had definitely turned. After whipping a couple of asses, word got around that "these two Mickey Doolans" (Catholics) were good to go.

Secondary school (grades 8-11) was hell on wheels. Once again, the

Private Alan Brosnan – recruit class 137, January, 1977

Private Michael Brosnan – recruit class 136, Waiouru, New Zealand, January, 1977

good Brothers attempted to impose order and discipline on us out of control pubescent bastards, who at this "tender age" were only interested in girls, fighting, boozing, and rugby in that order.

For many of us they did not quite succeed, and it did not surprise me as the years progressed to learn that a former classmate of mine was in jail, had been killed, or had died from a drug overdose. It was a tough crew brought on by fairly hard times. Like many physically oriented kids my main motivation for remaining in school was rugby. I loved it with a passion that nearly rivaled my interest in women, which would plague me throughout my life until I found and married my wife, Elaine. I was fortunate to represent my high school's premier rugby team from my freshman year, as well as having the honor of representing my Province of Otago. It was 1976, I was seventeen and as fate would have it, I broke my ankle during a game and that was it for me. The season was over and as far as I was concerned, so was school. Pissed off, I immediately quit school and took various laboring jobs till I was old enough to join the Army, six months later. My first job was a short-term contract that required under pinning and strengthening the town hall. My school-mate, Steve Morris, hooked me up with this and it certainly got me into shape for the months to come. A front-end loader would dig a flush hole down the side of the building approximately 5-6 meters deep. Steve and I would then be sent down there on a bucket with a jack-hammer and shovel. One of us would work the jack-hammer and dig the dirt out the required distance under the building while the other frantically shoveled it into the bucket where it was hauled up and removed. Because of the difficulty and strength required to

Private Garry Brosnan (now Lieutenant Colonel RNZIR) – top recruit of class 186, Waiouru, August, 1982. I was fortunate enough to have had my name inscribed on the same shield five years earlier.

work the jack-hammer, we swapped out after each bucket load. Once we had dug in and leveled our hole, the experts would come down to insert and weld the supporting I beams in place. This continued until the building was completely reinforced. Being winter, it was extremely wet, cold, and miserable, but that didn't matter as we were getting NZ$100.00 per week and that was a fortune for a young man. Twenty dollars went to Mum for board and the rest went to having a good time. My next job was with the Electricity Department laying cable all over the city. Again, my part was to dig the ditches so the experts could lay the cable. I became an expert at "digging in," an indispensable survival skill in the military. Regardless, both jobs assisted in preparing me physically for the months to come. After leaving school, I continued to keep in touch with my close mates from that era. Steve became a top publican in Dunedin, Mark Holmes evolved as a master chef, Ricky Michael turned out to be a top-notch salesman, and David McBride moved to Auckland to marry and pursue his dreams.

My younger brother, Garry, came along about five years after me and it was great bringing him up and coaching him in the evil ways that Mike and I had mastered. In the end, he was too smart for us and adopted a very sensible and responsible lifestyle. Maybe that's the difference between

Ruperts (officers) and enlisted personnel. They are less prone to pursue the forbidden things in life that are so tempting and so damn much fun. And, if you manage to get away with it, the feeling of satisfaction can be intoxicating. This is how risk takers are developed, or the so-called type "T" personality. Give them a brain, so they can appreciate a complex situation and they will epitomize the "Dare," in "Who Dares Wins."

My younger sister, Judy, was someone I never really got to know until later in life. When I joined the army, she was only about nine, but since 1985 she has played a huge part in my life, both professionally and socially. While I was in the SAS, she moved up to Auckland, New Zealand's largest city and home to the Unit, to experience life in the fast lane. Elaine, my wife, and I had just bought a house, but rather than live in it, we decided to stay in Army housing and rent it to Judy and some friends from Dunedin. Over the years, Colleen, Janet, Mary Jane, and Kaye were to experience the rigors of army socializing first hand. I am sure it was an experience that will stick in their minds for years to come. The day I left to join the army, Judy cried fiercely. From then till about age thirty, she would always cry whenever I came home for a holiday or left again. Our bond has remained extremely strong to this day, but it was with great regret that I missed her wedding to Neil in 1997. I had been away for twenty years and I believe that Judy understood. Alice and Ray, my Mum and Dad, were the best parents that one could wish for. We got our fair share of ass whippings from Dad, but truth be known, we probably deserved much more. As a young boy, I remember living in a grocery store that Dad managed, but was probably owned by Ollie and Dave, his parents. I guess that didn't suit him, because the remainder of his life was devoted to managing hotels. What a hard life that must have been and I guess it exacted a heavy toll from him. Eventually he became very ill and spent many years in and out of hospitals, before losing his bat-

My sister, Judy, with husband, Neil, at my home – Walls, Mississippi, May, 2000

tle with cancer the day after Christmas, 1995. Mum remains to this day to be great at what she does and I look forward to my trips home to get spoiled the way that only she can do. Her caring commitment to her family, friends, and anyone who happens to just stroll in for a cup of tea can never be disputed. Mum's chosen profession was as a primary school teacher. By the time I reached intermediate school (grade 7-8), Mum was employed as a music teacher at our school. Additionally, as an accomplished pianist, she was also responsible for whipping our school choir into shape. I guess that I must have been the "Barney Fife" of the choir and it wasn't long before Mum had to remove me from the stage. It was a bit of an embarrassment, but not as much as my next assignment. She made me stand by the piano and turn the music pages for her. The boys still give me shit over this to this day, but such was life as a school-teacher's son.

It was also during this time that I had my first run-in with the law. Once a week, we would march as a group down to the girl's school to take swimming lessons. On this particular day, as we marched past the local police sub-station I noticed a police car pulling into the driveway with a surf board that had been snapped in half and was sticking out the window. I guess that the officer must have had better hearing than I thought, as he apparently had no problem hearing the obscene remark that I mouthed off. Before the screeching sound of his brakes faded, his door was open and he was out on the pavement. He growled, "Who the hell is the smart ass then?" It was pretty obvious who the smart ass was as 50 heads immediately turned my way. Without hesitation, he strode over, grabbed me by the ear and dragged me into the station. Talk about being scared shitless. My whole life flashed before me, especially its future with my Dad kicking my ass black and blue. I remember looking back and seeing all the other kids and the teacher scuttling away from the scene as fast as they could without looking too panicked. I knew then that it was going to be every man for himself. He threw me in a cell and left me there for about 30 minutes. I was sweating bullets when he came back and demanded, "What's your name boy?" I stammered, "Alan Brosnan, Sir, please tell me I am not in trouble." "Boy, you are in the shit up to your worthless neck. Is Kevan Brosnan your Dad?"

"No sir, he is my uncle."

"Who is your Dad then?"

"Ray Brosnan sir. Please, please don't tell my Dad." After another 30 minutes of sweating it out, my Uncle Kevan showed up and dragged me out of there. Having to sweep the police station out after school for the next month wasn't as bad as the six licks of the cane I got on the ass when I got back to school that day. I will always be grateful to my Uncle for not dobbing me in to Dad. Apparently, a surfer had been attacked and killed by a great white shark that day and, understandably, the cop wasn't in the best of moods.

Mum's parents are still alive, and even though they are both in their nineties, my Granddad, until very recently, mowed Mum's lawn each week. The three of them are inseparable and it is great to see families like that enjoy each other's company so much. With my risky lifestyle, I don't expect that I will be around when I am ninety, but it sure would be nice to have my daughter, SeanBenet, look after me if it happens. I devote as much time as possible to my Grandparents, Leo and Audrey, and I certainly look forward to seeing them on my trips home. When I was 11-12, they only lived about a kilometer from my school. I used to love going to Grandma's for lunch because she would always get me a mince pie and spoil me rotten. Of course it was illegal to leave the school compound for any reason during lunch-time, but so was borrowing someone's bike from the neighbouring school yard to get to Grandma's and back in time. I used to make a habit of sleeping over once a week and that is when I got my first taste of firearms. Granddad had a .22 caliber rifle, and I would spend countless hours sitting on his porch steps sniping targets stapled to the wall of his shed.

When I was ten years old, I met a man that had a profound influence on my life. Dad's uncle Lenny owned a big sheep farm in Temuka, South Canterbury. My parents thought it would be good for Mike and me to experience the rigors of farm life first hand, so for the next couple of years, we would alternate school holidays and head north on the train for a stint under Lenny's earthy guidance. Lenny was definitely a hard charger. Small and wiry, but tough as old boots, he could swear like a trooper, especially when his dogs would fuck up. For those of you who have never seen a farmer work his sheep dogs, it is a unique experience. I remember my first morning on the farm well. I was "gently" nudged out of my semi-sleep by Uncle Lenny's penetrating voice, "Get your hand off it boy, breakfast is ready." I glanced out the window and it was still pitch black. "Fucking hell," I thought; what the hell was going on, it wasn't even dawn yet. Lenny had issued me a woolen shirt, an old pair of army pants, and a set of gumboots. Auntie Bertha whipped us up a huge breakfast, then it was out to the cow shed for my introduction to milking. What an abortion that was. Lenny was one of those guys who would show you once and then leave you to it. After about 30 minutes, I still hadn't covered the bottom of the bucket. That cow turned around and looked at me like I was an idiot. After that, it was off to the paddocks to do the rounds and assist the ewes that were having trouble giving birth.

Mode of transport was the tractor and my position was on the back in the tray cage with the dogs. Lenny drove like a fucking madman and it took me all my strength just to hang on and stop from being tossed out.

The dogs loved it and the faster he went, the more excited they would get. The dogs really came alive when they got wind of the sheep, because they knew that the fun was about to begin. Being working dogs, they weren't happy unless they were jumping fences, pounding the paddocks and nipping at sheep legs. A female sheep having trouble giving birth would be lost if she could not get the lamb out. Consequently, Dr. Lenny would spend the day lubing up his arm, sticking it up a pregnant ewe to his elbow and yanking out the young one, solving the problem. By the end of the day, I guess he was getting sick of it, because he looked across at me ordered, "Get over here boy and roll your sleeves up."

With that, he lubed my arm up with Vaseline, sat on the sheep's head, and told me to get on with it. "Go on, get it in there, more, more." I had run out of arm and he was still urging me to get it up there. I thought I was about to be swallowed up in the lady's vagina as she protested my crude and painful attempts to extract the lamb. I was sweating buckets and the raw experience gave me a whole new perspective on sex and procreation. "Sluuurp and pop," out it came and I didn't know whether I was going to puke or faint, I felt like I could do both — whew! At day's end, the dogs and I would also be accompanied by a number of dead sheep and lambs in the cage as we lurched back to the yard. Nevertheless, changes occurred after a couple of weeks, I was a different kid and had learned to really enjoy the outdoors. The rolling hills, clear crisp days and the rugged lifestyle appealed to me.

I remember being at the dinner table one night when Dallas, his son, screamed out to Lenny, "There's one in the vegetable garden, Dad." With battle stations alerted, Lenny was off like a rocket, grabbing his shotgun on the way. "Get out here boy." Oh shit, I thought, what now? A Wallaby (small kangaroo) was running amok all over the vegetables. He had no problem getting in, but couldn't figure out how to get out of the patch. He was obviously in a bit of a panic and kept bouncing off the hedges, doing back flips. "Alan, take this and shoot the bastard," was Lenny's order. He shoved a 12 gage double into my arms and just as quickly jumped in behind me. Fucking hell I thought, the damn thing was bigger than me. Oh well, no worries, I'll just treat it like Granddad's .22 rifle. Yeah, right! I know now why Lenny jumped in behind me. "KABOOM!" He caught the big bore before it clattered to the deck, but let me fly backward and land flat on my butt, back amid the daisies. The shot nicked the Wallaby and dug a hole under his ass, prompting the beast to make a giant leap out of the garden and into the night. There was general chaos with the sheep dogs chasing the Wallaby across the farm and Lenny and Dallas laughing their heads off as I slowly got to my feet while rubbing my aching shoulder. What a great life I thought, as I was getting on the train for my journey back to the city, but taking care not to aggravate my sore shoulder. I would definitely be back, and Lenny heartily approved of my intentions.

The older that I got, the more cunning and daring I seemed to get. Stealing a few pennies from Mum turned into a shilling, then a pound, and as broke as we all were in those days, the folks must have known what was going on. What really scared me was when Mike and I would take Mum's car for a spin when she wasn't home. At the time, neither of us had drivers licenses, but that didn't seem to matter. Mike brimmed with confidence and had the whole act squared away. Prior to moving off, he would use chalk to mark the exact positions of the tires, and, sure as hell, the wheels would end up in the same place upon our return. Like all kids growing up, I now regret the disloyalty and disrespect that I showed toward my parents. I only hope that SeanBenet never treats me the same, and if she does I will try to remember my past transgressions before I discipline her. However, it sure can be fun when the shoe is on the other foot!

The army allowed me to travel to parts of the country that I had never even heard of before and it seemed that every friend I made wanted me to experience life in his home-town. I was often happy to comply with their wishes, because as a young man, what else was there to do in life other than party and enjoy the World? As a young soldier, I came under the influence, both good and bad, of a number of people. The good influences were my boss, Captain Stan Pilbrow and his wife Denise. On weekends, they would often take me under their gracious wing and I owe them a great deal for their friendship and guidance. However, the bad influences were far more numerous and some of them nevertheless, turned out to be among my best mates. There was George "Tee Hee" Eruiti, Warren Richards, Hori "Hit Man" Hern, Dave "Shifty Eyes" Ngarewa, John Boy "Two Dogs" Collier, and Vern Pomana to name a few. Yea, we Kiwis have some weird nick-names and just as many unusual true names that have been promulgated by the mixing of the Maori and largely British cultures.

In 1979, I met Elaine Brown, who was to become my wife eight years later. She is of Maori descent, and when she told me where she was from, it meant absolutely nothing to me. Te Hapua is a small, extremely remote community located on the northern-most tip of the country. In fact, if you went any further you would fall into the South Pacific Ocean. When I first visited her hometown it was pure culture shock for a naive white boy from the south. The town sits smack on the ocean and is comprised of some twenty odd families. All the men and some of the women worked in either the forestry, sheep farming or fishing industries. With thirteen brothers and sisters, that meant inexhaustible amounts of firewood and seafood in the Brown household. What a great family, and to me, the life they led had to be the ultimate ideal. Away from the cities, the kids were brought up in the

Elaine and I, both Sergeants in the New Zealand Military (Army and Air Force, respectively).

traditional way and learned to respect family values that are so lacking these days. Elaine's Dad, Joe, and Mum, Lovey, are extremely proud of their fourteen kids and forty-odd grandchildren, and there is nothing better than to spend vacation time in that part of the world with the entire clan present. Warren was the eldest child, followed by Bradley, Elaine, Yvonne, Lloyde, Edith, Donna, Vivienne, Bethnie, John, Lewis, Lisa, Bobby-Joe, and Selina. You can forget about the luxuries and life's frills, but that is what makes it so worthwhile. The only road was gravel and transport was usually limited to bareback horse, motorbike, or four-wheeler. There were no shops or other amenities. TV channels were limited to two, if you were lucky enough to receive them, but the closeness of the people, particularly among the elderly, was extremely gratifying.

One would think that raising fourteen kids would take its toll, but Lovey always seemed to have everything under control. The family is top heavy on females and the nine girls always kept the house spick and span. The boys took care of the outdoor tasks, such as fishing, cutting firewood, mustering the cattle, hunting wild pigs and tending to the horses. It wasn't a farm, but all the animals were quartered into the back yard. The horses, in reality, had free reign, but the pig dogs were caged inside a make shift wire mesh fence. Occasionally, a stray sheep wandered into the yard and, of course, never made it out again. Joe would always cook a traditional Maori hangi meal that was prepared in a hole in the ground with hot stones, covered with dirt, and steamed for every Christmas or New Year's Day. On one occasion, when an errant sheep paid the family what was anticipated would be a permanent visit, Joe told Lewis to tie it to the shed so he could slaughter it the next day. However, when the sun arose the next morning, the sheep was gone and Lewis got one hell of a verbal whipping. He was told to saddle up and not come back till he had that sheep strapped across his horse. He was gone for two days. I guess the poor bastard didn't want to face the music and was too honest to even consider flogging one the neighbors batch. Sheep rustling was not condoned, but it appeared that "wild sheep" that wandered onto your property were considered fair game. Lovey was also as hard as nails, but a great woman. When she said jump, all the kids asked, "How high, Mum?" She ruled with an iron fist, but with a ton of siblings and the normal rivalries that surface, that is the way it had to be.

When Elaine and SeanBenet were there for an extended visit, my daughter went to the local Kohanga Reo (Kindergarten). Elaine's sister, Vivienne, and her Mum ran the school and even though SeanBenet was only one-and-a-half-years-old, she just loved the atmosphere and being with all her cousins. The only language spoken during school was Maori, and Lovey and Vivienne were excellent tutors. The Maori heritage is extremely important and I will always ensure that SeanBenet will be able to return to Te Hapua frequently to spend time with the family.

Like every town, there are always your ubiquitous, little local bastards that manage to piss everyone off. Te Hapua was no different, and once while I was lying in bed I heard Lovey cursing at the top of her voice about 200 meters away from the main house. Apparently, the local hoods had a habit of covertly sneaking their horses onto the greenest back yards in the neighborhood to graze and feed. Their mission was always performed well after dark when the lights were out, and prior to first light, the horses would be quietly removed. It wasn't the fact that the animals would be denied their rations, but rather that someone had to scoop up the ton of horseshit left by the visiting culprits. I would have hated to be in those little bastards shoes if Lovey had got hold of them.

Elaine and I with SeanBenet. Since her arrival in 1997, work hasn't slowed down but I certainly look forward to being at home more often.

Most Christmases were spent at the family's private beach at Tom Bowling Bay. The only way to get to it was by four-wheel drive vehicles. Stores and tents were hand carried down the hill to the awaiting horses that were eager to do their bit for the cause. We had a little tin, motor-less boat that we would load up with kids. Bradley would tie the boat to a horse's tail, jump on its back, and streak across the marshy estuary to dry land. What a blast, and the horses seemed to love it, especially when the boat turned over dumping everyone into shallow water. The next two weeks would be spent soaking up the sun, diving and fishing, eating fresh seafood and keeping the kids happy. They were simply great times, among great people. On Christmas Eve, the locals traditionally went to the rugby club for a party and for many of us, a huge piss up. Joe and I always downed considerable amounts of Coruba Rum, and this night was no exception. Elaine's brothers, Bradley and Lloyd, eventually joined us, and throughout the evening other relatives and friends would swing by and spin the shit. Among them were Chappy, Booksie, Joe, and Lena. Simon and Squidly were always in line ready to drain a bottle as well. Both of these guys were mischievous little buggers who did their best to keep up with their larger brethren. Usually, both of them would end up blowing their asses and wanting to take on the world. Every night however, would end up the same for them. Their better halves, Debbie and Maro, could be seen dragging them out by their ears as they continued to curse anyone who was within earshot.

Through my liquor-induced haze, one guest in particular caught my attention. "Who's that?" I asked Bradley. Equally opaque, he slurred a little, "That's Paki, our preacher, and he's conducting midnight mass tonight." *Bloody hell* I thought, and by 10:00 pm he was as shit faced as the rest of us and was falling all over the place. I like clergy that tipple with the common man. They have a good grasp on life and are able to appreciate what the average slug goes through when he commits his transgressions. However, at the appointed time Padre "Paki" drew himself up and with great dignity proceeded to the church's altar to deliver the Christmas message.

The church was a small building located between Joe's house and the Rugby Club. It had no electricity, so the procedure was for Lovey to run an extension cord from her house to the church to provide lighting and power the electric organ. Close to midnight the rum had won, and when I finally buckled I knew it was time to withdraw. This might sound easy to accomplish, but in fact became an extremely daunting task. There were no streetlights and it was as black as a coal miner's ass outside. Besides moving by feel, I learned after my first Rugby Club piss up that you had to count your paces from the building to the road. I knew it was exactly 72 sober man's strides and then I had to turn a hard left. However, at this stage of my celebrating I was alternating between staggering and crawling and was thoroughly disoriented. After a lengthy close target recce from a worm's perspective, I managed to find the road and began to rely on my hearing to get oriented. This proved to be a huge effort and I thought about sleeping it off where I was, but my fear of being run over by the milkman's wagon or similar conveyance caused me to renew my journey. The sounds from the church were receding and I knew within another 65 paces I would be able to see the dim porch light of Joe's house. I also knew that if I screwed up I would either end up in a storm drain or fall into the ocean. The thought of either fate did not appeal to me, and a shot of adrenalin must have sobered me up enough to get home. Five minutes later, Bradley and Lloyd arrived and decided that it was time for a feed. If it wasn't boiled cuisine, it was fried, and tonight steak and eggs were looking mighty good. By this time, the midnight mass was in full swing. God only knows how Paki did it, because he couldn't even utter an understandable sentence earlier in the evening. It had to be a minor miracle. Bradley went up to the stove, pulled out an extension cord plug and replaced it with the electric frying pan. Within minutes, our steaks were popping, sizzling, and smelling delicious. We were having a great time when suddenly the front door flew off its hinges. I thought it was a police raid and began to raise my hands. It was worse than that, however, as Lovey, with fire in her eyes, charged through the door at a great rate of knots. What the hell was her problem? I had made it a point to be extra nice to her tonight. By the time she breached the kitchen door, she already had her assault broom in hand and proceeded to bayonet and butt stroke anyone within range. I hit the deck and took cover under the table. Lloyd did a runner right through the rear door. Bradley, however caught the brunt of the banzai attack, and rightly so, since it was him who pulled out the extension cord, thus plunging the church into total darkness during the benediction. Apparently this caused Paki to become disorientated, lose his balance and end up in a couple of parishioner's laps. She had the element of surprise and it was ugly; I think Lovey originated the principles of Surprise, Speed, and Violence of Action.

Things haven't changed a great deal in New Zealand over the years and as much as I enjoy going back to visit the family, two weeks is about my limit. The low crime level, fantastic scenery, laid back lifestyle and of course, rugby makes it a treasured haven for living the good life. However, in all honesty it is a little too quiet for my liking. The people are great and extremely proud of their culture, history and achievements, be they during war or peace-time, on the athletic field or in the entertainment industry. Being kind and hospitable is not something Kiwis are taught to do, but rather a trait that they are born with.

The Mud, the Blood, and the Beer

Duke's Story

Vietnam, Singapore, and Malaysia

The RNZAF flight to Vietnam was uneventful and we landed with limited fuss or fanfare. A quick reshuffle on the ground and we prepared for the trip by vehicle convoy from Vung Tau to the Anzac Fire Base of Nui Dat. The company mounted the trucks and sat facing outboard, weapons tightly clutched and wired up ready for anything. Like most of the other guys in my platoon, I fully expected the Vietcong, or North Vietnamese regulars, to make a sudden appearance and brass us up big time. Most of us were completely over-awed by the situation that first couple of hours. After clearing the hustle and bustle of Vung Tau, little did we realize that it would be our last glimpse of civilization and pretty girls for the next three months.

Once in Nui Dat, Phuoc Tuoy Province, we settled in to the Whiskey Company lines. The four-man military tents had wood palettes for floors and were protected by sand bagged walls. We were now members of the ANZAC Battalion. and along with our Australian counterparts. we had the honor of maintaining the Anzac fighting tradition. As a Kiwi, it was sometimes difficult to accept the fact that the Australian military contingent and commitment was much larger and better equipped than ours, but unlike our "down under" brethren. all Kiwis were volunteers. Many Kiwi soldiers serving in Vietnam had originally started out as National Serviceman (under a ballot system of conscription). However, before being assigned duties in this theater they had to volunteer for service with the regular force infantry and meet its training requirements.

A glaring example of the negative aspects of conscription and, therefore, involuntary service happened a short while after our arrival in Nui Dat. A disgruntled Aussie grunt rolled a grenade under his platoon sergeant's cot and sent his non commissioned officer into the next world. However, in this case Murphy's Law had prevailed, because the troubled troopie was actually targeting his platoon commander.

We lost all sense of time in Vietnam and, truthfully, didn't care. The only dates that mattered were rest and recreation timings and our scheduled flight home. We were all volunteers, with a sense of immortality, and as professionals most of us were looking forward to the challenges and tests of combat.

In Malaysia, our belt order, packs, and the majority of our military kit was British issue. Uniformity in N.Z., and to a lesser degree in Malaysia, was still the name of the game and only issue kit could be used. However, in Vietnam, combat rules applied, and we were allowed to use just about anything we wanted, so most of us adopted the U.S. webbing and belt order. The final configuration was up to the individual wearing it and the only thing that was sacrosanct was that the field dressing had to be loosely taped to one of your web suspender straps.

I finally ended up with an ARVN pack mounted on a Special Forces frame with signaller's bum pack. This held my rations of five to seven days, which were normally a mixture of freeze dries and American C-rat cans. Rations had to be broken down, and it was difficult to carry a complete U.S. 24-hour rat pack because of it size. C-rats consisted of three heavy and bulky cans per meal, smokes and goodies, and while excellent tucker, were a determent to bush movement. On the opposite end of the field cuisine spectrum were the lightweight freeze dried food packs, they sapped our limited potable water supply, and over the long haul, lacked the *oomph* necessary to restore our required energy levels. Americans ate well, but our Kiwi priorities were ammo and water, in that order.

I carried four to six water bottles on my belt order and two in my pack's side pouches. This was further supplemented by an Aussie water bag, also attached to my pack. All water bottles/bags needed to be easily accessible for refilling purposes and, in turn, this exposure made the bladders prone to puncturing and tearing. I rationed myself to one water bottle a day for all purposes, but this changed when we contacted streams or other water supplies. In the dry season, we suffered and took and purified water wherever we could find it. During Monsoon season, we cursed the deluges. Even though I loved a full brew of coffee, I seldom took the trouble to make it. When I was able to indulge in such a luxury, I would boil the water with a marble of plastic explosive and use half for the freeze dries and the rest for the brew. I had no problem eating C-rats cold, and most times in the late afternoon when we invariably harboured up, were too tired or idle to cook it up. Other than ammo and operational kit, you were not checked on what you carried. For me, the extras consisted of a spare shirt and trousers, my British lightweight woollen blanket, and a Lilo tube cover to lie on. I also packed a liberated VC hammock and a lightweight shelter half, this was my full boonies compliment and once packed away I was "hot to trot." For Sergeant Dave, mosquito nets were not tactical and he frowned on them. Because of the heat and humidity, I never wore socks or cotton skivvies and was lucky that the crotch rot and athlete's foot left me well alone. These lessons were learned back in the Ulu (jungle) of Malaysia.

Our section composition and roles remained the same as it was during our jungle training in Malaysia. Billy Kahaki and I were the cover and lead scouts, Graham "Black Harry" Harris continued as section commander, Grame Edwards was our 2IC, Ginge Phillips carried the M79 40 MM grenade launcher, and Paul Carmichael served as a rifleman private. Our section, by hook or by crook, acquired two M60 light machine guns. Peter "Titty" Harris and Scrubber Ryalls handled gun one, and my tent mates, Rau Te Haara and Ben Te Namu, were on gun two. We conducted bush ops lasting between five to nine weeks and were re-supplied every five to seven days.

We all carried a 100-round belt of 7.62 x 51 MM link for the machine guns, two fragmentation grenades, a selection of colored smoke grenades, a minimum of eight fully loaded 20-round magazines for your FN Self Loading Rifle, and, in my case, I further augmented that with an extra bandoleer of rifle ammo. With the exception of the machine gunners, we all carried a claymore mine, a trip flare, extra radio batteries, and a starlight scope. Other odd items of team kit were also distributed among the section. The Signaller humped his radio, personal gear, and a lightweight M-16 5.56 x 45 MM rifle. Both M60 gunners carried the gun and 1000 rounds of linked ammunition, and pistols. Their assistant gunners were laden with an SLR, a spare MG barrel, and as much link as possible for them to carry. Being an M60 team was not for weaklings, but amazingly, most gunners weren't big men.

We usually deployed in company strength into our areas of operations by helicopters or armoured personnel carriers (APC's). Occasionally, when we had promising intelligence on large enemy concentrations, the entire battalion took a whack at them, but more often than not contacts were limited to platoon-sized engagements. It's a stirring sight to see several hundred men in battle dress and loaded for bear lining the airstrip in their respective sticks, waiting for the helicopters to take them up-country. Even today, when I hear the thumping of those blades, it brings back distant memories of the excitement of an ANZAC air assault.

Once on the ground we would fan out in a defensive perimeter to cover the bird's withdrawal and wait for any immediate enemy reaction. On command, we would quickly regroup, check our compass bearing, and get the fuck out of the area. We never operated at full strength, and for various reasons a platoon rarely exceeded 25 men. 2 Platoon normally operated as two elements. Invariably, our section ended up with Sgt. Dave Haywood as our commander, and Lieutenant Bobby Upton operated with the other element.

Jungle operations for the Kiwi infantrymen was traditionally a well-drilled routine. It was developed and perfected during, the Malaysian and Borneo campaigns in the 1960's. We were fortunate to have had a six-

Danny Campbell, Duke, Big George Winiata, and Barry Boylan – SVN

month workup in the Malaysian jungles, which is similar in topography and climate. We were jungle bunnies no doubt and extremely confident in our abilities to fight and survive in this environment. Ideally, through disciplined, stealthy movement, we wanted to be able to spot the enemy first and initiate the fire fight on our terms, rather than react to a contact firing at us. This can only be achieved by carefully following time tested SOPs and maintaining alertness on a 24/7 basis. Danger areas such as track systems, ridgelines, creek beds, roads, saddles, or any other natural routes, were to be avoided. People who ignored these basic rules did so at their peril and frequently paid the price in the form of a devastating ambush. Eyesight, sound, and smell were all involved in discerning the opposition, but we frequently heard them first before spotting them. Sound can carry a long way in the jungle, and noise discipline was paramount. Our enemy displayed serious discipline also, but was more apt to stick to existing track systems, perhaps so they could move at a fair rate of knots. And, at times, he got punished badly for this breach of tactics. We did not, as a rule, patrol or move at night, and since we operated in a free-fire zone anything that moved after dusk was considered fair game and was challenged. Halts required sentries and outposts to be deployed. Packs and webbing remained on unless the situation required us to lie in firing positions. Because of our operating procedures and style of patrolling, we did not travel great distances, and frequently only covered a 1000 meters between night harbor positions. Ambushes were usually set up at night, so most of us enjoyed only a few hours of sleep in our harbor sites. The "killer group," or the troops that covered the designated "kill zone," consisted of an M60 team and banks of claymore mines. The claymores were the favored method of initiation and the M60 and riflemen would not engage targets in the zone unless it required cleaning up. A claymore-initiated ambush could be misidentified as mortar or artillery harassing and interdiction fire and, therefore, would not compromise the patrol.

Contacts were sudden and frequently close, and although training and

Armored vehicle assembly area – SVN

discipline were key fundamentals for survival, lady luck, as always, had a hand in it. For the uninitiated, contrary to the way war is portrayed in the movies, the noise generated during a fire-fight is immense. Verbal control is almost impossible to exert when the balloon goes up. All orders are delivered blind because most of the combatants are hugging terra-firma very early in the contact. With green troops, the instinct for survival will often override training until leadership overcomes the grip of fear.

In the jungle, the ability to land navigate was paramount. The thick foliage made map reading an art form and was a skill that not everyone could master. It was very similar to night navigation and you had to count your paces and adhere to pre-set compass bearings. In addition to getting from point "A" to point "B" in the time estimated for a scheduled aerial re-supply, accurate artillery and close air support hinged on your ability to give the correct coordinates of your location. Misread the map or report the wrong coordinates and you could be on the wrong end of a 500 pound bomb. It's called fratricide in genteel company, but killing your own and doing the enemy's job for him was a big no-no. Many times we huddled in our shell holes as our boss Bobby, Sgt. Dave and the M Fire Controller huddled over a map, calling in high explosive rounds and taking quick fixes on the fall of the shot with back azimuths and map resection. This was an expensive but effective method of determining our own position when there were no terrain features to orient on.

There's nothing like the scream and crump of high explosives, with shrapnel whistling through the trees, to get you to get acquainted with the worms and other local vermin scurrying around in your partially sub-merged crater. When the big ordnance got a little too close, it didn't take much to convince you that it would be a whole lot easier on the nerves and sphincter muscle to perfect your traditional navigation techniques than opt for the "boom" method.

Early in our tour, we still thought we were invincible, but our first enemy contact changed that erroneous belief. We had been patrolling in platoon strength for several hours, during our thirty-day deployment in the bush. We were following a pre-determined compass bearing with our sec-tion and me as point in the lead. From the map recce and patrol brief that morning we knew that we should be approaching a creek junction in the next hour or so. We finally stopped for a break and, as always, because I was a non-smoker I was pushed out on sentry. Sergeant Dave signalled Ben, the M60 gunner, to accompany me. Peaches Brown was positioned to our right flank. We hadn't travelled more than ten meters when the familiar crack of an SLR round whistled past us from Brownie's position. After let-ting loose with a couple of rounds, all was quiet from his direction. The boss yelled out for a contact report. Sergeant Dave shook his head and sig-nalled us forward a couple of feet to take up a better defensive position. I was scanning the creek bed to our front when I suddenly glimpsed move-ment ten to fifteen feet out to my front. A flash of black — shit, there he was, a bad guy flat on his stomach and facing down the creek towards the platoon's right flank where Peaches had fired from. I was standing motion-less and slightly crouched. He must have sensed my presence or he was just checking his arc's because he glanced my way and our eyes met. He looked more surprised than afraid, and with what felt like slow motion, I instinc-tively shouldered my weapon, sighted in on his chest area, and engaged him with a 20-round magazine. With each hit, he flopped around a bit and it all seemed very clinical and clear to me. There was no emotion at this moment and I was simply doing what I had been trained to do. Searching for additional targets, I dropped to a knee, quickly changed magazines, and re-charged my rifle. For insurance, Ben hosed the guy down with his M60 and then covered the far bank and bunker systems that we could now see. Then things got quiet again as we all lay motionless, sucking in air and contemplating what had just occurred and what might happen next.

Eventually, we all three looked at each other and the ear-to-ear grins said it all. Fuck it, we were all right.

Peaches had observed two VC strolling down the creek bed towards his position and opened up with his SLR, knocking one ass over kite and wounding the other, who did a runner and got away. The soldier we had engaged was also wounded and could have been Peaches's first target.

During the Platoon follow up we discovered we were, in fact, already in the bunker zone, not a pleasant thought. After clearing the immediate concern and checking for further enemy, time forced us to move back and harbour up for the evening. It was getting dark and when the curtain descends, it's like someone switched off the light bulb. With the additional bunker complex across the creek, it looked like things could get serious so we pulled back and prepared for a rather anxious night. After our stand-to stood down, we set our listening posts and sentries. With us being in the enemy's neighborhood and he being pissed off about it, the boss did not have to worry about anyone on stag nodding off.

The next morning, with machine guns sited for support, the platoon got on line and advanced through and cleared the main bunkers on the other side of the creek. It turned out that they were not fully completed and only partially manned. Had it been otherwise, the fire fight that would have undoubtedly ensued could just have easily gone the other way.

Sergeant Dave had taken several of us under his wing, and although the memories have faded, we would have followed him anywhere and pretty much did. On one of several occasions, he took me on one of his more interesting escapades. We had located a camp of 30 to 40 VC and they were quite relaxed and unaware of our presence. They were making plenty of noise chopping down trees, yelling out to each other and quite confident that they were safe while they were engaged in building a base camp and a couple of bunkers. Upon hearing the sounds of chopping, we immediately moved into a perimeter defense and listened for an hour, trying to build a mental picture of enemy activities. The boss had radioed the company commander and advised him of our find. We held and the next day the balance of Whiskey joined us for a company-sized attack. About 4:00 pm, Sergeant Dave grabbed one other grunt and me and gave us an enlightening brief on his planned close camp reconnaissance. At the time, I was only nineteen and totally indoctrinated in contemporary infantry tactics. But, after five minutes with Dave, he had the other lad and me setting some of this doctrine aside and adopting the SAS techniques that he had developed in Borneo and elsewhere while in combat.

We made our preparations and he inspected us. Our faces and hands were camouflaged and we had removed our boots. Instead, we wore two pairs of socks, which I had to borrow, because I had no use for them in the jungle, to muffle our foot-falls and eliminate leaving footprints. Webbing had been discarded for this mission and I only carried a bandoleer of 7.62 x 51 MM around my waist and five 20-round magazines. A loaded magazine was placed in each pocket of my trousers and shirt and one on the weapon. We moved out, creeping in at various points, stopping and listening to the VC chorus and then creeping out again. Dave was establishing the location for our advance and start line for the company assault and trying to determine the parameters of the enemy encampment. We needed that information so our flanks would not be exposed to an enemy counter-attack. When we returned to our platoon position everyone carried on with the hard routine. No talking, no fires and keep the fuck still. Any food consumed was eaten cold or not at all. We all held our breath until sunrise.

In the end, it was all a waste of time. The following morning, 2 Platoon pulled back a couple of hundred meters and the rest of Whiskey Company regrouped on our new position. The Company Head Shed in the boonies and Aussie taskforce bosses back in the Dat, worked on a battle plan and the big picture. Murphy's Law, sure as shit, intervened and from the grunt's perspective this promising mission was a failure. The enemy camp was prepped with artillery, air support, and helicopter gunships. Everybody wanted a piece of the action, but the most effective weapon of all in this terrain, the light infantryman, was left to huddle impotently on the deck while this awesome display of firepower impacted a couple of hundred meters to our front. On cue, when the prep lifted, we did our thing, and it turned out to be the proverbial walk in the sun. The grand total for tons of expended ordnance was one confirmed enemy KIA, 30 odd packs quantities of rice, and some abandoned weapons and equipment. In hindsight, a better plan would have been to set out area ambushes Kiwi style and pound the camp with artillery or gunships under our direction. When they felt our pain, the VC would di-di into our kill zones and it would have been a turkey shoot. However, there was one consolation generated out of all of the fireworks. Our gunships caught an enemy group and chewed them up as they bolted across open grasslands trying to escape.

Relationships between the Aussies and Kiwis in Vietnam was a healthy one, although we swore up and down that the Aussie high command gave us the dirty end of the stick on operational taskings. Although there were

Rau Te Haara preparing to board the infamous floating patrol.

numerous punch-ups and bloody brawls between Anzac allies back in base camp and on liberty in Vung Tau, there was no malice intended. It was simply a continuation of the age old ANZAC friction which remains part of our N.Z. culture even today. I am firm believer that the demands jungle operations place on the grunt require frequent venting. A good controlled scrap usually did the trick, and hell, we even fought each other if there was no one else around. Out in the scrub where it counted, Aussies and Kiwis worked extremely well together and I have nothing but grudging admiration for the Aussie diggers who represented the majority of the ANZAC Task Force.

Rau and Duke awaiting helo exfil in the dry season.

Our platoon had moved into

a new AO and we were in the process of setting up the platoon harbour area. A small clearing patrol under Wally Goodman had moved out. Sergeant Dave snapped up Barry Boylan and me to recce a water-point located a short distance back. We hadn't travelled more than a 100 meters when all hell broke loose. A long ripping burst of M60, punctuated by individual SLR rounds, was holing the air in our general direction. This was accompanied by the now familiar cracking of AK47's giving it shit as well. We found a shallow depression and Dave monitored the PRC 77 radio he was carrying. Wally's group had hit it big time and several of his men were down with the fire-fight still in progress and building. Sergeant Dave took the lead and pushed Barry and me forward to the sound of the guns. A three man group, pepper potting forward towards a resounding little gun fight. Through head high scrub and jungle is not a pleasant task, and we were all wired pretty tight by the time we got to the battle zone.

Rex Ryan and his cover scout, Dave Wright, were leading the clearing patrol through fairly open jungle canopy when they engaged a small group of VC very close to our harbour site. Rex initiated the contact and the enemy group bolted with the boys hot in pursuit. Rex had barrelled a male teenager in the first exchange with his SLR, but the kid had kept going a couple of yards before dropping. The patrol charged into an area of consisting of high grass and low scrub with a wide, but old, APC/Tank track of some sort running at right angles to their axis of advance. The youth was crumpled up on the deck at the edge of the clearing, either dead or dying and clearly out of the fight. Reaching the clearing, Rex had dropped to his knee to reload while Dave Wright continued to hammer the fleeing enemy that were moving to his left down an old armoured vehicle track. Within seconds, they took incoming from a determined and extremely courageous one-man hasty ambush. At a range of only a few feet, the lone ranger stay behind force opened up with his AK on full auto and Dave was smashed to the ground with several hits. George MacLeod and his M60 was the next recipient of VC lead and it got worse. By the time we got there, Wally had wounded a couple of his own boys with a well-intentioned, but poorly placed grenade. Danny Campbell had gallantly and correctly responded to George's problem and under considerable pressure from the VC trooper, cleared the M60's stoppage. He then proceeded to stitch the Dink with a full belt of 7.62, effectively stopping this one-man army. Dave was down but still conscious, while poor old George, speechless for the first time in his life, had been ignored were he lay. Rex and I patched up Dave as best we could. He was fairly comfortable considering the extent of his wounds and calmly related the contact to us in his normal and dry manner. George, having recovered his wits and caustic tongue, could be heard complaining bitterly about his useless fucken mates. "Don't worry about me, ya bastards," he waffled on, so we knew he wasn't too bad. An LZ was cleared and secured to case-evac the two casualties back to Vung Tau military hospital. Dave's injuries were fairly substantial, with entry and exit wounds in his pelvis and upper torso. George had a couple of 7.62 x 39 MM rounds through one of his legs, but had lambasted his mates so viciously that he had sprained his tongue.

Dave and George were patched up and repatriated back home for better care and convalescence. Dave's injuries required further specialist treatment in Australia and he wrote a letter to Rex and the boys from the Aussie hospital. Unfortunately, he died from complications a few weeks later. However, when I finally caught up with George 25 years later, he was fighting fit and none the worse for wear.

All good things must come to an end and six months into our tour, Sergeant Dave Haywood was posted to the Jungle Warfare School at Johore Baru in Malaysia. Undoubtedly, he was responsible for keeping a whole bunch of us alive and his leaving was a critical blow to me; my focus was not the same without his professional presence. Sergeant Harry (Black) Hemana was his replacement and filling Dave's boots was no easy task for anyone.

When we returned to Nui Dat, our first priority was to clean all weapons and inspect, clean, and return any unexpended munitions, followed by cleaning and washing personal equipment. We only had a few days of respite, so priorities were well established and clear-cut. "Gear before beer," was our mantra and while the clean up and maintenance was going on, the company medics would carry out foreskin and foot inspections (FFI) and check us out in general for the inevitable jungle rot and fungal diseases that seemed to thrive on unwashed bodies. Clean ups were always accomplished in record time and the team-work was unbelievable. We were supremely motivated, because we knew that when we were done it was BBQ and Whiskey Company Piss Up Time. Capt. Jim Brown, the company second in command (executive officer), was built like the proverbial brick shit house and "took no prisoners," Kiwi or Viet Cong. He had risen through enlisted ranks, complete with Borneo and Malayan campaign medals with a mention in dispatches for bravery. He was a formidable soldier and man. He was a leader and always made the rounds upon our return to base, checking weapons, joking with and teasing the boys. This was his subtle method of getting soldier feed-back on any potential welfare, morale, or other issues. Because of our protracted periods in the scrub and our methods of operation, this was the only chance for anyone outside our section to catch up on what happened in the field to us. J.B. was a Maori and a staunch one to boot, and he still revealed glimpses of his previous military status when he tossed a few beers down with the boys. However, he maintained a proper relationship with the troops and certainly had no qualms about dispensing justice when he deemed it necessary. It made little difference to him whether you were black, white, or brindle. Stuff things up and he was going to come down hard on you. Probably his style was more suited to a crusty old Warrant Officer than captain, but it didn't matter — he was the Man. On one occasion, I was the recipient of some of his sage advice while I was up to my elbows in aviation gas with Titty Harris and Ben Tenamu cleaning the section's M60's. My SLR had been worked on until it was gleaming and it was propped up near me. J.B. appeared from nowhere, seized my weapon, checked it for safety, and then gave it the once over. Apparently unimpressed with my sterling effort, he uttered in his deep, but quiet, voice something to the effect that if I didn't lightly oil and pull through the barrel before he came back, he would shove the barrel up my backside and pull the trigger. We loved Big Jim, even though nine times out of ten whenever he spoke to you it was usually involved some sort of reprimand. His mere presence habitually boosted morale and confidence sky high.

Captain Brown was seconded to an Australian rifle company halfway through our time on duty, and his successful style of leadership was instrumental in raising the morale and capabilities of our Anzac brethren.

By late afternoon, all showered and cleaned up, we would front up at the Whiskey Company Baggies Bar for steaks and beer. Before this got underway, Major Torrance would call the role and single out all the boys that had turned 21 during our last stint in the scrub. He was a master at handling the men, although most of us had developed fairly cynical and hardened attitudes during our brief but intense time in-country. However, old E.T. convinced us all, for at least a short period of time, that achieving one's majority and celebrating it with a traditional birthday cake was still important even in the middle of hostile Vietnam. Every birthday boy would be called forward to receive a quick handshake and the major always managed to make some personal and relevant remarks to each individual. Included in his and the Company's best wishes was a 21st birthday cake. We all stood around in a loose formation for the informal ceremonies. Once the cake business was over it was down to the real deal of getting rat-arsed as quickly as possible.

Beer cost 15 cents a can and we tried our best to drink at least five dollars worth. Even the tightest wallet could afford to shout his mates in the Dat. The guitars would come out, and for the first time in weeks, sometimes months, we would catch up with our mates in the other platoons. We were close and totally committed to the W-3 identity and nothing, in my mind, other than for the passage of time, has changed that.

If we were lucky, the company would get a 48-hour pass and travel as a unit back through "Indian country" to the whorehouses and bars of Vung Tau, the nearest Vietnamese city. This was a great place, but we only got three or four trips to this passion paradise during the year we spent in-country. Considering that W-3 spent 325 days in the bush during our TOD, the boys were always "hot to trot" when they disappeared from the Peter Badco Club, our company drop off point. Propelled by our groins, we would fan out with amazing speed in search of bar girls and whores acquired on previous visits. Hours later, many of us would inevitably meet up at the Grand Hotel and, along with Captain Jim Brown, get absolutely legless.

The Australian military provost marshal must have had a bounty out on Kiwi scalps because we always ended up with our share of guys in the cells after a wild night on the town. He was a prize wanker and we hated him almost as much as the dreaded "White Mice," the South Vietnamese military police.

Our final operation started off the same as any other, but the company experienced an incident during our last week in the scrub that seriously marred our tour. Two call signs from one of our platoons mistakenly engaged each other and it turned into a case of force-on-force fratricide. Unfortunately, this was not an isolated incident. and at times other Kiwi companies that preceded us faced each other's gun muzzles. Our contact resulted in Tommy Cooper's death, Alan Herd with spinal injuries, from which he has only partially recovered, and Sammy Samson with gunshot wounds to his legs.

As a cohesive unit, we were totally devastated; when we returned to base, there was no joy in the Dat that night. However, in Vietnam death was not something we dwelled upon. Historically, alcohol has served as a valuable anti-depressant for the soldier and it was never more valid as it was in our AOR. Other than for the Padre and memorial services, we had no shrinks to help us cope with grief. This is something you had to resolve either with your fellow grunts help or on your own. Booze seemed to grease the skids of recovery, at least for most of us. Don't get me wrong, we were professionals, and in the bush we were cold stone sober, but back in Nui Dat these rules didn't apply, and us young guys were always ready for a bit of fun or general mischief.

We heard that Sammy and Alan were still in the hospital at Vung Tau and some bright spark suggested we travel to "Vungers" and visit them. Titty Harris, Scrubber Ryalls, Gannet Mullins, and half a dozen more of us, carried out this hasty plan. Half-pissed, we travelled through the Badlands lying on the back of a large Aussie steel tray truck. It was not the most comfortable journey, and when I looked around at our happy crew I was surprised to see Hank Puata from Victor 5 with us. How the hell he got there is still a mystery to me. Somewhere along the way, we got a little side tracked and ended up contributing to the welfare of the bars of Vung Tau and ended up taking an unofficial rest and recreation break for a couple of days. We raised merry hell and had a great time before our money ran out. Finally, the MP's rounded us up and herded us into the Aussie military cells. Our commands were duly notified and they reluctantly claimed their military "criminals." We were shipped back to Nui Dat in considerable disgrace. Most of us were stinking of beer, grubby, and half dressed. We looked like fugitives from a chain gang rather than soldiers. Gannet, a couple of others, and I had sold our military issue boots for beer money and we stood there barefoot in the dust awaiting the verbal firing squad.

I deeply regret the embarrassment and shame we caused our Whiskey Company hierarchy. We were a damn disgrace, but Sammy really enjoyed the visit and was deeply touched when he realized we all went AWOL to see a buddy in distress.

Fronting up to the Company Commander and CSM left us in no doubt as to the fate awaiting us in Singapore — we were all promised 30 days jail in the British Military Prison. Damn, not the best way to start a six month TOD in that fabulous city.

There were no brass bands or ceremonies as we boarded our aircraft to take us back to civilization and we departed much the same way as we had arrived a year ago. As we gained altitude, we were relieved to be out of the war, but the whole departure had been anti-climactic. I knew that for a lot of us it would take time to readjust. Going "cold turkey" from a combat routine to relatively quiet garrison life was going to create problems for some of the more field-oriented boys. For most of us, six more months of service remained prior to our discharge date, and the majority of Whiskey 3 Company was posted to Nee Soon Military Camp, Singapore.

When we landed, the First Royal New Zealand Infantry Regiment's Maori Cultural Party gave us an official welcome to the battalion lines and Tu ma Tauenga (the Infantry Battalion Marae). The ceremony was pretty moving and quite a few guys both Maori and Pakeha shed some tears that unmemorable day.

As newly returned veterans we believed that we were a cut above, or at least had some acquired some warrior mana within the military circle we had just joined. But, we were badly mistaken and it wasn't so. We were both envied and disliked by all ranks in the reinforcement companies. Oh how quickly we had forgotten our own discomfort over being the new and untested boys just a mere eighteen months earlier. Battalion morale at the time was at danger low. Many of these men had dedicated eighteen months of hard training specifically to see combat in Vietnam. With N.Z.'s decision to withdraw from the Vietnam conflict, all they had to look forward to now was a year to a year and a half of service in garrison. My young brother found himself in this unenviable position. To acquire campaign ribbons and professional credibility, Neil rejoined the military in 2002 (having retired in the early 90's from the NZSAS) as a 50 year-old captain and served in East Timor.

Whiskey 3 Company was not going to be replaced in RVN, so the practice of training up and passing on combat expertise to the new company's was no longer a priority. In turn, our command was mostly left to its own devices for the period we remained in South East Asia. Like processed food, we had a "use by date," and our packaging date indicated that our time was almost up. Our SNCO's and officers were replaced with new ones and we became a surplus item. Our new mission was playing rugby, drinking beer, and chasing bar girls in the seedy bars and back alleys of Geylang. All of which I carried out to the best of my abilities. I left Singapore with barely enough hand luggage to fill a suit cover. Six months of bar hopping had been a lot of fun but had drastically depleted my funds. I could have taken home my lovely and eager Asian bar girl and other trophies, but, atypically, reason prevailed and I walked away from those potential responsibilities once again. Many of my comrades had very little in the way of material possessions after two years in South East Asia. Sadly, for some, mental anguish was the reward that burdened them. But, for me, it had been a great life experience and I wanted more of it.

I stood in the city of Auckland with a couple of other guys from W3, for the first time in two years. It was mid-evening and after finally escaping from military madness for the next three weeks, priority number one was a good old feed of fish and chips, Kiwi style. The boys had all scattered from the airport, and for many of us our next reunion would come twenty years later. The welcome home was non-existent. We had been made aware of the anti-Vietnam movement and were prepared to expect some flack, and we were not disappointed. Whether young or old, it seemed everybody had an opinion on bloody Vietnam. I didn't pay much attention to their misinformed, biased bull shit, and still don't.

After a somewhat awkward home leave period, I couldn't get back to Burnham Military Camp quick enough. Rather then spend time catching up with family and friends, the mates I had in the military were the guys I wanted to be with. I was not prepared for the family or civilian scene, and like many servicemen from previous wars, not ready, or, in my case, willing to give up the camaraderie and comfort derived from my Vietnam companions. I rejoined the infantry for another three years.

I completed a two months posting to the Camp Training Wing while waiting for the formation of a new rifle company. Sergeant Tom "The Rat"

Rautau, a slight, but extremely tough little SNCO and former NZSAS member, was the driving force in our cell. Sgt Maxie Lawrence, Corporals "Hooks" Mathews, and Lehi Kaira, veterans of the Malayan, Borneo, and Vietnam campaigns provided him with able assistance. Sometime during this period, Lieutenant Bernie R.I. arrived as our training officer. He was a true blue Kiwi and one of the last to graduate from the British Military Academy at Sand Hurst. His slight build, aristocratic manner, augmented by a swagger stick and meticulous appearance, coupled with his British Rupert traits, belied what we naturally expected from such a stuffed shirt. He certainly did not seem to be the type to lead a bunch of rambunctious young infantryman from the wilds of rural New Zealand. He sure fooled us, because during Bernie's over twenty year military career he not only served as a troop and squadron commander, but rose to the much coveted position of colonel commander of 1 NZSAS Group. He was a consummate leader and a great guy. I consider myself extremely fortunate to have served under his command, both in the infantry and later while a member of the NZSAS.

With our withdrawal from Vietnam, training for such operational deployments was no longer a priority. This had a detrimental effect on troop morale and direction. Eventually, a new concept of soldiering developed and the "peace time, peace keeper" became the new mantra of the military. Instead of focusing on soldier's fighting wars defending N.Z.'s security and interests, the hierarchy became obsessed with packaging a product for UN export.

In Vietnam, soldiers were promoted based upon their performance during active service. Privates like John Nichols and Billy Kahaki successfully took over patrols as section commanders and some were promoted accordingly. It is doubtful that John or many like him could, or would, easily adjust to the new military system. An example of emasculation of responsibility was with the Mortar Fire Controllers. In Vietnam they were corporals, but this all changed, and months later, in the peacetime and contrary to lessons learned, the billet called for a sergeant to perform the same tasks.

Sour grapes on my part perhaps, but even years later I continued to receive course reports for infantry modules required for advancement that were excessively lengthy and required a brain surgeon to decipher. It seemed some instructors and course developers were writing to impress each other rather than for the aspiring grunt. Nonetheless, all of the courses I attended at the School of Infantry were totally professional, well presented, and invaluable to the students. The staff was extremely polished and focused. Unfortunately, too much weight was given to the course report for establishing "Top Student" status. In my opinion, the course report should serve as an indicator of potential performance and actual on the job achievements should be the primary method of career evaluation. In Vietnam, my end of tour report consisted of only three lines and that terse description of my performance meant a hell of a lot more to me than anything else ever written.

For the next three years I continued working in the rifle company scenario, which also included another two-year tour assigned to the Sembawang Garrison, Singapore. I became one of the many so called professional privates, guys who simply wanted to soldier outside of N.Z. rather than follow a more sensible career path plan. We did not see ourselves as losers or non performers, we were just not interested in the peacetime structure period. Bar girls, guitars, and rugby topped off with generous amounts of alcohol ridden holidays in South East Asia was the quest. Without us in retrospect the battalion would have struggled to fill its foot soldier quota? "B Company" Sergeant Major Danny and his wife, Jo, adopted many of us so-called single soldiers under their wing. He was a wiry, tough, incredibly fit individual and the consummate professional. Most of his military career had been in the NZSAS, and like a lot of career soldiers at the time he was taking the opportunity for an accompanied two year posting. Upon his return to N.Z., he would return to the SAS again as SSM (Squadron Sergeant Major). Under the supervision of Danny, HQ Section , B Coy became his own ten-man reconnaissance group. Lehi Kairau had been demoted to lance corporal again and Dave Lyver, Mike Sullivan, Ralph Matchitt, Mike Ngahue, Neville Prince, and the rest of us, did our best to emulate Danny.

Fitness was never a problem in those days and Danny had us jumping out of our skins. He led by example, whether it was rugby, bush time, or during the outfit's frequent booze breaks. It was the ANZAC's and Commonwealth SOP to "stand to" or to establish 100-percent alert before first and last light while operating in the jungle. It was a tactic adopted during the Malayan Confrontation days. Depending on the terrain and situation, we would be behind our guns in our fighting holes, huddled together in our wet clothing and belt order, with torrential monsoon rains bucketing down and totally pissed off. Suddenly, out of the gloom, Danny would appear in full kit and sit with the boys. He could have been sitting with the boss in the only hooch near the perimeter, drinking Milo and eating cakey buns, but that was not his style. On rare occasions, he would relate to us some of his adventures and war-time experiences. He would also talk about his soldiering in many countries and the various armies that he had deployed with. This was great stuff and provided me with motivational rocket fuel. Danny, like many of his SAS comrades, made an extremely positive contribution to the regular infantry and a very positive impression on the young and impressionable soldiers of the Singapore Battalion. Company Sergeant Major's Fred B. and Danny W., Sergeants Dave T., Dick K., and Corporals Jack Curtis, Roger M., Tom H., and others, injected the conventional military units with a much needed tonic. Their outstanding presence did more to promote the SAS than any other efforts. Coincidentally, Phil Cairns and I were the only members of Bravo Company under Danny's command that eventually passed SAS Selection.

During the two years in Singapore my company won most of the unit competitions. In the 1974 Battalion Skill at Arms Competition, we took first in everything, save for two second place finishes. In those days, the Skill At Arms teams were not pre-selected from the company roster and then formed into a dream team section. Everyone was a competitor and Danny was there to help spark even the least motivated to strive a good deal harder. Good old fashioned cursing, solid kicks up the arse, and the inculcation of the all for one and one for all philosophy usually got winning results. God help anyone who didn't give their all. It did not matter if you were a big, fat, and out-of-shape Mutha. As long as you kept going and gave it 100-percent, Danny would give you encouragement and credit for having heart.

Double timing as a unit around the bloody airfield every time somebody fucked up was something new. This included the Officers and NCOs. Guys like Steve Afamasaga, who could be counted on to open his suicidal mouth at least once a week while on company parade, were Danny's ready excuse for more physical training. Even before "Afa's" cockhead comment was completed, Danny would be cranking us up for his dreaded five mile run, which was extremely entertaining for the rest of the Battalion. Although the bar hopping and drinking continued with traditional enthusiasm, Danny's torture and group discipline was paying off in fitness dividends for me.

The combination of feeling I was ready for the Olympic trials, the positive role models projected by former SAS members, and the gnawing pain of having failed on my previous attempt, I decided to attend another SAS Selection course.

In 1974, the SAS ran their first Selection outside of N.Z. This took place in Singapore and Malaysia.

Day one, 0730, 84 others and I fronted up at Selection's initial parade. Accompanying me were my brother, Corporal Neil Henry, and Private Mosey Rangiwai, who, in the future, was to become my brother-in-law. Good old Warrant Officer Eric Ball, the meanest son of a bitch in the Universe, recognised me immediately and my day started of with a storm of, "CLOSE YOUR FUCKEN EYES HENRY, BY THE FRONT, SLOW MARCH." With that gracious greeting, I marched towards the six-foot deep open storm drains, completely at the mercy of this SAS fruitcake. Mosey, who at the time was a member of the battalion rugby team as a loose forward and certainly in the prime of his career, was built like the proverbial brick shithouse and incredibly swift for a big man. He was not easily intimidated, but he was also not stupid. Upon E.B.'s non-negotiable directive to me, Mosey stepped forward and announced that he was pulling off the course. E.B. went fucken ballistic and screamed, "YOU CAN'T FUCKEN PULL OFF, 'CAUSE WE HAVEN'T FUCKEN STARTED YET."

Things went down hill from there and for the next twelve hours, confusion reigned as far as we were concerned. We were quickly formed into squads and run all over camp and the airfield with no particular destination. The SAS staff hounded stragglers until they quit and then attacked the fitness freaks that were up front trying to impress everyone. Stick to the middle of the pack and become the grey man was something that I had learned the first time around this insane asylum. Duck walks, press-ups, mud runs, fireman's carry, and timed races in the Olympic swimming pool, while wearing full kit, were a few of the treats that we digested during that first day. In those days, physical beasting and mental bashing were in vogue.

At 5:00 pm, following a strenuous muscle boggling session on the confidence course, we were ordered to stand down for ten minutes. Paul Mokomoko, Paul Macfadden, Murray Rowe, Dick Witehira, Zukhov, Hoani, a half a dozen others, and I, had survived the initial fusillade of physical sickeners. We were barely half way through our first 24-hour test period and only thirteen candidates remained. On the old Selection course, a satisfactory performance on the first day and night was crucial. As always, first impressions were usually lasting ones. On the second day, the emphasis shifted to individual efforts, such as jungle terrain map marching and the start of long tabbing.

It wasn't all physical, and seated in the Band room building, pen and paper was distributed and we were told to write down our life stories. Since we received only one sheet of paper it appeared that this was merely a ploy to keep us busy. The instructors were unusually quiet and, for some reason, appeared uncomfortable.

The officer in charge of the Selection team slowly walked in and made one of the most jaw dropping statements that I had ever heard in my 23-year old life. For reasons beyond his control, Selection would stop and restart all over again at 0730 the following day. However, the biggest kick in the balls was to follow. All of the 84 original candidates were instructed to start again. We were totally pissed off and extremely disillusioned. I know I was fucken broken and I walked out of the room back to the barracks completely devastated.

I have never fully understood why or who made this incredible decision, but I have good reason to believe that the battalion commander, who had been a troop commander in the original NZSAS, was bitterly disappointed with his Battalion's performance and insisted upon this unprecedented re-start. It was a bad call and threatened to corrupt the process. Back in N.Z. the SAS would have never acknowledged such pressure.

Well, I spat the dummy and refused to start again. The next morning, along with a handful of others I was marched into the battalion head shed and reprimanded for not restarting. Contrary to all Army Rules regarding Selection details, I had to sign a statement regarding my reasons for not following the directive. Without hesitation, I did so. This incident destroyed any motivation for me to remain in the military. So, for the next six months I simply soldiered on and once I returned home, I wanted out.

TeAo, my Kiwi girlfriend, arrived in Singapore and we were married. With the support of Wally Joe, Roger "Bushy" Henry, Mattie Phillips, Margy and Trevor Good, I survived a horrendous stag party and managed to stumble through our military wedding ceremony. It was brilliant and the Maori Culture Group under Huia Brown (Jim Brown's wife) gave it the special aura it deserved. A tremendous wedding reception followed and the battalion's extended family of wives and dependants completed the event. Danny and Jo, along with many others, made it all happen. However, one glitch occurred. We had to have a substitute Father to give TeAo away. Tui Stirling, her cousin, was nominated. Unfortunately, Tui, in true East Coast fashion, ended up at the wrong damn church and someone else's wedding. Again, in typical Coasty fashion, he was not in the least a bit fazed and remained there enjoying himself at Stan Martin's reception. TeAo hurriedly grabbed another substitute and Sergeant Sonny Lakatani, currently the Premier of Niue Island, did the deed. Almost thirty happy years later, with three grown up children and two grandkids, I am not complaining.

In retrospect, Singapore had been an interesting period for me, but in no way did I wish to continue serving in a peacetime infantry battalion since the emphasis was now on coursemanship and looking good. Teeth Arm soldiering requires active service to separate the chaff from the wheat. Vietnam, in spite of its negative aspects, certainly exposed the non-performers. Nevertheless, my military future was very dim, and since the force's new direction disappointed me, the die was cast.

To Ani Wiki, Neville Prince, Tom Rogers, Mike Ngahue, MacKenzie Maaka, Vern Pomanma, Les Collier, Bun Cribb, Phil Cairns, Keepa Paenga, and a host of others, had we been given the opportunity to serve together in war I am confident we would have conducted ourselves with typical Kiwi honor. One thing would have been guaranteed, under Danny's leadership we would have been a bloody sight quicker and fitter than most.

Since 1974, CSM Danny has been the inspiration for much of what I have achieved and is without peer. To this day, his efforts and professionalism continue to inspire me. I am truly grateful for those two years in Singapore under his uncompromising guidance and occasional, but effective, kicks up the ass.

Ngati Porou Pursuit

Duke's Story

Civilian Life on New Zealand's East Coast

As explained in previous chapters, my early childhood was not a happy one. I was an extremely shy individual who had suffered all the typical growing pains of a country youth, and in my case, was significantly increased by my confused feelings regarding my parents broken marriage. My two blood brothers and I were never as close as we should have been and about the only thing we had in common as young adults was that all three of us had served in New Zealand's infantry battalions in South East Asia. Additionally, Neil and I served together in the N.Z. Special Air Service in the mid-eighties. The situation has certainly improved in later years, although my mother still struggles at times to understand my frequent lapses of compassion when she is involved. Divorce was not something unique to our clan. Dad's parents; my grandparents, were also divorced, so my concept of marriage was probably not a very positive one. That was before I met "TeAo Puangi Angi Rangiuiaia — Rangiwai." This red-haired, fair-skinned Maori maiden from the East Coast curbed any further desire for my bar hopping and stopped my old South East Asian antics dead in their tracks. My six-year apprenticeship and subsequent long-term commitment to the sleazy bars and fallen women of the Asian region ceased to be part of my travel routine. In spite of my pre-conceived notions and personal experiences of a disrupted family structure, I was now determined to be a good husband.

On the long flight returning home from Singapore, I was well aware of the significance of my first visit to TeAo's hometown of Ruatoria. The step I was about to take was far more serious than anything that I had ever taken before. I was about to travel deep into the heartland of Ngati Porou Maoridom with few credentials and little preparation, except for my glowing and pregnant young bride. In my mind, these were not great odds, and it was an understatement to say that I was a bit hesitant when I disembarked the aircraft at Gisborne City.

TeAo's sister, Rio, picked us up, and we drove what seemed like hours to get the obligatory homecoming visit out of the way. Rio was an extremely shy and private person and struggled to say more than a couple of words during the two hour trip. However, this changed once we got to know each other and she quickly became my favourite sister-in-law. Steven, TeAo's red-haired, four-year-old little brother sat on my knee during the entire journey. If I had been aware of the mischief he was capable of causing I would have wrung his little neck then and there. Since that initial ride, he has upset me at least a million times, but it is impossible not to have a soft spot for Steve. He has a heart of gold and now, as an adult, he can be counted on whenever trouble looms. Being a Pakeha (European) did not appear to be a problem for my new in-laws. However, I am the first to admit that I gave them plenty of reasons to question their daughter's choice of husband for a number of years. It took quite awhile, but eventually, over the oncoming years, I began to fit into this tight knit clan.

Maggie "Makere" Rangiwai (*nee* Pipi) was my new mother-in-law. She was a shy, modest woman who was perpetually fussing around her numerous children and mokopunas (grandchildren), but definitely the dominant force in the family structure. Bill "Piri te Aruhe" Rangiwai (Rangiuiaia), a tough East Coast Maori (Ngati Porou) and my father-in-law, measured six foot plus and weighed over 15 stone (210 lbs.) He was very much a man of the land. Maggie, although Maori, had a fair complexion that she passed on to most of her children. The red hair and freckles originally came from George (Hori Punehu) Taylor. This Irish ancestor of hers had jumped from his whaling ship in the mid 1800's, married locally, and resided in Whareponga for several years. Bill was proud of his reputation as a hard working, honest individual and his motto, which he shared with his crew of mates, was definitely "work hard and play hard." Considering my lack of social skills and knowledge of Maori etiquette, things went fairly smooth between the two of us. Bill's first comment after introductions were made to one and all was one of resignation, "Oh well, at least he's not Nga Bush." The "Nga Puhi (Nga Bush) Tribe" from up North, had raided throughout the East Coast and caused considerable mayhem in the early days of Maori tribal warfare. So, bringing home a white man wasn't quite as bad as marrying a dreaded Northerner.

James Pope, my great, great Grandfather had trekked through the East Coast in the late 1800's and early 1900's as the first inspector of Native Schools. Unfortunately, he was long gone and I wasn't too confident that his reputation would do me much good now. At the modest family house, the dining table was covered with loads of great East Coast food. There was fry bread and golden syrup appetizers, wild pork, *kumara* (sweet native potato), watercress, topped off with a sack of *kinas* (sea urchins) in the kitchen sink. There was also more *koura* (crayfish) than I had ever seen in my life before. After a quick hug and introductions, the meal began. Bill and Maggie had thirteen children. At least ten of them were peering intently at the new brother-in-law and the meal was constantly interrupted by the arrivals of curious relatives. It was quite a crowd. Only those who have experienced large family gatherings can understand how I felt. The welcome was simply brilliant and I considered phase one was complete.

Although I had met a couple of TeAo's sisters in Wellington and served with Moana (Mo or Mosey), her older brother, in South East Asia, I still had a few potential obstacles to deal with. First and foremost, I had to front up at the local pub and meet the rest of the Whareponga-based relations. As in all small rural communities, everyone knows everyone else's business and secrets do not exist. Rumour control was a living thing, so when I walked into town my presence had been noticed and my appearance at the local pub was anticipated long in advance. I stood in the shadows of Bill's house at 449 Amiria Avenue, deep in thought for several seconds and solemnly anticipated the next phase of my welcome. My mind raced back to Singapore and my first encounter with Mo, two years earlier. The Kiwi battalion rugby team was playing a visiting team of British rugby players that included several former internationals. One of them was big Campbell Lamerton. He was a giant of a man and had represented England in numerous international tests. Although somewhat past his prime, he was still a fearsome sight when in full lumbering flight with the rugby ball dwarfed by his enormous hands. I had recently returned to Singapore, for my second two-year stint while Mo was completing the last stages of his twenty-four month South East Asian and Vietnam tour of duty. The game was well underway when Campbell grabbed the ball from a line out and starts to rumble down the field like a Centurion tank, shrugging off tacklers with ease. All of a sudden, a red-haired, jet-propelled, 5-foot 8-inch Maori missile streaks forward and smashes into Campbell, front on, at groin level. There was a deafening impact followed by an agonising tangle of legs and arms and down went the ex-British Lions player for the duration of the game. Mo had done something that the hard men of New Zealand and South African rugby teams of the late 60's and early 70's had never been able to achieve. He had cancelled out one of the toughest guys of that rugby era with real guts and seemingly with comparative ease. That was my first and lasting impression of Mosey.

Bill and I strolled down to the pub as the evening shadows grew. Not a lot was said and I'm sure he was wondering what the hell he was going to do with this young pakeha boy if things turned bad inside the Manutahi Pub. I managed to stumble every now and then in the potholes and rain corrugations in the crushed gravel road. Sidewalks were non-existent then and things haven't changed much since. Even now, 28 years later, Amiria

Avenue, the earliest Maori Affairs sub-division in Ruatoria Township, is still waiting for the local Gisborne City Council to plan and build sidewalks for the residents.

At that time, the Manutahi Hotel in Ruatoria was the one and only drinking establishment in this small town of 5000 residents. The East Coast was then, and still is, considered the Wild West of New Zealand. The bar patrons conveyed this with their plain mode of dress and country manners. Ginge Kaiwai and Mac Fox enthusiastically backed up big Knobby Mackie, the chief barman. Knobby was a large and imposing Maori in his late forties, and a perfect gentleman. He was always immaculately dressed, soft spoken and low key no matter what the situation was. However, he ruled the Manutahi, with an iron fist and there was no trouble when Knobby was behind the bar. One look at his huge mitts as they enveloped mine in a welcoming handshake convinced me that his outward demeanour could be hiding a real terror if he was sufficiently provoked. After crossing the bar's threshold, my trepidation caused me to quickly glance around its interior. A rough-looking clientele had bellied up to the bar, all elbows on the counter top, with the inevitable hand-rolled, burning fag hanging from their lips. Numerous jugs of draught beer and large quart-sized beer bottles were at hand and the ongoing conversations were rowdy and deafening. All patrons, mostly hard working farmers, were in their work clothes and also wore the tools of their trade: a scabbard containing a lethal looking "butcher knife" and sharpening steel. These knives were the shepherd's tools of the trade and used mainly for slaughtering and dressing meat. A certain professional pride was evident and men did not willingly share their knives with just anyone.

All fights back then were usually settled with fists, although on the odd occasion some loser might slip in a quick kick to the ribs. Fights were seldom stopped, and if you started a ruckus then you better give it your best shot, because until someone went down the pounding would continue. I found this out early. Once on the ground, it was over only if you stayed down. It was the universal admission of surrender and time out. I never heard of or observed the "butcher knife" becoming a weapon in a brawl, no matter how desperate the situation becomes. Although knock down, drag out, bare knuckle fights were frequent and swift, heaven help any scrapper who resorted to low down and dirty tactics.

I anxiously searched for a friendly face, but couldn't find one. I had accumulated considerable experience in the South East Asian bars, dives, and brothels, but I was hard pressed to remember seeing such a concentration of capable looking cut-throats in any one place before. It was going to be a long night; however, after a couple of stiff shots of Square Gin I was beyond any pain and my anxiety went with it. At this stage, I had only been introduced to the Aunties: Maggie Tak, Lady Rose Moeke, Teo, and Mama Tamati, so things were going to require a fair amount of fortitude to get through the evening.

The local Maori farmed most of the land, but there were a few Europeans in the community. Maoris of the Ngati Porou are fiercely proud of their identity and it didn't matter that a fair percentage of them sported blue eyes and fair complexions. Many also possess surnames like Walker, Biddett, Hovell, Mackie, Collier, and Fox, but above all they are Ngatis and damn proud of it. I moved around the pub trailing behind Bill. The respect he received from his peers was obvious. His early stature as a sheep shearer was legendary throughout the East Coast. These days he worked with the Waiapu County Council and was the master grader driver for the community. He excelled at this vocation and had acquired a tremendous network of friends throughout the coastal area. At least once a week Bill, driving his giant grader, would return home through town with a dressed mutton or wild pig draped over the blade. Farmers and close relations always appreciated a little extra help with private roadways, blocked culverts, and gateways, and this was work that Bill freely did above and beyond his official obligations.

The military has always attracted Maori and a significant majority were, and still are, from the Ngati Porou regions. At one stage in the 1980's, John Collier, Dougie Walker, Eddy Tuhaka, and Sam Awarau, all East Coast born and bred, held the top warrant officer positions in the infantry. My friends in the infantry battalions included East Coast men like Geese Nepe, Henry Banks, Paul Moana, and Marbo Fox. Unfortunately, none of them were home when I needed them. I slipped over to the pool table and was introduced to Bill's close friends, many of whom were cousins and uncles, and the handshakes and smiles were genuine. From that day on, I have never looked back. Much can be said about how rural people tend to congregate, assist, and help in times of need, and Ruatoria was no exception. The men and women worked hard during the week and then drinkers and non-drinkers alike would stroll down to the local pub to catch up on the gossip and daily commerce of information. Television, with its one channel and poor reception, had just arrived. The picture hall had been boarded up years earlier and the few shops closed when it got dark. The pool and billiard saloon catered to the teenagers, while the Manutahi Hotel was the primary source of recreation available to adults.

Among the distinguished crew that gathered at the Manutahi on Thursdays, Fridays, and Saturdays, were Harry Ngarimu and his younger brother Pine. Harry was severely wounded while a member of the famous 28th Maori battalion during World War II. Their brother, Moana nui a kiwa Ngarimu, who was killed in action, was the only East Coast Maori

Victoria Cross recipient. Hook Kaiwai was the best one-handed pool player on the Coast. Pinto Pete Taewa, also a member of the legendary unit, was a tiny little guy. Facing hardened elements of Rommel's Afrika Corps, he and members of "Cowboy Company" boldly carried out the traditional "haka," or Maori war dance, in front of the enemy prior to launching a bayonet assault. Laughing, Pinto reckoned that he jumped so high at the end of the haka that he took a wild 8mm Mauser round through one of his balls. No worries, he had another one, and when he got back to N.Z., he generously contributed to the gene pool by producing several sons twice his size. Joe Brown was an eccentric Korean Vet and could be relied upon to be wearing anything from safety pin earrings, gaudy bandanas, or a Mexican sombrero. Harry and Johnny Rei Haenga, the terrible twins from Whareponga, kept us fed with *kai moana* (seafood) and anything else that grazed along the sides of the road. Guy Tamati and Big Bill Tangera added considerable size and muscle to this awesome group.

At long last, closing time arrived and I staggered out of the pub barely aware of what night it was let alone what time zone we had entered. This was the first time I had trouble leaving the Manutahi, but certainly not the last. Significant volumes of beer and a healthy wallet had assisted bonding. I was no longer a total stranger. I had been introduced to the Whareponga and Jeru whanau and in about twenty years time, if I played my cards right, I could, on a good day, almost be considered a local.

However, for TeAo and I, our problems were only just beginning. Some serious thought regarding our next stage in life had to be made. The infantry battalion's lifestyle was certainly not conducive for generating a sound platform of marriage between two young people like us. My deep-seated suspicion and newly acquired jealous nature would have destroyed our relationship in months under the military system. Therefore, the choice was obvious. I would take my discharge from the services and become a civilian again and avoid the hazards of long periods of separation and stress that are commonplace in the military. The service had proven to be a God-send for me. The harsh infantry system coupled with the Vietnam conflict had given me the opportunity to rediscover my self-esteem and develop deep bonds of friendship and loyalty. But, a simple taste of the great East Coast life and Teao's family made the decision making process relatively easy. I barely gave the previous six years of military service a thought, and the decision to leave the army, once made, never became an issue.

TeAo stayed on the Coast awaiting the birth of our first born under the protective umbrella of her numerous aunts, cousins, and ever-present Mum. I returned to the military and sat out the two-month period of service left on my military contract. With my military obligation completed, we were finally reunited and now had a lovely blue-eyed baby daughter, a couple hundred dollars in the bank, no car, no house, and no job. However, the birth of my first child overshadowed any concerns about my future prospects for the moment. Nevertheless, determined to do the right thing I took my family back to my Mother's home in Taranaki, so she could enjoy being a grandmother and also to have a base to work from. Mum was over the moon with Tanya, since she was the only girl in her family and, never having had a daughter of her own, she had missed out on having any feminine companionship. Tanya was her first grandchild and granddaughter as well, so Mum was understandably chuffed.

As a 24-year-old ex-infantryman with absolutely no civilian skills, I felt more apprehension going out and competing in the private sector than I had at any time during my stint on active service. Through my younger brother, John Smart, I was introduced to the foreman of the New Zealand Dairy Board Cool Stores, in New Plymouth. John was blessed with all the brains in our family and the only one who opted out of the military. Mind you, he couldn't hold a note or sing worth a damn, which are very important qualities if you wished to live on the East Coast. So in my mind the trade off was a fair one. In those days he was an astute young university student who worked in the off-season to gain the cash reserves needed to pay his university fees. Today he is an extremely successful bio-chemist, happily married and a doting father, but still a completely humble and helpful individual. My hiring consisted of a brief conversation, a handshake, and the foreman's approval to start work the following day. Although I was making good money with plenty of overtime, I hated it. After eight to fourteen hours of loading and unloading crates of cheese and butter into, or from CONEX containers and railway carriages, I felt like a bloody robot. Although a certain amount of endurance was required, it wasn't too physical. It was the mindless repetition and mundane environment that forced me to chuck it in. At night, all I dreamed about was damn cheese and butter. There I was, every day with my work gang, throwing crates of butter and cheese onto the rollers, a job that monkeys could do after minimal training. After three months of tedium and total job dissatisfaction, I was out of there.

We moved back to Gisborne and this seaside, low key, back water city became our new home for the next four years. TeAo's parents home was only an hour and a half away up the Coast in Ruatoria. TeAo and I had a tiny, one bedroom flat right in the town's center and, not having a car, walking distance to various amenities was crucial. I was fortunate and entered into an adult apprenticeship program with Lorry Gray in the painting and decorating trade. Pay was extremely low and things would have become drastic if the family had not helped out. My new workmates were all good guys, but Bo Te Aho became my main companion along with his family. His Mum was a lovely women (European) and his dad, "Big Bad" Basil Te Aho, ran Watties Canneries for many years with his charm and iron fists. Bo was a chip off the old block for sure. This 25-year-old muscle beach guy, complete with Harley Davidson, tattoos, earrings, and pony-tail, had all the old pensioners and elderly people we worked for (painting their houses) completely mesmerised. Bo would sweet talk them with polished ease and they loved him. In the mornings when we got to work he would pick up the milk bottles from the gateway and deliver them to the old girls in person, then in the evenings take out the rubbish tins for refuse pick up. Nothing was too difficult or inconvenient. He genuinely enjoyed chatting up these old girls, and before we knew it they would have the stoves pumping. And, as only the old nannies could, they would bake wonderful cakes and cookies especially for our smoko breaks. What a man! The very same night he would be down at the local boozer, cracking heads and arm wrestling the local heavys.

TeAo and Tanya would travel back to Ruatoria on Thursday evenings, courtesy of the bus driver, who also happened to be her brother-in-law, Chris Palmer. I would take the bus back on the Friday after work and invariably get rat-ass drunk at the pub. Instead of sleeping in, I would get up and play rugby the next day. Rugby in those days was a serious business and you couldn't just play for anyone. It was like tribal warfare and you had to represent your whanau. Since I had no choice in the matter, I played for Hikurangi, which was Teao's and most of Whareponga's team. Eighty-year-old Charlie Ferris was our club patron and he still saddled and rode his horse as a regular means of transport around the area. We played every weekend, and often the game required the team and supporters to travel by bus to outside venues. This was an experience in itself. Our supporters were blatantly one-eyed, and losing a game was the ultimate disgrace. This often caused tempers and "rugby rage" to be openly displayed by the supporting cast. Sometimes there was more action off the field than on. As one of the only pakehas on the field, I could usually count on receiving minor medical care after each game. The East Coast theory at the time was that white men were the cause of all the problems in the world, so any of them foolish enough to set foot on a rugby paddock deserved extra attention. The universal East Coast tactic was to nail (smash, crash, or bash in a tackle) the pakeha early in the game and check out his recovery rate and pucker factor reaction. This was not a problem for guys like John Cameron, Ian Smith, Peter McGranaghan, and many others who played for years on the East Coast, Ruatoria circuit. In the Army, no quarter was ever given or asked for during any physical activity so this was not something new to me. My skills as a player were only average, but nevertheless, after several broken noses and split eyebrows, I was proud to have contributed in some small way to

Hikurangi's considerable success over a five year period. Team mates such as V.J., Johnson Takarangi, Grope, Gina and Bone Dog Morice, Les and Jim White, Bart Keelan, Blue Kawai, Bob Moeke, J.P. Pohatu, Peter McGranahgan, Tiger Pohatu, Morgan and Goon Reedy played with their hearts and souls.

The referees on the Coast were unabashedly biased. On one occasion, a co-opted individual, Mr. Reweti Green, seriously handicapped our team. We were playing Tiki-Tiki on their home turf and the opposing halfback retrieved the ball from a stoppage in play. While the ensuing scrum was packing down for the restart, the halfback looked at the referee and asked, "Whose ball, ref?" Without hesitation, Mr. Green replied, "Ours."

The crowd frequently got intimately involved. One spectator was banned for life because he tackled a player who had out manoeuvred around the opposition and was galloping for the try line. However, in my opinion, the wildest part of the game was the return trip home, particularly after a hard-won victory. After one great victory, we staggered out of a pub in the vanquished neighbouring town of Te Araroa. Guitars were being hammered to accompany our raucous voices that were raised to their maximum decibel levels. To be sure, to the victor went the spoils, but to be honest we partied just as hard when we lost, which fortunately in those days, was not too often. We finally boarded our charter for the one-hour journey back to Ruatoria. The bus was rocking. Crates of beer were stacked along the bus aisle and bottles of Square Gin made the rounds as the singing continued. Eventually, bladders began to protest and the inevitable comfort stop was in order. We were at Mimi Hill, miles from nowhere, surrounded by farmland and bush covered hills. This was rural New Zealand, at its best. "Piss stop folks, men to the left and women to the rear." "Ahhhh!" The collective sounds of relief were almost as loud as the constant background of songs and laughter. Colbert's buses had to have been the most pissed on coaches in N.Z. Lizards and ladies drained, we clambered back on board and the guitars it seemed had barely missed a lick.

Our triumphant arrival at the Manutahi Pub was only eclipsed by the victory parade held years later when we whipped Dennis Connor in the America's Cup Yacht Race. We had three local teams in Ruatoria, and the competition was fierce. Winning teams totally glorified their achievements and we were no exception. The doors were flung open and we made our grand entrance, welcomed by the cheering and deafening verbal accolades from the whanau and supporters that formed an informal advanced party. However, an hour or so later our celebration was diluted somewhat when a group of weary stragglers entered the pub. This time the entrance was less enthusiastic and the bus driver became a target for abuse. It appeared that he had driven off from our comfort break without conducting the usual head count and left a couple of our longer pausing women behind. They had been stranded in the darkness on a lonely, secluded country road and had to walk several miles while hoping that a friendly vehicle would come along. Bedraggled and angry, they were not a happy group. No worries, nothing a few cold beers couldn't fix. In short order, the singing and celebrating resumed.

Uncle Harry "H" Ngarimu and his Whareponga homestead hold special memories for me. He took me under his wing and showed me many of the old ways. He was a master in the art of gathering seafood. His approach was a semi traditional one and after intensely studying the tides and moon states on the Maori calendar, we would find ourselves patiently catching crayfish from the under water ledges, in the dark, by bobbing. In this traditional native method you cut a manuka pole at least six feet in length. On one end is a pod made out of chicken wire, in which you place Paua (N.Z. abalone). The crayfish leave their craggy ledges and try to snatch the bait, but usually became hopelessly entangled in the wire. He also took great joy in introducing me to diving for Kina, Koura, and Paua, taking me to many of his "secret" diving locations. No matter how cold the water was, his only insulation was a woollen bushman's vest and pair of old overalls.

After a couple of hours of diving or bobbing, we would load up his patient old pack horse with our booty and return to his home situated only a couple hundred meters from the ocean. Waiting for us would be the beer and nips of gin to warm up the insides. Nanny Sani and Harry's numerous daughters would start the cooking process and the seafood would get prepared for the big cook up and BBQ. Unfortunately, Harry's twinkling eyes and humble manner hid a deep-seated desire to ensure that anyone who frequented his home and took advantage of his hospitality could only leave on a stretcher. That old guy was the champion East Coast beer drinker, and to my knowledge, has never been beaten. Those that dared to attempt to keep up with Uncle Harry paid the price and, young or old, all went down well before he retired for the night. In the summer months we would spend hours in the evening together mesmerized by the hearty outdoor fire that seemed to burn perpetually. That fire was like a beacon that lures the proverbial moth, and for some deep-seated reason, I couldn't ignore its interruption of the darkness.

During those wonderful early days I would often find myself galloping at breakneck speed along the sea's shoreline mounted on a sturdy Ngati steed, with young Steve holding onto me for dear life. We charged around the beach towards Waipiro Bay. We had to get to Mataahu and complete our hand line fishing expedition prior to the sand sharks invading the area at last light. All this nocturnal activity was not done for sport, but rather to put food on the table. We were subsistence hunters and fishermen well before the term became fashionable.

My wife's brothers and relatives were a great crew. One of the cousins, Campbell Keelan, had taken a "friendly" M-16 round through the back of his calf while in Vietnam. It tore up his leg, but he seemed to ignore any of its after effects. Along with Cam, there was Rocky Pardoe, another brother-in-law, and young Bartoria Keelan, one of TeAo's numerous brothers. Rocky came from a large family that lived in Manutuke, eighty miles away. The Pardoe's were a prominent crew in Poverty Bay and the East Coast regions. Rocky's pakeha Dad, C.P. Pardoe, was definitely old school and quite a man in his day. Rocky was a hard working sheep shearer and kept this difficult lifestyle up until his late forties. This, in itself, is quite a feat. He frequently lamented that he wished he had done a tour in Vietnam. Unfortunately, as a youth he had destroyed his potential military career when as a conscripted soldier under the compulsory military training program, he went AWOL for some long forgotten reason. Bart also maintained the family tradition and was also an accomplished shearer. Sheep shearing requires considerable strength, stamina and skill. It was a major occupation in N.Z., but sadly the youth of today have little desire to take on this extremely difficult lifestyle. Having said that, 20 years later, Bart's youngest son, Hemi, is well on the way to becoming a shearer of considerable promise and his tallies are up there with his Dad's. Bart and I hunted wild pig together, played rugby on the same team, and occasionally worked for Cam's painting business. At times we made poor old Cam's life miserable, but he would get his own back by physically punishing us on hunting trips. Bullet wounds or not, he was a walking fool in the rugged hill country. It was all pretty much Foreign Legion stuff, "march or die," he waited for no man.

John Kershaw, another good mate from my army days and boyfriend of one of the Rangiwai sisters, was passionate about playing the guitar, singing, drinking, organizing darts competitions in the pub, and rugby. Considering that he had taken a North Vietnamese AK47 round through the throat area, his vocal capabilities were amazing. The wound in no way impeded his capability to swallow alcohol either. Weekends were rich and full and devoted to rugby, diving, pig hunting, and drinking beer, but not necessarily in that order.

Pig hunting East Coast style, is extremely simple, but potentially dangerous. Captain Cook, the early British explorer, originally introduced these wild boars to the country. They are commonly referred to as "Captain Cookers" and are a tough, savage, and mobile adversary. One or more men on horseback and a couple of good pig dogs form the hunting party. Hunters ride or walk into the pig's habitat, then the dogs take over. The dogs, known as finders and holders, will perform one of two tasks. Finders will cast about in large sweeps trying to wind or scent a pig's sign or activity. Once they have picked up a lead they will begin the chase. The holders follow in close pursuit, ready to take over once the quarry is run to ground. The dogs are trained only to bark when they have made contact with the beast. Excited barking mixed with roaring and squealing from the boar indicate that the dogs have been successful and the hunters need to move in quickly before the dogs get gored. To prevent the pigs from escaping, the holders will go for the boar's ears or ball bags and this often results in dogs being ripped or killed by these tuskers. Once the pig is stopped and held, the hunter moves in for the kill. You have to move quickly before the dogs tire or get maimed. The dogs must remain locked on to the animal or else the situation could become extremely awkward for the hunter. The hunter grabs the animal and flips it on its back. The dogs are still chewing hell out of the animal's ears to keep the head secure. While the screams and snarling of the dogs and boar gets pretty daunting, it's sweet music to the true hunter's ears. Simultaneously, with his "pig sticker" knife he thrusts down through the pig's lower throat into its heart. The pig quickly bleeds to death, but as long as it twitches or shows signs of life, the trusty dogs will hang onto the animal.

The hunt generally culminates with a long and difficult carry of the carcass through the scrub to the waiting horse. Because of the "blow fly" problem, the animals are normally carried guts and all to the vehicle for final transportation to the chiller. Considering the size of the animal, an "entrails in" haul is an energy and strength sapping experience. Wild pigs are covered with a coarse matt of long hair or bristles and the best method of cleaning the animals is to singe them over a brush fire using creek water and a knife. The heat and ensuing steam works wonders. Once the animal has been singed, then it is gutted and cleaned. Done properly, the animal is a smoky but glowing tan color and ready for refrigeration. Back home, wild pork is definitely considered a delicacy.

These feral animals are savage creatures and frequently rogue boars and sows will develop a taste for young lambs during the lambing season. Both the ewe and lamb are extremely vulnerable at this time and are frequently attacked, ripped apart, and eaten by these pigs. Some boars have attained almost mythical reputations because of the large number of dogs they have killed in battle. Mobs of wild pigs cause unbelievable damage to pasture land, rooting up the grass and turf with incredible ease. To the local farmers they are not a just a source of food, but are a genuine concern because of potential loss of livestock and the denuding of grazing land.

The Whareponga Marae was TeAo's tribal base. The tribe and hapus (clans) have an ancient lineage with a history that was frequently characterized by wars and violence, long before Captain Cook staggered ashore in nearby Poverty Bay. They are a strong, resilient, and self-reliant people, and I have developed a tremendous admiration for many of them. For the last 30-odd years, I have listened intently to the stories and living history imparted by the elders and eagerly participated in the celebrations and marae-based festivities. I have, when required, helped dig the graves and bury relations at the family *urupa* (cemetery) and I trust that when my time comes, my final send off will be from Whareponga Marae. Hopefully, by owning a pub, it will guarantee that at my wake the mourners will not run out of liquid refreshment.

Prior to the mid 60's Whareponga was a bustling little settlement; however, a genuine lack of amenities and a new housing project in nearby Ruatoria forced people to reconsider their options and relocate. As the men were predominately shearers and away from home during the work season, it was up to the elders, women, and children to augment the family larder. The women would plant large vegetable gardens which supplement the abundance of game and seafood. The people were poor by today's standards, but in retrospect, they had much more to show for their efforts. Nobody ever went wanting, mainly due to the close family ties and support systems that were truly the greatness of that generation. Everyone was semi-productive and had some input to the whanau cupboards. TeAo's grandfather was a stern old advocate of the day, and the morning toil invariably began with the rising of the sun and finished when he deemed the day over. Sunday was the one and only day of rest. There were few if any idle hands at the "Gunga" (Whareponga) in those days.

The nearest hospital was at Te Puia Springs. Pregnant women travelled six miles by horseback around the beachfront to Waipiro Bay. This trip was normally negotiated during low-tide, or in emergencies, mid-tide. With rising seawater, the horse's progress was seriously impeded. After this wet ordeal, the last leg of the journey would be in Jim Morrissey's cab. Every now and then a newborn took their first look at the outside world through Jim's car windows.

Toss Mato Senior, another local stalwart and Bill's brother-in-law, once told me that whenever the shearing was finished, the men would buy a keg of beer and obtain groceries before making the perilous night time journey home around the beach's treacherous shoreline. Toss owned a packhorse that was worth its weight in gold. Every now and then, he and his Whareponga cronies would break into the back of the general store at Waipiro and abscond with some goods. They would carefully load it onto the horse and then send it home around the six-mile beach to Whareponga. The late night requisitions completed, they would then continue drinking at the bar. Later, at their leisure, they would openly depart without any of their misbegotten gains in evidence. Like a homing pigeon, the trusty pack horse would be found dozing under the trees by the Mato house, waiting patiently to be unloaded. Not withstanding the frequency of the journeys, or the state of the inebriated horsemen, Toss and Bill could not recollect losing a keg of beer on this rugged ride, but the same couldn't be said for the groceries.

Johnny Rei, Daisy and Harry Haenga, Mama and Roy Rose, Guy Tamati, Darkie Tamati, Toss and Kura Mato, Mo Keefe, Uncle "H" and Sani, Honey Bee, Nanny Fan and Dave Morice, Piri and Maggie Rangiwai, although many have passed on, they had a gigantic impact on my life. Hopefully, I, in turn, can pass on similar messages and traditions to my grandkids and young nieces and nephews coming on the scene.

Although I was quite happy with my civilian lifestyle, my thoughts frequently drifted back to the military and my former comrades. My failed attempt at SAS Selection was still a burning issue with me. In my mind, only success could purge the festering guilt trip and embarrassment for not making the grade. I knew I had to eventually make good and pass Selection. I was 29 years old, totally recharged and ready to go. Sergeant Lucky Monroe, an old friend of mine, was the Army recruiter in Gisborne. I knew I could count on him for straight answers. His news was not good. The Vietnam War was over and limited recruiting reflected deep military cutbacks. The last thing they needed was a married, low ranking soldier, with children. Lucky's advice was both discouraging and simple, "Try again next month."

Frustrated, I decided to take a different route. Much to TeAo's mirth and amusement, I wrote a letter stating my case to Sir Robert Muldoon, then our country's Prime Minister. As expected, he replied, and within a month I was wearing an Army uniform again. I was promoted to lance corporal and assigned to 2nd Field Squadron, Combat Engineers. I specifically rejoined so that I would be eligible for SAS Selection. Also, I needed that time to facilitate the heavy training that I would have to go through in order to prepare myself for Selection the following year.

At that time, my new unit was involved in constructing the N.Z. embassy in the Soviet Union. On duty for only a month, I was notified of my intended posting to Russia for an extended period of time. This assignment would completely disrupt my ulterior motive and there was no way that I could accept it. There was one possible way out of this posting, however. According to Army regulations, no soldier can be refused the opportunity to apply for SAS Selection. The only thing that can negate this is not being able to meet the pre-Selection requirements.

I began by hassling Captain Johnny Locke, the unit's 2IC. He was a ex-British Parachute Regiment officer, and for some reason he was sympathetic and helped me through the orderly room process. By rattling the chain of command, I was finally granted a session with Major Anderson, the 2nd Field Engineer Squadron Commander. He was a large, former enlisted man, and as tough as nails. I literally shook in my boots as I stood at rigid attention before him. I told him about my desire to attend the SAS Selection course. He looked up at me, staring right through my unfocused gaze. His comments are still clear to this day — the key to selection had been turned. "Henry, you had better pass, because there is no fucken place for you here if you fail. March out!"

Both the 2nd Field Squadron Sergeant Major, Winky Mulloch, and Captain Locke, were undoubtedly relieved to get rid of me; they sure as hell did not need a trooper who had no intention of following the company line. Aggravating this, I also attracted my share of attention in the Junior Ranks Club. Alcohol was a constant source of trouble for me during my early military days, and for that matter, it remained a problem throughout my military service.

My personal training continued for the next ten months, and during that period, TeAo and my two infant daughters, Tanya and Paula, joined me. For once in our lives I was earning a decent living and had acquired more good friends. Furthermore, my young family and I were experiencing an enjoyable lifestyle together.

For me however, this was not enough and I was unable to remain in this comfortable status quo scenario. The SAS Selection was my sole reason for rejoining the military and nothing was going to get in my way.

Two Wet Blankets And a Groundsheet

Alan and Duke's Story

New Zealand Special Air Service Selection

Alan

It was a typical cold and forbidding June winters night in 1978. Hori Hern, George Eruiti, Warren Richards, and I were working strenuously at repeating last weekends' drill during our tour of duty at the Waiouru Army Camp getting shit-faced in the Corporals Club. It is uncanny, but it seems that all the largest military bases in the world are located in the most remote locations with little, if anything, for single servicemen to do when off duty. Waiouru is situated on 200,000 acres of New Zealand's barren Central North Island desert plateau. Since World War II, it has been "home" to several thousand servicemen and their families and without a doubt, considered one of the most "hard luck" postings in the Army. At the time of this writing, the political emphasis had changed considerably and the military establishment had been restructured and down-sized. It was the main training depot for the New Zealand Army and was staffed by instructors from every Corps, except the Special Air Service (SAS). I was to find out later that this mysterious and low profile unit was headquartered in Papakura, South Auckland. At this juncture in my life, I had served for one and a half years in the infantry but I knew very little about the shadowy SAS.

Our beer-lubricated boredom was suddenly interrupted when I noticed three guys stride into the bar. It was difficult not to spot them because they were dressed in full camouflage uniforms and wearing blue corps belts. In those days, only "full time" field soldiers wore cammies on a daily basis and these worthies stood out in stark contrast to the bar full of garrison instructors. "Who are those guys, Hori," I quickly asked. Almost casually he replied, "SAS blokes from Papakura." To me, that meant absolutely nothing, so I just kept pouring it down and minding my own business. Several pints later, the camo-clad crew visited our table to chat with one of my buddies who had served with them in South East Asia. Hori introduced me to Charley, Blade, and Sam who at that time spoke little of their unit. Even I, as a nineteen-year-old young infanteer, could tell that these men possessed a certain warriors' aura that compelled instant respect from anyone around them. Other than for their distinct uniforms, there was nothing particularly special looking about these men. They were only average in size, but they presented themselves in such a confident manner that told me they would be comfortable in any environment, whether social or professional. I enjoyed their company and listening to numerous war stories and adventures that got better as the night progressed. I was impressed to say the least. During my Selection, which occurred two years later, both Sam and Blade were deployed to Rhodesia for a six-month tour of duty. Later on, as a badged member of the SAS, I found out the real truth about these guys. They were among the most mischievous bastards I have ever encountered.

While at work the following Monday, I immediately started researching this special force unit and the more I learned, the more I thought I wanted to be part of it. It was and remains a volunteer unit of soldiers who desire to prove themselves worthy of being in the Army's most professional and elite unit. Even though a professional antagonism prevails between the conventional or regular military and the so-called elitist units, there is obviously a need for such special entities. This has certainly been highlighted by the deployments and operational tasks that have been carried out since the mid-seventies and has reached its zenith in Afghanistan. United States Navy SEAL's, Delta Force, USMC Force Recon, US Army Special Forces, Canadian JTF2, British SAS and SBS, Rhodesian SAS and Selous Scouts during the Rhodesian War, the Australian and New Zealand SAS units, are just a few of the special teams who have remained active throughout the globe. In many ways these teams are different, but the one universal aspect that these teams have most in common, is the rigorous selection and weeding out process that each candidate is required to undergo and successfully complete before being "badged" and accepted as an operational member.

Since the inception of the British SAS during World War II, the SAS units of Great Britain, Australia, and New Zealand and, prior to independence, Rhodesia, have continually proven themselves to be among the best-trained and professional soldiers to take up arms in the modern worlds fighting forces. The respect that they have acquired worldwide is a direct reflection of their mental and physical toughness, coupled with their ultimate collective desire to dare and win at all costs. It is no secret that the Selection process is long and extremely rigorous and only a small percentage of candidates prevail and pass. I had already done parachute training, so repeating that phase during Selection would be no problem. However, I soberly anticipated that it was the other ninety percent of the process I had to worry about.

In early 1979, Hori and I took off for a weekend and wandered into a small pub in Rangitaiki. A veritable booze oasis, it was situated deeper still in the middle of nowhere and about a two-hour drive from Waiouru. Being a Saturday afternoon, the suds were flowing real smooth, the jukebox was pumping out rock and the drunker we got, the better looking the local "Sheilas" became. Hori's dashing good looks and his ability to bullshit the women meant that there was never a shortage of them hanging around our table. I always seemed to be the last in the line for the lovelies and whatever was left would normally require at least a half a bottle of rum to drink pretty.

Through my alcoholic haze I vaguely noticed several Army Land Rovers pull into the parking lot and their uniformed occupants head into the public bar where we were located. I noticed Hori's face light up as he recognized a burly, blond headed bloke as he strode towards us. Little did I realize that a strong and enduring friendship between. Earle (Duke) Henry and I would develop from this chance encounter. Duke and Hori had served together overseas before and it had been sometime since they last shared a brew. Duke and his guys were working in the local area and decided to drop in for a mince pie and a cold pint of Dominion Bitter (DB). After the intros, Duke mentioned that he was going to attend an SAS Selection course next year and asked if Hori wanted to go up as well. It was a challenge, but Hori in mild protest replied "fuck that" and deftly shifted attention from him to me by loudly announcing, so everyone in the pub could hear, "but Bros is planning to do one." Yep, that was I with a belly full of beer and ready for anything. I just smiled with my shit-eating grin and nodded to the affirmative, but at that point I would have volunteered for the French Foreign Legion, or Russian Spetsnatz, because I was feeling very little pain. In one long chug, Duke drained his handle of DB and eyeing me over the top of his empty glass, he studied me for a moment. Apparently satisfied that I was not another wanker wannabe, he ordered another round and we solemnly shook hands while agreeing that we would meet again a year hence at the SAS camp. This was the first time that I had met Duke and he hasn't changed much in the last 25 years. Although pushing middle age, he remains a youngster at heart and still loves the action. To this day, he still possesses the same dry sense of humor and "ice man" mentality, because nothing ever seems to faze him. You could tell him that his best friend had died, or he had won ten million in Lotto and you would get the exact same blank expression and grunt for a reply. A sort of, "who gives a fuck," unperturbed response. Duke's prevailing philosophy was that there is a job to do, so lets get on with it and whatever happens in the process happens and we'll handle it. From the start he possessed a typical warrior's mindset and continues to deal with life's trials and tribulations. Life is complicated enough, so "KISS" (Keep It Simple Stupid) is what he lived by.

In May 1980, I was in the best shape that I had ever been. During the four months prior to Selection, I would run the twelve miles separating Otahuhu, from camp and then pile on another five miler at lunch just for the hell of it. Mentally I felt confident and physically I was hard. At the grand old age of twenty years and eleven months, I felt I was ready for any challenge.

Pre-1980, there was not a lot known about the SAS, or more to the point, the type of training that was required for a man to be able to survive the rigors of Selection. Those who had passed and were badged were very coy about what was required and it was pretty much a "front up and find out for yourself" attitude. As I was soon to learn, it was not merely ten days of physical stress, but was ten days and nights of intense mental and physical pressure. It didn't matter if you could run a marathon in 2 hours 15 minutes, you wouldn't have a shit show in hell of passing if you couldn't TAB (tactical approach to battle) with a 60-pound rucksack on your back over extremely rugged terrain and arrive fit for combat.

Duke

Selection's Initial Obstacles

Forming up on day one of Selection is an accomplishment in its own right. However, looking back on the process, sixty-percent or more of the Selection applications are negated, because many of the candidates are unable to pass the paper barrage that is required to obtain approval to attend, let alone front up on the first day. The psychological testing team is a crucial element in the pre-Selection process and is continuously present during the ordeal and training cycle phase. From the outset, the psych team has total control over who is allowed to attend Selection and if you don't satisfy the mental profile you simply don't go any further. The next stage consists of a meticulous medical board, which can at times border on the ridiculous. Many a good soldier with serious active service behind him has been medically downgraded because, for example, a marginal hearing loss is detected, or some other minimal defect is uncovered and they are denied the opportunity to proceed further. Nevertheless, they are permitted to return to their parent units and actively soldier on for many more years. The last immutable standard remaining is the Armed Forces Mental Agility Scale, or the PSG factor. This test is taken as part of your basic recruit induction process and the results from that day appear to be recorded in stone. If you are not in the top third of the scale, then irregardless of your proven soldiering ability, there is no way you can attend SAS Selection. Unfortunately, it does not recognize the soldier's potential for maturity and intellectual growth. I believe it should be repeated some time during a soldier's subsequent re-enlistment. History has validated this stringent process and to my knowledge, there were only one or two instances in the last 25 years where former NZSAS members went haywire and became undesirables in the real world.

Alan

During our era, Selection was broken down into four phases: The four-week parachute course conducted at Auckland's Whenuapai Air Force Base started the festivities. This phase was of great benefit to us, because it gave us time to get to know each other, work as a team, and increase our motivation for what was about to follow. Besides, if you binned it after phase one, at least you left with a set of parachute wings.

Phase two got more serious and the two-week pre-Selection course concentrated on assessing and upgrading individual soldier skills, such as map reading, basic medical knowledge, fitness, weapons, and communications.

Phase three consisted of ten days of ball busting navigation and tabbing. Those that survived and passed were given the following weekend off, prior to starting the final phase.

Phase four lasted seven months and this training cycle prepared you for operational duties within the unit. Successfully completing all phases was mandatory for being accepted for service in the SAS.

Day one of this nine-month Selection process saw us on parade in front of the SAS Training Wing for the course introduction from E.B., the training officer. E.B. was one of those hard old bastards — tough as nails, who seemed to hate the world and everything it stood for. Deep down, I am sure that besides being an exceptional soldier, he was a great guy, but right now it was difficult for us to make eye contact with him without quivering in our boots. He was one of those guys that if you saw him come around the corner, you would look for a hole to crawl into. Consequently, we were glad to be on the trucks and out of there for a month's holiday, courtesy of the Air Force.

Duke

Of the thirty or so odd guys on our Selection, half a dozen had just completed two-years in South East Asia and in fact, arrived in country only days prior to the course start dates. The jungle boys were all infantry and displayed a definite attitude. Several others and I had come from the Engineer Corps. The rest of the wannabees consisted of an Army physical training instructor, several gunners from the Artillery, a burly infantry sergeant, a young infantry lance corporal by the name of Alan Brosnan and a trio of infantry officers. At age 29, John Shepherd and I were the oldest candidates and six of us, including two of the officers, had attended, but failed previous Selections. For many, ultimately triumphing was the only way to remove the shame of defeat and I was certainly one of those with a point to prove, especially to myself.

As Alan mentioned, E.B. was a sadistic son of a bitch and knowing he was there exacerbated my pending sense of doom. SAS Warrant Officer Dave Heyward, my old platoon sergeant in Vietnam and someone I had a tremendous amount of respect for was also prowling around the perimeter. Undoubtedly, he was really motivated for the upcoming events and did not look friendly at all, so I wisely and carefully refrained from making any eye contact. Because I had failed Selection on a previous occasion, my goose was cooked the minute my name appeared on the Selection roll muster. Lucky for me, there were others in a similar predicament and the wrath would be spread around a little. However, I was well aware that this was my last chance, so as far as I was concerned the Directing Staff (DS) could all go and get fucked, because I had nothing left to lose. After five discontented years on Civvy Street agonizing over my previous Selection misadventure, the word failure had been eliminated from my vocabulary. Eight years earlier, Private Phil Cairns and I had soldiered together throughout South East Asia as riflemen. However, now as a sergeant in the SAS, he coldly stalked the parade area and acted like a total stranger. Becoming a gray man and disappearing within the group was a prudent strategy. If no one knew you, there was a good possibility that they would mostly hassle those that they did.

Alan

An elite team of SAS parachute jump instructors awaited our arrival at jump school. They were supported by an equally competent group of Air Force counterparts. Warrant Officer Ernie, a legendary character from the early NZSAS days, headed up the team. About 5 foot nothing, Ernie was as hard as a rock and balls to the wall with whatever he did. With his shaved head, bandy legs and war torn rucksack, he was never far from the front on the frequent forced marches and runs. Habitually at the front, was Sergeant Pompey. He pushed relentlessly and drove us past our limits. Sergeant Jack Curtis, completed the trio and I cannot speak highly enough of his professional soldiering abilities. Duke and Jack had been good friends and colleagues in South East Asia, but at this juncture in Selection there were no friendships, past or present. We were simply all numbers. These three men represented our first sustained exposure to the SAS and they set the tone and highest example of the professional military conduct for the remainder of the course. They were all hardened combat veterans and possessed the attributes that we aspired to possess.

Duke

Because I had already completed a basic parachute course months earlier as a prelude to my Selection buildup, I possessed a bit of an edge at this early stage. Among my contemporaries, it was common knowledge that I was one of the world's worst parachutists and I still found it somewhat of a chore after thirteen years in the unit. Thank God the Amphibious Troop conducted water jumps, where at least the landings were softer and C-130 tailgate, instead of side door, exits were the norm. To this day, I have never been able to understand those free fall clowns in Air Troop and their insane desire to parachute day in day out.

Others in the course shared my distaste for plummeting towards the Earth, hoping that a bit of cloth and nylon would save you and succumbed to this anxiety. However, there was no way in hell that I would have buckled at the door like the big, burly infantry sergeant did. The poor bastard froze and opted out of jumping, making the long ride back to terra firmer as a dejected passenger and worse, a surveyed candidate. To survive in the unit you have to ignore, or control, your phobias and overcome the pucker factor. Fear it, but do it!

Not all of the jumping was grim and we discovered humor when and where we could, even if it was of the gallows variety. We had these little, rag-tag Malaysian Commandos on our course. As far as they were concerned we gave them fucking hell. When they exited, their slight bodies literally flew in the slipstream and we could hear the thumps from their helmets bouncing against the C-130's fuselage as they streaked toward the aircraft's tail. Generally, their exits were not forceful enough and for their lack of aggressiveness they paid a painful price. These and other humorous incidents helped to entertain us throughout the course. In this game you can't be thin-skinned and political correctness doesn't exist. You have to give as much as you got, because it was a dog eat dog environment.

Alan

Parachute training continued and I thoroughly enjoyed it. All we had to do was complete a minimum of eight jumps that initially involved clean fatigue exits, followed by descents with equipment and weapons, both day and night. Besides, it didn't take a great deal of effort propel oneself from the belly of an aircraft doing a lazy 120 knots at 1000 feet. The best part of it was that when we weren't jumping, we were played touch rugby, did pack walks, or took long boot runs.

At the halfway mark of our military "holiday," the tempo of drinking and partying picked up considerably. Everyone fucks up once in his life, or should I say gets caught, and now it was my turn. On our last night, after a huge piss-up in the bar, Mac and I decided to visit the womens' barracks to bid our manly farewells. Unfortunately, the Military Police had anticipated our impending operation and at 0500 hours, they assaulted the barracks from multiple entry points. As I hastily pulled on my clothes, I groggily contemplated putting my highly honed bailout skills to the test. Thankfully I didn't, because a perimeter containment team was eagerly waiting complete with growling German Shepherds. Mac was being warmly hosted in the next room and being a midget, he was able to hide in his lady's closet and avoid capture. Partially dressed and therefore, caught in the act, I was marched out by two club wielding MP's and booked for being in an out of bounds area. However, this was the easy part. It was now Friday morning and we headed back to SAS Lines at Papakura Camp, with me destined to face the inevitable music. And, I knew it wasn't going to be a long song. Every young soldier has a military mentor that he tries to emulate and I was no exception. My SAS career was greatly influenced by Bill and I considered him a friend as well as my teacher throughout my time with the unit. Initially, he was the training warrant officer during our Selection and training cycle, but I didn't get to really know him until six years later when I was posted to the Training Wing as an instructor under his command. He was an exceptional soldier who had a professional track record that few could surpass. Bill saw active service in the Borneo conflict during the early and mid sixties, but really made his name as an SAS patrol commander during the Vietnam War. A small man, who still looks years younger than his age, he had in particular a professional, no-nonsense demeanor about him and the innate ability to instill the fear of God in anyone. As our truckload of newly minted and re-minted parachutists rolled into the compound, word of my transgressions had naturally preceded me. I had broken one of Bill's golden rules (don't fuck up) and I was about to find out up close and personal how pissed off he was. Before the truck's wheels had stopped rolling, I could hear him screaming out my name and for me to get my ass into his office — now! As I rocketed off the truck, I bid a hasty and what I anticipated would be a final farewell to the boys, because I honestly thought that I would not see them again. However, double jeopardy raised its protective hand and since my "venal indiscretion" had occurred on Air Force turf and they had cited me, I could not be charged again under Army law. One trait Bill possessed was that he had the ability to swear like no one else I knew. Shaking with anxiety, I knocked on his door. His ominous order for me to enter and close it sounded like what Saint Peter, I imagined, might announce throughout heaven when he checked your earthly credentials. To this day, I can never understand why he required privacy because I am sure that they heard him screaming half a mile away at the front gate. More likely, he wanted to cut off any escape route. "Get your fucking heels together, cunt..." and with those terms of endearment he proceeded to give me the bollocking of my young, lustful life. I was unable to stand up straight because my knees were shaking from fear. Running through my mind was the image of the guys jumping off the truck, diving for cover and wondering throughout my verbal flogging if their name was going to be roared out next. Fortunately, Bill never held grudges and was not vindictive. He would bawl you out expecting you to learn from your mistakes, wipe the slate clean, and then it was time to get on with life. Bill was finally commissioned, and after 32 years of proud service retired from the SAS as a captain. It was leaders like him that I will always remember and respect and I did my best to model myself after him.

Duke

The two-week pre-Selection phase was a difficult period for me, because we were under the constant scrutiny of the Training Wing. The opportunity to fuck up in front of the DS was a real possibility and no one desired any extra attention. The daily routine started at 0600 hours, with a savage group physical training session before breakfast. This was followed by relentless navigation exercises and map marches for most of the day. All activities, except for the selected physical training sessions were carried out with candidates carrying packs, SLR rifle and belt order, which was our field service marching order for the following ten-day test period. Most evenings were spent under the dubious tutelage of Corporal Max, a small, but very nasty,

SSgt Phil Cairns training new SAS Troopers during the mid-eighties. A proven operator who attained the rank of Sergeant Major in three armies – New Zealand, South African, and The Oman.

tattooed, ex-British Parachute Regiment member and one of the unit's non-badged medics. He, like most other non–badged personnel when given the chance, seemed to particularly enjoy beasting Selection and cycle candidates. Up until the early 1980's, all ranks within the unit, whether badged or non-badged, wore the international Parachutist's red beret. The airborne and parachute tradition prevailed within the SAS and all members double-timed everywhere they went while in garrison. We were certainly no exception to this practice and we ran as a squad to every assignment. Whoever was in charge of the formation appeared determined to get the lads moving at a maximum pace during his period of command and heaven help the last man that arrived at the group's destination. The slightest sign of apprehension or display of weakness was mercilessly exploited by the eagle eyed DS. Accordingly, the weaker candidates fell by the wayside and returned to their parent commands. Captain John, a DS sidekick of E.B.'s, ensured that my time on this phase was a trial by fire. He and other former so-called "friends," namely Phil Cairns, made the most of the occasion and doled out generous helpings of terror and punishment in a sadistic frenzy of power. Upon reflection and to be fair, at least they were consistent and generally fucked everybody around. I was greatly relieved when they left the unit several months later. Phil departed to soldier with 32 Battalion in South West Namibia and John joined the Sultan of Oman's Special Forces.

Alan

The pre-Selection, or "hurt phase," helped us run off all the booze that we sponged up, courtesy of the Air Force, during the previous month. Attitudes began changing as we more soberly anticipated what was lurking in wait around the next Selection corner. Personally, I was relieved to finally start the ten-day Selection phase and I was eager to get on with it.

In those days, you didn't have to be a rocket scientist to complete the ordeal. You just had to be physically strong and, in a way, cunning. Our course was one of the last that was run the traditional way. In that era, the instructors had a great deal of subjective influence over who passed and who failed. If a particular instructor had a hard-on for you, then the outcome was predictable — you were not going to get the nod, or the bastard would drive you into the deck until you were forced to withdraw. I believe that the NZSAS took a giant leap forward around the mid-eighties, by standardizing the course and placing the emphasis on the individual to perform. If one desired to pass, it would be entirely up to that soldier to satisfy all requirements, meet the course objectives and pass himself. Basically, you had to hump for the ten days with Bergen weights and distances increasing progressively, while still maintaining the required pace and mileage over varied terrain.

While the Aussie SAS emphasizes team-work and spontaneous group leadership, the Kiwi and Brit Selections rely more on measuring individual performance. We believe that the essence of good teamwork is strong individual performances. If each soldier performs his responsibility 100-percent, then the team will click and perform credibly as a unit.

The ten-day ordeal was sub-tended into four phases that involved among other events, tabbing day and night. As Duke previously mentioned at the outset of pre-Selection, we were issued pack and webbing; two woolen blankets; one change of clothes; an FN 7.62x51 MM self-loading rifle, minus its sling; ANPRC 77 ground-to-air radio set; spare battery, and other items that were of no value other than for keeping our packs at the required weight level. I could see everyone's eyebrows lifting higher and higher as the guys carefully placed the gear into their packs. We were all thinking the same thing. It's winter, so where is our sleeping bag, ground sheet, tenting, wet weather gear, and most importantly, food? To somewhat allay our concerns they did give us a 24-hour ration pack, but that was for emergency use only and for no other circumstances, other than impending death, was it to be touched. It was excruciatingly difficult to stare at the packet when you were absolutely starving, knowing full well that opening it could result in failure. I heard that in the "good old days" they use to issue the candidates a live chicken and razor blade. Reportedly, some of the hard cases still had the chicken with them on day ten, having saved it for company more that anything else. I sometimes wondered what sort of company it provided! The instructors were obviously going to make it as uncomfortable for us as possible by not issuing any water proofing bags. After the first rain, you and your precious belongings suddenly weighed twice as much.

Personally, the times I enjoyed the most on Selection were the ones when I was tabbing on my own. This was the case for about 80-percent of the course. You had an objective and it was your responsibility to get there the easiest and fastest way you could. There was less stress here because there were no instructors around and you made your own decisions, be they right or wrong. If you wanted to sit down and rest then you did that. If you fancied walking on a road to save time and effort, but were willing to risk getting caught then that was your prerogative. Hunger and the subsequent loss of energy was the biggest problem to deal with throughout Selection. We probably consumed a total of three 24 hour ration packs over the ten days. Everyone knows that it takes food to give you strength to enable one to cover the required distances in the allotted time. These normally consisted of canned foods such as baked beans, beef stew or corned beef and because of time restraints, would most often be eaten cold.

Duke

It was every man for himself while tabbing in the Woodhill State Forest. The penalties for collaborating with other candidates, walking on roads, talking to or taking advantage of civilian property would result, if caught, in dismissal. However, even with heavy penalties many among us broke the rules as they saw fit and believed that fortune favored the bold. I was under no allusion regarding my ability and had no interest in transgressing any regulations, regardless of the calculated benefits that such risks could involve. On one of the tabs, while paralleling a road, but well within the tree line, I observed a civilian vehicle scoot past three or four times with one of the lads relaxing in the back seat. He didn't get pinched and passed, so good for him. However, as fate would have it, his deficiencies eventually caught up with him and he only spent a few years in the unit before opting for a more comfortable life style in the regular Army. This supported my theory that those who habitually seek the easy way on Selection will eventually decide that the SAS is not for them. Two other good mates of mine openly told me they were getting a lift on a certain leg and lo and behold two hours later a decrepit old Kiwi Ute (Station Wagon) trundled past with the two "Ronnie's" snuggled up on the back tray. However, the downside of this audaciousness was they were spotted and nobbled for their indiscretion. I arrived at the final check point early without getting snaffled by the SAS hunter force and as was the custom in those days, rewards for good performances were occasionally passed on. Staff Sergeant Buzz grilled me on my activities over the previous 24 hours. Apparently I passed muster and rolling his big eyes he tossed me a gift that was worth its weight in gold. It was an ancient, but complete 24-hour ration pack, which from its bedraggled appearance was probably originally issued during the Malaysian Emergency, 25 years earlier. Suddenly, I was extremely content with life and, as if on holiday, I languished in a hasty nest of pine needles under the canopy of a huge forestry plantation. I was soaked, footsore and bruised, but totally oblivious to the drizzle and cold. For the first time since Selection had started I had a full belly and a bit of solitude.

Alan

The most feared exercise during Selection was the "infested swamp." It was the only event that was conducted in teams. The primary reason for a "buddy" system here was because a candidate drowned in these fetid waters several years earlier. It got underway on the third day of Selection and lasted for twenty-four hours. We were broken down into four man teams and each team was assigned two instructors. My team consisted of Myself,

Duke, Como, and Ants, who was a Rupert (officer). The reason for the two instructors was that this was the phase that most of the candidates choked on, so someone had to walk the withdrawing soldier out while the others slogged on. In addition to our normal equipment and rifle, each four-man team had to carry three, six-gallon jerry cans of water, each weighing 42 pounds. The point man was exempt as he had the ball-busting job of forcing his way through the reeds, vines, and trees, blazing a trail for the team. There was no easy way to haul the water cans. Hand carrying them meant that your arms would eventually drop off. Tying it to the top of your pack would mean that your legs would buckle and, furthermore, sagging shoulders would inhibit respiration. Floating or dragging them through the water meant that they got tangled up every few feet or so. Most of us settled for the pack option because it was just a matter of head down and ass up. We would rotate the bush-whacking point man after about 50 yards, but this distance got progressively shorter as the fatigue-inducing hours accumulated and exacted its toll. Time is a great healer, and it was funny as shit now that I look back on it. One minute you would be up to your knees in water, and the next, after stepping into a hole, completely submerged. You were forever stumbling over logs and tree roots, getting hung up in thorny vines, and plunging into deeper and colder areas, spluttering and cursing like hell while struggling to resurface. At the start of the exercise, everyone was trying to tip toe through the slime in a futile effort to stay dry. Yeah, right, may as well just take a fall and get it over and done with. There was no way you were going to stay dry, unless like our Navy SEAL brothers, you could walk on water! After the all-day "swim," somehow we ended up on an island in the middle of the swamp. Lips blue and shivering from exposure, I hunkered down with my team as the medics came around, lancing our blisters and injecting the sores with antiseptic. Talk about bringing tears to your eyes, the pain momentarily took my mind off my raging feet. Most of the withdrawals came when the instructors lined us up after a short break and said that we were diving back in (as if it wasn't obvious that we had to get back somehow). The mental shock and challenge was far more taxing than the physical. Here we were, in the middle of winter, soaking wet, freezing our balls off, and about to spend all night repeating our dog paddle through that liquid crud. My attitude was one of resignation, so I muttered, "What the hell, let's get going." More importantly, it would be a hell of lot warmer on the move rather than sitting here bitching and freezing. Miraculously, our four-man team was still intact, so that was an encouraging sign. Throughout the night, we could hear parallel teams cursing and swearing as someone went under or got poked in the eye by a branch.

It was about 0400 hours when we hit dry land again and that was when the real pain started. The sky was cloudless, a full moon was up, and Jack Frost was out and making the rounds big time. The instructors had us lie up in the bush by the edge of a road, told us to maintain a radio watch and to get on the truck when it came by. Of course, the truck would not be stopping, so we would have only one opportunity to get on board or we would be walking home. Damn, I didn't even know where home was from here.

Duke

I had negotiated the swamp phase once before, so it wasn't a shock to me. Not that this is a great advantage, because you still had to bull your way through it. Alan was easily one of the strongest mentally and physically on the course. And, he continues to maintain the same persistent, single-minded approach when confronted by any obstacle. He simply takes it head on and usually overcomes it by climbing over it, or by smashing it aside. Along with several of the other young "thrusters" he seemed to be eating Selection up. Nevertheless, the relentless hard slog day in and day out, with minimum sleep and marginal food was a great leveler for everyone, irregardless of the shape you entered Selection in. The cold and continuous emersion in deep slime and swamp water habitually turned out to be the final straw for many. Como and the officer hit the wall on the back azimuth and essentially became passengers during the night. However, even if you threw in the towel you still have to extract under your own steam, so we continued to press ahead. With this reality in mind, Alan and I handled the donkey-work during the night slog. Although all of us were walking wounded, I was, barring unforeseen injuries confident of completing this phase. Alan began to slow down because of his hamburgered feet and was moving forward in serious discomfort. I knew that there was no way he was going to quit, but it was obvious that Selection had now become a real test of will. I was thankful for having another kindred spirit with me, resolved to do his utmost at the sharp end, but at the end of the day Alan's problems were all his own. To show compassion and assist fellow candidates on Selection can be interpreted as either a positive or negative act, and it was best not to take the chance. For Alan, it was simply going to be a long and stressful night. If you don't shrug it off and suck it up, you are done. Pain is your constant companion and after awhile you learn to ignore it more and more. Big Dave was the only guy on our course who seemed completely unaffected or stuffed by the series of ordeals. Serious physical deterioration occurred for most of us after the swamp. However, fucked up feet and massive crotch rash were the least of our worries. Some of us had incurred serious cuts, abrasions, and sores that had become infected, as swollen and painful lymph nodes testified to this threatening condition. A simple sprain or muscle strain that could impede your mobility and speed was a virtual death knock on Selection's door. Luxuries such as foot powder and dry socks were figments of someone's medical imagination and did not materialize on our Selection. I chuckle to myself when I recall Max, the medic's, adamant pre-Selection briefings on the dangers of water immersion and the importance foot care, admonishing us to use copious amounts of powder. What a load of bollocks, and it just confirms the old adage: never trust a non-badge.

Alan

The four of us sat down in the barbed gorse bushes and scrub along the roadside. Our mission was to monitor the traffic and log it down for the DS. Yeah! Fucken right! Duke issued the order.

"Okay boss, you take first radio watch and wake Como up next."

"Roger that, Duke," was the Rupert's reply. Duke and I crawled about ten meters away and found a spot to hide in where, hopefully, Como and the boss wouldn't find us. As we huddled there feeling sorry for ourselves, Duke whispered, "Sure am hungry Bros." "Yeah, me too, Duke," was my shivering reply. We were both on the same wave-length and we dove into our rucks and retrieved our emergency ration pack. After studying them intently to decide what we could eat without its absence being noticed, we demolished some candy, cunningly replacing it with little stones. A mouthful of honey was the next to go and then about eight raisins each. Shit, although it was token chow, it felt like a banquet. "Duke, my feet sure could use some fresh air," I moaned."Yeah, mine too," was his equally pained reply. Within minutes, we jettisoned our boots, socks, and in my case, my soaked trousers. Since Duke didn't wear underpants, he felt more comfortable leaving the dripping things on. We laid our items of clothing over a log and tried to insulate ourselves from the cold with a groundsheet between us and the sodden ground, and two wet blankets wrapped around our freezing bodies. Cuddling up for body warmth, we savored these precious moments of frigid peace. However, every time Duke moved, he would kick the blister on my foot. "Duke for fuck's sake, be still," I growled. Besides inflicting needless pain on me, he would shift the blankets and let cold air in. In spite of all my complaining, I must have crashed for a bit because the next thing I knew was that I was jolted from a deep sleep by Ants screaming that the truck was coming. Of course, he and Como were good to go, but Duke and I had shit scattered everywhere. We had only slept for about an hour, but it seemed like a lifetime. Like Laurel and Hardy, both of us leapt to our feet, ran around in circles, collided, and fell over. Realizing that we were in various states of un-dress, our puckered peckers recoiled against the cold as we scampered about trying to find our socks, boots, and my trousers. Forget it, they were frozen solid. I remember slamming my trousers against the log trying to unsuccessfully crack them open. Everything that was wet was just as solid, so down the front of my shirt they went.

Sprinting for the disappearing truck as it trundled down the road, something didn't feel right. I looked down and noticed that I had put my boots on the wrong feet. Even with my feet facing East and West, I still managed to beat Duke to the truck by a good 30 yards. Shit, it was every man for himself. From the truck's darkened interior, the other candidates grinned as we struggled to pull ourselves up and over the tailgate. I wasn't the only guy to experience the "outward feet" problem. Two years later, Duke's younger brother Neil found himself in the same predicament.

The final hurdle of Selection was the arduous "60-60" endurance march. Our packs matured to 60 lbs. and we had to cover 60 rough-terrain kilometers as quickly as possible. Once again, it was in the forest, but you could use the roads. It was a straight out sprint, but at this stage my body was completely knackered all over. My shoulders ached, the small of my back was raw from my pack rubbing against it, my legs felt lifeless, the groin was red-raw, and, of course, my feet were generously blistered. It takes immense self-motivation to push oneself forward through the accumulated fatigue and pain at the required speed. You can't walk without healthy feet, and it was amazing how much one little blister could handicap your movement. It angered me when guys less fit than I just breezed past me as I limped on. There was no strategy here. It was simply a matter of head down and ass up, the infantryman's traditional position. It was alluded to earlier, but the mental toughness displayed by some of the candidates on the course was truly amazing. I watched men peel off their socks at the end of a tab and half their foot with it. All that was left were huge oozing and searing blisters that turned into red, raw skin. When it gets that bad and the body really rebels, it doesn't matter how tough you are, it's impossible to cover the distances in the allotted times. The worst thing that you can do was the thing that felt the best and that was to listen to your protesting body and sit down and take that heavy weight off your shoulders. Ooooh shit, it felt sooo good. It felt so good in fact, that you didn't want to get up again. Just one more minute, you keep saying yourself and in the next minute you are fast asleep and losing valuable time. This happened to me during a break I took during the night portion of the 60/60. I sat down for a brief rest and immediately dozed off. Coming too after rolling off the boulder, I was sitting on and realizing what had happened, I jumped up in a panic and raced off, leaving my precious map behind. That was a serious balls-up, but luckily, it was a straight dash to the finish line and my compass was pre-set on the correct bearing.

At the time, we had no idea how far we ultimately had to walk or for how long. Once again, it was a mind game, so it was just a matter of trying to maintain 4-5 kilometers (3 miles) per hour until they told you to stop and get on the truck. The instructor checkpoints were spaced anywhere from 10-16 kilometers apart, so you can imagine the effect it had on morale when you thought you were at the end, but instead, the instructor rewarded you with another six figure grid reference.

At the end of "the end," I could feel the sensation of relief being exuded by everyone in the back of the truck as we were returning to the compound. Strangely, everyone was rather somber and there was no cheering, or back-slapping. The guys still seemed to be in their individual "bubbles" and remained deep within themselves. Some of us fully expected to be dumped out at some God forsaken location and told to get on with it until we collapsed. However, it was really all over, and quite honestly, whether I had passed or failed, I was just happy that I had been able to finish. To me, that in itself was the ultimate personal achievement. Passing, so I could move onto the next phase, was the big bonus. You could discern the deeply etched fatigue on everyone's faces as the survivors slowly shifted around to get as comfortable as they could while being jostled around by the bumpy dirt roads.

Duke

I agree with Alan's assessment that the 60-60 endurance march was a real ball buster. Navigation was critical and the lack of discernible landmarks made it difficult for even the most seasoned map-reader. If you miscalculated your checkpoint prior to commencing each leg you were out of the running. The night time tabbing was unreal and at times, I began hallucinating. My feet were lumps of throbbing meat and my groin was on fire from ill-fitting Selection issue trousers that had been wet from day one. Somehow, I made the final checkpoint and for the first time since South Vietnam, I caught a glimmer of a smile from my old mentor, Dave Heyward. Not that it lasted more than a second or two, because his next message rocketed in with a veiled threat to sort my fucken kit out and get my weapon ready for inspection before we arrived back at camp, or suffer the consequences.

Although the boys being shielded by the flapping canvas on the back of the lurching R.L. Bedford had triumphed over the last ten days and were internally chuffed over this, our candidate status remained the same. In short, we had about as much rights with the DS as the bad boys in "Gitmo's" Camp X-ray. However, this time we were aware of our destination and in several uncomfortable hours we would be back at Papakura

Camp to face Selection's panel of judges. Sitting on our burdensome packs, we huddled together trying to shield ourselves as best we could from the wind and sleet driving in on us from the front of the vehicle. There was always an SAS member present and you had to resist the temptation to fall asleep or talk to another candidate. If this happened, or you got braced for any other "criminal activity," punishment was swift and collective. The old SAS adage, "one in, all in," meant that individual infractions resulted in the entire group being disciplined, which did little for the popularity of the offender among his peers. Staff Sergeant Joe, a slender and quietly spoken veteran, commanded my full attention whenever he bothered to address us. He had us doing somersaults trying to get up a sodden, slippery, clay bank early one morning near the "Mere Mere Swamp." Frustration did not do justice in describing the futility of our efforts as we battled environmental conditions trying to succeed in this task. To this day, it still remains unclear why we expended so much precious energy over this activity. I can only presume it was merely included to wake us up and keep our sleep deprived bodies moving. Joe didn't yell, carry on or bluff, but his threats were always ruthlessly carried out. When he talked, you had better be listening and

SAS Counter Terrorist Team Troopers with MP5 A3 SMG – Papakura, New Zealand, 1984

Prime Minister Sir Robert Muldoon during a visit to the compound. A former WWII soldier and great friend of the SAS – Papakura, New Zealand, 1983

respond quickly, or else you paid for your in attentiveness with blood, sweat and tears. To everyone's surprise, he became a top echelon anchor man for National Maori Television after his retirement.

Alan

Once we reached the compound, everyone seemed to come back to life and look halfway alive. This was in part due to massive relief and furthermore, we were not going to give the staff any indication that they had beaten us down. We were directed into an open area and told to clean our weapons, and that proved to be a considerable task. Cleaning gear was limited to what we carried in the butt of our SLRs and they were completely fouled with ten days of rain, frost, swamp, mud and pine needles. However, I had no doubt that these excellent weapons would function if called upon to do so. I learned to like the American Armalite (M-16), but it could not have taken a beating and kept on ticking like the FN. The FN was heavier, held fewer rounds and had much more recoil than the black rifle, but it was more flexible over various combat range conditions. It also shared the same round as our beloved "Gimpy," FN's General Purpose Machinegun (GPMG). Little conversation occurred between us and individually, we were ushered into Major "E.B.'s" office for the infamous "tick or flick." Reporting in, my dirty, stinking and ragged, but rigidly held body was greeted by an inspiring sight that Duke and I would never forget. Arrayed with the major were Squadron Sergeant Major (SSM) Jack, Training Warrant Officer Bill and Senior NCO Cadre Kevan, Ben and Dave Heyward, who was tragically killed a couple of years later. These senior SAS warriors were all staunch to the bone. Between them they wore a variety of campaign ribbons that mutely attested to their combat experience, which would have been difficult to rival and could not be questioned. I was very fortunate just to be in the same room with these men and as the years and my career progressed, I learned that outside of their professional demeanor, there was also a friendly and humane side to them as well. However, at this moment, our military future rested totally in their hands. It was nothing elaborate, there were no emotions, and it was either, "See you at 0700 Monday," or, "See you later." If a man failed, he was either told it would be worth his while to have another go, or to just give it a miss. I knew that if I failed there was no way I would be going through this shit again. This was definitely a one-time deal for me. At the end of this fateful day, nine of us out of thirty starters were accepted for the next training cycle phase. Although they gave it a good whack, Wake, Brian, and Ants missed the mark and were immediately returned to their parent units.

Duke

Waiting to find out if I had passed or failed was most excruciating. I finally got the nod and fronted up before the dreaded panel of judges and jury. Nevertheless, the decision went in my favor, so I got out of the room as rapidly as possible in case E.B. changed his mind. SAS Selection is the ultimate test within our military forces. Selection is an individual effort and as was previously mentioned, compassion, fair play or assistance to other candidates although morally correct, is discouraged when striving to meet strict timings or conditions. It supports the mission first concept, but it is the only time in the SAS that you ever consider yourself acting alone as an individual. Once Selection was completed, teamwork is paramount to enable one to successfully navigate through the training phase, let alone ultimately survive as a member of this elite unit.

Alan

After the weekend respite, nine of us paraded in front of the Training Wing on Monday morning. What a sorry looking group, we looked more like Selection course rejects rather than successful candidates. Our cycle had a good cross section of interesting personalities and characters. There was the Aussie, John Shepherd. "Shep" had been a surf life-guard on Bondi Beach in his younger days and then did his stint in the Australian infantry in South Vietnam. Like Duke, he was the only other married troopie on the course. His gravely voice and deliberate manner was a source of constant amusement for all of us. He was a tough fucker and not shy about competing physically with us younger guys. However, coordination was not one of his strong points and he continually displayed this short-coming while sparring on the close quarters battle course. He just couldn't pull a punch and my bruised body graphically attested to that fact!

Richie Tolich, my future best man, was definitely the "mischief" maker of the group. Raised in the Far North and of Maori-Dalmatian heritage, he would win, hands down, the prize for "party animal of the course." If there was music, beer, and women, and not necessarily in that order, then look no further, Ritchie would be there, leading from the front, guitar in one hand and six pack in the other. Hohepa Skipwith, alias "Skippy," another Maori from Rotorua, was the complete opposite of our group comic. Skippy was cool, and like a coiled cobra, he would usually sit back in the shadows of the various drinking spots just waiting to strike. Nine times out of ten, after Ritchie had done all the hard work with the ladies, Skippy would end up with the women. Never one to panic or rush, his professionalism, strength, loyalty, and friendship was as solid as Gibraltar. Although some of the old "war horses" in the unit were unsure of Skippy's new-age manner, we, his Selection mates, had no reservations.

Pete Madden was a young Engineer Corps corporal. A tall, well-built, former cadet soldier from the East Coast, Pete's European/Maori bloodline resulted in him possessing extremely good looks. Undoubtedly, the social threat imposed by Pete, made Ritchie apply himself with all due diligence at the bar scene. Pete was a strong individual and although lacking a lot of basic infantry skills, he displayed excellent potential in the unit, but like Ritchie, his preoccupation with the ladies became a concern at times.

Stu was the only officer to make the grade and as a repeat candidate he was extremely happy and relieved to be in the final line up. Anyone who took bets at the start of Selection on the three officers attending would have agonized to place a wager on Stu, but in the end he stood tall with the rest of us. Stu was almost as laid back as Skippy and knew how to mingle with the lads without compromising himself. However, there were times when both parties forgot he was an officer and he was a welcome drinking partner whenever the chance arose. It should be understood that the relationship between special operations personnel and their superiors is a casual, but respected one and the NZSAS is no exception to this phenomenon. If an officer had the respect of the men, he was called "boss." If he didn't, he was habitually responded to as "sir." Poor and marginal officers as well as non-commissioned officers did not last long in the unit. DS were often harder on the officer Selection candidates, because of the unusual professional and leadership demands a unit such as the SAS, imposes on a leader. In truth, however, the NCO's ran the show.

Como Compton was our proverbial gray man and would have made a great undercover operative. He was a slightly built, non-descript individual and considered the odd man out on Selection. He was one of those guys who never stood out in a crowd or caused any dramas. Like a few others in the candidate crew, he was determined to get through and become badged and wasn't interested in "stuff it up" with the wild antics the rest of us seemed to thrive upon.

Similarly, Big Dave displayed a serious attitude and he completed the team. Dave was a tall, rangy individual who had did not appreciate his own strength. He was totally honest, and, at times, quite out-spoken, and you knew where he stood on all issues. Nevertheless, he was a professional soldier and could party, but like Como, postponed any antics until we were actually badged. Dave and Como proved to be our most focused peers and they always appeared more squared away at Monday morning's muster. With the exception of Shep, who went home when he could to his family, the rest of us derelicts in uniform aggressively hit the bars from Friday's Happy hour until the Rugby Club closed on Sunday evening.

Duke

Becoming badged was every candidate's Holy Grail and the only object of our quest. However, there were some pleasant unit distractions and most of us took advantage of them. The SAS in those days, encouraged group drinking sessions as one of many means to develop camaraderie and promote bonding and unit cohesion. However, you were expected to control it and most could. It also served to relieve stress and enabled men to vent in a controlled environment and what was said usually stayed there. The NZSAS was unique in that all ranks drank together on Friday afternoons in the Squadron "smoko room." Assembled, we would receive a spiel from the boss on the week's activities, learn of promotions and get news in general on what was going on in the world that could affect the unit. This normally took a couple of hours, sometimes considerably longer, depending on the gravity of the subjects covered, before we moved on to our respective mess venues. However, this can only work within established protocols and guidelines if the organization has a strong RSM. As a unit, we drank hard and played hard. However, regrettably for some, this tradition got out of control and destroyed many promising careers. Nevertheless, I enjoyed

Duke being presented with his beret and belt from Col Rennie, the original SAS commander – 1980

these gatherings immensely and it sure made Monday mornings most interesting.

Alan

We expected that our first day back after completing Selection, was going to be a great one for us. Instead, E.B. and Captain Wally, who was a plank owner from the original Malayan Emergency days, sorted us out super quick at the 0800 hours briefing. We were pointedly reminded of our lowly status in the military and that to become troopers in this elite unit, every one of us, excluding the officer, was to revert to the rank of private and enjoy the status and privileges accorded to such lowly positions in life. This was not a problem, but what was difficult to understand and accept was how even the non-badged support dickheads seemed to have more clout than we did. It was going to be a difficult seven months.

All of us were hobbling around, grunting and groaning from the numerous pains and injuries that had been inflicted upon us. Everyone had lost a good deal of weight and looked forward to easier times now that the nightmare was behind us. Ironically, the most difficult part was just about to begin. The next seven months would prove to be the real test, and the pressure would be relentless. The focus would be on determining whether we could master and perform the necessary skills to become a functioning member of an operational SAS patrol. These skills were both broad and varied, but each one was essential for the successful functioning of a patrol. In spite of the emphasis on individual performance during Selection, in reality, the unit wasn't interested in the soldier who was a brilliant soloist, or one who only excelled at one or two skills. They ultimately wanted men who were strong across the board and were able to fit into any scenario or patrol position, whether as a leader or follower. Communications, medical, patrolling procedures, helicopter operations, small boating, climbing, demolitions, unarmed combat, and special warfare (counter terrorism) were the main subjects covered during the cycle phase. Of course, weapons proficiency with longs, shorts, and crew-served weapons were continuously emphasized throughout this phase as well as during our entire careers. Bluntly put, SAS operators were expected to hit what they aimed at under all conditions.

Combat Survival Training.

Combat Survival was added to an already rigorous schedule a couple of years later. This demanding training concentrated on survival while living off the land, escape and evasion,

SAS Combat Survival Training. Captured and now awaiting the feared interrogation phase – Waiouru, New Zealand, 1985

and resistance to interrogation.

The final test for Patrol Procedures involved a two-week deployment to the tangled jungles of Fiji. With new patrol commanders assigned to us from the Squadrons, we were formed into patrols, issued our orders, performed a number of rehearsals and completed preparations at our base in Auckland. From isolation we would board our C130 aircraft, fly directly to Fiji and insert via parachute. Mission: Perform recon and ambush operations. Our enemy would be seasoned members of the SAS and Fijian military. Everything would be real with the exception of an exchange of live fire. I wondered to myself whom would be ambushing whom?

Alan in a jungle base camp, Brunei, 1987

As we filled the C130 aircraft with our personnel, equipment and parachutes, you could sense the tension. In two weeks, if everything went as planned, we would be badged and posted to our squadrons as full-fledged SAS operators. Our consummate training would enable us to deploy anywhere in the world to conduct operations that the SAS had become famous for. Our five-man patrol consisted of Skippy as lead scout; Dave as medic; Como, rear security, or "tail end Charlie"; Sergeant Phil Cairns functioning as patrol commander; and me as radio operator. Because of my comms responsibility, I would be positioned in trace of Phil. In addition to the ANPRC 64 Morse Code radio, my bergen was crammed with a variety of personal and team gear. Food, water, weapons, and ammo made up the rest, which resulted in my decent weight exceeding 250 pounds. No worries, I had done this many times before, but I was a bit concerned about getting a tree branch up my butt. The pilots, God bless them, managed to locate and drop us into the correct country. I waddled up to the gaping ramp and was impolitely ushered out of the aircraft. This was a static line descent and as I performed a controlled plunge to Earth, all I could see was a great green rug-like mass below me waiting to swallow us up into its dark depths. The LZ was supposed to be cold, but I had learned never to assume anything, so I mentally rehearsed my actions upon impact, particularly the part about un-hooking and accessing my weapon. It would be just like Training Wing to have a hot reception prepared for us. I glanced around and the patrol appeared to be in good order. The ground was coming up fast, so it was time to put the brakes on. Greatly relieved as I decelerated, I could make out details on the ground as I steered toward the largest open area on the DZ. My next burst of prayers was for a good and injury free landing. Some of us were close enough to yell at each other, but we religiously maintained operational silence. The great game was on and we would learn that the Fijian jungle was every bit as tough as the wiry warriors that inhabit it.

After performing our controlled crashes, we quickly fanned out and formed a defensive perimeter, where we stood-to and waited, watched and listened. In the jungle, you hear things first before you see them and the ears aim the eyes. After a tactical interval, we rallied around our patrol commander. He ordered me to inform HQ that we had successfully inserted and had not been compromised. This was my first sustained contact with Phil, who was an old mate of Duke's. Although Phil was not involved in our Selection, he had been a member of the unit for several years. I felt that it was good that we had not seen him a great deal during the previous seven months because this would allow him to make an honest assessment of our capabilities.

Phil obviously had his shit together and he immediately impressed me. It is vital that patrol members have complete confidence in its leader and Phil created an atmosphere for success. His was a no-nonsense approach and he expected you to perform any task given to you. Always thirsting for action and practical combat experience, Phil, true to his calling, went on sabbatical to participate in a conflict in South West Africa shortly after our jungle gig. I suspected that he used the two weeks as a warm up for the actual thing. His two-year contract saw him constantly on operations as a member of an elite reconnaissance unit. After an additional two-year stint in the Middle East, Phil returned to the unit where we became close friends while working together in the SAS Training Wing. Later on, we served together as operational members on the newly minted counter terrorist team. Phil became the sniper group commander, while I took control of the assault group.

The hard slog we had been exposed to over the last seven months started to pay off. All the patrolling, live fire training, communications, medical, demolition skills and discipline that had been instilled into us proved to be critical when operating in this primitive environment. This was particularly true for me, since I was the only soldier on the cycle who had never been exposed to this type of close country combat. Even though the fundamentals of patrolling remained the same, the harsh operating conditions of the jungle were vastly different from the frequently freezing native bush that we were accustomed to in New Zealand. Additionally, there were no nasty creatures other than wild boar, inhabiting the N.Z. bush that posed a threat to your well-being. Peace of mind prevailed in knowing that there were no snakes, scorpions, poisonous centipedes, tigers, elephants and the like to stuff you into the surrounding decaying matter. Habitually, this was a hugely positive factor when heading into the scrub back home. However, as I patrolled along behind Skippy and Phil, thoughts of danger presented by the local flora and fauna evaporated as I concentrated on the task at hand. The heat and humidity was unbearable and with no time to acclimatize, your personal fitness played a huge part in your survivability. I constantly watched and imitated the actions of the other guys when it came time to perform certain skills that were new to me. Whether it was moving past or through certain foliage that could prove hazardous to your health, erecting a hammock at night to keep the bugs and snakes off your body, or detecting and avoiding a hornet's nest, there was always something to learn that would make me a better operator in the years to come. My individual task within the patrol was to transmit and receive via Morse code to and from the patrol base. This mission also involved encrypting Phil's outgoing messages and in turn, decrypting all incoming messages. An immense amount of concentration was required to accurately perform this skill, especially if the signal was weak and when monsoon rains poured bucket loads of water down your back, let alone when under fire. There was no doubt after this trip that my confidence and ability to operate in this theatre had greatly increased, even though I still had a long way to go.

The seven-month cycle taught you the SAS way to operate, and although audacity and thinking outside the box was encouraged, it was literally "our way or the highway." Thus, there were not a lot of shortcuts available and if the job required that you go hard routine, i.e. no cooking, no overhead shelters, no smoking, shitting into plastic bags and carrying it out with you, then that is what was done. The instructors were hard, but fair and in the end, the foundations had been firmly laid for our new careers. Although the married men on our Selection had been separated from their families for seven months, their priority was the same as those of us who were unattached — passing the cycle and receiving the ultimate jewel in the crown, acceptance as an SAS operator. It's a hard fact, but within the SAS and Special Forces in general, work often comes first. As an operator, you never turn down or withdraw from a deployment because of family or other personal reasons. To do so could jeopardize your growth and progression within the unit. Therefore, divorce rates among us were quite high. There is a saying among operators that, "Women love to marry warriors, but try to turn them into farmers." Whatever the attraction is, the SAS definitely appeals strongly to the warrior spirit.

Duke

I joined the SAS as a 29 year old with two young children and all that goes with it. SAS wives or partners quickly become aware of the demanding lifestyle and the camaraderie their men enjoy. This solidarity is equally as strong among the families. The ability to handle this lifestyle and establish their independence is a must. Those who could not adjust either divorced, or with their husbands, disappeared from the unit.

Duke and TeAo at Government House for his British Empire Medal investiture, 1995

A significant proportion of the wives and soldiers within the SAS infrastructure are Maori. I cannot recall any occurrence of racial disharmony within the SAS family and a true spirit of brotherhood prevailed throughout the unit. This common bond was undeniably created through a Selection process based totally on individual performance. TeAo was familiar with the script and completely accepted my love for the military and adventure. It was my choice and although I gave Civvy Street a go, she had no interest in changing me. Unlike some others, the SAS in no way impaired the development of my marriage. If anything, the experiences both TeAo and I shared as members of that select family have strengthened

Duke Henry, BEM, with Governor General Sir Paul Reeves, 1995

our resolve and commitment a hundred fold. In spite of my risky and fractured life style, we are still together and although no longer part of the active SAS, the friendships and camaraderie we, as a family developed over the years, remain strong today. However, the SAS is a closed club and it is folly to think that girlfriends and wives, who are often propelled head first into a completely alien culture of strong egos and male elitism, will find the adjustment an easy one. Sorry ladies, but it's definitely a man's world behind the SAS compound's fence and there is no way that it will ever change. Surviving as a healthy family unit requires the woman to accept many of the normal tasks and functions that her partner would perform in ordinary military life. Long, lonely hours and weeks apart with constant upheavals created by rapid deployments and interruptions to daily schedules, coupled with the possibility of death waiting in the wings, will strain the strongest of relationships. However, if a family can weather all this turmoil and drama, then the rest of your married lives will seem a hell of a lot easier and simpler.

Alan

In the end, the seven-month ordeal seemed to have passed quickly. I had learned a great deal about the SAS, but most importantly, I was able to become intimate with myself and reflect on my true character. I, with the others, became pretty transparent when pushed to the limit. Some of what we saw of ourselves and in each other we didn't like and inwardly I resolved to work hard on my weaknesses. In our minds we had reached a fairly exalted status, but although we had proven ourselves to the Training Wing staff, it now remained for us to demonstrate our worth to our fellow operators, the men we were expected to fight alongside with. We were promptly and unequivocally reminded of this when we mustered in front of our troop room after returning from Fiji. Tip, our new troop sergeant and future SAS Regimental Sergeant Major inspected us and with his distinct air of regimentality made no bones about the fact that we were the still the new boys on the block and had a long way to go to get up on the first rung!

Duke

Injury is always a big threat to unit members. Realistic, high-risk training and routine operational demands exact their toll. Como and Shep departed it after three years of service. Como returned to farming in his beloved South Island and Shep went back to the conventional infantry. Upon retirement, he did a stint as a civilian prison officer and then worked the security circuit in Angola and currently, in Zimbabwe. In addition to gunshot wounds, Skippy was seriously injured in an explosion, both occurring on separate occasions over a five- year period. This helped convince him that there were undeniable benefits for working on civvy street after completing his degree at university he now resides in his hometown of Rotorua. Ritchie had a bad fall while rappelling and broke his pelvis, and guitar-playing arm. He received a medical discharge, and after a remedial period, amazed everyone by passing police training and becoming a front line cop in the tough South Auckland streets. Later on, he became a private investigator and proud father of several young Tolich's up in Whangarei. Stu completed his two-year assignment as a troop commander and being the ultimate chameleon, he simply blended into the mainstream military and relative obscurity. Dave, son of a former RSM cruised through the rank structure of the SAS with considerable zeal and speed. He had strict standards and couldn't be faulted for his work ethic. Eventually commissioned, he left the SAS after eighteen years and is now an airline pilot in the South Pacific. Dave was the only guy from our cycle not to sustain any meaningful injuries. Alan took a hunk of lead shrapnel in the arm from a nasty explosive shaped charge that stuffed him around for a while. In turn, I absorbed a 9mm round in the forearm while conducting CQB training in the "kill house." We paid little attention to the routine knee, ankle, back, and other ailments that went with the job, and at one juncture, when we were on the counter-terrorist team, we almost had a permanent bed at the local hospital. Obviously, the SAS is not a place for the faint hearted, but it's definitely worth it.

Alan was a raw, young soldier on Selection and even then he was extremely focused and committed to the SAS cause. He and I shared many trials and tribulations during Selection, and we roomed together for seven months on the cycle. The next nine years, we served together in the same squadron as troopers and senior NCO's, both in the conventional role and as members of the counter terrorist team. Our wives became great friends,

Amphibious Troop after Phoenix exercise – South Island, New Zealand, 1983. Aussie Trooper, Handles, Duke, Mattie Boy, Pop, Henry.

my kids called him Uncle and it was common knowledge amongst the SAS tribe of children that Uncle Alan and Aunty Elaine always had ice cream and loads of goodies in their refrigerator. On Sundays, the young,"Iron Man" Bros would frequently play host to half a dozen children from the Henry, Williams and Brausch clans. We were not quite sure how it started, but there he would be sitting on his steps suffering from the inevitable Sunday morning hangover and dishing out ice cream to his numerous adopted SAS nieces and nephews.

We worked hard, socialized at every opportunity and thrived within the SAS community. It's hard to recall what we saw in each other that appealed to us. I was impressed with Alan's aggressive attitude optimism. On both internal and external courses he habitually excelled. The role models we had in those days gave rough diamonds like most of the guys coming through Selection every chance to refine and develop themselves. Loyalty was a key ingredient, and Kevin, one of our early RSMs, along with his core of senior NCO's, molded the new lads coming through with their unique style of leadership. All the SNCO's were Vietnam veterans and totally in sync with what they wanted coming through the Selection process. There is no doubt that Alan and I along with our peer group were the lucky ones. To those crusty old warriors Kevin, Whee, Bill, Babs, Wings, Dicko, JT, Ben, Kerry, Jack, Vic, Poni, Joe, Paddy, and many more, I fervently hope that you have as many fond memories of your time in the Unit as Alan and I do. I would give my left nut to be 29 years old and starting the SAS life all over again. 2002 has been a significant one for spe-

Duke and Mattie Boy – Amphibious Troop, 1989

Duke with Orang Asli (indigenous Malaysian Tribe) – Malaysia, 1991

cial operation professionals and once again they are being committed to tasks and roles that they have been trained for and comfortable with. Leave the confusing UN "peace keeping" missions to the conventional troops and let the "hard core" get on with the real deal.

Alan

Between us, Duke and I would spend a total of 22 years together in the SAS. We readily recognize the fact that we were extremely fortunate to be able to work alongside men of the highest professional caliber as well as

Alan's Sudanese Special Forces tracking team during his attachment to them at the commencement of their civil war in 1983.

Preparing an RPG 7 prior to patrolling. These SF operators had never fired a live rocket before our arrival. Money and supplies are always available, it just often takes a good war to bring them out – Alan, Sudan, 1983

learn skills that would help prepare ourselves for a future on "civvy street." The opportunity to work with our foreign counterparts, particularly the Brits and Americans, throughout Africa, Asia, Europe, Central America, and the South Pacific, was a most rewarding experience.

Test firing the General Purpose Machine Gun (GPMG) prior to patrol – belt-fed ammunition was new to these guys. The annual ammunition allowance for their personal AK47 was a "staggering" 60 rounds per man, per year! Alan, Sudan, 1983

Many good men have attempted Selection, with nearly as many failing since the unit's inception in 1955, to fight alongside our British comrades in what then was called Malaya. Included in the list of successful foreign candidates are a large number of Pacific Islanders, the odd Brit and even an American Special Forces operator who completed Selection "just for kicks," in the mid eighties. After finishing the course, he simply bid all a friendly farewell and returned to the States, a contented man.

We have always held our parent unit, the British 22nd SAS Regiment, in extremely high regard because of their historical origins, vast operational experience and successful track record in a wide variety of theatres. Duke and I were fortunate to spend lengthy attachments to the Brits at their base in Hereford. Additionally, we were able to deploy to countries with them that we normally would not have had the opportunity to operate in. Some Kiwi SAS members were sufficiently impressed that they joined the Brit SAS after completing their Selection process. It may not be well known outside the two units, but Kiwis along with the Fijians have made up the largest contingent of foreigners to serve with the British SAS since its formation in 1941. Even though 12,000 miles of oceans and land-masses separate both countries, the military bond formed between these two members of the Commonwealth has remained remarkably close.

I am confident that our former unit is in great shape these days and ready for any assignment. Under new and visionary leadership, sustained by on-going operational deployments, fresh ideas have been introduced and implemented with great enthusiasm and vigor. Today's soldiers are more educated and technologically advanced, which is a direct reflection upon society and its progress. However, as a member of a Special Forces unit in the New Millennium, it could be fatal to accept what the media says about future technological warfare. Pilot-less aircraft, artificial intelligence, smart bombs, and computers may bode the future for winning large conflicts, but as far as the SAS is concerned we will always rely on cooperation and interaction with allied units, particularly the Americans. Solid, current, and realistic training, good boots, a strong back, and a reliable rifle will guarantee future success in battle.

Pulling The Pin

Alan's Story

Why I Left the SAS and New Zealand

The darkest day for the New Zealand military, and in particular the SAS, occurred on July 26, 1984 when David Lange was voted in as Prime Minister. It was an event that will make my stomach turn until the day I die. How on earth could a country with such a proud military history see fit to vote in such a left-wing, liberal, anti-military pacifist? We were sitting in the team shed in stunned silence the morning after the election results were confirmed. The reason we were so concerned was that we knew, politically and militarily, what lay ahead. Lange had focused his election campaign on what seemed like a one issue agenda — making New Zealand a nuclear-free country by banning all nuclear armed or capable vessels and aircraft from New Zealand's territories and its waters. To even think that such an issue would become a reality was beyond our wildest belief. It appeared that I had completely misunderstood the thought process of the mainstream Kiwi and what they considered important for themselves and their families. To me, there is nothing more important to a civilization, than security from external and internal threats to ensure the well being of your family and country. It is the most basic governmental obligation to society. For a small country such as New Zealand, it is obvious that we have to rely heavily on outside security support, hence the formation of the South East Asian Treaty Organization (SEATO) and more importantly, the Australian, New Zealand, United States (ANZUS) Alliance. It is critical to remember that these alliances are not only about assisting each other during "regional conflicts," but also dealt with the issues of mutual close cooperation in the form of military equipment, training and intelligence matters. Obviously, both Australia and New Zealand relied heavily on the superpower status of the United States to guarantee this international concept. What better friend could one wish for than to have the United States flexing muscle on your behalf and in support of your policies and decisions? In return of course, the United States and Australia both expected the same sort of commitment and support from us. This support was normally in the form of troop transfers and training, sharing of military and other forms of intelligence that affected national security, the hosting of American troops, aircraft and naval vessels and providing sites for intelligence gathering facilities. Additionally, New Zealand was seen as a potential staging area for the U.S. Pacific Fleet and fixed wing aircraft for any major conflict that occurred in the South Pacific or South East Asian regions. No politician can easily ignore these commitments, which were historically anchored in our allied response to Japanese aggression during WWII, but somehow Lange and his administration erased much of this tradition.

Under any conditions, one of the deadliest mindsets that a country can adopt is to think that it has total control over its strategic assets and borders and has nothing to fear from its "neighbours" or today's radical terrorist organizations. Let's not forget the murderous maritime bombing of the Greenpeace Flag Ship the "Rainbow Warrior" by French Intelligence Agents while anchored in Auckland Harbor on July 10, 1985, or the hijacking of an Air New Zealand 747 in Suva, Fiji in 1987. Both of these invasive incidents occurred while Lange was in power. It is interesting to note that U.S. Intelligence was aware of the impending attack that was orchestrated by the French Government against the Greenpeace anti-nuclear flag-ship as it was transiting through Auckland, en route to the French nuclear testing site at Moruroa Atoll in the South Pacific. I agreed with the American decision not to inform the New Zealand Security Intelligence Service because of our frosty relationship. Stand by to start accepting the long-term consequences of your decision, Lange! After his administration was voted out of office, the consequences of his abortive policies have nevertheless persisted for decades. I am by no means a supporter of the organization known as Greenpeace. Quite frankly, I think they are a bunch of anarchist troublemakers. Typically, they are liberal college graduates (or drop-outs) who should focus their attention on getting decent haircuts and good jobs rather than meddling in the affairs of foreign governments.

On the other hand, the French are by no means a popular nation in anyones' books. Not quite sure where their loyalties lie from one day to the next, they tend to chase the money and spend a little too much time supporting Arab nations with somewhat dubious terrorist track records. I remember being present at a private airport just outside Paris in August 1989 on a VIP protection detail waiting for our Principal's aircraft to arrive. In flew a Soviet Military cargo plane that was loaded up with two military helicopters, each bearing Libyan Airforce markings in Arabic and English, plus two CONEX boxes full of what could only be military supplies. I also think it ironic that the same type of helicopters were also used by Israel to kick sand in the face of their enemies during various wars of annihilation and frequent Spec-Op missions.

In line with that, they also refused U.S. warplanes, on orders from President Reagan, permission to fly over French airspace en route to bomb specific Libyan targets in the mid-80's.

I think that the French government employed extremely bad judgment and displayed their consummate arrogance by infiltrating a friendly country's territory and executing a military style operation that resulted in death and destruction. It was obvious that they grossly underestimated the investigative ability and rapid reaction of the New Zealand Police and Security Intelligence Service. As a result of their disrespect for sovereignty and massive miscalculations, they ended up looking like idiots all over the world.

The operation, including the actual placement of the two mines and subsequent sinking of the ship, was carried out by operators from France's intelligence and covert operations bureau, Direction Generale de la Securite Exterieure (DGSE). Christine Gabon, an intelligence gatherer with the unit was infiltrated into the Auckland office of Greenpeace in April, 1985. Her mission was to gather information pertaining to the "Rainbow Warrior's" next mission to Moruroa Atoll, as well prepare for the arrival of subsequent operatives. The next to arrive were Major Alain Marfart and Captain Dominique Prieur. Acting as Swiss husband and wife tourists, they were sent to N.Z. to arrange necessary support matters, prior to the arrival of the saboteurs on the yacht "Ouvea." They were not involved in the physical placement of the charges, however they were caught a couple of days after the bombing while returning their rental van in Auckland. By this time, "Ouvea" was steaming rapidly toward Norfolk Island, carrying the DGSE agents who were responsible for placing the two mines on the ship. They were subsequently uplifted by a French submarine and taken to Tahiti. To avoid further embarrassment to the French government, and ensure that that facts of the mission were never made public, Marfart and Prieur pleaded guilty to lesser charges of manslaughter for the death of one crewman and willful damage. On November 4, 1985, they were subsequently sentenced to ten years in a New Zealand prison. In June 1986, a deal was brokered by Javier Perez de Cuellar, Secretary of the United Nations. France was ordered to pay USD$6.5 million in compensation to the N.Z. government, plus make an official "apology." In return, Marfart and Prieur would be released from New Zealand's custody and transferred to a French Military Base on Hao Atoll for a period of three years. To top off the whole deal, both "prisoners" were released from their holiday camp prior to the three-year period. Marfart returned to France due to illness in December, 1987 and was never sent back to Hao, while Prieur was welcomed home to France in May, 1988 as a hero. Prieur was pregnant at the time of her release due to the fact that her husband was granted permission to join her on Hao Atoll. Once again, the United Nations "comes to the rescue and does a terrific job."

Personally, I didn't really give a damn because their operators were following orders, just as we would have done, except they committed the ultimate sin — they got caught. Additionally, at that time I was a team leader on the counter terrorist team and it provided several months of interesting work for us, up till the day, under UN direction, we transported the two undercover operators to the Whenuapai Air Force Base to load them on a C-130 that took them to their "private prison" on a sunny beach in the South Pacific.

Lange's electoral promise to ban all nuclear type vessels was implemented immediately upon his election as Prime Minister. Some New Zealanders obviously have a very short memory as to our professional and emotional association with the United States. New Zealand troops have operated gallantly and with great honor alongside United States forces in WWI, WWII, Korea, Vietnam, and the Gulf War. Additionally, our forces operational deployments with the British during the Malayan and Borneo campaigns did nothing but enhance our total commitment to not only our allies, but also to putting an end to communist inspired guerilla insurgencies and terrorist campaigns in our region.

What a total sellout to all the veterans of my country, not to mention the fighting men and women who gave their lives in the line of duty. New Zealand has a small, but extremely proud and professional military force and for over 130 years has fought and died with honor and distinction alongside their allies. From the Maori Wars to the Boer War, Gallipoli to North Africa, Europe, the South Pacific, the jungles of South East Asia, and more recently Ethiopia, Lebanon, Cambodia, Sierra Leone, Bosnia, The Sinai, Laos, Bougainville, East Timor, and Afghanistan, they have never backed down from a good and righteous scrap. What was going through the minds of these veterans now? All active duty personnel and I felt extremely embarrassed over this decision and a sense of mass guilt toward our American colleagues. Our government, it seemed, was doing its best to alienate us. During my time as an operator with the SAS, and since opening my school in the United States, I have trained extensively with members of the U.S. Navy SEALs, Army Special Forces (Green Berets), and members of the 1st Special Forces Operational Detachment, commonly known as Delta Force. I consider these men to be some of the most competent and dedicated warriors that I have ever worked alongside. Many of these professionals have become my great friends, work mates, advisers and drinking buddies over the years. Included in this select group are former U.S. Army Delta Force operators Mike, Matt and Kit, all soldiers from the 70's to the 90's, skilled, smart and gifted operators who would be my first choice for any risky operation. Also included in this select group is fellow

Mississippian and former Gulf War Veteran, 82nd Airborne paratrooper — John Herron. After the war, John went on to become a special forces operator and eventually a commissioned officer and which time, he switched trades and became a Blackhawk helicopter and fixed wing pilot for the army.

The United States has produced many fine, brave and honorable servicemen over the years, but there is one who stands above all others in my eyes. I have had the privilege to work overseas many times with my good friend Amado, a man that I consider a true warrior and patriot. In April of 1961, Amado was one of the 1500 Cubans from Brigade 2506 who went up against 100,000 of Castro's finest during the U.S. sponsored Bay of Pig's invasion. As a 19 year old, Lieutenant Amado and his airborne infantry platoon parachuted into his former homeland to rid it of a communist dictator. Even though "his hot war" was short, his incarceration as a prisoner of war in Fidel's filthy and tortuous prisons was not. As a "Brigade" officer he and others were eventually "bought back" by the United States after two years of hell that was rotting their lives away.

Upon his return to U.S. soil, he became a U.S. Marine Corps officer, a decision that would have a huge impact on his future. After President Kennedy's assassination, he saw operational service in South Vietnam and the Dominican Republic with the U.S. Army's Special Forces.

After his military service, Amado contributed another 20 odd years to U.S. Government service worldwide until his retirement in the late 1990's. What an interesting and unique individual, and what a life this man has led! It is to patriots like Amado, who have fought tyranny since he was a young man, that we owe such a great deal. These men understood and completely embraced the meaning of commitment and loyalty to their country and commander in chief, something that I, sadly, could no longer honor in my own country.

As my buddy Duke once said to a high ranking, regular Army officer when questioned on his loyalties to Queen and country, "Sir, there is only one person that I am loyal to. It is not the Queen, Governor General, Prime Minister, or the Minister of Defense. It is the Commanding Officer of the Special Air Service."

What about the thousands of American servicemen who gave their lives during WWII in the South Pacific? If it weren't for them, we would all be pulling rickshaws and bowing to the emperor! It should be noted that after Lange and his liberal party were finally ousted, military activity markedly increased, with our troops deploying to troubled regions throughout the world on a variety of missions.

Of all the "dog and pony shows" (counter-terrorist demonstrations) that we performed for visiting VIP's, one stands out in contrast to the rest.

Without a doubt, the most memorable and motivating demo was for the best Prime Minister the military ever had, Sir Robert Muldoon. A WWII veteran and total supporter of the SAS, Sir Robert knew that every SAS operator was prepared to follow him back into the trenches of Gallipoli if that was what he wanted. Lange, on the other hand, was a total fuck up from day one. How he even had the balls to visit our unit compound, I will never know. I remember the day well. Morale was at an all time low and I had never seen the men so pissed off and despondent about giving a demonstration. We felt like we had absolutely nothing to gain from it.

The aim of the demonstration was obviously to show Lange and his new cabinet members the capabilities of the NZSAS counter-terrorist team, should he ever be required to activate us. The team was created in the late 1970's and structured along the lines of the British SAS counter-terrorist unit. The unit was responsible for responding to and confronting acts of terrorism that occurred within our jurisdiction both at home and similar incidents abroad that targeted New Zealand citizens or property.

Unlike the United States Armed Forces, the New Zealand military did have civil operational jurisdiction within its borders for tasks that were deemed over and above that which the National Police could be expected to handle. Being the Prime Minister, you would think that Lange would take this kind of demonstration extremely seriously, but not this son-of-a-bitch. To aggravate matters, he showed up with his two sons who were wearing "peace oriented T-shirts." What a fucking joke. Treating our efforts like a Rambo cinema, Lange walked out of the demo still not knowing which end of a weapon was the dangerous one.

Similarly, Lange's cabinet ministers were also as disliked as their esteemed leader. In fact, the boys held all members of the Labor Party accountable for the situation we currently were in. In the late 1980's, the SAS Association hosted the five-year reunion at the SAS lines at the Papakura Camp. Former SAS operators from Britain, Australia, and Rhodesia (Zimbabwe) tend to join the Kiwis for these occasions, so it is a special and personal get together for members dating back to the 1955 New Zealand originals. Many a pint was sculled as members reminisced and exchanged stories that had become larger and more perilous with time, regardless of the era you wore the beret, or the country you served. We all had one thing in common — the SAS family and what it stood for.

However, during the gathering, an incident developed that threatened to mar the seriousness and sanctity of the ceremonies. Duke, Ritchie, Brent, Gillie, and myself were standing in a corner sculling a few cold ones when Blade staggered over.

"Hey you guys, guess who the fuck just walked in."

"Who, mate," was Brent's instant reply.

"That wanker Prebble — that's who." Richard Prebble was a senior member of Lange's political party who held a cabinet portfolio. A "right plonker" to say the least, he had a lot of nerve poking his head into an SAS reunion. Apparently he was brought in as a private guest by one of the former members who claimed to be a "buddy" of his. However, it didn't matter because he wasn't officially invited (and never would have been) so in our minds, he wasn't welcome. The former members who were now out of the business may have felt differently, but to us serving members it was an insult and totally unacceptable. He was one of Lange's hardcore peacenik no nuclear wankers, which meant he was responsible for us not training with the Americans.

"Go drag his sorry ass over here Blade," was the first thing out of Gillie's mouth.

You really need to know Blade to understand him. I don't know how he got that nickname, but his other alias was "Winegum." Two sniffs of a beer cap and he was on his way. A stocky little bugger and great rugby player, Blade was always ready for a fight, regardless of rank or the size of the opponent. Without further ado, Blade made a "B-line" for Prebble's table where he was mixing it up with the Ruperts and tapped him firmly on the shoulder.

"Oi, the boys want a word with you over in the corner."

Making sure that his "request" in the form of an order was instantly obeyed, Blade escorted the Honorable Richard Prebble to our corner. As he approached, he tried to seize the initiative and feebly attempted to mollify us and ease the tension by the salutation, "Good evening men and how is everyone tonight?"

"No bloody good, we need to ask you a few questions," was Gillie's threatening retort.

With that, Prebble's back was pinned to the wall and he was surrounded and brutally questioned by six, over-aggressive and liquored up troopers, lusting for blood. The questions were geared toward recent operations that we were either involved in or meant to be. After about ten minutes of relentless interrogation, Prebbles's host came barging in and tried to rescue him, but the boys weren't finished yet. He was respectfully acknowledged by Blade with "fuck off mate, you aren't invited to this meeting."

The Ruperts, knowing what was going on seemed to turn a blind eye and just let the boys get their frustrations out. Like a true politician, Prebble blamed every other man and his dog for his party's decisions and ended up becoming totally confused and frustrated, while babbling on like a fool, and not as a leader of our nation. I thought at one stage that Blade was going to leap in and put the chocker (strangle) on him — it wasn't a pretty sight. Consequently, Prebble, sensing imminent disaster, made a hasty retreat from the hall. If the wanker wasn't already aware our feelings toward the Labor Party and its legacy, he certainly was now. An un-professional act on our behalf you might say. Yes, looking back on it, you are probably right, but such was the mood and friction level caused by politics back in those days.

I guess that everything in life happens for a reason and in May, 1987, something fateful happened to me. At that time, I was an instructor in the Training Wing responsible for conducting internal training courses for the squadron operators. One of the programs under my supervision was the Unarmed Combat Instructors' Course. This course involved taking selected operators from the squadrons and training them to become unarmed combat instructors.

To assist the unit in this process, the SAS employed the services of Mr. Jack Sims, the President of the New Zealand Chidokan Karate Association. Since 1968, Jack had been designing and implementing mission specific curriculums for the unit that addressed armed and unarmed confrontations in extremely close quarter environments. I cannot speak highly enough of the contribution Jack made to the unit over the years. A small unassuming man, Jack possessed a presence unlike any other I have seen. His adult life had been dedicated to the pursuit of excellence and perfection in an art that he lived for. The respect that he had from the operators of the SAS was unquestionable and there was no doubt that he had the undivided attention of every man for the fours hours each afternoon we spent in his dojo.

One afternoon, typically drenched in sweat and bodies aching from the constant poundings received during the numerous sparring sessions, the boys changed partners for one last time. I squared off against Bryan Fitzpatrick, who was Jack's top black belt and a meticulous exponent of the art. Out of the corner of my eye, I noticed a big guy standing at the back of the dojo. During the next break, he walked up and introduced himself to me as Mark Lonsdale, an ex-New Zealander now residing in the United States who was visiting from Los Angeles.

I listened intently as he explained what he did in the States and I was fascinated as to the extent of his business. Besides running a full time security operation for a Forbes 400 businessman and his family in Beverly Hills, he also conducted training for police and military special operation teams throughout the United States. Prior to leaving, he handed me his card and said to call him if I felt he could be of assistance to me "in any way." At that stage of my military career, I was still happy with what I was doing. Although the military was still suffering terribly from the Labor Party's policies, decision time for me actually came a year later. I had now reached a level in the unit's rank structure that began to slowly take me away from the "action man jobs" and move me more in the direction of supervisory

Two true warriors and friends – Amado and Bob Taubert. After meeting at U.S. Army Ranger School in 1964, then fighting for their country throughout the 1960's, they would devote a further 25 years each serving their country at government level worldwide – Puerto Rico, 2001

roles. Not yet ready to turn my M-16 in for a desk job, I retrieved Mark's card and decided to give him a call to see if his offer of sponsorship still stood. Sure enough, he was still motivated, so we started the process with the United States Immigration and Naturalization Service to obtain a work visa for me. This was a huge decision for me, because there had been no doubt in my mind that I absolutely loved the Army life and was convinced I was a "lifer." However, because of the distasteful political climate, my decision to "pull the pin" was not as gut wrenching as I had imagined it to be. Nevertheless, the most difficult thing for me to do was to front up to my mentor, Bill and reveal my dire decision to him. It was men like Bill who made the SAS what it is today. Out of respect to him and because he contributed so much to my development as an SAS-SNCO, I didn't want him to hear the news second hand. He listened and there were no arguments. He trusted my judgment and being the profound professional that he was, he simply wished me luck and got straight back into his work.

Another SAS operator that I had a great deal of respect for was Phil Cairns. Phil was my patrol commander during our final jungle exercise on selection. Shortly thereafter, he disappeared into the "dark continent" for several years to acquire further operational experience. He had a great deal to offer the unit, particularly after his return from his overseas shooting stints. He may not have been noted for "pushing paper" among the unit's senior NCOs, but as far as the operators were concerned that was not an important attribute on the "two-way firing range," which is a large part of the SAS's "bread and butter" tasking.

Nothing can rival experience in actual operations, be they conventional or in the counter terrorist arena. The realities of violent conflict act as a proving ground for one's training and theories about armed confrontations. Sometimes, what you learned to expect is diametrically opposed to what you actually run into. I believe that those who survive and benefit from these encounters have a great deal to relate in the area of lessons learned and serve to eliminate myths associated with small unit warfare. An unfortunate, but common problem often exists within small, elite units that are made up of strong-willed men.

Frequently, there are some sensitive egos holding command positions that actually appear to resent members who take leave of the unit to fulfill their professional and personal quests. They fail to appreciate that men like Phil are mission- rather than career-oriented and probably would have been quickly commissioned in any other command. Phil acquired operational experiences that many could only fantasize about, but never have the balls to make a reality.

In my opinion, given the opportunity, Phil would have made an excellent Regimental Sergeant Major (RSM) for the unit. Unfortunately, for whatever reasons, this did not happen and he retired as a Warrant Officer Class Two, a rank he achieved in three different armies (New Zealand, South Africa and Oman) during a career that spanned some 25 years.

Although that anxious formality was relatively uneventful, my official farewell from the unit was a great piss-up. When Steve, my Squadron Commander, presented me with the customary unit plaque, he stated that I would not last a minute on "civvy street" and my return to the unit would be imminent. Being the stubborn mule that I am, I looked him in the eye and said, "no way boss, once I walk out that gate, you won't see me again." Ultimately however, he was right, but not in the way he intended his remark to be interpreted. Eventually, I did return as the owner of T.E.E.S. and a U.S. citizen, to see old mates, catch up on the news, and offer employment to the young operators that wanted to experience training and operations worldwide. After proclaiming my bold intentions, in the back of my mind I was fervently praying that my U.S. visa would come through, because up till now, the ink was definitely still wet and my application was probably at the bottom of a three foot high stack of applications in some junior bureaucrat's office in Los Angeles.

I did not burn any bridges, but my pride would not let me lose face by asking for my job back. At the conclusion of my send off, I staggered out of the compound, with my unit's blessing, closed the gate, and did not look back.

Since leaving, my relationship with the unit has remained strong. I have maintained a professional rapport with the officers and men, something I hope remains in the years to come. As for Lange, the mere mention of his name makes me want to vomit. The damage that he did to New Zealand was serious, but to a large degree has been rectified by the country's willing commitments to various peace-keeping efforts and by participating to the international outrage and response to radical, militant Islamic terrorism. New Zealand's loyalties, thank God, are no longer in question. I was a soldier, and a casualty of a fucked up political party. What soldier in any country isn't affected by political decisions sometime throughout his career? I am sure that many American servicemen felt similar frustrations during the eight-year tenor of President Clinton as their Commander in Chief. Finally, under intense pressure, Lange resigned his premiership on August 8, 1989, after five disastrous years in office. Letting him off the hook that way was too easy. He should have been tarred and feathered for the setbacks and damage he inflicted upon our country. One thing for sure, as far as the military was concerned — there would have been no shortage of volunteers to carry out the task.

Embracing America

Alan's Story

From Hollywood to the Mississippi Delta
— Realizing the American Dream

In May, 1989, I set an extended foot on U.S. soil. Under the Immigration and Naturalization Service's Alien Status criteria, I was classified as a "Teacher/Expert Counter-Terrorism." I was sponsored and brought into America by Mark Lonsdale, founder and director of the Los Angeles based Specialized Tactical Training Unit (STTU) to teach law enforcement and military personnel the lexicon of skills and trade-craft associated with counter-terrorism and high risk special operations. Our programs were specifically designed for personnel operating in military (green), police (blue), and counter terrorist (black) roles. Even though I had traveled to this vast continent in the past, I was about to see a whole new side of this amazing country. I spent my first two years working for my sponsor in Los Angeles. The majority of my time was spent as a personal protection officer for Mark's other company, tasked to provide security for a prominent businessman and movie producer who is currently worth approximately $1.2 billion. I found Mark's security company, International Diplomatic Security (IDS), to be an extremely professional and well-run organization. There was absolutely no confusion regarding what was expected of you, or the absolute requirement to perform your duties in a highly professional manner. The work involved extensive travel within the United States and abroad. Compensation and benefits were excellent, particularly for a raggedy assed Kiwi coming in from a poorly paying military career. In addition to my security responsibilities, Mark and I conducted a number of courses for military and law enforcement special operation teams. Training revolved around close quarter battle skills and forced entry/hostage operations in buildings, buses, and aircraft. Our first trip was to Reno, Nevada where we worked with the Reno Police Department and Washoe County Sheriff's Department in skills ranging from close quarter tactical shooting to room combat and explosive breaching. I must say that after a lengthy layoff from this type of work, it was great to get back amongst the dust, grime, and cordite associated with this type of work. Next we were off to

Ohio to present a seminar to a variety of law enforcement agencies. It was here that I got to meet a man that I would come to respect immensely. Ken Hackathorn was a U/S/ Army special forces veteran who now devotes his life to passing on the skills that he has gained over the years in the business of gun fighting and special operation tactics. Next stop saw Mark, Max Joseph, fellow Kiwi and martial arts exponent, Bryan Fitzpatrick, and myself landing in Camp Pendleton, California — home of the United States Marine Corps. It was near the end of 1990 and during the course, Sadaam Hussein invaded Kuwait, which in turn activated the largest U.S. and allied military mobilization since WWII. Our guys were set to travel on the first ship out, but their commanding officer saw fit to ensure that all the live fire range training was conducted by us prior to them shipping out. It felt good to be part of a team that had the opportunity to prepare these guys for war.

After two years of protecting the elite Hollywood crowd, I felt it was high time I moved on and did more of what I was bought into this country to do — teach tactics. Dave, my team leader at IDS, had an incredible background in explosives as a result of his time spent as a special agent for the federal government. Additionally, his expertise with weapons was second to none. He was an accomplished shooter and consistently rated among the top ten combat shooters in the world with the handgun, shotgun, and rifle. His speed and accuracy coupled with his overall knowledge of firearms was amazing. In action, he was extremely motivating and thrilling to watch. While in the SAS, I considered myself an above-average handgun shooter and was very familiar with the popular 9mm Browning pistol. In the U.S., I transitioned to America's pistol, the .45ACP 1911 A1 Government Model. However, I was frequently humbled when I started shooting alongside real pros like Dave and Mark. I learned that when performing a physical skill, you often don't realize that you may be doing it incorrectly, or that there is a more efficient way, until you compete against someone who is better than you. I learned a great deal about combat shooting and weapons in general from Dave and Mark and, subsequently, my skill levels increased tremendously in a short amount of time.

During May, 1991, Dave and I reluctantly left IDS to open the Tactical Explosive Entry School (T.E.E.S.) in Memphis, Tennessee. With Dave's knowledge in explosive handling and shooting and my expertise in explosive breaching and tactics, we felt that we had a quality product to offer the special operations community. Predictably, as with any new business, it was a slow start, but our perseverance eventually paid off. In little more than a decade, T.E.E.S. has trained thousands of domestic military and law enforcement personnel and operators from over thirty countries. The school's motto is "train for the worst case scenario" and is strongly reflected in the realistic and thorough manner in which I approach all aspects of my training.

Dave left the company in 1993 to pursue other interests and I assumed full control. With assistance from my world-class adjunct cadre, which consists of Senior Instructor Max Joseph, Department of Energy Master Breacher Bill Yaegle, Former Delta Force operators Mike Smith and Matt Mann, SWAT Officer Todd Taylor, former FBI Agent Bob Taubert, Texas SWAT Officer Tim Bulot, former Kiwi and British SAS Trooper Adam Hamon, T.E.E.S. Brazil partner Kevan Gillies, and, of course, my SAS colleague Duke, we developed the company to where it is today. However, the man who held the team together was not a former SWAT cop or special forces operator, nor an instructor or tactician extraordinaire. He was just an ordinary man from the South, but one who could shoot a black powder gun like no one else. Bill Duke, the "Sar Major," as he is commonly referred to, is also affectionately called the "grumpy old bastard" of the company. His Fatherly leadership was exactly what us young bucks needed — someone to kick our ass and keep us on the straight and narrow. Bill's background as an aircraft engineer enabled him to become exceptionally skilled in the art of "fixing," or construction. He basically took a sixteen- acre sandpit and turned it into a highly functional and workable training facility. Dave, however, was the key reason why we moved to this part of the country. He had been stationed in Memphis as an agent and knew a lot of people who could assist in our risky endeavor. Geographically, the location was ideal because it was within a day and half driving time from a significant segment of the country's population.

I eventually established my residence in nearby DeSoto County, Mississippi. One of my first priorities was to apply for reserve deputy status with the local Sheriff's Department. Coming from a mili-

Great mate and fellow T.E.E.S. instructor, Max "Ranger" Joseph – former U.S. Marine Recon Sergeant (Semper Fi, Ranger).

tary special forces background, I felt it was important for me to obtain a sound understanding of police work if I was going to make a career out of training law enforcement officers. Obviously, there is no better way to do that than to get out on the streets and perform those duties. In due course, I was commissioned as a deputy within the department, but it was made very clear that my primary responsibilities would specifically revolve around SWAT operations. In my wildest imagination, I could not have asked for anything more than that. After nine years of service, I was promoted to my present rank of captain.

Most of us will agree that America can be a violent and dangerous country. I had been in Memphis for approximately a year when the reality of this infamous attribute hit me. A local businessman that we purchased range supplies from thought he knew Dave and I a little better than he really did. One afternoon while we were at his place of business, he took us aside and bluntly asked us if we would kill someone for him. Without hesitation, Dave quickly informed him that he had just made his first big, legal mistake and he best zip up. Nothing further was said, but we quickly severed our business relationship with him.

The T.E.E.S. "Sar Major" Bill Duke after a successful coyote hunt – Arkansas, 2001

As an American citizen, I am a strong supporter of the National Rifle

Association and the right for law-abiding citizens to own and bear arms. There is nothing more important in life than being capable of protecting yourself, your family, and property. The only way that this can be guaranteed in a democratic and free society that owes its historical freedom to armed citizens is to possess them for personal security as well as for sporting and other legitimate purposes.

With tens of thousands of murders, rapes, assaults, and armed robberies each year and an incarcerated population of approximately 6.6 million, you would think that our laws would lean more toward protecting the law abiding citizens than coddling the criminal. It is my habit to never leave home without a handgun concealed on my person because I refuse to be a victim. I am convinced that there are no victims, but only volunteers when it comes to human predators. They will always avoid the "hard target" and instead prey upon the weak that project vulnerability. Most of us are familiar with the old saying "it is better to be tried by twelve rather than buried by six," and I believe that many innocent Americans have been victimized because they obeyed the cosmetic laws passed by politically correct politicians. The political liberal elite can afford body-guards and high walls.

Hypocritically, many anti-gun legislators possess firearms for protection, but don't want the "incompetent populace" to have access to them. Without the right to own firearms, because of government distrust, you become a subject, not a citizen. There is no way in hell that I, or my family, will be harmed by some scumbag because a politician established a law that prevents me from defending what is legally and morally mine.

During my early introduction to life in the South, I was involved in two altercations that required me to display my pistol. In the first instance, an aggressive use of "justified force" with my weapon convinced one offender that he had created a serious problem for himself and I was not going to be an easy mark. In the second, the would be predator (and his mates) immediately stopped his aggression when he saw the barrel of my Sig P226 zeroed in between his eyes. These social misfits only understand and appreciate strength, force, and pain. If you attempt to reason with them, or beg for mercy, they will kill you. They only relate to brutality because that is what their entire life revolves around.

While driving home on two separate occasions, I spotted dead bodies dumped on the side of the road. This appears to be a common occurrence in my area, because my county shares a common border with Memphis, Tennessee. Murders are committed in Memphis and the bodies are fre quently disposed of by transporting them across the state line and dumping them in Mississippi. Criminals do this to involve more than one jurisdiction in an effort to complicate the investigative process and hamper the legal system as much as possible.

While living in a quiet rural area of North Mississippi, a black Memphis prostitute had her throat cut and was hastily buried in a shallow grave about ten yards off the road I lived on. As part of my fitness regime, I ran past this spot everyday and was always accompanied by my neighbors yapping dog. Eventually the dog got wind of the decaying body and decided to investigate. He dug up the corpse, gnawed off the head, and did what any well-trained dog would do — took it home to the boss. It was around Halloween, so that added a little more drama to the rest of the story. The neighbor's ten-year old son came home from school and found this decomposing and partially eaten lady's head perched on the back door step. Although he didn't panic, he immediately called his Mother at work to inform her of his macabre discovery.

"Momma, Momma, there's a dead Black lady's head on the porch."

Bearing in mind that it was Halloween, the mother angrily replied, "Stop being so stupid, Benny, now get inside and do your homework."

"But Momma, I swear, there is a dead Black lady's head on the porch."

"Benny, it's Halloween and someone is playing a joke, now get inside and call your Grandma before I come home and kick your butt." With that stern admonition, little Benny picked up the phone and cried into it, "Grandma, Grandma, there's a dead Black lady's head on the porch." With that plea still ringing in her ears, Grandma rushed over and nearly suffered a heart attack. Little Benny wasn't so stupid after all, although he could be a little nuts now!

Some people might be surprised to learn that the United States has approximately 900,000 law enforcement officers involved in fighting crime. This number could be increased to a million and they would still not be able to keep up with the amount of crime that sweeps the country on a daily basis. The majority of officers are overworked and grossly underpaid for the type and amount of work they are performing. On average, between 60-120 officers lose their lives each year in the line of duty and thousands of others are injured or psychologically affected because of work-related stress. It has also been said that America has more lawyers than cops, and this is certainly reflected in the judicial system. Quite simply, it is a joke, and it is no wonder that the public gets frustrated over the manner in which violent criminals are pampered. Sentences grossly incompatible with the type of crime committed are routinely handed out, and with time reduced for good behavior the criminal is back out on the street before victims have been able to adjust to their losses.

The causes for this criminal justice disaster can probably be narrowed down to overcrowded prisons, civil libertarians, lenient parole boards, and a plethora of defense attorneys. The death penalty should be mandatory in every state for criminals who are without a doubt guilty of crimes that warrant their extermination. The serial killers, murderers, rapists, and child molesters who are convicted beyond reasonable doubt should be taken out the back door and immediately shot. Why should society be required to pay millions of dollars while they occupy death row for several years while appealing their case? If true justice has been realized, then their sentences should be carried out swiftly.

The Chinese not only believe in a speedy trial, but a speedy execution as well. Additionally, they make the family of the felon pay for the bullet that terminates his life. Litigation oriented attorneys are another huge problem in this country. All they seem to do is inundate the courts with frivolous lawsuits in an effort to find ways to bleed the institutions of this country so they can make big buck settlements. If, as in the United Kingdom, losing plaintiffs and their attorneys here were forced to pay the opposing party's legal fees, this would give them pause when contemplating messing with people's lives.

The prison system is a growing business in this country. With approximately 6.6 million (1 in 32 adults) in the nation's correction system, and growing on a daily basis, space is at a premium. Some of the larger penitentiaries and jails house five to six thousand inmates. I have visited these institutions on a number of work-related occasions. In the South, many of them are referred to as "prison farms." Some consist of up to 20,000 acres of land and qualified inmates are put to work each day in the fields to perform a variety of tasks.

These work gangs march out into the fields in company size formations, complete with rakes, shovels, hoes, and other tools required for the job. Guards control the work detail mounted on horses and armed with lever action carbines, shotguns, and handguns. The guards normally form a triangle around the work party and everyone knows the rules. Move outside the imaginary line drawn between two horses and you are fair game for the guards. The rules are very simple, cut and dried. Occasionally, mentally unstable prisoners attempt to commit suicide by guard, but are usually detected ahead of time and isolated for treatment.

The Mississippi State Penitentiary in Parchman is one of the most notorious of all prison farms. Situated 90 minutes south of Memphis, it is located in the heart of the hot and humid Mississippi Delta. I regularly visited my good mate, Skipper Phillips, who is the Penitentiary range master, to conduct training or just to bullshit. Usually, State Trooper Bobby G. Reed would accompany me on these visits.

Customarily, on the large farms there are several satellite "camps" dispersed throughout the facility. Each inmate would be classified according to the seriousness of his offense and sent to the appropriate camp. The inmates assigned to the minimum, medium, and maximum security facilities run the gamut from bad check passers to serial rapists and killers on death row. Most of these institutions possess their own SWAT or special operations teams to handle major confrontations. The Parchman facility was no exception to this practice, and their team was also responsible for training and maintaining the dog section. The prison dogs are broken down into three categories. There are drug dogs (Labradors), attack dogs (German Shepherds), and tracker dogs (Bloodhounds). Kenneled in a huge barn, the dogs are well taken care of by trustee inmates.

There are not a lot of places to run to if you break out of Parchmen. Surrounded by the rice and cotton fields of the flat Delta, no visible landmarks exist to orientate on. Running in the summer's heat can easily result in death by heat stroke and Delta denizens, such as its huge mosquitoes, mean unrelenting torture at night or possibly a bout with the feared "West Nile Virus." It gets pretty frosty during the winter, and getting wet from surface water or perspiration could induce hypothermia at night, that is, if the Bloodhounds don't tear you up first.

In 1998 I applied for and obtained my U.S. citizenship during a brief five-minute ceremony in the Memphis office the Immigration and Naturalization Service. This was an important step for me in the fact that it could open me up to more lucrative work opportunities at government level. Additionally, by becoming a citizen, it was also a way of "giving back" something to the country that presented me with a unique work opportunity nine years previously.

A number of the police officers have asked me if I miss the SAS lifestyle. Of course I do, but I never let myself become convinced that it was an all-consuming issue. The SAS taught me the skills that enabled me to operate as a soldier anywhere in the world, doing the things that I loved to do most, with people who meant everything to me. Furthermore, without my SAS skills, it would have been unlikely that Mark would have sponsored me into the United States. Additionally, without U.S. Citizenship I would not be the owner of training facilities in the United States and Brazil, a commissioned law enforcement officer, a contract instructor for the U.S. government, or had the opportunity to perform security details worldwide.

I will always be indebted to Mark Lonsdale for giving me the opportunity, as well as the men who mentored me, and especially to the ones that I operated with. Most importantly, it was ultimately reassuring to have received their blessings for what I have accomplished in training and operational arenas. How did I do it? It was actually very simple. I adopted the SAS's universal motto, "Who Dares Wins." I dared and I believe that I won!

American Express

Duke's Story

Introduction to T.E.E.S. and DeSoto County Sheriffs Department (U.S.A.)

After retiring from the military, I moved back to our family home in Ruatoria. It was a great place and not only my wife's family refuge, but also where we really wanted to be. We planned to sit back on our large veranda and let the world pass us by. TeAo and I had worked all our lives and at the age of 42, I thought I had cracked it and would just take it easy for the rest of my life. The biggest excitement of the day was watching the school bus pick up my teenage daughter and son. Boy what a life. Well, it got old real quick. Since I had part of my kneecap surgically removed prior to my discharge, it was probably a good period for convelesance. Nevertheless, pig hunting, fishing, diving, and socializing over a cold bottle of beer are great pastimes, but try to pay your electricity bill with a sack of crayfish or a hind quarter of wild pork. The barter system was no longer valid and nobody does business that way any more.

Alan had moved to Memphis, Tennessee to start his new project, the Tactical Explosive Entry School. He had also been given the opportunity to instruct in Baton Rouge, Louisiana with the U.S. State Department's Anti-Terrorism Assistance Program, which was dedicated to developing third world nations and emerging democracy's police forces. He was also working executive protection and security details for wealthy clients and, therefore, was spread thin. He not only needed help with his fledging enterprise, but required someone with the same expertise and experience to carry on with his programs as an assistant, or in his absence. He couldn't reimburse me in the conventional sense, so I came across Stateside for a 6 month vacation as one of his instructors. In addition to being well fed, I was afforded plenty of opportunities for raising hell without having to pick up the tab. However, more importantly, I was introduced to the close knit community of U.S. law enforcement personnel and American training methods.

I was extremely fortunate to be in a position to assist the local Sheriffs Department. During my initial six months stay, Alan and I conducted a training program that started the DeSoto County, Mississippi SWAT team. Alan, was a department deputy and responsible for training the team. The officers selected were good men and keen to learn. And learn they did. To date, their record is a good one and they have become a valuable asset to the department and surrounding counties. Alan meanwhile (2002) has been promoted to the giddy heights of Captain, I always knew he had this desire to be a Rupert deep down inside.

To help promote the new business, we participated as guest speakers and instructors at various police and military Special Operations venues all over the country. At one particular conference in Washington, DC, I ran into my good mate and former 22 SAS member, Mel, from the United Kingdom and his newly acquired friend, Gene Zink, who was a recognized trainer in the United States. After the usual dog and pony show we went to a local bar and began a serious drinking session. We had a number of other stalwarts with us, but most of them fell by the wayside pretty early in the evening. I remember Frank Mrozek, from Sentry Solutions, and Nancy, from Heckler and Koch, and even Dick Kramer gave it a try, but I guess that the savage drinking pace was a little tough for those that hadn't trained for it. However, we all considered that national pride was at stake, so no quarter was given and no prisoners were taken. We were finally asked to leave the Irish Bar we were frequenting. We started singing so loudly that the Irish band in the pub quit and joined us for a few ales and understandably the management got concerned. So, on we staggered to the next port of call and our bar hopping continued until the early hours of the morning. Through the fog of smoke and booze that surrounded us, I could tell that the current bar owner, staff, and decor were definitely Arabic. Mel was having flashbacks to the old Oman (Operation Storm) days and he was sitting cross legged and shoeless on the floor, rabbiting on to the elderly owner in what I can only presume was Arabic. My shattered brain was in full retreat and I knew I was about done when I could barely make out the sultry looking, big breasted bar maid. Poor old Gene was sitting their in a totally stunned condition, as we say back home "the lights are on but nobody behind the wheel." It was a great evening and the start of my close association with the American training establishment.

As the law enforcement groups and individuals came through T.E.E.S., more friendships and contacts were made, and many have withstood the ravages of time and distance. One particular course had a significant impact on me. Two senior SWAT team officers from Louisiana approached me and discussed a series of unfortunate incidents that had befallen their team. In the last six months, they had lost two officers during SWAT callouts. Death has a profound effect on those close to it and on small, close-knit, high-risk teams, such as SWAT, it can destroy unity and focus. The two officers were still mourning their loses and they needed to talk about it with a person removed from the incident, but one who could understand the gravity of the situation. Beer is the universally recognised lubricant for loss, and at our first opportunity we held a good old-fashioned wake for their buddies in a downtown watering hole in Memphis. It's a fact of life in the military, law enforcement, and other danger courting careers that death is a constant companion.

At the conclusion of the training, they asked me if I would like to come down to Louisiana and check out their team. I was keen and so it happened. They flew me down and I stayed for a week or so with Mike, the team leader and his family. I trained during the day with the SWAT team, and at night they exposed me to their operations. On the first morning, I met the team at their operational headquarters. They looked like most of the teams that had attended T.E.E.S.'s training, but were unique in their personnel. They had funny talking Cajuns, skinny white dudes, a damn cowboy, and one guy who must have been seven foot tall. Good old "Stretch" made for a formidable figure when decked out in full battle dress. They were a professional group of individuals and well versed in police matters. Another thing they all had in common, they loved their job.

As we drove to the Shreveport Louisiana Police Training Academy, Mike filled me in on the training programs he had been running with his guys, their strengths and weaknesses and areas of training that they would benefit from. He had stressed that while at our school several weeks earlier, that it was the first time that they had been involved in training while wearing gas masks. The Heckler Koch MP5 sub-machine gun is an excellent close quarters battle weapon, but its sling configuration presents a potential problem when used with gas masks. The sling must be adjusted to the correct length and tension. If it is too tight, the sling can ride up during the gun mount and compromise the mask's seal, resulting in a gut full of disabling gas. This, and the fact that it is difficult to establish a good sight picture while wearing a mask, is the main reason the British SAS employed a loose sling in the past and punched out with the SMG when engaging close targets. With all that in mind, I started out with chemical agent training.

Very few look forward to gas training. It's a mongrel atmosphere to work in and creates visual problems that are almost as much of a tactical handicap as a leaking gas mask. Masks are hot and uncomfortable, fog up, and create claustrophobic conditions for many who are not used to them. Until the mask is on and the white stuff floats through the room, no one is overly confident in the operational status of his filters. Nevertheless, on went the rubber rascals and we all stomped into an abandoned, three bedroom house and resignedly stood around in a circle. "Pop" went the gas grenades and everybody held their breath and hoped that their mask was working. I forced the men to talk by asking them questions, and after a few cautious breaths, confidence returned, and everyone was sucking in healthy volumes of air. I thought we were batting 1000, but our average was marred by a muffled curse and the frantic scuffling of a team member as he made a break for the exit. Life's a bitch when your mask leaks. I gazed around and the smug looks coming through the eye-pieces said it all. "Fuck you," you Kiwi bastard. We walked outside and moved up wind from the large, billowing gas cloud that was escaping the confines of the house. Three gas grenades had been initiated, so there was a lot of particulate lingering in the area.

At the same time we were at the Academy, a basic police recruit class was in session. It just so happened that down wind from us, a large squad of recruits were engaged in callisthenics. The instructor was barking out commands and cadence. The gas cloud continued to move sedately toward this group and there was nothing we could do but watch. We were quite impressed by the students who never uttered a word in protest, but just kept on doing their sit ups. Suddenly everything turned to shit, and without even dismissing his troops, the instructor bolted from the scene, snot and tears exiting his facial orifices. The students were not quite so savvy and had to take a couple of deep hits to figure out what was going on, and then pandemonium followed. What a sight and what a baptism of reality for these lunch-heaving, red-eyed, snotty-nosed recruits. Ten minutes later we were suffering just as badly, as an indication of the down side of gas training it is advisable for the operators to experience the adverse effects at least once. Under my control we all walked back in to the gas zone inside the house with masks on. On the command "masks off," I had popped a canister then charged outside as quickly as possible. It was a mad damn scramble and every man for himself, coughing and dry retching all the way. I can guarantee one thing, the boys on the team may have forgotten everything else we talked and trained with but all who were there will still cringe thinking of the dreaded gas induced nausea and heaves. Welcome to police work, warts and all.

Later in the afternoon, we received our brief for the evening's operation. I was impressed with the orders format, which is often foolishly neglected. I should not have been surprised, Mike had been a Marine and seen service in Vietnam before joining the sheriff's department. With no further questions, the team was stood down and rested up for the night shift.

Our target was literally a drive up drug service operated by a gang of youths. They were working out of a house and selling crack cocaine at the roadside. I was detailed to work with Mark the Cowboy and one other deputy. We were dropped off by vehicle a block away from our observation point. Using available cover and concealment, we stalked, crawled, and slithered through back yards and hedgerows to get to our OP. We were lying under a small hedge approximately 50 meters from our target. After a listening pause, we set up our night surveillance equipment and began reporting. We were well camouflaged, but were extremely close to the sidewalk and road, and both were fairly busy. I was not comfortable, but Mark was in the lead and his confidence was extremely reassuring. For the next couple of hours, we relayed by radio vehicle descriptions, registrations, and number of persons doing business with the gang. This information was provided to our cut off groups and arrest teams concealed several blocks away in marked and unmarked police vehicles. It was a good system and worked well.

Near the end of the operation, a decision was made to force entry, bust the sellers, and search the house and property. This was my signal to move back to the forming up point and rendezvous with the arrest team. Subsequently, we were inserted by fast moving vehicles and as they converged on the target we bailed out. There were people running in all directions. I ended up two blocks away covering a six-foot wall that my suspect had scaled and escaped. I returned to the crack house and assisted in carrying out the arrest procedures. Mark and his boys almost split their sides laughing while watching me try to get a young hood to put his damn hands on his head while he was lying on the ground. It wasn't working at all and I was getting pretty worked up, "Get your fucken hands on your fucken head, ya fuck," I demanded. For some reason the punk wasn't responding and I was about to "nudge" him with my boot when Mark sauntered over. "Interlace your fingers and assume the position," he commanded in a stern, but not overly loud voice. The dude's response was instantaneous. Later, the subject asked the arrest team, "What was that cop saying man? Is he from Naw Lins (New Orleans)? I couldn't understand a thing he said?" Obviously there was a clash of cultures and a Kiwi accent in the South can be a handicap.

For the next couple of nights we carried out mobile buy-bust, jump out arrests around Shreveport. A plainclothes officer in a van would drive around high crime areas buying crack from the numerous street sellers. However, this was a Trojan horse set up, because a team of SWAT personnel were hidden and geared up in the back waiting for the word to make the arrest. The driver would cruise the area and patronize the drug dealers. Once a deal was completed, he would utter a key phrase and we, the snatch team would rocket outside and in the best rugby tradition, crash tackle the bad guys, one high and one low. Once they were cuffed and searched they would then be transferred to a processing team. It was a simple, but extremely effective method. It was so successful, that we continued locking people up until the early hours of the morning. Drug dealers have big balls or just don't care because at times, we operated only a block or two away from the central police station.

Off duty one night, we spent it in the cowboy bars of Shreveport. "Work hard, play hard" was my motto and Shreveport's "Jump Out Boys" enthusiastically shared it. Deservedly, they had earned a big rep, and to a degree, there were even reluctant kudos from the teenage drug dealers and gang bangers after being busted by Mike's team. Mike and his boys where definitely a cohesive unit and made me feel welcome. I returned to their department in 1997 and again, worked with them in Memphis in 1999. There were a lot of new faces the last time, but the team still had retained a good number of the older hands, including Mark, Jimmie Ogden, Mark Holley, and Stretch.

Hey! You Shreveport bad assess out there — "Stay off dem streets, else dem Jump Out Boyz will get you for sure."

Allan's service on his county SWAT team also led to my periodic involvement with them. As the years have progressed I am impressed with the level of expertise and planning that team members put into their call outs. They are a far cry from the bunch of good old boy originals and have become a highly prized county asset. They may not all possess the physical attributes of the fulltime, train incessantly, metropolitan teams, or have acquired the high dollar gear and equipment of units like the Los Angeles Police Department. But one thing is for sure, they can and often "do the deed" when called upon.

One callout that I participated in involved a disturbed Vietnam veteran. Reportedly, he was a former Army Ranger and everything else that can make life difficult for the police. Old "Ranger Danger" after starting to knock back the beer he had stocked up for Christmas, had fired several shots around his property and given his suffering wife sufficient cause to flee their home. The barricaded suspect's residence was in a wooded area, and by the time we got there, it was blacker than Chris Raikuna's butt. However, he suddenly turned on his external building lights, making it difficult to approach without detection. The negotiating team were doing their best, but were experiencing considerable difficulty in getting any response.

All options appeared to be exhausted and the Sheriff finally committed the team. Big Randy Doss was its team leader and Alan assisted him in the planning. During daylight hours, a helicopter had been used to acquire aerial photos of the house and surrounding acreage. Family members had provided a detailed description of the internal layout of the modest, two story home.

From the holding area, we kitted up and moved to our forming up point. While the negotiators continued to try and at least distract the suspect, Alan led our element across the horse paddock and halted a short distance from the house. We had to scale the horse fence and form up at the wall nearest to our final assault position, which was a large wood door. It was decided to make an explosive breach and I had the folding linear charge that, hopefully, would negate any problems with door locks and a suspected barricade augmenting the door's security. I looked at Alan and I mentally prepared for my next move. I repeated to myself for at least the hundredth time the charge placement drill and firing sequence for the device. Suddenly the door flew open and out staggered our combat veteran, drunker than he had any right to be. We tensed for the worst and I strained to see if he was carrying a firearm. Momentarily, I thought this was going to be a suicide by cop, but before he could advance much further, team members coming in from his flank wrestled him to the ground. Randy had gotten on the throw phone and made a last ditch man-to-man appeal to him and he quit before the command post could alert us. We started breathing again, made a tactical entry, and searched the house. He had a number of firearms scattered around the house and he could have made it very difficult for us had he chosen that way out of his misery.

Several years later, I had the pleasure and great relief to inform Sheriff James A. Riley that the DeSoto County Reserve Deputies identification card he honoured me with had saved my sorry hide in West Africa while I was the reluctant guest of Guinea's Gendarmerie. On hearing that, he replied in his deep Southern drawl, "Hell son, that's amazing, that little piece of paper wouldn't even stop you from getting a traffic ticket in downtown Memphis."

I make it a point to visit Alan's school as often as I can. Besides a long and enduring friendship, it is my only real chance to catch up with new variations in weapon systems, law enforcement tactics, and to rekindle the numerous and wonderful contacts cultivated over the years. Southern hospitality is not a myth and people like Harry and Julie Sergeant, Bobby Reed and Melissa, and of course, good old Sar' Major Bill Duke, make it a reality.

God Bless America!

Plumes and Arrows

Duke's Story

Security Contract in Papua New Guinea

In 1995, I received a call from Sledge, a former NZSAS mate who was working in Papua New Guinea. He was second in command of a security organisation based at an extremely remote mine site in the Western Highlands. The contract was for a period of ten weeks and the company was trying to augment its security force as quickly as possible. These measures were required because of an ever-increasing problem with a local criminal element called the "Raskols."

Tensions had mounted dramatically, and prior to my arrival the main accommodation camp at Suyen had been attacked and over run by local tribesmen that were incensed over the shooting of one of their clansmen by a police officer. When faced with an overwhelming and blood-thirsty force, the officer and his mobile contingent retreated and took refuge in the mine's accommodation camp. When the situation escalated, they did a runner, but their temporary presence was enough of a reason for the tribesmen to take the camp out. No foreigners or indigenous employees were killed, but a number of women were raped and terrorised. In addition, one expatriate was taken hostage for several hours. However, the tribesmen had their hands full with this particular hostage, who was an extremely eccentric Irish computer technician. They quickly released him because his odd behaviour was even too much for them. Like the American Indian and other indigenous races, they historically consider the "mentally challenged" to be possessed by demons and will not contemplate harming such a person.

After a one-hour flight from Australia, I literally stepped back in time. My Grandfather's sister and her husband, Reo Fortune, who was previously married to Margaret Mead, were among the first anthropologists to visit PNG (pre-WWII) to study the native population. My initial impression was that the terrain and situation had not changed much since they were trekking around this wild country.

After the pleasant flight from Cairns, Australia, we arrived in the wild and woolly Mount Hagen Airport. Damn, what a place. After passing through customs I walked a couple of hundred metres to the Heavylift Helicopter Terminal, carefully dodging the remnants of ochre stained buai spit that almost totally covered the walk way. Locals here chew a mixture of betel nut and lime (buai) and this gives them the pickup and buzz required to get through the work-day. It has a mild narcotic effect, but similar to Vietnamese bettlenut, it stains the teeth and colors one's spittle a bright red and is expectorated without much thought everywhere.

With the new shift change of mine workers I tossed my gear on board the company helicopter, which was totally Russian including its crewmembers. You can imagine the impression this caused on new guys like myself. Here we were on the PNG version of Aeroflot, going into the infamous "Crash Alley" where no one, to date, had survived a plane crash. In their version of "coffee, tea, or me," the former Kremlin crew was all smiles and responded with hand signals, but couldn't speak a word of English. Matters were further exacerbated because all safety messages and placards on the aircraft were in bloody Russian. A local PNG lad acted as flight attendant, but his English on a par with my Russian, which is zilch. If we had an emergency, it was going to be every man for himself and I mentally prepared myself accordingly for the 40-minute flight.

My companions consisted of a bizarre assortment of individuals. Crocodile Dundee would have looked like a rank amateur next to the grizzled Aussie veterans of the underground mining fraternity. Mix in a couple of New Zealanders with a few of their Maori brethren sporting Mohawk haircuts, Ray Ban sun glasses, and multiple earrings, throw in the odd Grizzly Adams American, and finally, some local PNG employees, and it added up to a rather eclectic group of nomads. The PNG boys wore a colorful mix of second-hand clothing and down to and including indigenous "arse grass." This simple garment, consisting of a traditional loin cloth with a hand full of grass covering their rear end only. This could be topped off with sunglasses covered with stickers from Sunkist oranges and bubble gum transfers. Anything that shined or glittered, or appealed to the eye of the beholder, was deemed to be a fashion statement and worn with great pride. The men will don anything that could be a potential winner in the mating ritual, and in so doing, imitate the Highland's beautiful Birds of Paradise that strut their stuff to attract the female of their species. They truly ascribe to the philosophy that clothes do indeed make the man, and PNG is one of the biggest importers of second-hand clothing in the world. One of our dog handlers wore a tartan dressing gown to ward off the chill while on night watch. Another down-town warrior had a slinky, shimmering, sheath dress for that special occasion.

Huge, mountainous outcrops swathed in thick clouds surrounded us.

As noted previously, loses of light aircraft frequently occur in the Highlands and the rugged terrain yields few survivors. Shuddering violently, the veteran Russian military transport touched down at our landing zone. Several armed members of the company security detail greeted us. Dog handlers stood by with their wicked assortment of ferocious canines, while all bags and personnel were checked for alcohol and pornographic literature. Bringing in anything like Playboy magazine was a definite no-go in PNG, even though the local hill country maidens often suckled young piglets while breast-feeding toddlers without meriting a single glance. Possessing a photograph of an unclad pin-up girl would be enough to cause a small riot among our hill country lads. Bringing in alcohol resulted in automatic dismissal, and the offender, without a scintilla of appeal, went straight back onto the aircraft he had just arrived on.

I looked around and inhaled the surrounding view and it was totally impressive. The camp was nestled among several, craggy mountain peaks that compartmentalized the valley. The vegetation, trees and intermingled grasslands were a thick, lush, dark green, which was ribboned by a rushing river of brown, foamy water. The river and immediate area's tranquility was further augmented by natives who were washing and swimming in its waters. Cooking and drinking water was also drawn from this vital resource.

My attention was drawn to the huge, open mine face, which was dotted with large vehicles scurrying back and forth, and the mining plant itself. However, like an ant-hill, much of the mining was carried on underground. Other helicopters slashed through the sky and were engaged in hauling large, external loads. The entire operation was a veritable beehive of activity. It was also ideal guerrilla warfare country.

When I finished moving my gear and freshening up in my assigned quarters, I was introduced to the new security personnel. Charlie, a Maori and former NZSAS mate, along with a contingent of Australian police officers on leave, comprised the security force. After one day of indoctrination on the mining process, I became operational. However, the anticipated problems between the landowners and the local agitators never materialized and after ten weeks of relative peace and harmony, I returned home.

Several months later, I was recalled and became a full time member of the mine's security department. By this time, the company and government came up with a novel way to combat the growing criminal activities in the area. In addition to the expanded mine security force, they formed a 50-man mobile force. The native community had grown considerably since the mine started, and people from outside the district were migrating to the area to find work, or otherwise reap benefits from the newly created wealth the mine was generating. The augmented main security force consisted of

Australians, Brits, and New Zealanders, many of who were former Aussie and Kiwi SAS, or policemen. Kiwis Colin and Ben were good mates of mine, and we had been together in the same squadron for several years. "Whee" had been our regimental sergeant major, and Paul had also served in the unit. It was a coincidental reunion of sorts.

Duke [on right] and Charlie in an underground Porgera mine site – Western Highlands, PNG

The foreigners were employed as shift team leaders, made up the gold shipment teams, and were responsible for conducting all mine site investigations. The mobile force officers were mainly PNG nationals with a considerable appreciation for the policing services required for the mine and Western Highlands area. The two security forces enjoyed a good balance between new and veteran personnel and were held to reasonably high standards. In addition, men with PNG military or police experience filled the ranks of the mine's main indigenous security.

The mine paid for the government's Royal Constabulary to conduct a training course and its successful completion authorized selected security force members to act as sworn members of the PNG Police Reserve. With sixty men, broken down into three 20-man shifts, this enabled us to provide a mobile response for the mine site, the nearby settlements, and more importantly, the main highway, which was our primary lifeline through the Western Highlands. The highway was plagued by violent criminal acts of every description. Unguarded re-supply convoys experienced thefts, hijackings, and armed robberies. Innocent civilians travelling around the province in small, twelve-seat vans were held up, raped, and murdered on a weekly basis. Local Raskol gangs were the perpetrators of most of the road's mayhem and the provincial police seemed incapable of stopping it.

Our duty schedule required that two foreigners were assigned to each twelve-hour shift. This, at times, made night shifts a lonely and somewhat difficult duty. However, in order to maximize the impact of our indigenous security force on the local bandits, training became a top priority.

Bruce Grey, our security boss, had visited Alan in Memphis and was suitably impressed with the training and equipment that he saw at T.E.E.S. Upon his return, a comprehensive package for the Mobile Team was advanced and approved. The company provided excellent weapons and four-wheel drive patrol vehicles, gas masks, body-armor, ballistic helmets, and numerous other items of security equipment. For three months we drilled with FN Browning 9mm pistols, Sig Sauer rifles, shotguns, and less-lethal, civil disturbance systems. My function was to develop and administer firearms and tactical training programs appropriate to our extremely difficult area of operations.

Because of my association with American police SWAT and T.E.E.S., I was able to create such a course, and at the conclusion of my version of the ninety-day wonder program, all hands, foreigners included, exhibited vastly improved weapons and tactical capabilities.

PNG has an ancient Biblical, eye-for-eye type tribal justice system that is still very much in force. If an individual or group commits a crime, such as murder against a person or persons from some other clan, immediate and violent retribution generally follows. However, payback does not have to involve the person who actually committed the crime. Any member of the opposing clan will do. As a result, one never knew when the bushman's Sword of Damocles would fall on them, and therefore, any travel around the Province was at times extremely risky. Inter-tribal wars were common and many feuds continued off and on for years. In one such instance, I was sleeping off my night shift when I was jerked out of bed by a highly agitated local security guard and told to get to the main gate as quick as I could. Half dressed, I grabbed my radio and shotgun and raced to that location, where I came upon a scene straight out of a Hollywood movie. Women, with all their belongings were rushing around helter-skelter. Howling children were hanging onto their mother's legs and their stunted dogs were baying like castrated banshees. It was always a bad sign when the women packed up with the kids and scarpered. Most of the security force's day and night shifts rallied and the superintendent briefed us on the situation.

A young man from a distant clan had just completed his university education in Port Moresby and arrived at the mine site for a job interview. As soon as he had disembarked from the four-wheel drive vehicle, all hell broke loose. Several local tribesmen immediately identified him as being a member of an offending clan with whom they had a perpetual feud. Completely surprised by the attack, he had no chance. He tried to run, but was hacked, slashed, and chopped down with a myriad of long handled tomahawks and razor sharp bush knives wielded by a half-dozen or more assailants. His body lay on top of the burned out vehicle and it stayed there for 24 hours, while various acts of gratuitous violence raged around his remains. No one dared take responsibility for his mutilated body. Because his murder had occurred on the narrow road between the mine site and the Suyen village, there was going to be even more serious problems for our shift workers in their bus convoys if this fracas continued.

Alleviating or aggravating the situation, depending on how you looked at it, the local police mobile squad roared up decked out in their paramilitary uniforms and armed with M-16's, shotguns, gas guns, and bandoleers of ammo. On top of this array of modern weaponry, their features were highlighted with ancient tribal war paint and crowned with headresses made of surrounding foliage. Truthfully, they looked damned intimidating.

As soon as we got to the body, a "platoon" of equally fierce looking and chanting warriors from the murdered man's clan trotted up. They had run a considerable distance on foot and were primed for blood. Six foot long shields made of roofing iron, bows and arrows, long handled tomahawks, and home-made shotguns were in abundance. The warriors were colourfully adorned with mud in ochre colors. Twigs, leaves, feathers, and other natural forms of garnishment made up their formidable headdresses. This was part of the pre-combat posturing and designed to make a warrior look taller, bigger, more aggressive, and, hopefully, more intimidating. All Western Highland combatants convey threats through posturing, preening, and colourful and aggressive displays, reminiscent of the Mountain Gorilla. When confronted by an enemy, the male gorillas make a great deal of noise accompanied by a lot of bluster, chest pounding, and general destruction of the surrounding foliage in an effort to intimidate so that actual combat can be avoided. "Uniforms" were as varied as the weapon systems carried and ranged from traditional ass grass to jeans. The grand prize for "best dressed warrior" had to go to the fighter who wore a full 14mm-thick diver's wetsuit. After the lengthy and broiling run to the battlefield, I could understand why he might be extremely hostile.

Undeterred by the armed presence of the police, they immediately started burning the grass huts and destroying the tin sheds belonging to the opposition. There was no resistance because the villagers and offending warriors had prudently vacated the area. The age-old tactic of scorched earth was in effect, and everything, including livestock, gardens, and livery were razed. The slaughter of the clan's pigs was a particularly grievous loss since they are considered a unit of wealth. The average sized adult animal is worth approximately PNG$1000. Since it was our job to monitor the attack and ensure the safety of mine personnel, we did not get directly involved. However, the blazing fires began to spread toward an abandoned civilian diesel and petroleum storage area and the intense heat was beginning to destroy power lines. At this juncture, we intervened and were able to coordinate fire-fighting efforts without stepping on the toes of the vengeance seeking warriors.

Homemade weapons that were confiscated during a raid on squatter settlements by police and mobile mine teams.

A large snapping and crackling power line had fallen across the road and it appeared that some fools were tempted to touch it. With much leaping and chanting, the clansmen had worked themselves up for their next phase of attack and were coming perilously close to the hot wire. Oblivious to it, they seemed to be in a collective trance-like state. PNG had some peculiar customs and in this situation, the company would be held responsible for any injuries incurred from the snaking line since the mining concern had erected it. Any deaths would result in large compensations, or could precipitate even more violence.

However, every tense situation has its element of humour and this one proved to be no different. Bruce Grey and I stood on one side of the flicking cable, holding our weapons in a non-threatening manner. Although we were ready, two men against sixty or more hyped-up "Bone Suckers" were

PNG natives wearing everyday dress, complete with nose flutes.

poor odds, so dialogue was the only way to go. On the other side of the very lethal line, ranks of rioting tribesmen were closing in. Confronted by this pyrotechnic mayhem and general chaos, Bruce, speaking in Australian accented English, yelled, "Hey guys! Watch out for this cable, it's still alive!" With his "Number 7" (Highlands tomahawk) in hand, the crew's leader turned around and calmly replied in even better English, "No problem." He and his men paused momentarily and then, quite nonchalantly stepped over the wire. Once everyone negotiated the wire and were accounted for, they ignored us and carried on with their marauding.

For the rest of the afternoon, company fire fighters attempted to suppress the fires, concentrating on involved huts and buildings that threatened the power line. Of course, these efforts were made under the armed protection from our mine security personnel and Mobile Police Patrol. After the smoke had cleared, it took several months for the evicted clansmen to return to their devastated village. On top of their losses and diminished respect, they were required to pay compensation through the intricate tribal justice system.

In contrast to this episode, traditional warfare in the Highlands was not always as violent. In years past, once blood was drawn on either side, the fighting would cease and payback negotiations would begin. Today, home made shotguns and the odd factory weapon were changing the whole retribution equation.

The Western Highlanders, both criminal and cop, embraced this time-worn philosophy. This reaction to violence, real or imagined, was one of the more difficult practices to negate with our standard operational procedures (SOP). The Mobile Team was totally convinced that in any ambush or shots fired situation, their justified and instant reaction was to fire off a volley of their own. They argued long and hard with us that it was the "warriors way" in the Highlands, or the opposition would not take the Mobile Force seriously. I am a believer in" if it works, why fix it," but in those days I was still trying to prove a point. My advice to those of you contemplating working with the contemporary indigenous warrior is to be extremely flexible when it comes to structuring rules of engagement. The loss of respect by your opponents because of the imposition of Western, "civilized" standards for armed conflict is inestimable and in many cases, doomed to failure.

Training continued and I made it more realistic by introducing the men to steel reactive targets. Now they were able to derive instant feedback and they loved banging away at targets that rewarded their efforts with audible hits and reactive movement. The police teams were thrilled with their increased levels of competence, which for many, including military vets from the Bougainville and Solomon Island conflicts, was superior to any training they had experienced previously.

The Provincial Chief of Police quickly recognized their newly acquired capabilities and began to use our Mobile Force members, including our foreign supervisors, to assist his officers in serving high-risk warrants. Having signed and sworn the oath of allegiance, they could not refuse because they were now members of the Royal PNG Constabulary. This created a problem, because the Mobile Team and selected foreign officers had attended the police-training module simply to appease the PNG government and legalize the security process. It was not a healthy situation and several of the guys quickly handed in their police badges. I had opted out of attending the police course for similar reasons.

Our camp was many hours away by road from civilization and the capital city of Port Moresby. The British High Commissioner had compared Port Moresby with Beirut, as far as general crime and law and order were concerned. Perhaps civilization was the wrong word? In one particular incident, we had a vehicle that had to be returned to Port Moresby, which was a long and arduous drive through "Indian Country," at the best of times. Desiring a little rest and relaxation, our gallant lads from Mobile Force's Bravo One Section nevertheless eagerly volunteered for the mission. Bright eyed and bushy tailed, they jumped into their leave clothing and took off. After several hours of bone jarring travel, Roy Arkis, the driver, noticed that all his mates were asleep in the van. Feeling a bit soporific himself, he rounded a bend and ran smack into a Raskol's roadblock. Surrounded by the gang, they were stripped, not only of their valuables, but clothing as well. Pleading for their garments, they were forced to drive on to Mount Hagen naked as jay-birds. Although it sounds funny, and they were teased for months after the incident, had they been identified as policemen they would, without hesitation, have lost more than their dignity.

Duke with Roy (No Pants) Arkis in the Sag Mill area, the scene of a recent Raskol gang shooting.

My shift partner, Phil S., was a small Londoner and former member of 22 SAS. He was an old hand at this and had worked in PNG for several years. What he lacked in size he more than made up for in heart. During the early hours of one morning, Phil and I were checking the mine site perimeter, when we observed that a gate leading into the mill area was opened. We were concerned because during the previous evening we had spotted a group of twenty or more armed clansmen that appeared to be sussing out that area, only 100 meters from the perimeter fence. We eventually dispersed them with gas and a show of force. We reported the open gate, and as per instructions, continued our patrol. However, those responsible never secured the gate. Several hours later, while having a brew of tea in the control room, two very excited young women arrived at the gold room perimeter gate. They had been working in the mine samples room when an injured local guard staggered into their office with axe wounds to his head and shoulders. He had been attacked by a group of tribesman who had gained access to the area through the unlocked gate. With him out of the way, they stole whatever they could grab and disappeared into the night. Those two girls had been damn lucky; rape is a team sport amongst the Highland Raskols and all part of the macho code. Although security was in effect twenty- four-seven, the site was simply too large to maintain complete and simultaneous control over.

On another occasion, Phil was acting as team leader on a dawn raid against a criminal element that had been organized by the Provincial police. While he and his Mobile team members were moving into position they were compromised and came under intense fire. At the end of the gun battle, Phil's lead scout was sporting a new haircut and rearranged facial features, courtesy of a buck shot round fired by one of the Raskols.

The mine site was a huge, sprawling area and the outer perimeter was virtually uncontrollable. Numerous compounds of various sizes were scattered throughout the work face and it was these fenced-off areas that we were responsible for. One such compound was Sag Mill. A foreign officer teamed with an indigenous security member was left there overnight. The Sag Mill had been targeted several times and armed intruders frequently skulked around in the shadows outside the razor wire topped, ten-foot high fence. Finally, on one black night they made their move.

A sextet of armed Raskols forced their way into the mill area. The security team confronted them and commenced to do battle. Results: one Raskol killed, courtesy of a solid slug from a shotgun, his leader captured, and one officer receiving minor shotgun pellet wounds. The arrested leader was jailed in the local slammer, but somehow managed to "escape" on the same day. However, his status among his tribe was precarious, because he had lost a man and was responsible to his survivors for compensation. His reputation as a leader was in question and, somehow, he had to make good. However, the way he chose to do this was through further aggressive actions against the mine. Rumours and death threats abounded. A week later, again during the night shift, one of our dog handlers surprised a couple of Raskols tampering with one of the company's helicopters. They immediately took off and it was discovered that they had poured gasoline into the aircraft and placed dry grass on top of the accelerant. Our helicopters were critical to our operation and this sabotage attempt was extremely serious because of its life threatening potential.

One of the mine site construction companies employed a significant number of Kiwis. Aussies and Kiwi's don't ask for much, but the boys were definitely unhappy over the dry camp rules concerning booze. They spent considerable time and effort engaged in smuggling operations and home brew set-ups. At great risk, they did their damnedest to by pass prohibition and get the dreaded alcohol on site. I had several good friends in this crew including good old Charley, who had worked the initial security contract with me. Instead of coming back as a fulltime security member he had opted for the construction scene because there were definitely more perks to be found in this work.

When the construction companies contract was completed, the whole crew departed the site via bus and began the torturous mountain road journey to the international airport at Port Moresby. Several hours later they arrived at Yumi Bridge, quite knackered and in no mood for the roadblock that a local clan had erected. However, this one was different. This Raskols had managed to dig up an unexploded WWII bomb and place it under the bridge. Demanding exorbitant tolls and engaging in other forms of extortion, they halted all traffic. What made the situation so dangerous was that the silly buggers had no idea how to handle the ordinance safely. At this rate, it was obvious to the construction boys that they were not going to get through to the Airport and catch their flight to Australia.

Charley took the initiative, and after having a long talk with the clan's leaders, he somehow managed to get the bus through. Some hours later, a huge "kaaruump" from the direction of the bridge indicated the bomb had erupted and demolished the bridge. Now the main highway was completely stuffed and no traffic could get through. The responding police units were severely mauled and their vehicles over-turned and burned. Chaos and mayhem, Highland Warrior style, was the order of the day for some time later and once again the road link between the capital and the Western Highlands was totally blocked until law and order restored.

Several months later, while having a beer with some friends in Australia, I overheard a discussion about a Kiwi who had bribed his way through a blockade of Raskols by showing them how to detonate a piece of dud ordinance. Apparently, they built a fire around the bomb and literally "cooked" it off.

The latest rumour reports that Charlie is currently sporting a foot long ponytail and earrings and is in charge of a mining security team in Tanzania, Africa. Hopefully, they keep him away from the demolition shed, the mealie-mealie beer, and any guitar parties.

Illegal miners also created problems for the mine, especially in the areas where ore was stockpiled. These sites involved huge deposits of quarried ore waiting to go through the crushers. As time progressed, the squatters became more organized and aggressive. They were able to monitor our radio net with stolen hand held Motorola's and keep track of our security forces. They had also started firing back with their homemade shotguns and bows and arrows when confronted, which proved to be a one sided battle. If a gun battle erupted, we would race to the scene, and with our police team, or static security force, dominate the high ground and lob gas projectiles into their ranks. Normally, that was enough to send them high-tailing it for the jungle, and work would again commence.

Large amounts of explosives were used both for the open pit and underground mining operations. The storage and preparation was on site, but completely handled by an outside contractor, who had a competent and safe track record. However, the site was almost completely flattened when several tons of it went high order during the preparation process. Ten employees were instantly vaporized and their remains never located.

Things were never easy in the Western Highlands, and logistical convoys to and from Port Moresby had to be armed and escorted where possible by police. The mine was saved considerable time and expense when W.W., sporting a shaved head and scraggly and bushy beard, took over convoy security. He could have easily passed as one of the bad guys. He would fly down to the capital, link up with the convoy commander, and then accompany the convoy, while coordinating the move with security control in Porgera. At a given point, the security mobiles (reserve police) would travel from our base, marry up with the convoy, and protect it while it passed through the trouble spots. W.W. was not the least fazed by the challenges the dangerous journey may have presented. He had "seen the elephant" numerous times while serving in the NZSAS in Borneo and South Vietnam, and after reaching the distinguished rank of regimental sergeant major, considered these excursions to be nothing more than interesting drives in the country.

After a decade in PNG, Whee is back in New Zealand and has settled down on the East Coast. Still as brusque and grumpy as ever, but underneath that harsh exterior is a real generous soul. As SNCO's in the unit, Alan, Charlie, Phil, Mattie Boy, Horse, Tex, Spence, Black Sam, and I were frequently taken hostage by Whee in the Sergeant's Mess. When he said "Senior non-commissioned officers report to the mess at 1600 hours," you had better fucken be there and forget about going home before daylight. When Whee called a parade in the bar, money was never a problem. That old bugger could drink with the best of them and all he ever had in his wallet were crisp, new $50 notes.

Late one afternoon, Security Headquarters was advised that the local police chief had created an incident and a crowd of uncooperative villagers had gathered on the highway some 10 miles from our camp. They had been demonstrating over some minor issue and had refused to disperse when the police detachment turned up. Deciding that discretion was in order, the regular force police detachment pulled back to a safe distance, and then for some intangible reason, they decided to fire a couple of warning shots. This backfired and it incited the villagers. Per SOP, the police then fled the scene. This was one of their immediate action drills, and in this instance, turned out to be a wise move. As a result of this careless action, one of the protesting warriors lay in the middle of the road with an M-16 round through his gut. Since the convoy was scheduled to pass through this area the next day, we had to attempt to mollify the situation. The next morning, Bruce Grey and I moved by helicopter to the problem area. At this stage, no mine personnel or interests had been involved in any way with this current drama and it remained a PNG problem. We landed well away from the demonstrators, and Bruce, along with a community relation's worker, convinced the villagers that we needed to get the wounded man to the hospital.

I checked his vital signs out and was pessimistic regarding his chances of surviving the move to the chopper, let alone the mission hospital. The poor bastard was covered with blood and barely breathing. The bullet had ploughed into him, but had not exited. Things did not look good for this poor bugger. Nonetheless, the semi-conscious patient was carted off to the waiting aircraft and the road was reopened. At the hospital, we placed the unfortunate villager onto the operating table where he expired during surgery. The .22 high velocity round had destroyed his organs and it was a tribute to his amazing inner strength and incredible pain threshold that he had even survived the night after the shooting. Although in some considerable pain during the move, he was still able to converse back and forth with his Wantok minder during the flight. Unfortunately for us, in the villager's eyes, because the mining company had transported the wounded man to the hospital using mining assets and manpower, we had accepted some responsibility. Accordingly, a compensation claim was submitted against the mine for his death.

The mine operated under serious limitations and the security force worked to the best of its ability to achieve non-violent solutions to the numerous incidents. Having worked on numerous similar operations in West Africa and the Philippines, I can only say that when it comes to security there is no perfect answer. Several years later, Bruce Grey and I met at a conference held in Davao, Philippines. He mentioned that that the criminal statistics in Porgera have dramatically declined since my two-year hitch in the Western Highlands. However, he could not say the same for Port Moresby, and it appears that anarchy is just around the corner for this troubled country.

Tribal fights in the Highlands have ratcheted up a cog and no longer involve mere posturing. It has now escalated to ambushes and short, but sharp, fire-fights with military high power rifles. Many of these weapons became available during the Bougainville confrontation and were either purchased or stolen from the military. Others were smuggled in and exchanged for "New Guinea Gold," considered to be the primo marijuana in nearby Australia.

In the midst of all this madness, Alan gave me a call and asked me if I wanted to join him on a short contract in Switzerland. It wasn't a hard choice to make. The cold and wet nights patrolling the mine site, the weekly power games with the illegal miners, and the occasional heliborne forays over problem areas, which involved dropping gas projectiles on scavenging looters, was getting old. I was ready for a change.

Nevertheless, I made numerous friends among both foreigners and locals in PNG. To all of you, take care and thanks for the memories. As they say in PNG pidgin, "Lookem Yu Behind!"

Controlled Agression

Alan's Story

SWAT Operations in the Deep South

Sir, They Stole My House and Won't Give it Back...

Terry Dunn, our team commander turned from the chalk board and barked, "Everyone here, Randy?"

"Yes sir," was Lieutenant Randy Doss's immediate reply.

Our DeSoto County sheriff's office SWAT team had been tasked to take down a McLean County crack house. Captain Dunn initiated his commander's briefing by orienting everyone to the location and situation with his terse and down to earth style. "Y'all know that the McLean SO doesn't have a tactical team and this caper has been determined to be beyond the capabilities of their narcotics squad. The target is in a rural area, totally surrounded by woods and segregated from the local population. The house actually belongs to a family who went away on holiday, came back and found their home occupied by a gang of crack-heads. These pricks have refused to leave claiming it was their crash pad now and unless the owners fucked off, they would end up buried in the yard. The owner has provided a sketch of the internal layout and the local officers have agreed to lead us to the vehicle drop-off point. Take a good look at the internal configuration. I want a plan and brief back in 30 minutes. We are mounting up at 2300 hours."

It was relatively simple to come up with a plan because the team had assaulted and cleared a number of similar designed houses in the past. However, the selection of an approach route was critical so we could reach our primary entry point undetected. Apparently, the gremlins were brazenly dealing a considerable amount of drugs from the garage, so the traffic in and out was comparatively heavy and constant. That meant the possibility that some customers could be hanging around who could compromise us en-route. We also had to strike when all the subjects were inside, otherwise we would be required to split our small force and send an element to the garage. Realistically, we didn't have the numbers to support the latter option, but nevertheless it became one of our contingency plans.

It was around midnight when we rolled into a vacant parking lot situated in the town's center. We had to wait for the McLean County Sheriff to come down and swear us in as deputies so we could operate in his jurisdiction. While we waited, the guys kitted up and commenced to apply camouflage cream to their hands, necks, and faces. Because it was a typical Mississippi hot summer and moon-lit night, wearing our Nomex hoods on the long stalk through the bush would have been unbearable. However, conversely, with the high humidity most of the camouflage paint would sweat off and run down our backs by the time we reached the target area. But, by that time it wouldn't matter. The guys had been talking and joking about the peculiar protocol associated with the "swearing in" ceremony during the ride to the county seat.

I was out of town the first time our team was seconded to this jurisdiction, but I was about to find out what all the gallows humor was about. Our jocularity was ominously interrupted by the throaty rumble of straight exhaust pipes from a big bore V-8, as they announced the arrival of The Man in this little part of the universe. In strode a small, unarmed Black man dressed in 70's style clothing. In stark contrast, twelve of us were aggressively arrayed in dark full battle dress, complete with helmets, low-slung pistols, and 9mm MP5 submachine guns hanging loosely from their slings. Sheriff Roger Jones's uniform was circa seventies rather than being compatible with the nineties and I assumed that it was probably around that era that he had become the law in this predominately Black county. Nevertheless he was all business and without even the slightest introduction, he started reciting in a deep southern country drawl, his obviously often-repeated speech as he approached us. "Y'all form up here in one line now. Y'all raise your right hands and repeat after me. Do you and all youse swears to uphold the Constitution of the United States of America — say I do?"

With equal seriousness we chorused, "I do." Continuing without the slightest hesitation, he asked, "Do you and all youse swear to uphold the Constitution of the great state of Mississippi, in the country of the United States of America — say I do?" Collectively we announced, "I do." He concluding with, "Do you and all youse swears to uphold the laws of the County of McLean in the great state of Mississippi — say I do?" Again we replied, "I do." Satisfied that a proper "posse" was formed, Sheriff Jones's personal, but also terse, words of encouragement and motivation were simply, "Okay, go get 'em boys." Without waiting for a reply, he about-faced and departed faster than he had arrived. As the sound of his engine roared into the night, I was relieved that I was in the rear ranks, because I was cracking up and couldn't suppress my laughter. I turned my head slightly in an effort to avoid being considered unprofessional and noticed that I was not the only giggling black clad figure in our assembly area. However, the comical aspect of this seriously-intentioned ceremony broke much of the pre-operational tension and each man relaxed a bit.

We boarded the vans and reached the drop-off point about twenty minutes later. With boots on the ground, it was into the boonies for a thirty-minute stealthy stalk to the target. I was assigned point, and reverting back to my SAS jungle days, I set a bearing with my compass and slowly starting to weave my way through the thick vegetation of North Mississippi. In addition to the human threats, this part of the country was thick with snakes and other nasty, natural vermin. New Zealand, in contrast, had none of these indigenous hazards to be avoided. So, with my uniform soaked and clinging to me, and in spite of being bombarded by squadrons of mosquitoes, I moved with extreme care. Even though we were still a half-mile from the target, the old habits still stuck — slow down, pick your route, minimize noise, stop and listen. The bush was alive with insect activity so it was difficult to hear much and I knew some of the lads were getting restless back there. They weren't as patient, or as familiar, with this type of uncomfortable environment and all they wanted to do was rush in and kick ass. However, as long as I was up front, it wasn't going to go down like that. Suddenly, I heard activity to my front and saw the headlights of a vehicle. We had moved more quickly than I had estimated and we were just 50 yards short of the target. I signaled the man behind me to get down and pass it on to the rest of the team. Now came the hard part as we spent at least a half hour crawling forward an inch at a time on our bellies. As I communicated with nature, I thought that I had given this shit up when I left the Special Air Service, but no, here I was trying to imitate the "keeni-meani" undulations of a snake through the grass and hoping that I would not attract the attention of a horny male rattler. If that happened, this raid was aborted as far as I was concerned. By the time we reached the edge of the clearing, the attitudes of all hands had shifted dramatically. Now, the focus was totally on the job and every man was concentrating on his specific task. Leaving the group, Randy and I moved closer for a team leader's close target recon and we immediately observed two people sitting on the porch. Vehicles were coming and going, and, sure enough, dope transactions were being openly conducted from out of the garage. As frustrating as it was to wait, we knew it was the best option. To get anxious and rush in would do us no good. Randy reported the situation via radio to the command post that was situated approximately three fourths of a mile to our rear. Our action-oriented boss, Sheriff James A. Riley, was standing by in the CP and we knew he was becoming impatient with the wait. Fuck it, we were on the target and we knew what was tactically right for us. After a short interval of time, our patience and resistance to a premature execution was rewarded.

All the suspects had apparently disappeared inside and the "shop" appeared to have been closed down, at least for the time being. If everyone was consolidated in the house, now was time for us to make our move. Our present location was designated as our forming up position (FUP) and all team members were brought in for a final situational update. Routinely, after Randy completed his brief, everyone physically checked all of his personal equipment. I started from the top and ran through my personal check-list: helmet straps fastened, goggles down and clear, flash-bang grenades correctly stowed and secured, MP5 magazine seated and safety on, Sig Sauer P226 handgun snapped in, magazine seated and spare 15 round magazines properly stowed. Prior to departing our FUP for the primary and secondary entry points, I reminded the men about our teams' golden rule, "Stay in pairs, always have a backup, and fill the gaps as they appear so that we maintain visual continuity." However, for this operation and the degree of coverage required, the tactical luxury of having a third entry man would have to be ignored. It is too easy during the excitement of the assault, with adrenaline pumping, for operators to move too fast and aggressively, resulting in them forgetting the basics. The first two officers moved in and established a position of containment at the back of the house, covering the rear exits and ready to deploy numerous distraction devices, when we breached and entered the front, or white side of the residence. The resulting detonations were designed to create a good diversion and assist us at this critical juncture by augmenting the element of surprise. Once they reported that they were in position, the assault element stealthfully moved forward to the main door for the mechanical

Tim, David, and Alan after a successful explosive breach during SWAT mission – DeSoto County, Mississippi, 1999

breach. My heart was shifting into overdrive and my mind was ratcheting toward condition red. I was not overly concerned with death or injury, but like most men, I was concerned about performing my job and not letting my colleagues down. A successful operation relies heavily on each individual operator performing well. If this occurred, then the team would function as a cohesive unit. Frank, our breacher, received his signal and crossed the door with the battering ram. Tim, the cover man, maintained forward focus on the door as I prepared to deploy my flash-bang diversionary device. Through my ear-piece I heard Randy report to the commander in the CP, "Team one is at the Final Assault Position (FAP)." Almost immediately, Terry replied, "Roger team one — this is the Commander. I have control — standby, standby, go!"

On "go," I stepped out and around the cover man as the breacher swung his ram, generating 20,000 psi, which almost obliterated the door as it was torn from its hinges. Being a "no-knock" entry warrant, we were not required to announce our presence and wait a "reasonable" time prior to effecting entry. Our appreciation of the situation concluded that the use of an explosive breaching charge as a primary means of effecting entry was not warranted and our estimate proved to be correct. We knew that a lot of traffic was moving in and out of the door, so we did not think it would be heavily barricaded. However, as a contingency, I was carrying an explosive strip charge on my vest should the situation change and its use become warranted. Constructed of deta sheet, this small amount of calculated explosive would blast any external door lock nicely and we also had a shotgun breaching capability for other possible internal obstacles. Three OMNI Blast 100 distraction devices detonated at the rear of the house as I quickly checked the positive results of the breach and made sure the doorway was clear of people. Door open, threshold clear, pull pin, and I lobbed the grenade about three feet into the first room to clear the immediate threat area and to temporarily disorient any suspects in the room. Immediately there was a brilliant flash of light, followed by a deafening detonation and concussive slap, which was heavily augmented by the night air's thick humidity. However, all anxiety vanished upon the initiation of the assault and now it simply boiled down to business, a business that we all loved. Weapons at the low ready, safeties on, but accessed, and all senses 100-percent tuned in, we penetrated the laundry and moved through the kitchen. We were maintaining our momentum and I sensed the raid was going well. Internally, the team was communicating well and the tempo of movement was tactically sound and manageable. Careful hurry, careful hurry, I mentally repeated to myself as we hit the lounge. "Contact!" "Sheriff's Department — don't move, don't move" resulted in six terrified men and women freezing in their tracks, subconsciously wishing that they were someplace else. Only seconds had elapsed and our rapid and violent penetration had denied them of their ability to make decisions. They had no time to regroup, attempt to escape, mount a counter attack, or let alone think about flushing the drugs down the commode. Operators peeled off the stack to cover the suspects they confronted, while the rest of the team continued to clear the structure. More male and female suspects were located in bedrooms in various states of undress. As they say, timing is everything, and I guess we had rudely interrupted their foreplay and other passionate activities. The anxiously anticipated command of "Dominate" was announced as the last room was cleared. This signaled all hands to slow down and to secure and search the suspects. Although the dynamic portion of the raid in the house had ceased, we reversed direction and moved outside to search and clear our second objective, the garage. Inner perimeter personnel had been covering it to make sure that no one exited it. Ka-Wham! My diversionary device announced our immediate presence and all kinds of shit fell off the walls and shelves from its concussion. There was no doubt in my military mind that it would ruin your day if you were hiding in there. As it turned out there was someone lurking just outside the garage, but he was quickly apprehended. Even though he was sprawled out on the ground with an MP5 barrel pressed against his head, it quickly became obvious that he was not going to cooperate. Crack cocaine had scrambled his brain to the point that he could not even recall his name, but all he wanted to do was whip our butts in the most evil of ways. He was handcuffed, but that still didn't shut him up. This guy wanted us bad. He was dragged inside and deposited next to the other suspects. There were nine of them total, all Black except for two crack-head, white-trash whores. Drug addicts and crack-heads particularly disgust me, but these two whores generated a new depth of revulsion. Lying there in just their bras and panties, worn out bodies trembling with fear, tears running down their haggard cheeks, they looked like human cesspools. How anyone could get aroused enough to sleep with him or her was beyond me. The whole scene was pathetic and I almost began to feel something for them as one human toward another, but reminded myself that these people were extremely dangerous and would kill without feeling or remorse. Fuck 'em, was my mental slap in my face and I got back to business.

They got themselves into this situation and now they have to pay the price. Until "Malcolm the Mouth" was dragged in, it was so quiet a dropped pin would have attracted your attention. He was still in his badass mode and continued to threaten to kill all of us. Besides failing to comply with our verbal orders, he started agitating the other suspects, so it was time to move up a notch on the response spectrum. Suspects dictate the level of police action and this dickhead was exercising his prerogatives.

Randy gave me a nod to pull his head back. As I did this, he gave him a generous squirt of OC pepper spray. About five seconds later, we noticed a remarkable difference in Malcolm's general attitude toward us. He no longer wanted to kill us, but he was begging us to kill him. This inflammatory agent can be absolutely devastating and a true leveler in most cases. In this situation it worked as advertised.

You could tell that it was burning him up and tearing his insides out. There was snot and mucus running out of his nose, mouth, and who knows what was coming out of other orifices. His eyelids were bright red and locked shut. I think the spray actually sobered him up.

"Oh God, oh Jesus, what's happening to me, I'm burning up, oh please officer, shoot me dead, shoot me dead." We could see the other suspects stiffen up with fear. They didn't know what had happened, but they had seen their immortal leader turn from a tough guy into a blithering wimp. One of the girls pissed in her pants as her trembling increased. What a disgusting and degrading experience to see how low people could sink. Needless to say, the house was returned to its rightful owner. Due to the filthy state of the house, the owner wisely opted to have it fumigated and thoroughly cleaned prior to moving back in.

This raid was flawless because of the pre-operational rehearsals that we conducted and the fact that we adhered to the CQB principles of "Surprise, Shock Action, and Speed." A substantial amount of crack cocaine was confiscated as well as several handguns, shotguns, and a rifle. There were no shots fired and no casualties resulting from our aggressive actions, if you discount any mental trauma that some of the suspects may have suffered. However, I was particularly relieved that none of our personnel were injured and I'll take those results in a heartbeat at any time. As we withdrew and returned to our holding area, I privately hoped that we could keep it that way. Thousands of raids like this occur annually in every city and town in the United States. Drugs are a billion-dollar business covering all corners of the globe, and the production and distribution of them might be slowed by the efforts of law enforcement officers, but will never be stopped, unless demand does.

Each prospective raid is looked at individually and the appropriate amount of planning is conducted according to the gravity, danger, and complexity of the mission. To me they are all serious because you are dealing with desperate people who have adopted or inherited this way of life. They don't give a damn about the law, morals, or values. They don't care that if they are poisoning our youth; it is all about money and getting high. Crack cocaine is an extremely addictive, low-cost drug and, subsequently, is very popular in many of the poorer neighborhoods. Consequently, that is where most of our thankless business is conducted.

The Split Option

As this raid was fading from memory, Randy, our team leader, pulled up while I was conducting a class at my West Memphis facility. He informed me that there was a big operation going down tonight, once again in Sheriff Jones's county, and to be at the command post by midnight. He advised that the raid involved several different departments and drug enforcement agencies, but our team would be making the actual hit. As a reserve officer, I considered myself to be in quite a unique position

Chief Deputy Charlie Brown and Sheriff James A. Riley with their DeSoto County SWAT Team after another successful mission. Alan standing second from right, middle row; Duke is fourth from the right – DeSoto County, Mississippi, 1997

within the department. I was taken aboard by then Sheriff Riley in 1992 with the understanding that I would provide as much support to the SWAT team as I possibly could. During my first two years, in addition to SWAT duties, I worked patrol because I felt it was important to get a grasp of the whole concept of local policing. My SWAT team support manifested itself in the form of monthly training, which was either conducted at my range or at suitable locations around the county.

It also included monthly evaluations of the team, recommendations on equipment procurement, and responding to all call-outs when I was in town. There was never any problem in meeting the last requirement, because this was our opportunity to put our training and approach to tactical matters to the test, both individually and collectively.

On this operation, we would be required to conduct a coordinated assault on two houses that were about 100 yards apart. Because of exposed avenues of approach and the reported weaponry in the strongholds, we would be deploying from an armored vehicle. Although my first thoughts were focused on the type of firearms we might encounter, I was also concerned about numbers, or more to the point, our lack of sufficient personnel to cover both objectives. With only thirteen men, I didn't want to stretch our assets out too thinly on the ground. Although I am a stickler for maintaining team integrity, we were able, after some negotiating, to borrow a four-man element from one of the cities within the county. Because of the increase in size, complexity, and frequency of these raids, the lack of qualified manpower was becoming a more acute problem. For this reason, we have formed county-wide alliances and train together more frequently.

We reluctantly decided to divide the seventeen-man contingent, with Randy moving on the largest house with twelve shooters and I would be responsible for taking down the other residence with a small five-man element. Since we were going to deploy with a limited force, Randy, being the leader that he is, made sure I had some of the more experienced operators with me.

All final preparations and rehearsals were conducted in a local carpet factory. Here we also had the opportunity to debrief narcotics agents that had been working this case for several months. They had both night and day video footage of my target, but it only showed the "white side," or front of the house. Those in the know told us explicitly that the door was constructed of wood and that it opened in. In addition, they advised there were two ferocious pit bull terriers tied up near the corner of the house and their chains were long enough to allow them access to the front porch. Damn, I had no problem eliminating them should that become necessary, but like an enemy soldier I appreciated the fact that they were there to be sacrificed by their "higher command" and I felt some regret for their predicament. They were just dumb animals, doing what they have been trained to do and owned by scum bags that were, in my opinion, lower on the evolutionary scale than any canine. Dogs have small brains and are difficult targets when they get moving. From my SAS days I learned that attack dogs could be tough to neutralize once they vector in on you. Once they get in among your boys, trying to drop them with a firearm can actually exacerbate an already dangerous situation. Furthermore, dealing with them would distract us from our primary mission, and without a suppressed weapon our approach could be compromised. I asked the case officer if there were any other available entry points. He replied that there was and described another inwardly opening wood door. Somewhat relieved, I decided that this would be our primary entry point. This breach point would also facilitate our small team's flow and it would enable us to maneuver down the length of the mobile home en-masse, rather than being forced to split into two pairs, moving left and right from the original entry point. No force likes to fight in two directions simultaneously unless it cannot be avoided. It creates all kinds of tactical problems and vulnerabilities. Because the occupants in both residences were considered armed and dangerous, I requested permission to use an explosive charge to effect entry into my target. Randy agreed to this, but ruled out the option for himself because his target was believed to contain a number of young children who were thought to be sleeping on the floor of the main entry point room. With what we accepted as "solid intelligence" on the door's construction, Mac and I went about constructing the explosive charge and rehearsing the charge placement drill while other team members continued to gather intelligence and complete the assault plan.

Our preparations were complete and we were ready to go. All that was required was for Sheriff Jones to arrive and give the team his legal blessing. Sure enough, at 0400 hours there was a screech of tires, this time from his truck, and in he strode. Dressed in his now signature bow tie and tweed jacket, he wandered up to us, hollering as he moved, "Y'all listen up now." Anticipating this, we were lined up and ready to go with right hands raised. It didn't matter how many times he did this; it seemed to get funnier each time. Here I am, an expat Kiwi, trying to decipher what this little Black man from the Mississippi Delta was saying. As soon as the last "I do" reverberated off the factory's walls, Sheriff Jones had already vanished and was getting ready to roar off into the early morning in his hopped up pickup. Randy and I ran after him because we wanted to explain to him about the explosive charge and get his approval. We intercepted him as he was cranking up his vehicles turbo-charged V-8. Yelling loudly over the lusty detonations of his big bore mill, Randy asked, "Sheriff, have you got a second, please?" With a pre-occupied look he bellowed, "Goddamn it, only about two. It's after four o'clock in the goddamn morning and I gotta get up for work real soon."

"Sheriff, we want you to know that we are fixing to use an explosive charge to get into one of the houses."

Upon hearing that, the Sheriff's back stiffened, his eyes widened, and without missing a beat, he covered both ears sounding off loudly, "You da boss, you da boss," and with engine screaming from being over-revved, wheels spinning and smoking, he launched out of that parking lot in a cloud of flame, smoke, and dust.

Randy and I looked at each other and roared with laughter as we returned to the team gathered in the assembly area. Facing a neutral wall, Randy ordered, "Okay, line up guys. MP5's — load. Handguns — load." Satisfied that everyone was "hot," Randy and I inspected each of our respective team members and individually checked all equipment. Any hint of fatigue disappeared as the men became instantly alert and properly focused. Each officer was quizzed on his responsibilities and only correct answers were accepted.

My breacher was sent away to safely connect up the charge and upon his return; I checked him out. "Are you happy with what you have to do, Mac?"

"Yeah, no problem." was his confident reply.

"When is the safety pin removed from the firing device?" I asked?

Mac replied, "Once you have placed the charge on the door, returned to my rear, and slapped me on the arm."

I had absolutely no reason to doubt Mac's ability, especially since we had served together for many years in the SAS, but it never hurts to question each other to confirm the small, but important, points that could ultimately affect officer safety. The positive use of explosive charges to affect rapid entry and augment shock action during high-risk operations has significantly increased over the last several years. Too many officers have been killed or seriously injured attempting to breach an entry point using mechanical means. However, explosive breaching is still considered the most advanced and potentially dangerous form of breaching and should only be employed by trained and competent operators.

An in-depth knowledge of the conventional use of explosives by itself does not, by any means, qualify an individual as an explosive breacher. Both an art and a science, charge weights have to be carefully calculated and constructed to be both "failsafe" and to limit any collateral damage that may occur, and to reduce the associated risks to all personnel.

We entered our tactical transport and as usual, you could feel the excitement and tension mounting. It was a ten-minute drive to the targets and, almost on cue, the team clown would tell the filthiest joke he could think of to loosen everyone up.

"Five minutes," shouted the driver. "Okay, no more talking. Everyone make sure your safeties are on, get your head out of your ass, and think about your job," admonished the team leader.

"Two minutes!"

"Turning up the gravel road now, team one — 15 seconds."

The door slid open and all hands blinked against the sudden glare. Bracing for the jump, we were ready. Per personal SOP, my heart started to pump a little quicker as I looked for the debussing point. I could see our target and, as briefed, the driver kept rolling as we bailed out in a close formation. Sprinting with weapons at the low ready, we burned through the twenty yards that remained in spite of each man being laden with extra gear such as breaching tools, ballistic shield, and the explosive charge. As we hit the side of the mobile home I damn near shit.

"Fuck it," I cursed to myself. There was no door; that useless prick gave us the wrong information. First lesson learned, never assume anything and confirm the intelligence you receive. This practice was routine in the SAS and I was pissed at myself for being so naive. Continuing with our forward momentum, the point man led the team around to the residence's rear side in an effort to locate another door. If one was not available, I contemplated going through a window. "Be flexible, be flexible," I kept repeating to myself.

Upon clearing the house's corner, I heard the point man gasp as he ran directly into the two pit bulls. I don't know who got more of a fright, the point man or the dogs, but thankfully, they high tailed it back to their pens. It reminded me of a previous operation which involved blowing the door with an explosive charge. A small "rat like" dog was yapping and hanging onto Randy's BDU trousers as he raced up to the door to place the charge. Refusing to let go, the dog was dragged into the stack. However, the moment the charge was detonated you couldn't see the little bastard for dust.

I ran past Mac and passed the firing device to him as I moved toward the door. I could hear Randy's team deploying flash-bangs and that meant that they had effected entry. It was motivating to hear their explosions, but this was supposed to be a coordinated hit and we were tardy with our entry because we had incorrect information. When we accessed the door I damn near shit again. Not only was it not a wooden door opening in, as briefed, it turned out to be a metal door opening out. This presented me with a serious problem because our charge was specifically constructed for an inward opening door.

"Fuck that useless prick," I muttered as my mind raced. Maintain concentration, I said to myself — now was not the time to be distracted by thoughts of revenge. I still had a job to do. Without too many available options and our loss of critical time, I hastily affixed the charge to the door and raced back to my position in the stack. Checking to see if the blast shield was in position and with my fingers crossed I slapped Mac on the shoulder. "Boom!" Without hesitation, three quarters of an ounce of sheet explosive knifed through the obstacle, and in spite of the shield, I felt the slap of its spall along the wall. We charged forward through the lingering smoke because it was vital to maximize the shock effect that the blast had created inside the stronghold. We were lucky because the door had bounced open. Gun lights were stabbing through darkness because it was pitch black inside and pre-blast junk and debris was scattered everywhere. As we stumbled through the dump, my number-two man and I entered and cleared the first room, while the next two peeled off into the bedroom. MP5-mounted white light beams swept the interior as operators cleared to their respective corners and then merged and overlapped in the middle of the room, visually inscribing their arcs of fire. Room coverage had to be guaranteed and no part of the room could be left unaccounted for.

"Clear left, clear right, go!" followed, indicating that it was safe for the following team members to continue on through the stronghold. Intra-team communications punctuated the darkness as we continued to clear, search, and probe for occupants. Commands were loud and clear not only to let all hands know what was going on, but as part of our command presence and psychological effect it projected. We were letting potential adversaries know in no uncertain terms not to fuck with us or there would be severe consequences. Finally, louder than any of the preceding commands, "Contact! Sheriff's Department — don't move, don't move." A few seconds later that was followed by, "I got 'em, you go!" Todd and Scott had encountered two suspects and froze them in place with their weapon lights while the rest of us continued to flood the structure. Firearms were pre-positioned all over the house. In spite of the short delay in penetrating the structure, enough surprise was preserved by our rapid exploitation of the breach once it had been effected so neither suspect could get within arms reach of them.

"Dominate," music to an assaulter's ears, was relayed throughout the mobile home and it communicated that the last room had been cleared. I quickly rendezvoused with Scott and Mac in the bedroom and found them covering a suspect and a female as they lay in bed. Both were naked, filthy; and extremely nasty looking. He was a huge, obese man and had to weigh a good 300 pounds. They looked compatible because Momma was no lightweight and I figured the bed had to be reinforced with steel girders to support this load of adipose tissue.

His grossness was probably of benefit to us because even if he wanted to reach for the pump 12 gage lounging lethally in the corner, he would not have been able to get his fat ass out of the bed quickly enough. One of the most repulsive and dangerous, from a health standpoint, was that we had to eventually handle, search and secure these cesspools of humanity. However, without a scintilla of hesitation, Todd announced, "Cover me." Mac responded immediately with, "Covering," The suspects were rolled out of bed, handcuffed, and dragged from their boudoir through all their shit into the living room, where they were proned out and covered. After getting a better look at the two beached whales, I was thankful that our SOP dictated that we wear gloves and that our hepatitis shots are kept current. After receiving a status report, I reported to the commander that my team was "secure and covering." That meant the good guys were OK and we had suspects in custody. Although it seemed like the proverbial eternity, our mission took no more than 20 seconds to complete after entry.

Thank God that the two dogs opted out of the fight, and the fact that we struck at 0400 hours while they were in a deep sleep was also a factor in our favor. However, I knew I owed Lady Luck big time for this one. Randy's team also bagged a number of suspects, and when we got more light into our residence, I could see that it was littered with weapons, drugs, and associated contraband. People who live like this literally become animals. The house stunk like hell, so you can imagine what the people were like. However, the real tragedy is when you encounter young children in these places. No wonder they grow up to become problems for society. Their dysfunctional parents are drug-addicted assholes, so the cycle repeats itself unless some kind of early and meaningful intervention occurs. Satisfied that the objective was safe and secure, we called the narcotics guys and other technicians in to seize and document evidence. I spotted the agent that gave us the bad info and my blood started to boil. As I was leaving, I hissed into his ear, "We need to talk once this is all over, partner." He knew he had fucked up and I believe he regretted it. I realized that they were there for different reasons. They want the contraband and to make the collar, and they frequently think we are too cautious and detailed-oriented.

We want to get in as quickly and safely as possible and neutralize the threat with the minimal amount of drama. To us it is extremely personal and the intelligence we receive could mean the difference between life and death. As many other teams have learned the hard way, the only people you can trust are the guys on your own team. My only words of advice to the intelligence gathering community is that if you don't know, or are not sure, then tell us that. We are interested only in cold, hard facts. Don't dream up shit just to make us happy.

Randy's assault also went well. As they were fighting their way through the stronghold, one of the suspects was throwing drugs out the window into the waiting arms of one of the narcotics officers. Dumb bastards. The other house was much bigger than ours and it appeared that every time this suspect made some money, he would buy some plywood and add a room onto the existing structure. What a maze it turned out to be.

Ten people, including infants and young kids, occupied the house. The main suspect was locked in his bedroom, and by the time the guys broke in, he was lying on the bed pointing a pistol at them. Exhibiting tremendous restraint, Tim and Frank raised their MP5's, safeties snapping to fire as they did so. I guess it wasn't a good day to die, and as slack was being taken up on the sub gun's triggers, he lowered his pistol. Things happen very quickly in this job and decisions have to be made in split seconds. Coincidently, the officers mutually and without communicating overtly with each other, choose not to shoot him. This tactical telepathy derives from extended periods of time working together and frequently and intuitively surfaces during high-stress events. The decision has to be subconscious for it to be made so quickly. Nevertheless, it was their decision and no one can fault them for it. What would my reaction have been? Like anyone, I don't like people who point guns at me. Would my military or police mind-set prevail? It's hard to predict, because I wasn't in that room at that specific moment. Bottom line, the bad guy made a choice that enhanced his longevity.

One of the reasons Randy led the assault on the larger house was because he had been inside the residence once before while issuing an arrest warrant. They were voodoo worshippers and it seemed that they remembered him as well. Hanging from the tree outside the house were numerous mirrors that momentarily distracted the entry team as their white lights flashed off them at all angles. Stapled to the front door was a dead red bird and underneath it on the porch was a pouch containing hot peppers, a chicken's foot, sliced up garlic, and a piece of paper with Randy Doss's name on it. It seems that they had cast a voodoo spell on Big Daddy, but I think it would take more than that to perturb him.

Our small team had come along way professionally since its inception. I completely embrace the old saying that, "The more confident and competent with firearms you are, the less likely you are to inadvertently shoot someone." Officers that lack confidence in their own ability often tend to shoot before thinking. Shortly after joining the team, we were returning from a raid when we were tasked to support patrol officers who were involved in a vehicle chase. The fleeing vehicle apparently contained a murder suspect who had crossed over from Tunica County into our jurisdiction. Patrol managed to drive the suspect's vehicle off the road, and on arrival at the scene the gunfight was in progress. I remember exiting the vehicle with my Colt .45 firmly in hand and sliding behind a huge log where two of our officers were laying down lead toward the tree line. Brass casings were being ejected rapidly as trees were being stripped of bark. "Cease fire, cease fire," I yelled over the noise while at the same time banging the closest officer on the head to get his attention. "What the fuck are you shooting at?" was my immediate question. "He's over there — behind the tree." Yeah, right, that bastard was about half a mile into the woods by now. Discipline, discipline, discipline!

The Refrigerator Option

For a period of time, our fugitive division had been on the look out for an individual wanted for suspicion of committing murder. The suspect's sister showed up at the department one day and Big Daddy Doss, head of the Investigative Division, ended up interviewing her. She volunteered that her brother would be home this Friday night and advised that if he detected the police before they got in he would either hide under the bed or in the refrigerator. The fridge part sounded real bogus to Randy because this guy was no midget, so he threatened her with imprisonment if she was lying. Being a good Southern Baptist, she pulled out her Bible from her purse and swore that he would be there. With that kind of Godly assurance, the team was assembled. After the initial sweep, Leon was nowhere to be found and all you could here was Randy cursing and threatening the sister with the slammer. A secondary sweep produced similar results. One of the younger deputies sheepishly reminded "Big Daddy" that she said he would hide in the fridge. Randy, who was a good-sized man in all directions, slowly turned and staring down on the officer who now regretted bringing it up bellowed, "Don't be so fucking stupid, no one is dumb enough to hide in a perfectly good refrigerator and freeze his balls off." Realizing that the young buck was only trying to help and was as frustrated as he was, relented and addressing the appliance said, "What the hell, let's check it anyway." With that, John positioned himself to open the door and Randy took up a covering position and brought his .45 pistol to bear on its door. With a nod from Randy, John yanked on the door only to have it wrenched from his grip and slammed shut. Somewhat shocked, John stammered, "Holy fucking hell, he's in the fridge."

"Goddamn it Leon, get your fucking ass out of the fridge," screamed Randy. From the white box's interior came a muffled reply, "Nooo sah, I ain't cumin out of dis ice box." Again John tried to rip open the door only to have it yanked back out of his hands causing the appliance to almost fall over. Things were getting testy and Randy began to doubt his deputy's manhood. Totally pissed, Randy ordered, "Goddamn it, get a man's grip on that door and open that son-of-a-bitch." With an enormous grunt, John nearly tore the door off its hinges, and sure enough, there was Leon scrunched up in the fetal position, unfortunately with his hands in a low ready position. "Boooom!" The noise was deafening as Randy's .45 auto discharged and sent a high velocity 230-grain hollow point into Leon's center of mass. Before the ejected case struck the floor, the next bang was young Leon's perforated body toppling to the kitchen linoleum. With him came a box of corn dogs, a half eaten chicken, a gallon of rancid milk, but no weapon. Recovering, Randy questioned the rather ill Leon.

"Leon, Leon — where are you hit?"

"Officer, I'm hurtin' all over," was his immediate and painful reply as he rolled around in a rapidly increasing pool of blood.

When the team withdrew, the deputies who were able to view the kitchen as they moved outside appeared to be more upset over the incident than Leon's sister was. She just wanted to know who was going to clean up the kitchen.

Lessons learned — do not move or posture in a furtive or threatening manner when a police officer has the drop on you, and never overlook any potential hiding place, no matter how impossible it may appear to be.

Luckily for Leon, he survived the gunshot wound. He was given trauma first aid and transported to the hospital by helicopter, ultimately living to see his day in court. At the moment Randy fired the shot, Leon's arm was across his center chest and the round collided with his forearm first. The slug expanded as advertised and made a mess of his arm. He was eventually sentenced to life in prison at the state penitentiary for his past misdeeds.

The Mississippi Militia

I frequently involve my New Zealand SAS colleagues in my work throughout the United States. During my two years of security assignments in Beverly Hills, I would give them a tour of my principal's seven-acre mansion, familiarizing them with the intricacies of the multi-million dollar security system that protects both the exterior and interior of the property. It was vastly different and more elaborate than what they had been exposed to before, and when they traveled the globe on similar assignments they understood what enough money could buy. On occasions, when visiting Mississippi, they were invited to deploy with our team to get a taste of what it was like to operate on a SWAT Team in the deep South. Pete, a rugged Maori, who had recently left the SAS, was in Memphis working as a bodyguard for a wealthy friend of mine. During his days off, he would often travel to my range in order to work on and improve his individual shooting skills, then hang out at my house during the evenings. One visit to the house coincided with a major call-out we had. Having nothing else to do in the evening but drink beer and chase Southern belles, he was recruited to do something useful and join us on the op. Hell, I had to think of something to keep him out of trouble.

This situation involved a hardcore member of the "Mississippi Militia" and well-known survivalist, who had been playing hardball with the authorities for the last five years. Through the exercise of eminent domain the airport had bought out his entire neighbourhood, including his home, but he refused to move. Every house around him for 150 yards had already been demolished. This leveling of the surrounding terrain created excellent fields of fire and observation for him from his fortified residence that was perched on the geographic crest of a knoll. His utilities had been cut off and he was surviving on generated energy, ration packs, and considerable support from militia groups from neighboring states. His son was being home schooled and neither he nor his wife left the house at the same time. Undercover officers from various levels of law enforcement had infiltrated some of the militia organizations that provided support for this family and all had arrived at the same conclusion and that was he was hard-core and would resist any attempt to dislodge him with deadly force. Every month we trained for this eventuality, because we knew it was only a matter of time before the final court eviction order was signed. Because of the exposed approach from any forming up position that we could select we concentrated on contact/immediate action drills and fire and movement with our .223 caliber carbines. Since he had similar weaponry, our body armor and Kevlar helmets would be of little value, but we would wear them anyway to cope with any lesser threats we might encounter. Of particular concern to us was whether his wife and son were also shooters. No one relished having to defend himself against a mother and her kid, so the element of surprise would be extremely critical.

Result after an explosive charge was placed on a Militiaman's front door – Southaven, Mississippi, 1999

A judge finally signed the order ending his long string of appeals, and that was our signal to swing into action. We made a final recce and cammied up for a night sortie. We approached from what we considered the house's blind side carrying in minimal gear, with everything capable of generating noise padded and taped. We dropped to the ground and paused about 150 yards from the home's green (left) side. Here we armed the linear door charge that would effect our initial entry, as well as the internal door charges that both Tim and I carried. As the designated breachers for this operation, Tim and I discussed which of us would place the charge and who would fire it. As was customary, we would rotate positions each operation to keep it fair. There was no doubt that placing the charge was much more dangerous as your body often became exposed in front of the door, depending on the type of charge and which side of the door you were approaching from. I knew damn well that it was my turn to fire the charge, but I issued the challenge anyway.

"Whose turn to place the charge, Tim?"

"Yours, Alan," was his split second reply.

"Fucking hell," I said to myself. I can't sit here and argue with him in front of the boys. Bastard!

"Roger that Tim — no worries." I definitely owed him for this one.

My mind was now preoccupied with that crazy bastard inside. If he heard me placing that charge, he was just the type to start sending AK47 rounds zipping through the center of that door. The charge that we chose was a simple wood strip charge that contained detonating cord. It was designed to run down the complete length of the door on the hinge side. What made this worse was that he had a steel burglar bar door on the outside of his regular door, and the door was set into a porch so there was absolutely no way that I could avoid standing directly in front of the hatch.

Prior to departing our FUP, four of our riflemen positioned themselves in a fire support overwatch should we come under fire during the approach. The assault team now moved forward, hoping like hell that luck would be on our side. The point man armed with an AR15 led the way. I followed, carrying the charge and firing system. Tim was next with his MP5, followed by the remaining team members. I made sure that the firing system and I were tucked in behind my cover man. I could not afford for a round to strike the blasting cap and evaporate the team and me en route. On reaching the white/green corner of the house, we signaled for the rifle support team to move to us. Phase one was now complete. Four yards short of the door, my cover man stopped, indicating that we had reached our firing position. I passed the firing device back to Tim, so that he could remove the PVC pipe holding the shock tube lead line together. Only his eyes were exposed, but I could see a fucking huge cheesy grin behind that mask. "Double bastard," I swore to myself. I squeezed my cover man and forward we went — sweat now dripping profusely down my back, mouth dry, but most importantly maintaining concentration on my task. The burglar bar door was eased open in a series of loud squeaks, "Fuck, fuck," I hissed as I shut my eyes waiting for hot lead to rip into my body. The linear charge was placed and I slowly closed the grill door to hold and tamp the wood strip in place. I could not get out of there fast enough and I accessed my AR15 before I rejoined the stack. Phew, what a relief. The hard part was over for me, at least for the moment, but now I would have a weapon in my hand and my mates there to back me up during the entry.

On hearing the first "stand-by," I stuck my left finger in my ear and tucked my right ear hard against my raised shoulder, because I knew this would be a loud bastard. "Boooooom" — damn right about that!

The entry was now unobstructed. The metal door was lying outside and internal door was flattened immediately inside the doorway. The lounge was first to be cleared, followed by a split stack. I ended up heading down the hallway to the bedrooms as Tim and three others heading to the right to clear the dining room, kitchen, wash house, and garage. Still no contact — what the fuck? We were now at the last bedroom, so for us, this was it. He was sure to be barricaded in there, positioned strategically with his AK47 stock slammed into his cheek. "Signal white" was the call and we all new what that meant. There was no way we were going in there without banging it first. "I have the door," yelled Woody. "Bangs on me," replied Scott. On that, the door was breached and an OMNI 100 distraction device was lobbed just inside the threshold. I mistimed this one badly and my ears were not covered. The shock wave was reflected straight back to us and slapped the shit out of us – fucking hell. I don't care how many times you have been exposed to those devices, you just never get used to them.

"Room clear, room clear," yelled Woody.

From the other end of the house, I could hear Tim yelling for an internal door charge (IDC). When I made my way through to him, we noticed that a chain had been wrapped around the handle of the door leading into the garage. It then ran its way up the frame and into a door ringer's metal container. Based on this guy's background, there was no way we were going to touch the knob. Tim made the right decision. I snatched the plastic strip charge from his vest, handed him the firing device, and placed the charge between the doorknob and frame. By this time, he had retreated to a safe location down the hallway where everyone was shielded if, in fact, a secondary explosion occurred. "Disappear," I yelled to the cover-man. On ensuring the area was totally clear, I slapped Tim on the arm and the charge was detonated. This was nothing compared to the external charge or distraction device. Measuring only six inches long, it was designed to dislodge the locking system and lay it down just inside the room. Sure enough, there it was, eighteen inches inside the garage.

There was absolutely no room inside the garage to move, let alone effectively clear. It was completely stacked to the roof with military rations, gasoline to run the generators, blankets, ammunition, gun safes full of weaponry, $167.000 in cash, and an abundance of South African, Canadian, and Mexican gold coins. Additionally, long guns and handguns were placed strategically throughout the house to cover all entrances and vulnerable points. Not a bad haul. It took three detectives seven hours the next day to count the loot.

Major problem — we still haven't located the suspects. There was only one place left to check, the attic. If there was ever a more dangerous aspect to this mission, this was it. What idiot would ever stick his head up there just to have it removed by a high velocity round? "Scott – get your ass over here," was Tim's order. Scott was our resident tunnel rat. Measuring five feet and bit and weight a buck and a quarter, he was the perfect choice. Prior to inserting him, we utilized Southaven Police Department's SWAT team's tactical pole mirror and one of their dogs. They had been waiting in support and it was at times like this that their presence was greatly appreciated.

Disappointingly, the family had been tipped off earlier about our impending raid. They hastily vacated the residence and it was the first time in five years that they had left the house together. Quite honestly, this was one mission that I did not regret that the house was empty. As far as I was concerned, the man came to his senses and made everyone's job easier. It definitely could have turned ugly if he had stubbornly maintained his normal mind-set.

When we left the scene, I noticed an eighteen-wheeler container truck and a flatbed, with a big yellow bulldozer on its deck waiting down the road. When I drove past the incident area the following morning, the house was completely gone. Only the dozer's track marks remained. Immediately, the Israeli-Palestinian conflict came to mind, where the Israel Defense Force destroys the families of convicted terrorist's homes with explosives or bulldozers. This man had not broken the law, it was just the fact that his final appeal had been exhausted and the administrators were sick to death of him. Only in Mississippi!

Don't misunderstand me, I am a strong proponent of the Second Amendment and one of the first things I did when I came to this country was join the NRA. However, these were not firearms ownership issues. This involved individuals and groups that advocated guerilla warfare against the United States for a variety of conspiracy and other paranoid political theories. And law enforcement officers were high on their list of potential targets.

On another occasion, Randy and I were part of a three-man recon team that deployed to a remote area of a neighboring county to gather intelligence on the Mississippi Militia while they conducted a range training day. This occurred before we had acquired M-16's, so our MP5 submachine guns were the most effective weapons we had. We were able to navigate into the general area by following the Militia's coded signs that had been positioned along the roads during the early morning hours. After hiding our vehicle, we had our air support fly over the area at a safe and inconspicuous altitude. In a short time, he was able to pin point their parking location for us. From there, it was just a matter of performing a map study and locating likely terrain where they could conduct their shoot. After patrolling for a few klicks, we were able to zero in on their gunfire. When we reached their woodland range and bivouac area we set up a hide and observation point (OP). Randy and I occupied the OP and the third officer acted as rear security. What a racket. There were several dozen shooters and almost as many spectators. The atmosphere was almost picnic like and they cranked off rounds ranging up to .50 caliber M2 Browning machine guns. Noise discipline therefore, was not a concern, but we maintained it anyway because they had posted armed sentries around the site. When one headed in our direction and stood right in front of our position, we decided to withdraw as soon as he moved on. However, this guy must have had a case of the "for reals," because he kept his FN-SLR .308 rifle at port arms and really eyeballed the wood line before he wandered back toward the firing line. I looked over at Randy who kept a bead on him with his MP5 and signaled him to move out. As I left the OP I picked up point and Randy brought up the rear. We hadn't moved more than fifty meters when a dog spotted us and started barking. We immediately proned out and froze. The last thing we wanted was to get into a shootout while severely out gunned and out manned with a bunch of paranoid people who would not hesitate to mix it up with us. I had a strip of beef jerky in my pocket and when the dog came closer I tossed it to him. After a quick sniff, it took him a New York minute to snatch it up and take off to feast on it. After 100 meters of careful movement we periodically double-timed, to put as much distance between the Militia and us. After digesting our intelligence, investigators searched the site the following Monday morning and found a generous amount of physical evidence that confirmed the Militia's presence, the weaponry employed, and possible intentions for future operations.

Escaped Convict
— Catch Me If You Can, I Ain't Going Back To The Pen

Duke has assisted me in teaching several Special Operations schools in the U.S. His involvement with the DeSoto County Sheriff's Department goes back to the mid-nineties. He also got intimately involved in the department's SWAT team training and development, particularly when I was out of town. His reputation as a skilled operator and exceptional instructional abilities, coupled with his relaxed demeanor, made him an instant hit with the guys. It wasn't too long before he was accompanying the team on raids and advising them on matters of tactical importance. Shortly thereafter, Duke was renamed "Deputy Dukey Dukester from Down Under."

Our department was faced with a particularly complex operation and Duke's wisdom and tactical savvy contributed materially to its successful resolution. An escaped convict from Arkansas had been on the run for three months before he was located in our county. It was his second successful escape and his taking of two-prison guards hostage facilitated this one. He was a hard core, no nonsense criminal who categorically stated that he would never return to prison. His wife resided in DeSoto County and reportedly they would frequently meet in the woods where he was holed up in a van and domed tent. The number of weapons he had acquired and his van's mobility presented us with substantial problems. Furthermore, we had never executed an actual van assault before and if he detected our approach, he most likely would greet us with his collection of ordnance. Frank, our intelligence officer held up his rap sheet and let it unravel. Frank is 6 feet, 3 inches and even with his hand raised high above his head, the fax was still rolled up on the floor. This guy's time had come. He knew it and we knew it. We only hoped that his wife, or anyone else, would not be present to become potential hostages.

The basic plan was as follows. A sniper-observer team would be inserted by helicopter a good distance from the suspected location. They would stalk through the woods and locate the suspect's lair. Once that was accomplished, they would contact the entry team via radio if he was there, or when he arrived. After several tense hours, just prior to last light, the snipers reported that a darkened vehicle had moved down a nearby dirt road and its occupants had parked inside the tree line. Was it our boy, or was it two teenagers looking for a place to get to know each other? Either way, they were in for memorable experience and perhaps their last.

Aft of his hiding place was a huge lake, and although we considered an amphibious approach, we decided this was not the time to experiment with a new and unfamiliar insert technique for the team. Other terrain considerations dictated that the assault team's direction of approach would be from the front. The radio came alive again and the Ghillie-suited snipers advised that two persons exited the vehicle and disappeared into the darkness. They requested permission to move closer to re-establish visual contact, but it was denied. We were now at the make or break stage, and it was time to close in.

Our ten-man assault force augmented by Duke, was dropped off some distance from the dirt road. I could see that Duke was in his camo-clad element. With the exception of his M-16, (Duke carried an FN SLR in S.E. Asia) he might as well have been back in Vietnam. With the aid of a night vision scope, we cautiously inched our way toward the suspect's location. However, the undergrowth was extremely dry, and, therefore, noisy, so we had to abandon a more covered route and, against all training doctrine, had to use a dirt track as our avenue of approach. At this critical point, sound was our greatest enemy. Tim had point followed by myself, Duke, Big Daddy Doss, then the remaining seven in trace.

Tim suddenly froze and slowly motioned to his left. The woods were so thick that even with the monocular device I could just make out the van about 30 feet off to my flank. I swallowed the "oh shit" that welled up into my throat, because there was no way we could even whisper without compromising our presence. We were close enough to hear muffled sounds coming from the van, but that meant if we could hear him he could hear us if we were not very careful. I hoped he was knocking the bottom out of his old lady, because his focus at that moment would certainly not be on his security.

Our plan was to create an aggressive diversion, break the van's rear windows, then insert a can of CS/OC agent to incapacitate or drive him out of his vehicle. However, donning our gas masks was out of the question because we were so close. The team faced left and prepared to assault as rehearsed. The first element lobbed seven flash bang diversionary devices at the vehicle to initiate the assault. It sounded like a mortar barrage going off and hopefully got his attention while the chemical agents were being dropped into his vehicle. The second element consisting of Duke, two others, and myself, were responsible for locating and clearing the tent which was thought to be well concealed somewhere behind the van. There it was, about 15 yards further into the woods. It was a four-man dome-type tent. Prior to accessing it, we bracketed the tent with two flash-bangs to cover our approach. According to plan, we flattened it rather than stick our heads into what would have amounted to be a dark bag and try to clear it. Our action reminded me of a Maori attack on a British encampment during the early colonial days. After the sentries were quietly eliminated, the Maori war party crept into the camp and collapsed the tents by cutting the ropes. They then waded through the mass of captured chaos, hacking and slashing anything that moved. By day break the entire command had almost been wiped out. The tent was flattened and we stomped through it in an attempt to discover anyone inside. It was empty.

By this time, the buck-naked suspect and his wife, who was wearing "long johns" to ward off the chilly night air, had been extracted from the van and handcuffed, face down in the dirt. Feeble gasps and cries were coming from their mouths and snot was running freely from their nostrils as they felt the full effects of 22,000 cubic feet of gas that had filled their tiny van in seconds. Without our masks, most of us had a bad case of the sniffles too. Sure as shit, inside the van were two rifles, one shotgun, and two handguns. The tent was hauled to the department for evidence and deposited in Randy's office for the night. Everything else that could be documented was, and other than the weapons, a large quantity of crystal methamphetamine was also seized. The next day, Randy unzipped the tent to inspect its interior and he damn near shit. Out crawled a black snake over six feet long that the guy kept for a pet. By not warning us he probably thought he would get the last laugh. I guess that he wanted to exact as much revenge as he could. When Randy asked why he was stark naked on a chilly night he unabashedly told him that when he heard all those "cannons" (flash-bangs) being fired he was getting a blow job from his wife. When he reached beside him for his rifle, "A million pieces of glass fell on me and then suddenly I couldn't breathe and my eyes closed tight." The next thing he remembered were blinding lights, being dragged out of the van, slammed to the ground, and handcuffed with someone's knee driving his snot-covered face into the mud. He was real pissed, because if we had waited just a little longer his wife would have been able to do her thing and he would have been ready to give us a good fight. After the shock wears off

Two-time prison escaper from Arkansas caught by our team in DeSoto County with his wife in 1998. Besides a large quantity of methamphetamines he also had numerous handguns and rifles in his hideout.

and they know they are going to live, most of these punks suddenly become macho men again. What an asshole. Regardless of all that, he now had to face the music and the possibility of up to 20 years added to his time for forcible escape from an Arkansas prison.

Dave "Magnet For Trouble" Meredith

Since I have been in the United States, I have literally trained thousands of American police and military special operations personnel and similar operatives from some 30 foreign countries. It has been a most gratifying and rewarding experience. Over the years, a number of common similarities among these domestic and foreign warriors have emerged. For starters, all are extremely underpaid and over extended for the dangerous work they are tasked to perform. The equipment provided to the majority of foreign officers is sub-standard and, shockingly, too many American police show up at TEES with gear that is inadequate. In some cases, protective items like body armor has to be loaned to them during the training because their issue Kevlar was unsafe. And appropriately, they bitch and moan about the lack of this and that, but when they see what the foreign cops show up with it puts things a little more in perspective. Many times the overseas visitors leave TEES with their bags filled with gear that sympathetic American officers give them. After bonds of brotherhood are formed through shared training experiences, I have seen some cops literally take the shirt off their backs and insist that their foreign counterparts accept them in friendship and admiration.

The typical SWAT officer's dedication to the job and mission at hand can never be disputed. I believe that this commitment to both the job and fellow officers results from the fact that they are all volunteers, which means that they want to be there, to be part of a select team, the broader special operations community, and to be the best that their department has to offer.

Every team has its characters and ours was no exception. David, who's nickname was "Contingency Dave," was an officer who absolutely lived for law enforcement. Being a bachelor, almost every cent he made would be put to good use by purchasing the latest equipment or weaponry. He was extremely proud of his personal arsenal and carried a tactical assortment in the trunk of his patrol vehicle, "just in case!" It must have taken him thirty minutes to load and position everything prior to commencing his shift. We worked together on many successful raids, but there was one where he was extremely lucky to have survived.

We were executing an arrest warrant for a felon who was wanted in Texas, but living in the vicinity of my residence in a house trailer. We were advised that his trailer was filled with stolen goods. This also including the truck parked in his driveway. Intelligence also indicated that every room in the trailer had a firearm positioned in it.

Upon entry, SWAT's universal calling card, a 175-decibel OMNI Blast 100 flash-bang was deployed, and the first two men quickly cleared the living room. When they peeled off to sweep the kitchen, four of us split left across the living room and moved toward the hallway. I was slotted third and David was our rear security.

Three men remained outside to establish an inner-perimeter so that they could prevent any breakout attempts. As we moved quickly across the floor, I noticed that our weight was causing the trailer to shift and bounce. I also became aware of a double-barreled shotgun leaning up against the wall near the hallway. Our lead element had cleared the corner and I was just past the big smoothbore when my focus was shattered by a tremendous blast. Christ! My immediate thoughts were that the guys in the kitchen must have made contact and clobbered someone with the Benelli, or worse, one of us was on the receiving end. Although tempted, my element couldn't stop because our sector had not been cleared. Once we dominated, I returned to the living room to find a badly shaken David, frantically examining his groin area. Apparently our aggressive movement had disturbed the trailer's equilibrium and the resulting motion dislodged the 12 gage. It must have had faulty or very light triggers, because both barrels let go when it hit the floor. Since it was close, the two shot patterns were tight and passed directly between David's legs as he was in mid stride. He said it was so close he could feel the shot's wake as it tried to occupy the same space his balls were in. But that was not the end of the pellet's errant odyssey. Continuing at a good clip, three more targets would not be so lucky. Max, who was working the perimeter heard the blast and immediately noticed a snakeskin cowboy boot come flying toward him at a high velocity. This boot had been positioned by the front door and absorbed half of the shot. Simultaneously, he felt several pellets of the steel shot slam into his chest. I bet Max gave extra thanks that he was wearing his ballistic vest.

David was a magnet for trouble. Wherever he went, it either preceded him, or followed him. If communications reported shots fired, invariably David would be the one laying them down. One night, while patrolling the southwest corner of the county, he heard the call go out that a hot pursuit was taking place. The fact that it was a good distance away did not deter David, who ended up at the front of the formation as the convoy reached the Tennessee State Line. As expected, the suspect crossed the line into Memphis and David continued his pursuit. City officers laid a spiked chain tire trap across the freeway and, as scripted, the bad guys tires were shredded. Not to worry, the fugitive ignored that little mishap and drove onward in a shower of sparks until his rims almost melted. As David pulled up and paralleled the slowing vehicle in an effort to force him over, he was rewarded with the customary finger and verbal abuse. No worries. With his MP5 lying beside him on the seat, David proceeded to intimidate the suspect by indicating rather aggressively that he should reconsider his intentions. The next 400 yards produced nothing but sparks and debris as the suspect's car disintegrated right there on the freeway. Other pursuing officers said they were looking for a parachute, anticipating the subject's bail out at his first opportunity.

When both vehicles ground to a halt the gun battle began with the suspect hunkered down behind his hood busting caps at David's car as he returned fire with controlled bursts from his sub-machinegun while positioned at the rear of his cruiser. Switching to single fire, David tried to pick him off and end it quickly. Oblivious to the drama unfolding near them, motorists blithely continued driving on the interstate as bullets flew. Before what was going on registered, they were well past the scene. David had gained fire superiority, and when the suspect ran out of ammunition, he desperately began to look for a way out. Back up units kept arriving and he found himself threatened on both flanks. He had the woods to his left, and a still active four-lane freeway on his right. Under stress many of us do dumb things and this guy was no exception to this common phenomenon. The woods were his best option, but instead, he turned to his right and sprinted toward the freeway. I guess that his battle blinkers were on and all he could envision was freedom on the other side of the road and, by God, that was where he was going. No way, mate. He got no more than three strides across the first lane and splat, he was leveled by an eighteen wheeler doing 80 miles per hour. If it were me, I think I would have rather have taken a bullet!

The Mexican Mafia

Mutual aid in DeSoto County has always been an important issue for Sheriff Riley and Chief Deputy Charlie Brown. They have always been ready to assist the four city tactical teams in our county in any way. In turn, he has also not been shy to request support when we have required it. Being only a twelve-man team, we have often utilized the services of Horn Lake, Hernando, and Olive Branch PD SWAT teams. Now, however, it was time to join forces with Southaven PD for a particularly large operation. The Southaven Department comes under the command of Chief Tom Long and his Deputy, Steve Pirtle. Without a doubt, these two men are among the most administratively and operationally capable officers in the Mid South region. Both are graduates of the FBI's prestigious National Academy and have been around long enough to understand what is right and what is wrong tactically. This experience and knowledge reflects largely on the organization and exceptional capabilities of their SWAT team.

Living in the city of Southaven was a gang of mostly illegal Mexicans that were responsible for approximately 70-percent of all the major burglaries in the county, as well as the production and distribution of narcotics. Once the appropriate amount of intelligence had been collected, it was decided to issue arrest warrants for the major players. With this accomplished, it was established that the wanted personnel lived in four different houses within the city's limits. The problem for us was that three of the four houses were within shouting distance of each other. Because of this fact, it was obvious that we would have to hit all four simultaneously in order to maintain the element of surprise. That probably sounds a little easier than it really is. Because of the seriousness of the charges and the ability for the suspects to turn nasty on us, it was decided that we would use explosive charges to guarantee entry into two of the residences. The third and forth would be breached manually because one of them contained flammable drug producing chemicals and the other contained a considerable number of adults and kids who slept on floors throughout the house.

A total of 26 operators would be involved in making the entries. Planning for the mission took several hours at the Sheriff's Office. Detectives and narcotics officers briefed us and we also had the opportunity to interview one of the gang members who had been arrested and held in custody a couple of days earlier. The main questions presented to him related to entry points, internal layouts, and disposition of suspects, weapons, and family members. He spoke freely throughout the interrogation and appeared to be straight up with his information. A hit time of 0330 hours was chosen because we anticipated that all the players would be asleep. However, this can never be taken for gospel because drug dealers and the like could be up at any hour snorting or planning their next caper. Proceeding with this in mind, the raid force was broken down as follows:

Team one consisted of five members with me as team leader. We would be responsible for taking down the ring-leader's residence where he, his wife, their baby, his second in command, and the latter's girlfriend lived. We were to effect entry using explosive means.

Team two was commanded by Roger Clark and he was assigned four officers. They would take down the residence immediately opposite ours that reportedly contained approximately two gang members and their spouses. They were to effect entry using explosive means.

Team three, consisting of Southaven personnel, would neutralize the drug production house situated directly behind ours on the next street. They would gain entry employing mechanical means.

Team four, saw Randy (Big Daddy) Doss in charge and his five man team would clear and dominate the fourth house that held the bulk of the gang and a large number of Spanish-speaking illegal aliens.

Our raid commander, Tim Harris, and Southaven's Steve Pirtle quickly developed a coordinated plan that would enable all four teams to hit simultaneously. Woody Grantham, Brian Darby, and I put together two water charges to take out the metal doors. Additionally, small strip charges were constructed and placed on our vests to take care of any locked doors found inside the strongholds. The remaining team members were busy laying out rehearsal areas and going over the plan.

It was decided that a vehicle insert followed by a dismounted assault would be conducted using a Southaven truck and two of our vans. The vehicle drivers were briefed to stop approximately three houses short of their assigned strongholds. At that juncture, each team would advance to their final assault positions. It was critical for us to be able to covertly place our explosive entry charges without compromising ourselves. To assist in this, it was decided to hold teams three and four about 10 to 15 yards short of their entry points until teams one and two had placed their charges and reported that they were ready. Upon receiving that signal, the remaining teams were free to proceed to their entry points.

Everything looks good and sounds easy when you are planning it on a chalkboard, but oh how things can change once you pour out of the vans. Total disorientation tends to take over as you are adjusting yourself to the target area. What you envisioned to be on the right turns out to be actually on the left, and after executing a couple of 360-degree turns, we finally headed off in the correct direction. As Roger's and my teams moved down the road in column, we identified our targets and proceeded to split off from each other. We encountered our first problem as we stealthfully climbed the chain link fence that surrounded our target. When Brian passed me the charge while he scaled the fence, I noticed that the stairs moving up to the front porch were the reverse, or back to front from what the informant related to us. "Fucking asshole just got his first one over us," I murmured to myself. It was too late to worry about it. Paul, our cover man, made a tactical decision and we went with it. He placed us on the side opposite from where we had rehearsed, but, no worries, it was a good call since my shock tube lead line would not have reached from the other side anyway. At the FAP, Brian passed the firing device to me and squeezed Paul on the shoulder indicating that he was ready to move forward to the door. The lead line slinked out as they advanced. At the same time, I glanced across the street and observed Woody carefully moving forward to place his own charge. Teams three and four radioed that they were "ready at their FAP's." So far, so good, and the only noise being made was from a stray dog yelping, but that was to be expected. I observed Woody pass his lead line to Gary, his cover man, and proceed back to his firing point. Having Gary hold the lead line was critical because it would have been disastrous if Woody had hit a snag and pulled the charge off the door at this crucial phase. That is the primary reason I opted for a two-man charge placement drill, which meant that we paid the lead line out from the firing point instead of from the door. No problems, that was Woody's choice and he was doing a good job. I felt Brian squeeze my arm as he moved past me and then saw Paul, his cover man, drop down in front of me to assume point position. I then passed my thumb back and it was relayed to the rear point man that reported to the commander that we were at FAP. Ten more seconds elapsed and Roger finally reported in for team two. Everyone tensed as the anticipated command flowed through our ear-pieces. "All call signs, this is the commander. I have control — Stand by, stand by, go."

"Booom! Booom!" Two perfect breaches, both within a second of each other, and the assaults were on. Total focus was now on our own areas of responsibility and nothing else. Paul led me through the breach, and as he peeled right, I focused my attention to the left. As assault elements moved through the structure, they called out, "7 clear — 10 clear — go." Two operators immediately peeled off and entered the kitchen as the remaining three stacked in the hallway. "Signal white, signal white," I yelled to the man behind me. "It's on me," Paul replied as he accessed his flash bang, diversionary grenade. "Booooomm!" Damn, that bastard seemed louder than the explosive charge, and it was because we were now confined inside a very tight house trailer. Upon rounding a corner leading into the hallway, I was confronted by the wife holding her ten-month infant. Reflexively I yelled, "Sheriffs department — don't move." As I maintained control over her, the remaining members flowed past in pairs and on into the two bedrooms. There they found the main suspect and a female already standing in submissive arrest positions. The surprise, dynamic and aggressive impact of the assault took the fight out of them. Upon questioning the mother, she told us that her boyfriend was at another location where stockpiles of stolen goods were stored. Turning the subjects over to follow on arrest teams, we quickly regrouped, redistributed flash-bangs, and headed to the new address on the double. When we arrived, we radioed back to confirm the address and to get a verbal description of the residence from the woman. The last thing we wanted to do was interrupt a peaceful citizen enjoying a good nights sleep.

With one quick shot, the ram smashed down the door. We further heralded our entry with another Omni Blast. Paul remained outside to cover the other external door as we moved smoothly through the rooms. "Booom!" One more bang to cover our hall entry, which we considered a danger area. "Dominate," was passed from man to man, which signaled us to perform our secondary searches. Two of us quickly moved outside to join Paul and clear an outbuilding. "Signal White," resulted in a stunning blast that shattered the shed's windows. I felt sorry for any bastard who might be hiding in there, because he would have been jelly after that one. "Building's clear!" Completing our detailed searches we concluded that there were no suspects and in fact, no anything. The house had been stripped and cleared out. There was not even a knife or fork in the draw. It looked like their intelligence was better than ours and they had been tipped off, but only had enough time to move the stolen property. The leader sacrificed the others to save this stash.

All four strongholds were successfully breached and dominated quickly. While closing with a suspect, Woody ordered him to show his hands, which he concealed behind his back. After several seconds of defiant hesitation, a .38 Special revolver clattered to the floor. I speculated on what might have been going through the suspect's mind at the moment of truth. In that fatal moment, did he stifle his Latin machismo, or was he a cold stone killer that calculated his chances of survival and decided that discretion was the better part of valor? From that raid an extraordinary amount of stolen gear ranging from cameras, kitchen utensils, weapons, furniture, audio and video gear, household appliances, bikes, cars, and vans were harvested from the main targets.

The primary factor that creates a credible and proficient SWAT unit is team-work. And, strong individual performances are the ingredients that contribute to team-work. If each man performs his specific task to the best of his developed ability, then, obviously, the team will click. If one man fails to meet his commitments then the team will start to disintegrate and another operator will be required to fill the vacuum and pick up the slack. I believe that our twelve man DeSoto County team has performed professionally and with excellent credibility over the years. The support and trust afforded to us by Sheriff Riley and Chief Deputy Brown are major factors for our success. The rigid discipline instilled during training has obviously paid off and has been amply demonstrated during departmental operations. A great deal can be said for a well-trained team that employs good tactics, discipline, and command and control, versus a disorganized group that relies purely on aggression and luck. As we all know, eventually that luck

Shreveport PD SWAT Team during training at the T.E.E.S. facility. Known as the "jump-out-boys," they were feared by the many gangs controlling the drug trade on the mean streets of Shreveport, Louisiana – Memphis, Tennessee, 1999

U.S. Marshall Service Special Operations Group during T.E.E.S. training. "A fine team of true professionals" – Camp Beauregard, Louisiana, 2002

Members of the New Zealand Special Tactics Group, Victoria (Australia) Special Operations Group and Australian Federal Police after specialty training in New Zealand, 2001. The Kiwis are a dedicated group who have come a long way since I first worked with them in 1980. Acting Sergeant Peter McCarthy (standing, fourth from left) has been extremely influential in getting the Kiwis to where they are today.

will run out.

There are many fine teams throughout the United States that are considered "leaders in the field." As previously mentioned, they invariably host an unusual number of strong individuals and stronger leaders that clearly understand the mission, are adept at conducting tactical appreciations, can formulate and present a sound and workable plan, and, of course, perform in the arena as well. Men like Mike Odle and Rick Massa from Los Angeles, (California) PD SWAT; Todd Taylor from Des Moines, (Iowa) PD SWAT; Ver Dayrit from San Diego, (California) Sheriff's Office SWAT; Mark Davis from Shreveport, (Louisiana) PD SWAT; and my good friend, Bob Taubert, from the FBI's Special Operations and Research Unit are, to name a few, excellent tacticians and true professionals who have performed with consistent distinction. In the police breaching field, Captain Keith Frakes from Maricopa County (Arizona) Sheriff's Office Bomb is, in my view, one of the most competent breachers in U.S. law enforcement today and a leading proponent in the art.

Commander Stu Blackton from the Orange County (Florida) Bomb Squad is another officer who is pushing himself to be the best he possibly can in a skill that requires nothing but total dedication and commitment. There are many other fine operators in this country who put their lives on the line on a daily basis and constantly push themselves to the limit so that they perform these critical tasks for their respective teams on demand. All these men are consummate practitioners in the law enforcement special operations field.

Sierra Leone

Duke's Story

Escaping A Coup in West Africa

After working in Papua New Guinea I spent a fortnight in Switzerland with Alan on a T.E.E.S. training module and continued working with him for a couple of months in Memphis, Tennessee. I then returned to my New Zealand home and relaxed with my wife and teenage kids for a spell. The layoff was long overdue and it gave me an opportunity to refocus. It didn't take long to get back into the East Coast groove of hunting, fishing, and socializing — what a life. TeAo was really enjoying the challenges of the new business and, as always, after a respite of a couple of months I needed to get back to the work I knew best — again. By now my reputation was established globally with numerous organizations and companies.

Fred Marafono had contacted me a few years earlier regarding work opportunities abroad. As his surname suggests, he is a Fijian, but definitely not your average man by any means. He is a legend among the SAS fraternity and had been a career soldier in the British army for over 20 years, but was now well integrated into the West African security circuit. Unexpectedly, he rang me up with an offer for employment in Sierra Leone. Fred advised that it would consist of a twelve-month training program involving jungle warfare and close country tactics for a militia force. The wages weren't the best, USD$4500 per month, but a cost of living allowance was additional and there were good indications that the salary would improve when the contract was re-negotiated. Per standard operating procedures (SOP), I checked out the new work zone on the internet prior to leaving. It's always wise to have some idea of the terrain and situation before you commit yourself. Sierra Leone did not look good at all, but the only reason I finally accepted this contract was to establish myself in this new area of operations. The following article did not instil me with much confidence but I desperately wanted to get into the African circuit.

Sierra Leone has 25-percent of the world's known Rutile (titanium ore), massive bauxite deposits, and enough diamonds to support an illicit gem trade amounting to 180,000 carats a year. It also has significant gold, platinum, and oil deposits. However, even with all these natural resources, it is the sixth most impoverished nation on earth. In 1992, a military coup occurred and the country's President Joseph Momoh was replaced by Captain Valentine Strasser. Corporal Alfred Foday Sankoh opposed Strasser and led the Revolutionary United Front (RUF) rebel forces against him. Sankoh was trained by the British as a radio operator in the late 1950's, cashiered, and imprisoned for his part in an attempted coup in 1971. Amnestied in 1980, he fled to Libya where he met up with the Liberian rebel leader, James Taylor, who later established rebel bases in Sierra Leone for his own war against Liberia's President Samuel Doe. The rebel attacks created considerable problems for Strasser's administration. In 1995, "Gurkha Security Guards Limited" arrived to train the Sierra Leone Army. Several weeks later, the American commander and a former British Army sergeant were killed in a rebel ambush. This company fulfilled their contract and were then replaced by Pretoria-based Executive Outcomes (EO). Staffed almost entirely by former South African Special Forces personnel, they had arrived with a respectable reputation gained from operations in Angola against UNITA forces. After two years in the theatre, they did what the Portuguese Army could not do and helped force UNITA to come to terms with the government.

The five years of war that followed in Sierra Leone had been marked by unspeakable atrocities and ritual cannibalism on the part of the RUF, and sheer incompetence and their own share of war crimes on the part of the Sierra Leone Army. The international community pressured Strasser into accepting democratic elections. Strasser was exiled to Ghana, and the final round of elections was held during March, 1996. Ahmed Tejan Kabbah, of the Sierra Leone People's Party, won and promised to negotiate a peace treaty with Sankoh.

Amidst this background of turmoil, I promptly booked the appropriate flights and once more left the "Land of the Long White Cloud" (Aotearoa) as the N.Z. Maori refer to our N.Z. paradise. My commercial airlift to Freetown was one of the longest and most demanding I have ever encountered. I had to fly from Auckland, New Zealand to Los Angeles, then to Amsterdam, and finally Sierra Leone. Without any significant layovers, I was still shattered by the time I arrived at my destination.

The international airport in Freetown was a classic example of things to come. With my civilian kitbag safely slung over a shoulder, one hand on my passport and the other on my wallet. I pushed, shouldered, and scrambled my way through the melee that was supposed to be the airport's security staff on my way to the international customs and immigration desk. Soldiers and members of the Sierra Leone Police Force lounged against the walls, bedecked with weapons as is the custom there, eyeing up the women, frequently hooting with raucous laughter and making loud, ribald comments. Hardly a professional looking crew at all. After paying the inevitable bribes and so on I was processed and moved through to the helicopter departure area. The waiting passengers, mainly wealthy local men and women, stood in small groups and were apparently, completely at ease with the chaos that surrounded them. In contrast were the clusters of Europeans, and I couldn't help wonder what the hell they were doing there. Some of them resembled elderly tourists, while others were obviously missionary and church groups. One thing for sure they were all out of their depth and completely bewildered.

Finally, the pilots and crew of the helicopter ferrying the passengers into the city proper arrived and started the charter flight process. These helicopters were similar to the Russian birds we used in Papua New Guinea and were blue and white Mi 17's. As we clambered aboard it somehow came as no surprise to discover that the crew was Russian. The seating process was on a first come, first serve basis and we all grabbed a space as best we could. Without a ground safety brief or any further communication by the crew, we lifted off for the hotel DZ. The majority of the elderly tourists were suffering from culture shock and by now definitely aware that any trappings of civilization were rapidly disappearing as we clawed our way upward. As we passed over a wide and brown tinted river, I mentally rehearsed my exit plan if this crate went down. Our bags and luggage simply lay in a heap in the middle of the aircraft completely unsecured by any nets or cargo straps. If required, I selected a rapid exit via the helo's open porthole to my rear. As we rumbled through the sky, it got dark so little else could be seen, and I was relieved when we bounced onto the helipad of the Mammy Yoko Hotel. Little did I realize how infamous this place would become in the next few months during the 1999 military coup in Freetown. For whatever reasons, this hotel became the focal point/safe house for large numbers of foreign refugees and the scene of serious rebel fighting. My good mate and fellow worker, Will Scully, distinguished himself during the ferocious rebel assaults against the hotel. Arming himself with a light machine gun liberated from the totally ineffective ECOMOG troops, he managed to keep the rebels at a distance until American naval forces could evacuate them several days later.

Once the rotors closed down it became apparent that the crew had finished flying the aircraft. Just as abruptly, without any formal brief or signal, everyone stood up and disembarked, some of the old timers visibly relieved. In hindsight it would have been more prudent for me to have reboarded that relic of past African wars and gone back home. As I moved toward the gateway, I saw a lean, middle-aged individual waiting near the entrance. Spotting kindred spirits at international airports becomes easier after awhile. When you are involved professionally in the security industry, it seems that the majority of your time is spent lounging around third world airports while either on bodyguard assignments or similar duties. Former Special Forces military men tend to be fairly conspicuous if you know what to look for. Besides being in better shape than most tourists, they usually display a focused awareness or keen interest in people carrying weapons and in the ongoing security activities taking place around them. However, in this instance I was the only European fitting the bill and it was no surprise when he extended his hand and introduced himself, "How's it going, Kiwi, I'm Ray Harris." Without further drama we got into his vehicle, a battered old Mercedes, and drove off to meet Murdo MacLeod, the boss of Cape International. As he negotiated the primitive and rugged city roads through the inky darkness, Ray gave me a somewhat disturbing info brief. It was straight down the line with no bullshit and it prepared me for what was about to come. "The jobs not what it seems Duke, the money is shit, but Murdo is a good guy even though he was a Rupert. He has promised to sort the money out when the contract is renewed. Fred has gone native and definitely not the guy we once knew. As for me, I only have another month in-country and then I'm heading back to South Africa for my couple of weeks off." This was the first and the last time that I received an honest appraisal of Cape International and the situation in Freetown. I appreciated Ray's no-nonsense laconic manner and we became

Soviet-made Hind helicopter in Freetown, Sierra Leone, 1998 [photo by Al J. Venter]

Sierra Leone Army helicopter – up-country, 1998 [photo by Al J. Venter]

good friends, although we did not have much time in-country together.

Murdo MacLeod was an interesting chap. He was a middle aged Scot, still fairly trim and fit in appearance and very much the jolly old officer, but extremely likable and articulate. His enthusiasm was unbelievable and he had more projects and irons in the fire than any other man I knew, perhaps a few too many. As a respected former member of the RAF, he had an impressive background in the Falklands campaign as a Harrier jet pilot and later as a squadron leader. He had obviously moved on to (not necessarily) better things. Ray and Murdo were old friends both having worked for Executive Outcomes for several years. According to Murdo, he helped set up the EO Air Wing in Sierra Leone and became the air logistics administrator during that operation. Fred Marafono had worked with EO and their subsidiary, Branch Energy. Minky, the other member of this small team, was an old mate of mine and we had served in B Squadron in New Zealand for over a decade. However, he was currently up-country at the Yara Bush Camp.

We sat around the Spartan office in Cape House, which was previously the property of EO and home to their aircrews and pilots. Murdo had purchased this huge, two-storied building some months earlier, but somewhere along the line he had been shafted and the building's bare, bleak shell reflected this. The air conditioning worked in parts of the accommodation but standard furnishings were non-existent. A dysfunctional television, with an incompatible video player, sat desolately in the large open and undecorated lounge. A lonely, but welcome, refrigerator stood forlornly by the so-called bar area, but it seldom held any beer of substance other than for a dozen small bottles or cans of the local brew. In defence of the boss, I later discovered first hand no matter how much booze he put in the damn box or stockpiled, it was never enough to relieve the tension and boredom that accumulated while working in this volatile environment. Team members taking a break from up-country would voraciously consume anything that happened to be in there at the time. The kitchen struggled to give any indication of recent use or potential for cooking. Our cook was totally dependent on food supplied by Murdo. Since he usually dined out, frequently on pizza, and could consume more than any man I knew, meals prepared in the kitchen were a rare treat. Gripping one of the stubbie bottles of local, cold beer I slowly unwound and absorbed the atmosphere, or lack of it. Already, the seeds of doubt were germinating in my mind. As Murdo jollied on about how we were going to train the Kamajors, a secret society of warriors, and all the good things that were soon to happen, I distractedly looked around the "Cape Castle" with increasing reservations. Meanwhile, Ray sucked away on his stubbie looking rather resigned. I had a few more of those brief belts, but my mood did not improve so I went to my room to get some needed rest. "No worries, everything will look better in the morning," were my last thoughts as I drifted off to sleep.

The next morning, Ray prepared his kit for a vehicle run to the base camp. I got up and squared myself away, had a quick breakfast of eggs on toast with Murdo and Ray, and then took a casual walk around Cape House and its grounds. This had once been a fantastic residence, but not anymore. Back in the stark second floor "operations room," Murdo and I sat down and he explained the role that Cape International was going to assume over the next 90 days. At this stage, we were only training our local security force at the Yara base camp. Our connection with the government depended on Fred's close friendship and ties with the Minister of Defense, Chief Sam Hinga Norman. By various means, Murdo cultivated a healthy relationship with government officials and people in power, but Chief Norman was the linchpin. Fred later related that he had saved the chief from certain death during the previous war with the rebels and this man was eternally grateful. So there I was. Instead of training government forces in the arts of jungle warfare and close quarter battle, I was part of a damn Mine Exploration program training a primitive security force with bloody home-made shotguns and bush knives. Brilliant!

Ray returned that afternoon and I prepared to depart the next morning for Indian Country, six hours North of Freetown. Vehicle travel was risky even during daylight hours because of sporadic RUF actions in the area. Although many of the ambushes and acts of indiscriminate banditry and mayhem where carried out by the rebels, frequently drunken and maverick soldiers carried out atrocities on their own. At night, any overland travel beyond the city was definitely not encouraged. Shot up and burned out vehicles discarded along the roadsides bore mute testimony to the perils of travel in this volatile country. That night, Ray and I sat around drinking the odd beer while he continued to explain his appreciation of the present situation. Although Ray may have been pissed off about the inactivity, poor wages, and lengthy delay in setting up the training, he was extremely professional and remained loyal to the enterprise.

Solly, our driver, was a small native and, as with all the locals, ferociously loyal to Fred. I just hoped he had his driving act squared away for the coming "stagecoach ride" through the badlands. Our fate was clearly in his hands. As we got into the Mercedes, Ray added to my anxiety with his rather casual but cautionary remark that I need to keep my weapons hidden because we were not legally permitted to carry firearms in this shoot first, ask questions later country.

The previous evening, Murdo generously handed me an old Chinese AK47 with a folding stock. I stripped and cleaned the weapon, its magazines, and checked the ammo. I wanted to test fire the oriental "Klatch," but the urban situation hardly permitted such a check, and, furthermore, we were supposed to be a "low profile operation." With this latest revelation, I was not only plagued by mixed emotions, I was fuming. No contract, no confirmation of wages and allowances, a totally misleading job description, and Murdo's arming me with a firearm and not warning me about the legalities really pissed me off. I didn't fancy spending time in a local prison over possession of a worn out assault rifle that I was not even sure worked. Although it looked like I had been really sucked in, I hadn't travelled half way round the world to flick it at this early stage. I wanted to withhold my final decision until I had checked out the operational situation up country.

The vehicle dodged through the maze of heavily congested, litter-infested streets and eventually merged with the highway. The grand but decaying old colonial buildings hinted at what must have, at one time, been an impressive city. As expected, the highway was intermittently landscaped with the evidence of previous violent confrontations. Burned out hulks of derelict cars, trucks, and buses periodically punctuated the relatively pristine surroundings on both sides of the highway. Our travel was also frequently interrupted by a series of military roadblocks and police checkpoints. At these stops, the police and military often extorted payments in the form of "tolls" from passengers and drivers as a convenient and easy way of lining their pockets. Solly did all the talking, and for this first trip I was purported to be a South African doctor on his way to take care of the sick folks in Camp Yara. At Makeni, which was our link up point with any personnel returning to Freetown, we grabbed a coke and Solly took me over to the "half way house" where I could pick up a bowl of local stew. Sated, we travelled for another hour on the highway until we left that pot holed and debris-laden route, only to be assaulted by an even more treacherous dirt track. We belted along in the old Mercedes on tracks much more suited to four wheel drive vehicles. Alongside this torturous route scattered African villages punctuated the roadside. Rampant poverty was obvious, but it appeared that life in the rural areas was a hell of a lot better than in the city's cesspools. These people were surviving with their agricultural skills and simple lifestyles that enabled them to hold on to some dignity.

My driver seemed determined to break the Sierra Leone land speed record but his driving skills left much to be desired and on a number of occasions the thought of bailing out uppermost in my mind. After considerable gut wrenching and jolting while winding and climbing through the hill country, we negotiated a sharp corner and just as suddenly, Yara Camp finally confronted us.

A quick survey told me this was a security operator's nightmare. Through the clouds of dust our vehicle had generated, a familiar robust figure strolled towards us. Old Minky quickly thrust his mitt out and we clasped hands with genuine feeling. We first met on SAS Selection in the early 1980's, but, unfortunately for him, he was a candidate and I was a member of the staff. Needless to say it was great to see him again. Minky was a cousin of TeAo's and a good old Ngati Porou lad from way back. I stood there smiling at his new image. There he was, 5-foot, 10-inches, and 16 stone of thickset Polynesian muscle, but now sporting a Spanish lip goatee and a hairstyle from hell. Not one to be easily fazed, he carried on as if nothing was out of the ordinary. "How's it going mate," was his typical Kiwi greeting. "Fred's stuck on his back in the basha with a stuffed foot. He will give you a brief, Okey! I will catch up with you when I come back in a couple of days. Until then, see ya!"

With that laconic reunion, Minky tossed his gear and weapon into the back seat and climbed into the old Mercedes. Solly, apparently impatient so they could beat last light and the increased threats that accompanied it, was already at the wheel and gunning the engine. They roared off to Freetown and quickly disappeared in our constant companion — a cloud of choking dust.

Limping heavily on a grotesquely swollen ankle, Fred Marafono hobbled out of his basha, employing a large hand-carved staff as a third leg. Another typical Pacific Islander, he exhibited an unruly mop of hair, huge grin, and thickset physique. I tried to imagine what the locals thought

Duke and Minky at Camp Yara, Sierra Leone – 1998

when Fred and Minky did the rounds. They were bloody big guys. Fred placed great store in handshakes, and it was almost a ritual with him. We adjourned to a thatched roof dwelling, sat down, and had the traditional cup of Commonwealth tea.

Fred is extremely proud of his native heritage, but he is also staunchly British and a Royalist to boot. This alone made him a unique individual, and it was a pleasure to meet him. Although we had never served together, we had a wealth of mutual friends and acquaintances. I spent the next hour sitting and listening to Fred's stories and travels and one thing couldn't be denied, he had been there and back again. Fred's ankle was giving him hell, and about the only thing he could for it was return to his cot and rest it. I entertained myself by taking a second and more detailed tour of my surroundings and further evaluated the situation.

Yara Camp was an exploration base for The Wesley Mining Company and employed an African work force of one hundred, four British citizens, and a fifty-man guard force. The British team consisted of two geologists and a father and son mechanic and handy man combination. The mining side of the project was doing well and the geologists were confident that a promising opportunity was about to materialize for a successful mining operation.

Neil Walker was the owner of the company and mine site, and although a tough taskmaster, he was scrupulously honest with his workers.

Having started his profession as a worker on the mine face many years earlier and being steadily promoted to his present status gave an indication of his leadership and intellectual abilities. Although his rugby days were well behind him, he was no mug. When I met him some weeks later it was obvious that Neil was not a man to monkey with.

A flimsy, 12-foot-high wooden palisade perimeter fence ringed most of the compound and camp area. At the time, all the buildings were constructed of local materials and consisted of thatched roofs, rattan woven walls, and dirt floors. These dwellings were extremely basic, perfectly adequate in the dry season but a total disaster in the wet, as we would soon find out.

A security force of local tribesmen manned the main gate and they looked rather formidable with their homemade shotguns and company uniforms. Obviously, they wouldn't stand a dog's chance against the RUF with their AK's and heavier weapons, but they didn't seem overly concerned. This whole security situation was more than a little shaky and my sense of doom became even heavier.

The vehicle pits and mechanic's work area contained five steel CONEX containers, which had been modified into workshops and storage lockers. Guard posts were manned day and night but primarily served to mitigate theft and vandalism. In reality, even if our position was tenable we could not defend it against a determined attack. The boy's hearts might be there, but lack of expertise and equipment was too much to overcome at this juncture. However, it was the training team's task to change this and I was willing to give it an honest shot.

Ray, Minky, Fred, and I oversaw the security of the camp, which required two of us on site for a three week deployment. One of the crew performed mobile and radio watch duties in Freetown while the fourth member took R&R. After my first rotation back in Freetown, I remained up-country most of the time, preferring the rustic atmosphere of the bush camp to sitting in the bleak surroundings of Cape House while on radio watch.

Neil Walker was a hulking individual in his late 50's. He was blunt, but forthright, and his knowledge of local affairs was significant. He was officially deemed to be a Paramount Chief in the area, which was no mean feat considering that he was European and born and bred in Cornwall, England. However, to the native population that did not matter and they treated him like he was a God. Neil's in-country manager was Matt Needham. Matt was not an easy guy to get along with, but as a former policeman he was well versed in the ways and intricacies of the country. He was married to a local Fula (woman) and they had several adult children residing in the UK. Matt cruised around the area in an old Range Rover, wearing safari suits, and carrying a concealed 9mm Browning pistol. He looked like the proverbial

Colonial in all his glory. In his own way, he proved to be interesting and when the mood struck him, which wasn't often, good company. Unfortunately, it appeared that everyone else had experienced a falling out with him, and he had few friends. I got on fairly well with him, but like everyone else, when he appeared on site we all took cover.

Upon completion of his initial six-month tour in country, Ray returned to South Africa for a four week respite. Minky was also due to depart for his vacation within the next couple of weeks and, like Ray, was frustrated and burned out after spending 180 days in Sierra Leone. Fred had a mission in life, which seemed to be a sincere desire to help the poor and needy of the region, and he did this by using the company "float," or escape funds. We had no doubt that Fred was a humanitarian, but the problem was that working with him was almost impossible because of his hidden agendas. Serious problems were developing within our small team and it was becoming noticeable to the exploration group. After several meetings in Freetown, Fred returned with the news that I had been tasked as the new team leader, and I was not surprised. Fred and Matt Needham were not on good terms, and Minky, who was scheduled to depart shortly, was too confrontational for Matt. Ray was on leave, but it was obvious to everyone except Murdo that he was not coming back, so that only left me, so I was promoted by default. Murdo could have solved many of these problems with an occasional over-night visit to the bush camp. He would have experienced first hand the problems plaguing the group, but while I was there he stayed well away from Yara. Morale was the team's number one problem; Ray, Minky, and I had certainly not joined Cape to work as mine security.

Old Murdo would have been incapable of operating or living under the conditions we were experiencing. The rainy season destroyed our thatched dwellings on a daily basis and habitually soaked our bedding and what few possessions we had with us. Everything stayed wet because there was insufficient sunshine to dry and air our soaking bedding and blankets. After only a week into the rainy season, the musty damp odour of wet bedding and clothing became a permanent feature of our basha life. The only positive aspect of all this water was the sudden absence of snakes and scorpions from the thatched roofs. During the dry season, we had to rely on our mossie nets to divert the vermin's free fall as they dropped onto our cots in the dark. There is nothing like the dreaded anticipation of a nocturnal visit from a poisonous snake or insect to disrupt sound sleep patterns.

The food at Yara was atrocious. Our local cook fried everything in gallons of palm oil. The taste certainly appeals to the African tribesmen but we expat guys found it almost unpalatable, unfortunately there was no option other than pineapples and mangoes, the all-fruit diet.

Dennis, Ray, and Fred had all contracted malaria during their time in-country and suffered accordingly. During my second month I succumbed to a nasty cocktail of three different types of diarrhoea; life could be damn uncomfortable in Yara, weight loss was guaranteed.

During this period of declining health, Neil happened to mention the wages and shares package he had negotiated with his British exploration site workers and related that they were not that thrilled with the deal. When I learned what the package was, I was damn envious of it and said so in no uncertain terms. Neil inquired as to what sort of money we were receiving and he was not amused to find out. When Neil, Murdo, and Fred negotiated the original contract, Murdo advised Neil that the salary for the men he required was to be USD$10,000 per man, per month, minimum. It appeared that half our wages were being skimmed off the top and added to the contract fee Neil paid to Cape International as the security company. Neil was deeply troubled by this and when back in Freetown he confronted both Murdo and Fred about the situation. He told me it was none of his business to question our wage status, but he simply wanted to advise Cape International that he was aware of their profit margin and would not be part of the deception. We found out that Wesley Mining was not responsible for our skimpy wages, no medical insurance, and meager benefits being paid to us. We were being completely conned and the shit was about to hit the fan. Somehow, Minky was blamed for the leak and he returned to Yara pissing blood. Upon my return to Freetown, I fronted up to Murdo and took full responsibility for the backlash from Neil. Murdo was obviously disappointed and harped on the old adage about loyalty to the company and so forth. That night I made my final decision — I was no longer interested or sufficiently motivated to continue employment with Cape International. The next morning I advised Murdo of my intentions and gave him a month's notice to find a replacement. He was probably relieved to get rid of me.

The RUF had notched its activities up a cog and a United Nations mobile patrol was ambushed on the highway between Makeni and Freetown. Murdo sent daily situation reports regarding rebel activities in our area of concern. The increased rebel activity along with disturbing reports of the possibility of a significant attack occurring against the mine site was enough to convince the expats in the mining team that Mother England was beckoning them. The next morning they pulled the pin and demanded to be evacuated from the camp and returned to Freetown. Exploration nevertheless continued and the workers "protected" by our security force remained in place.

Murdo called and advised that a replacement for Ray was on his way from the U.K. And so, Will Scully joined Cape International. I levelled with Murdo and told him Will was a tough, no nonsense Londoner, a hard man, pretty much a thug. We had worked together in 1984 at the Hereford SAS base during a six-month military exchange. Even though I described him in harsh terms, I considered Will a friend, but more importantly I regarded him as an extremely capable individual and he would certainly demonstrate this during the troubled times that lay ahead. When Will finally arrived at Yara, he smiled, extended his hand and said, "So I'm a thug, am I, Kiwi?" Good one, Murdo. We both laughed and then got down to business.

For the next couple of days, Will acted as Fred's chauffeur for the monthly cattle auction. Fred had managed to do some serious damage to one of the mining companies vehicles, so this gave Matt Needham the opportunity to bar Fred from driving. Fred had a legitimate need to get out there and see his people, but the rest of us did not share his zeal and hated driving the back roads all over country. Unnecessary travel on the bone-shaking roads was reason enough to stay well clear of them, and the constant threat from Sankoh's boys augmented that wisdom. After a whirlwind tour of the area, Will was convinced that Fred's reasons for being in West Africa were not the same as his, so he too decided to leave the country.

Murdo listened to Will's comments and was uncomfortable with the suggestions he made. At the completion of Will's recommendations Murdo dropped a bombshell, although it was coming a little late for me. Cape International was finally going to train the Kamajors to assist military forces in the ongoing conflict against RUF. He had also received written permission for us to carry firearms. This was a significant change, and along with Will's suggestions, Murdo finally agreed, in principal, to rectify some of the conditions of service.

A week earlier, the RUF had been practicing their particular brand of terrorism on the terrified inhabitants of a village close to Kondembia. This was only fifteen miles from our base camp and gave us some cause for concern. Up until now we had been fortunate, and other than for armed individuals being sporadically sighted around the local diamond digs, no open threats had been received by our organization. These gunmen were more likely military personnel checking out the diamond dig's potential for their military commanders. The military was loath to leave the safety and relative luxury of the larger townships, and routine patrolling was nonexistent, unless it could be performed from the back of a vehicle. These were road-bound warriors and no wonder they were losing the war.

During the morning, our radio came to life and Minky reported that heavy explosions and sporadic small arms fire had been rocking Freetown since dawn. Except for the cook, house boy and a local maiden, he was alone and without back up. He was in a predicament and could not hole up for long; as always, there were never any extra supplies of canned food, bottled water, or other edibles at Cape House. However, in his favour, he knew his way around the back streets and alleys of Freetown better than most. Solly and the houseboys were there with him and the property was about 600 meters from the British Embassy, on Spur Road. Therefore, at this stage, we thought there was no real cause for immediate concern. I advised him to hang in there and give us an update in two hours. How wrong we were.

One of our security force members came bounding over to the radio shack holding aloft his tiny transistor radio, complete with electrical tape binding it together. This dilapidated piece of plastic and wires gave us some mind - boggling news. The good old BBC commentator gave us the ultimate kick in the groin by announcing that a military coup had occurred in the West African capital city of Freetown. In addition to blasting their way into the city, the mutineers released all the prisoners in the Pandema Road Prison complex, which included a number of military personnel awaiting trial for previous coup attempts. President Kabbah had escaped to Guinea, and one Corporal Gborie became the initial spokesman for the coup leaders. Major Johnny Paul Koroma eventually identified himself as being the coup leader. They cleaned out the treasury, robbed the banks, and spread mayhem in earnest. The released prisoners were given weapons and uniforms and became part of the new army. Koroma called upon the RUF to join his coup and help oust the Kabbah regime. This time the looting and pillaging was not limited to government buildings and institutions. The few shopping areas were next and then the rich, mainly Lebanese, civilian estates were targeted; unfortunately, Cape House was also on the hit list. The law of the gun prevailed.

Life became amazingly simple for me. Returning to Freetown was out of the question and I looked at Bill and we both burst out laughing. What a fucken joke. Here I was, a short-timer with only six days left in this rat hole, and now there's a friggen coup. Luckily, for some unfathomable reason I had kept my passport and airline tickets with me. This proved to be a good move. During the rest of the day we tried in vain to re-establish radio contact with Freetown and we hoped that Minky had made it out of there. Will and I discussed and reviewed our contingency plans. Our crisis response plans had been developed with having a friendly military and police force in mind.

With our ties to Chief Norman, who was not only the Minister of Defense but also the head of the Kamajor Warrior society, we had been lulled into a false sense of security. Now we had to completely rethink our plans and, just as importantly, remain in control at Yara, protecting our client's personnel and assets. Any animosity or ill feeling towards Murdo and the contract was immediately forgotten. We were really going to earn our next months pay. We quickly regained our focus and were determined to do the right thing. This was more to protect our own credibility as much as for anything else.

I gave our guards a quick brief on the situation. Before I had spoken to them the "jungle drum" rumours were already rocketing around the campsite and neighbouring village. Small groups of workers were clustered around the vehicle bay and became quite vocal regarding what they wanted us to do. Poor bastards, they were 200 miles from Freetown and their families with little chance of getting back to assist and check on the welfare of loved ones. Tiny transistor radios exacerbated the situation by describing in graphic terms the terrorizing of helpless civilians, lawlessness, and general mayhem in Freetown. The likelihood of anyone coming to liberate Yara Camp was nil.

That night we maintained a close eye on our security force. Understandably, for once, sleeping on duty was not part of their routine. In the quiet darkness afforded us, I looked around the compound and at the moonlit and serene surrounding country beyond our fence line. It was difficult to imagine for a moment that I was in the same country as the one now in total chaos that was being shown on the world's television screens.

Several hours earlier, Will and I completed a map study. The geologist's mining maps were barely adequate but at least gave us an indication of potential vehicle escape routes and cross-country movement by foot. To the best of my knowledge or recollection we were 100 kilometres as the crow flies from the Guinea border. The problem with the vehicle routes was that the military and police controlled them. We had no idea if the coup was supported country-wide or was limited to Freetown and its surrounding area. Bill and I alternated on stag throughout the night and we must have been the only ones that slept, because on my shift the workers and guards were all very much awake. The adjacent village was eerily silent for the first time in several months and the small fires flickering in front of most of the dwellings indicated they too were apprehensive. They had every reason to be afraid because their future and survival was in the hands of Freetown and its killer clowns.

The next morning we convinced the shift bosses that the coup was bound to blow over in the next couple of days and they should all get back out to the work areas and continue with the project. With considerable reluctance, they and their men mounted their vehicles and moved out to the various digging sites. About mid-morning, Fred established communications with us. He sounded deeply subdued and his message was confusing and lacked any significant content. He advised that Minky had survived a violent visit by armed coup members and although Cape House had been compromised, Minky had managed to escape and evade. Before I was able to cover some pertinent issues, Fred abruptly terminated his transmission. This latest message, from God knows where, was totally alien to Fred's communications technique. Was Fred being forced to contact us by members of the coup to confirm our presence? We had to seriously consider that Fred might have been captured and compromised, or possibly that he was transmitting from a hostile environment and unable to converse freely. A year later, I learned that Fred had in fact transmitted from Lifeguard's base station at Kono. Lifeguard had taken over Executive Outcomes security functions after the peace accord with the RUF had taken place. Some members of Lifeguard remained in-countryduring the duration of the coup and helped provide on site intelligence to outside agencies. However, this restrained contact and other factors indicated that our position at Yara was becoming more dangerous each day. We felt that it was only a matter of time before the rebels came hunting for us.

Whenever we required a telephone link-up while stationed at Yara, we had to travel two hours to Makeni. At this point this was not a viable option. Will and I decided to chance driving to the outskirts of Kabala to use the telephone at the Catholic mission. The French priest was extremely helpful, but the mission did not have a telephone and he was unable to shed much light on the current situation. Furthermore, he was not unduly concerned with the current problem and with a mere shrug of his shoulders dismissed the coup as being a Freetown issue.

The Sierra Leone Army had a substantial military force stationed in Kabala and it was not in our interest to meet up with them, until we were sure of their current allegiance. However, before returning to the mine site we stopped at the Paramount Chiefs residence in Kondembia. He was in the unique position of having lived in the United States for several years while his Father was on the throne. Upon his father's passing, he returned and became chief. However, he was an absolute failure and whenever I visited him he was usually stoned on the local ganja while sitting with his cronies in a state of bliss and completely unaware of the issues and responsibilities his position demanded. This day was no different, but had the mutineers entered his village I can guarantee you that he would have quickly sobered up. The Sierra Leone head sorcerer was also present, resplendent in his tribal attire and showing off his brand new Sport Utility Vehicle, courtesy of Wesley Mining. He was a gentleman of incredible nationwide prestige and power. Neil Walker had introduced us during one of his visits and I had accompanied both of them into the backcountry while he performed some magical activities on behalf of mining interests. Disgusted with the Paramount Chief's apparent disregard for the current situation, I had a quick talk with the head sorcerer. He confirmed that Freetown was in chaos, but the Kabala and Makeni areas on its outskirts appeared to be quiet, but that would not last long.

Back at our base, Will and I had our last brew together. He decided that he would attempt to reach the British High Commission in Freetown by vehicle. We had recently hired a former Sierra Leone soldier and he was keen to assist with the driving duties. However, he may well have been just as keen to get in on some of the action that his old military mates were enjoying. With this possibility burdening Will's mind, the vehicle was gassed up with fuel and water, while he loaded up some essentials and his weapon with a few hundred rounds of ammo. There was no need for any big farewells or good luck, because we were both well aware of the difficulties we faced. With a quick exchange of grins and a brief handshake that said it all, we parted company.

We were two independent operators focusing on the ultimate challenge — survival. Even though neither of us would have left the other in the lurch, we both concluded that we would have a better chance for success by implementing our own escape plans. I was determined that RUF boys were going to earn their money if they wanted my scalp, and my sense of doom and gloom that had been lurking in the background suddenly disappeared.

I ensured that I had as many plastic bottles of distilled water as I could fit into my small backpack, along with my antibiotics, mosquito repellent, and Silva compass. I foraged through the junk trunk and grabbed some shell wound dressings and a couple of M26 fragmentation grenades. The escape funds had vanished courtesy of Fred's largess, but all was not lost. I had drawn USD $300 from my last month's wages to sustain me over my long flight home; unfortunately it was in $100 bills. I kept $200 with my credit cards in a small billfold in my side pocket and secreted the third century note into my pack.

I re-studied the geologist's maps and confirmed that my vehicle and foot options still had their merits. Since the galloping diarrhoea had seriously weakened me, the forced march option looked less attractive. It was approximately 100 kilometers (60 miles) to the Guinea border. Once at the border, it was a further 500 kilometers (300 miles) to Conakry, the capital of Guinea, and safety. The North Eastern route I would have to take was typically West African and varied from undulating rolling hill country to the steeper hills of the Loma Mountain ranges. Vegetation varied from lush jungle to thinly covered bush country, which would afford some concealment. This appeared to be the safer of the two options because it would be extremely difficult to evade the military garrisons at Makeni and Pendembu. Furthermore, my diminished ability to do a runner from a compromised Land Rover had to be taken into consideration. My confidence in my bush skills was high, and if I was not being pressured by a hot pursuit, I could tab through the area by pacing myself based on my physical condition. I approached one of the local security team leaders. He was an incorrigible individual, but the most respected hunter in the area. Simbu, a true bushman, was a lean, muscular, and leathery individual, 30 to 45 years of age. Hunting was his true love, closely followed by his thirst for the amber fluid. Simbu and I had a fairly good relationship, although I had to give him the hard word on a couple of occasions for being late and drinking prior to his shift. Nevertheless, he was a good man and an excellent bushman. When I gave him a warning order and told him to make sure he had his swag packed and to stand by for a run to the border, he was overjoyed and managed to leave the bottle alone that night, which was a considerable feat for him. I did not reveal my intentions to the rest of the mine workforce, as they were becoming increasingly anxious, particularly when Will departed.

That night, I thought about TeAo and the kids very briefly, then just as quickly turned my attention to more pressing matters. I needed a clear head and total focus for the next phase of my plan. I hoped Murdo had done the right thing and kept TeAo apprised of the situation. I slowly rehydrated my system and mentally prepared myself for the next day. I catnapped through the night under the twisted tree near our cook-house, using my backpack as a pillow. Periodically, I would rouse myself, and with my backpack, belt order, and AK in hand, check the camp and the perimeter. Good. It looked like the guards were still keeping the flag flying.

Minky's racing rooster shattered the stillness of the morning for the last time for me. This little feathered fucker had been a pain in the arse ever since I had been here. As he was stretching to his full height and leaning forward to scream his second phase annoying squawk, I took his head off with a well aimed swing of Fred's wooden staff. Simbu and the boys were ecstatic and he quickly became part of an African breakfast.

Sometime around mid morning, the sound of Will's voice materialized over the camp's radio net. He had successfully gotten through to Freetown, but Cape House had been over run and trashed by Army lads from the nearby military barracks on Spur Drive. Minky was alive and well, but there was no sign of Fred. However, the old rascal seemed to thrive in these conditions, so no news was good news as far he was concerned. After I confirmed that things were still okay at my end and the camp site, we agreed to rendezvous on the radio at 4:00 pm.

I grabbed my new shadow, and Simbu and I made a vehicle run to Kondembia to check on one of our road crews. On the way, I decided to visit the chief again and see if he, or his head shed, had heard or seen anything of interest. Barrelling along the dirt road towards us was the head sorcerer in his gleaming machine. He stopped and waved over Simbu. After a quick exchange of words we resumed our journey, but five minutes later, as we approached the last corner before reaching the village, Simbu hit me with the sorcerers message. "Mr. Dook, don't go right into the village because the soldiers are there." Simbu's head and upper body jack knifed violently when I locked up the brakes and came to a swerving halt. As quickly as I could, I wrestled the antiquated machine around and raced back towards camp. My mind was going sixty to the dozen, but right then and there a decision had been made for me. It was immaterial to me whether the soldiers were there to plunder the local villages, or were on their way to Yara to give us a kick in the guts. I didn't give a fat rat's ass. I was fucken out of there. The vehicle E and E was definitely out, so it boiled down to "head down, arse up" and tabbing to the rendezvous point just like the old days. We raced past the camp gates and travelled several miles until the road ended. Leaving the keys in the vehicle and without a backward glance, Simbu and I started to stroll out of there. It was 2:00 pm on Wednesday 25, 1997.

Simbu was aware of my recent bout of diarrhoea and nursed the pace a bit for the first hour. The first leg was a steady climb on a non-descript animal track and the foliage was adequate to protect us from observation from ground forces. However, we would be in trouble if they had a helicopter looking for us. I drank sparingly, but frequently, and had an adrenaline buzz going that lasted for four days. I was excited but in control. Besides being a raw survival situation, my competitive juices were flowing and this was literally a contest between the bad guys and me, the hunters versus the hunted. As we passed over the first major terrain feature, I looked back at Yara now receding in the distance. I had anticipated that when the military reached the camp that all the goodies there would keep them occupied at least until late afternoon. We continued maintaining a steady pace but ratcheted it down a bit because I appreciated the fact it was going to take me three or four days to get to Guinea. While speed can be a form of security, it can make you careless and lead to mistakes. I was 47 and my left knee had been under the surgeon's knife twice, so I had to pace myself and stay alert. If I twisted a knee or suffered a sprained ankle I would have to lie up for awhile and that could prove fatal. As the afternoon wore on, my rhythm returned and although I was sucking wind on the hills, the knees and legs felt good. In contrast, Simbu wasn't even breaking a sweat. He advised me that the military did not routinely patrol these areas and since this was still part of his hunting domain, I was comfortable with that information. From my earliest military training and Vietnam days, the rules were simple — keep off roads and track systems, and avoid using ridge lines and creek beds as foot routes. But I also knew that I had only enough water to last for four days. Compromises had to be made. Simbu took point with his home-made shotgun and we maintained about a fifteen-meter interval. Automatically, we would drop into patrolling mode when we were in the vicinity of bush villages. When we approached a group of huts, we would sit back and observe for twenty minutes or so and then Simbu would stroll in and check it out. At dusk, he advised me that we were about an hour away from an American missionary family. Now we were moving on a four-wheel-drive vehicle track and, sure as shit, we not only came upon a group of native homes, but also a more substantial Western-styled dwelling located among them. Simbu had a cousin who lived in this area and, fortunately, she knew of the missionary and his wife. As Simbu knocked on the front door, I remained secreted in the shadows, AK at the ready. I was a mess and my black T-shirt and light tan fatigues were filthy and dripping wet. When the lady of the house appeared at the door, I approached her and explained who I was and where I had come from. Apparently unconcerned over my dishevelled and filthy appearance, she smiled and graciously extended her hand in greeting. I was completely taken aback and stammered some reply. Unexpectedly, she was an attractive woman and I was somewhat unsettled for a minute or two. Hardly what one would expect a missionary's wife to look like, especially in the middle of the African wilds. She was incredible, and without hesitation invited Simbu and me inside to meet her husband.

I stepped through the doorway and a young boy of 10 or 11 was sitting in an easy chair reading a novel. A pretty teenage girl was sitting at the table with her father, who was the minister. He was about my age and his whiskered jaw dropped open in amazement when he saw this filthy apparition coming through his living room holding an assault rifle. Suddenly, I became very conscious of my weapon, but at that moment, I did not know what to do with it. "Come in, come in," he stammered and immediately followed with, "Have you eaten?" "Please, please sit down," and he motioned over to a table and chairs. Americans can be among the most hospitable and open-hearted people in the world, and these people were no different. My evening with them was the best night I had had in the last three months. After showering and changing into clean clothes, I had a cup of coffee loaded with sugar and a couple of pieces of pineapple. I had absolutely no appetite, but had an abnormal craving for coke and other sweet soft drinks. They were a remarkable family and I hope that they were able to get out to safety, if that became necessary. They told me about a previous escape that they made from the country during an earlier coup. However, they were quite nonchalant and appeared unconcerned about the one that was spreading from Freetown. Their calmness made me feel a bit foolish when I thought about my assault rifle and hand grenades. Paranoia keeps you alive in this business, so before getting my head down, I made sure that my gear was all packed, the door locked, and I had familiarized myself with the window catches. If required, I could be out of there pretty damn quick.

I slept fairly well but kept waking every couple of hours. I would lie there motionless, listening intently for any change in the pattern of noisy African insect life outside my window. Then, almost as quickly, I would drift off to sleep again. Simbu was curled up in the other bed and he never moved. Talk about the sleep of the innocent. I had to shake him awake at 5:00 am. I reluctantly removed my dry clothing and slid back into my stinking, clammy, and now cold gear from the day before. In the kitchen, the good minister and his wife sat with us completely oblivious to our bush aroma and scruffy clothing. It seemed that nothing could faze them. We were offered an entire breakfast menu, but I wasn't hungry, so I sat back and watched Simbu demolish a couple of fried eggs and a dollop of baked beans. After I had a huge mug of coffee and plain piece of bread, we bid our farewells to the family. The minister kindly drove us to the end of the four-wheel track. Here we shook hands and our trek continued. However, I was not totally convinced that they were as safe as they seemed to think.

Our staying in their home for the night was extremely beneficial, but I was much happier back on my feet and in the scrub again. We were almost out of Simbu's hunting domain and now would have to rely on his ability to meet and contact relations and friends for directions and information on the bad guys. I was not only concerned about the obvious threat from the coup forces and police, but also from any RUF groups that might be around. My guides prowess and reputation as a hunter was widespread and wherever we went people heard of him, or knew someone else who had. We climbed through the lush vegetation of the hill country. A reasonably thick canopy of trees shielded us from the sun. The area was starkly different from the arid, harsh plains and undulating country we had to negotiate near the mine site. I slowly increased the pace and carefully tested my dodgy knee. It was holding up quite well. Simbu ambled on with his effortless bush gait and was absolutely tireless. If it was possible, we skirted the villages, but frequently Simbu would go in and check it out before I made my presence known. I had refilled my water bottles at the American's home and was confident that as long as my water supply lasted, my chances of survival were excellent. Local water was off limits because the return of the trots was my biggest fear. Late in the afternoon we found ourselves on the outskirts of a fairly significant village. The day had been fairly demanding and my energy levels were starting to ebb, so I moved into a patch of low scrub and lay down to observe and cover my hunter's recce of the camp. He was gone for at least an hour, and when he came back he was reeking of the local brew. I was not unduly perturbed because his rules and lifestyle were totally foreign to mine, and vice-versa. I had to trust his judgement, and, in reality, my safety was in his hands. At the Guinea border, I planned to give him my assault rifle, six 30-round magazines, plus 100 additional rounds, and two fragmentation grenades. For him, this would be a treasure trove of wealth and status. It could also get him in serious strife with the government and rebel forces. He watched me with fascination when I demonstrated firing techniques to the camp's mining guards and was well aware of my capabilities with firearms. Simbu had been keen to check out my assault rifle and I had given him every opportunity to do so. It's always a sound practice to let the lads see your abilities with the weapon systems in use. Not only does it set the standard and give them confidence in the operator's overall knowledge and skills, it also serve as a warning to the criminal element that you maybe too tough to tangle with.

Completely relaxed, Simbu squatted down next to me and whispered, "We should mebbe stay here tonight, Mr. Dook, tomorrow we have a long walk, but we can get to the border." That was good news to me. Periodically, I had been taking a quick fix with my compass and was satisfied that my navigation was accurate. I was getting knackered and although I did not have any intolerable aches, pains, or even blisters, I was very tired and lacked energy. Carefully, we moved closer to the village until we could see the outlines of an old shelter of some sort ten meters to our immediate front. It was well away from the main buildings and track systems, and adults could be heard talking with the chatter of small children mixed in. Simbu had met with some old hunting cronies and wanted to engage in a catch-up session with the boys over a few jugs of the local spirits. Resignedly, I sat down with my pack still on, and in a state of mild anxiety, awaited his return. I would give him an hour and then I would move out. I was both relieved and grateful when he came back with a couple of pineapples and a beaming smile. We ate the food and I prepared to wait for morning. Simbu excused himself and caught up with his mates. Alone, I sat on stag, dozing off in fits and starts, but unable to totally relax or lie down. Some hours later my faithful companion returned, stretched out on the deck, and was asleep in minutes. Using a twisted tree trunk root as a pillow, I settled in for the night. Abruptly, I awoke. Something was very wrong. Without moving myself, I sensed some movement to my immediate left. Straining my eyeballs almost out of their sockets, I couldn't fucken believe it. On my left, a shadowy figure of a man moved on his hands and knees within arms reach of me. He was quietly going through my pack. I am left-handed, so consequently my weapon was lying on the ground by my left hand. I was powerless and Simbu, supposedly covering that side, was in dreamland and no damn help at all. I had to do something and I had to do it fast. My right hand touched a hard, cylindrical object by my thigh. I now had a weapon. I slowly established a good grip on it and I violently rolled towards the threat and laid it hard on the side of his head. It sounded like a rifle shot when I cracked his skull. With a muffled grunt, he collapsed and ceased all movement. Crouching on my knees with my AK in hand, I searched the immediate area. There was absolute silence. I quickly put on my backpack and dragged the body into the undergrowth. If this turkey woke up in the morning he would have one hell of a headache, but the way he went down indicated to me that he was past all that. I quickly moved over to Simbu and shoved him a damn sight harder than necessary, I was real pissed off and told him it was time to go. He finally staggered to his feet and we moved silently through the village. My pulse was racing like a jackhammer and I was experiencing an adrenaline rush. Obviously, I wanted to put as much distance as quickly as possible between the village and us. I hadn't told Simbu about our midnight visitor. Hell, it might have been one of his drinking buddies.

After several hours of tabbing, the early morning daylight filtered in and we took a welcome breather. As things quieted down I heard a distant mechanical sound waft our way. It was the noise of a motorcycle and it was heading in our direction. About five minutes later, the bike rider appeared around the dusty track. Simbu stepped out of the scrub cover, flagged him down, and started plan B, the hiring of transport for our next part of our escape. It was my intention to rent a couple of bikes to quickly penetrate the border areas and transport me to Conakry. Guinea had once been under French rule and, consequently, that language was still spoken. Unless you were able to communicate in French, or in one of the numerous local African dialects, the passage through the next 500 kilometers to Conakry would be difficult. However, Simbu had convinced me that he was the man to assist in this department. I covered the motorcyclist from my position. The motorcyclist dragged his machine around, and with a wave to Simbu, took off in the direction he came from. I waited for a couple of minutes and then signalled my trusty hunter back in. The news was positive. The motorcyclist was a member of the Fula tribe, the so-called "Jews of Africa," because of their renown trading and business acumen. This guy was no exception and among other things, a diamond smuggler. He was going back to get his mate with another motor bike and, shortly I hoped, we would be riding to the border in style. I briefed Simbu and we bolted down the track for a quarter of an hour to establish a new and unexpected link up point and observation point. If they were going to bring any reinforcements with them in the way of police or military, we would sit tight until they had passed and then vacate the area. The BBC news stated that the borders to Guinea were open for refugees trying to escape from the chaos in Sierra Leone. I was still hoping that that continued to be the case before the coup leaders got around to sealing them off. While waiting, my thoughts drifted off to Cape House and the boys. I was informed later that Minky and the staff had managed to secrete themselves in the ceiling just as the rebels "knocked" on its heavy double doors with RPG's. Finding no one at home they "killed" the building with copious amounts of automatic small arms fire. Luckily, they never discovered my mates and the wild shooting did not clip anyone. I grimaced at the thought of some camouflaged douche bag wearing my Doc Martens, sporting my Ray Bans, and making good use of my Sony Walkman and Robert Cray tapes.

Two motorbikes in concert could be heard revving up in the distance. We readied ourselves as they continued towards us totally unaware of our new positions. They were clean with no hangers on. They almost shit when Simbu stepped out and stopped them. We couldn't muck about, and after five minutes of dicking around they suddenly became real interested when I offered them USD$100 each to get us into Guinea and deposit us at the nearest cabstand. Looking like a ninja with my AK on the back of the bike, we took off, with Simbu and his driver in the lead. We continued our Easy Rider venture for several hours, which convinced me that Simbu's estimate of distance and time were flawed. Finally, a village of significant size and substance took shape before us. Simbu indicated his desire to locate one of his many relations, and after questioning a passer by, within a couple of minutes we were parked in front of his home. This was where my disarming process was carried out and I although I felt naked and very vulnerable, I was clean. My next stop would be at customs and immigration. My plan was to front up at the police outpost and go through the departure process. Hopefully, I could convince authorities that I was a harmless back packer that was inadvertently caught up in the turmoil.

It was 5:00 pm of day three and I slowly got off the bike and stood in the dust near the border gate with my entourage. A corpulent official and his rodent-like cohorts ignored us for several minutes. There were about seven scruffily attired, but extremely arrogant, policemen manning the outpost. These guys were on a significant power trip. Oddly, they were not wearing uniforms, but the unmistakable bulge of handguns printed plainly underneath their shirts. Since I was an aberration, within ten minutes at least twenty more personnel stirred in the torpid heat and casually surrounded us. Now the group consisted of military members as well. I was getting real nervous. Porky finally came alive and proceeded to ask why we were here and what was my purpose for being in Sierra Leone. I surrendered my passport and one of the rat pack took it inside. I remained outside and followed the discussion as best I could from the veranda steps. My two guides argued valiantly and it seemed that we were going to be allowed through. No! Out of the blue comes this little skinny piece of shit with one hell of an attitude, and a real power merchant to boot. He turned the whole situation around, and as far as he was concerned the borders were officially closed as of that morning. No one was allowed in or out of Sierra Leone. This was a severe blow and my mind raced to try to figure out what to do. A couple of the more observant troops could sense my growing desperation and shifted their positions. My three musketeers solemnly approached me and we sat on the steps for half an hour while the discussion flowed around us. It appeared that we had some guys on our side, so all was not yet lost. Simbu and the lead rider went inside the police station for another session. Shortly thereafter, Simbu bounded out, grinning from ear to ear. We would get the nod if I "reimbursed" everyone for their efforts. I nodded in assent and went into the backpack for my last big bill, wondering if I was going to receive change. Well, I need not have been concerned because my money had disappeared. Instantly, I knew where it was. What a bummer, it was probably still nestled in the bag snatcher's pocket waiting for one of his buddies to find it. Damn, why didn't I check his hands and pockets.

Simbu staggered back inside and conveyed the bad news to the boys. They all stormed outside and gave me the evil eye. Nevertheless, some guys were still on our side and all for letting us through. In a tiny West African town, on a stinking hot day, it boiled down to a group of soldiers and police voting on whether or not we were going to stay or be let go. As we were waiting for a decision, local people were entering and leaving Sierra Leone under the watchful eyes of the law and no questions were asked. I sat quietly, making no eye contact with anyone and feigning disinterest in the debate going on around me. Eventually, one of the soldiers came over and quietly advised us that it would be best for us to leave. I stood up and slowly walked over to my bike. It took a lifetime, and when we were on board I prayed that no one would give us the command to stop. The engine fired and we roared out of there with the argument still in progress and going strong. We tried to crash through various tracks and animal paths that were used by the smugglers, but each attempt was unsuccessful. The riders were relying on local knowledge and information and it appeared that the border areas were being actively patrolled. The two smugglers gave me a one-hundred percent effort and if it had not been for them my problems would have been considerably worse, but they were not about to risk their lives for me.

About 7:00 pm, we reluctantly returned to Simbu's cousin's house and held another war council. As we sat around the simple room sucking on a boiling hot brew of tea, Simbu and my two roadrunners were deep in discussion. Finally, the cousin suggested that we seek council with the provincial Muslim leader. These old boys have considerable power and authority and I thought it might be worth a try. After a going like the clappers, dodging goats, chickens, and the odd young child on the bikes, we arrived at the cleric's residence. At the large double door entrance a small attendant, who spoke perfect English, met us and took me inside where a village meeting was in progress. The village elders were gathered in a semi-circle around the headman, looking quite imposing in their traditional Muslim garb. They barely acknowledged me as I was offered a seat, a jug of cool water, and a face cloth to cleanse my hands and face. The meeting continued for another hour, and after it was concluded I was left with the receptionist and this tall and stately man in his late sixties. His steady gaze and reserved demeanour quickly dispelled any thoughts that I had of trying to bullshit him. He offered me food and sweet tea, and when I had finished he asked me to tell him my story. I didn't reveal everything, but explained that I had escaped from certain military problems and upon reaching the border I was denied passage, allegedly, because the borders were closed. He spoke to his assistant and then shook hands with me and left the room. He returned with a towel and once again disappeared down the passageway. The assistant turned to me and said, "The headman will personally assist you across the border in the morning. He asks that you sleep here, but since you are rather dirty you should wash and bathe before you do so." With that strong suggestion, I promptly followed him outside to a small ablution area and had one of the best showers I have experienced. Buckets of cold water and plenty of soap, it was both cleansing and refreshing. I went to my room and sank into a deep sleep, but still waking periodically to check my six. I awoke early, washed, and waited for the household to start its daily routine. I wasn't hungry and once again a coke and couple of pieces of pineapple was all that I wanted. We boarded his Toyota Hi Lux, flanked by Simbu and our two motorcycle riders, and departed for the dreaded border post. The English speaker kept chattering for the entire trip and reassured me that this was a mere formality and I had no further worries. I would be in Guinea in mere hours.

We arrived at the checkpoint, but this time the atmosphere was totally different. The authorities were extremely gracious and cokes were served and then the talks began.

With a quiet dignity, the headman described the numerous issues and problems that were troubling Sierra Leone and during his ten minute lecture, basically told the police that, "This is my son. As you can see he is a White man. He is not from Sierra Leone and the coup is a Sierra Leone problem — nobody else's. I ask you to let my son go to Guinea." He then sat down and let the officials have their voice. It was obvious that my benefactor was completely in charge and the police were desperately trying to cover their backsides. This went on for an hour or so and ended with profuse apologies. My passport was duly stamped and I was granted official permission to depart. The Muslim leader stood up, clasped my hand, and without a word left. I am deeply obligated to this humble, but great man. The police chief hustled over and mumbled his sincere apologies and hoped that I would explain to the headman that he was deeply sorry for any misunderstanding. This fawning was augmented by everyone in the detachment, and now they were all good guys as far as I was concerned, but I just wanted out of there. The last guy to come up had a small camera. It was the same nasty little bastard that started all this shit. Again, he was so sorry and wanted a photograph to keep for his mementos. I wasn't quite so convinced that his reasons were innocent, but we all formed a large gaggle and the snap was taken. The ironic aspect of all this is that this runty piss ant was the nephew of the chief sorcerer who had precipitated my escape with his warning message to Simbu, back at Yara.

We bade our farewells and broke free from our newly acquired "friends." Outside, my benefactor was sitting with a senior police official, and with a brief nod and smile, he acknowledged my hand gesture of farewell and we took off for Guinea. I didn't hazard a look back. Did I have an epiphany? After all, the strangers that significantly helped me were faithful members of their respective religions. I am not very religious, but I have strong core values. However, their unconditional kindness and without proselytising gave me pause. I couldn't believe that I was finally out of Sierra Leone. My two smuggling buddies and Simbu were over the moon. The smugglers had been down this route many times before and were on a roll. Their humour and newly acquired confidence was infectious. Yeehaaa! Once again I was a free man. Five minutes into Guinea and we bumped up against its border guards. Damn, I thought things were tough where we came from, but in front of us stood two scrawny, under-nourished soldiers wearing tattered, nondescript green uniforms without boots. However, they had very serviceable assault rifles, which they held menacingly at high port, barring our way. The bargaining began again and for the lack of five bucks USD, we sat at this damned outpost for the better part of an hour negotiating. The smugglers were determined not to pay because it would set a precedent and stuff up any future illicit excursions. To their credit the "Jews of Africa" finally wore them down and we were disgustedly waved through. Like fucking traffic lights, we moved another two hundred meters and fell into the welcome clutches of customs. It looked like these boys had it a little better than the military and surprisingly we were shown every courtesy. However, the questions were not only thorough, but seemed endless. Their voices became a little more authoritative and aggressive when they broached the subject of "tolls." My guys had to shuck down and turn out their pockets and place passports and documents in one pile and cash in the other. At no time was I touched or badmouthed, but their insinuations were obvious. What was a White man doing with these two smugglers?

They suspected that I was a wealthy diamond smuggler and I should be able to pay my way into Guinea. They were not seeking a large amount of ransom, but they figured that I was holding out on them and did not think it was funny. Furthermore, this is part and parcel of doing business in the third world, and Guinea was no exception. In short, I was insulting their intelligence and embarrassing them by keeping my wallet closed.

Since French was now the language of the month, Simbu told me what was going on. With a reluctant sigh, I took off my Seiko diving watch and placed it on the table. "Non, non, we are not thieves," was the reply. "We just want a small something, whatever you can afford." After four hours of face-to-face, they discovered one of the smuggler's $100 notes and that was confiscated. Suddenly, we cleared customs and although the two smugglers were pissed, I was, once again, overjoyed.

But, it wasn't over yet, and a little further down that dusty road we approached immigration. The officials were extremely pleasant and briefly checked my passport before handing it back. We sat back and waited for the next shoe to drop, but no one wanted to raise the issue. After a few minutes of uncomfortable silence, the chief official, in passable English, broke it by saying, "Monsieur, the question of payment?"

After I related our sad tail of woe, he leaned back with his arms folded, looked at me shrewdly, and said coldly, "Monsieur, are you aware the borders are closed, that no persons can enter or leave Guinea?" God, I was done now, but just as quickly he slapped my passport back on the desk and left the room. His number two spat something out in French, which activated the two bikers. They leapt to their feet and dragged me out of the building. We travelled at full throttle for a couple of miles and finally stopped at a Fula tribesman's thatched roof mud hut. We sat inside this prosperous farmer's house and a meal was prepared for us. It consisted of rice and some goat meat in a curry or stew. It was probably delicious, but I was still not hungry. However, I did swallow a couple of mouthfuls so I would not insult the beautiful Fula girl that had prepared the meal. The smugglers came through this way each month and we were at one of their business contact's homes. He was part of the vast Fula tribal network that traditionally acknowledges no boundaries, borders, or government restrictions and they trade all over Africa. They were gracious hosts and wanted us to stay for the night and leave the next morning. As it was only mid-morning, I was eager to get on to Conarky and the British consulate. We had another 250 kilometers to go, and after twenty minutes we hit the main highway. I wanted to get to a phone and contact the consulate. Well, lightning struck this odyssey again, and two gendarmes pulled up and stopped us. There was very little talk and they took us directly to the local jail and charged us with:

1. Illegal entry into Guinea
2. Violating border restrictions
3. Smuggling diamonds into Guinea
4. Simbu having no documentation
5. The smugglers being in possession of several false passports

The immigration guys had screwed us good by not stamping our passports, so we were in the country illegally. And, since Simbu had no documentation on him at all, he didn't exist. The smugglers were going to do some serious jail time, their bikes were confiscated, and they were being charged for diamond smuggling and aiding and abetting my violation of the border closure. As for me, I was looking good for a return trip back to Sierra Leone. After all this effort, I reached the point where I finally switched off and lost interest in the hostilities swirling around me. Fuck them. As far as I was concerned, nothing I could do would change the situation. They were in complete charge and now my job was to remain in control of myself and take my chances if they came. French was the only language they would converse in and I had been completely ignored. My request to call the British consulate was either not understood or arrogantly rejected.

I was dozing away in the corner of my cell when I heard voices in the interrogation office become agitated and suddenly I was being summoned into the main office. I was courteously offered a chair and I cautiously sat down. Across the desk, the little fat guy held my passport and small canvas wallet. He appeared to be excited about a small white laminated card. In pidgin English he asked, "Are you a gendarme in America?" It was my deputy sheriff's identification card from DeSoto County, Mississippi, complete with official logo, fingerprint, and photograph. Without hesitation, I answered, "Hell yeah, for sure — as you can see, I'm a deputy sheriff in Mississippi." That small ID card from the good old U.S.A. was the talisman to my newfound popularity. Terry Dunne and Sheriff Riley of the DeSoto County Sheriff's department had saved my bacon.

The head of the police force came down in person. He looked like a 30-year old version of Muhammad Ali, and with great patience briefed me on the best way for me to obtain passage to the consulate. My three amigos were also released, with stern warnings to the smugglers about the perils of their criminal activities. I shook hands with my three companions, and like Houdini, they disappeared before things changed again. Some years later I received a rather sad letter explaining the misfortunes that were suffered by the two diamond smugglers back across the S.L. border, but that's another saga.

With a signed pass from the commandant, his cousin's rental car, a driver, and a policeman as my bodyguard, my trip to Conakry began. I had promised payment of USD$100 upon arrival at the consulate. I had no guarantee they would loan me the cash, but once I got there, who cared. The trip was made more difficult than it had to be. For the nine hours that it took to travel to the capital, I was continually hassled and hauled out of the vehicle for attempted shakedowns at repetitive military roadblocks. My papers and escort did not impress them. It was a long night and since it was in their monetary interest, I left it all up to my driver and bodyguard to get me through. I arrived at the consulate's private residence in the early hours of the morning, but the old gate boy refused me entry and would not wake the British consul. In desperation, I sought out the American Embassy. I have been a big supporter of grass-root Americans for a long time, and once again they did not let me down. The young Marine at the door was courteous and efficient and in no time I was sitting comfortably in a briefing room. I advised the embassy official of my financial problems, and without hesitation, he reached into his wallet and handed me a $100 bill. With relief, I paid my debt to my escort and returned to the embassy, safe at last. A quick call home and all was back to square one again.

Eventually, the embarrassed British consul came bustling in with her son. She was extremely helpful and sympathetic. My dealings with her over the next couple of days reinforced my admiration for her efforts. That morning, I visited a French doctor who drained a blister, checked me out, and declared me fit and healthy. I flew out of Guinea days later on a special chartered flight that was absolutely packed solid with every nationality.

Next stop, New Zealand.

Postscript —

My trip home was uneventful, but a great time to reflect on what could have been and how much my true friends and family meant to me. I called Teao and then Alan from the L.A. airport and it was a great feeling. However I wasn't completely satisfied until I stood under the massive Oak Trees at the Kaharau Homestead; only then in the close proximity of my wife and family did I feel truly free again.

Will Scully put together one meritorious performance in his command and control of the refugees that had congregated in Freetown's Mammy Yoko Hotel. For his skill and bravery, he was awarded the Queen's Gallantry Medal. Hopefully, sometime in the next few years we will catch up with each other and share a few laughs over a pint or two.

Fred, Murdo Ray, and Minky all survived their own ordeals in that troubled region, but other than the odd e-mail we still haven't met since those turbulent days in Freetown.

Rabby Woods, thanks, mate.

Thirty Years On

Duke's Story

New Zealand Vietnam Veterans Official Welcome Home

I placed the quart bottle of Lion Brown beer back on the surface of the bar leaner, and trying to taste every molecule, I slowly swallowed my mouthful of liquid gold. I was relaxing and shooting the breeze with a couple of mates in the infamous Manutahi Hotel. It was another blistering hot day on the East Coast of New Zealand. The bar was fairly empty, since most of the patrons were down at the local sports ground taking part in some televised promotional venue. Warren Richards, a whiskered and definitely heftier version of the Kiwi (Singapore) Infantry Battalion's swimming champion of the early 70's, was slumped beside me. His swimming records still remained on the battalion plaques decades after he left the military. His drinking ability was certainly standing up against the test of time and was an adherent of "practice makes perfect." Near the end of his military career, he was the Company Quartermaster Master Sergeant for the officer cadet school. This position was of obvious benefit as he was seldom seen not wearing his cammies or remnants of military clothing. Wayne Wright, the district's recently posted police sergeant, was with us as well. He had left the so-called hot spot of Ruatoria several months earlier to take an even more volatile position in Otaki. He was back visiting and enjoying the tranquility of our Ngati Porou environment for the weekend. We were quietly discussing various humorous incidents that occurred during the previous couple of years that he had lived in the community. I should add that Wayne was a straight up guy and although he had his share of enemies, he also had a certain amount of backing and respect from the lads on both sides of the law. He was a keen rugby player and a staunch member of the City Rugby Club. After a hard rugby game and a matching session involving the amber brew, "Koro Pants," a five foot high, Maori leprechaun, accused Wayne of having a bad "altitude." To back up his accusation, Koro promptly unleashed a ferocious upper-cut to Wayne's chin. Unfortunately, all poor old Koro accomplished was cutting air because he didn't have the reach. Wayne gave him a stiff thump behind the ear to get him to relax and then continued on with the more serious business of discussing the pros and cons of the city rugby club's woeful performance that season. Wayne made an excellent police officer and certainly understood the men of the notorious East Coast.

Out of the corner of my eye I casually observed Leon Higgen's unlatching the double door catches, no big thing really. Suddenly both doors burst wide open and a horse and rider stationed themselves in the entrance. The horse rolled its eyes and snorted a little, but the animal didn't flinch, and without any further hesitation stepped inside. The rider had to lean over in the saddle as he came through the doorway, so he would not brain himself on the doorjamb. Animal and rider did a quick tour of the bar, circled the pool table, and waltzed across the dance floor without acknowledging anyone or saying anything. We continued to drink and talk, but kept an eye on the horse and cowboy. I was a bit glazed over, but I finally recognized the saddle tramp and things got ugly. The horseman happened to be young Steven Rangiwai, one of my numerous brother-in-laws, and, as usual, he was up to mischief. Steve was giving us a gratuitous display of his horsemanship. As a horse breaker of considerable merit, he needed to promote and market his animals, today was obviously one of his promotional days. Mohi Haenga and Roy (The Rat) Ratahi, both distant cousins of his, were not in the least amused by this intrusion and disruption of their game of pool and promptly hauled him off his horse. It looked like something from Custer's Last Stand. Without direction, the rider-less horse slid and skidded on the dance floor, crashed into our drinking space, and almost destroyed the bar leaner. Warren's military training took over and he managed to save our beer before it was toppled to the floor. With bottles in hand, we all withdrew a couple of paces and carried on with our drinking. Leon held the door open and the horse bolted outside to the safety of the car park. Steven and his Whareponga cousins were now engaged in a fairly intense swearing contest, but other than a few choice epithets and very colourful language, not a lot of damage was done. Eventually I caught the animal in the car park and Steve remounted the now saddle less animal. He was a little worse for wear and suffering from a few dozen too many bottles of Steinlager beer, but he still managed to gallop down the main street and out of town. It was just another sleepy day in Ruatoria, I thought, and had to smile to myself. It was great to be back home. I had returned only a couple of days prior after finishing up a couple of months with Alan in Memphis and Florida. My immediate intentions were to attend the Welcome Home Parade for the Kiwi Vietnam Veterans, which was to be held in Wellington City. As a member of the Vietnam fraternity, it was a belated event that I viewed with mixed emotions.

Whiskey 3 Company had an official reunion 20 years after our deployment to South Vietnam. It was organised by the guys and the special efforts of the incorrigible Peter "One Tit" Harris and Dick Schwass for spreading the word around the country. Interestingly, it was held right back were it all started in 1968, the Waiouru Military Camp. This was our first attempt to get back together as a complete group, and for most of us, it was long overdue. At national level, the Vietnam Veterans Association holds reunions every two years and many issues concerning welfare and other pertinent topics are discussed. The official welcome home parade planned for Wellington in 1998 was a much more significant event by far.

For most N.Z. Vietnam veterans, the official 1998 "Welcome Home Parade" was a long time coming and, unfortunately for many, much too late. Upon our return to New Zealand, we were left to discover, without the support of our mates, the harsh realities of hostile national and global reactions to the Vietnam War. However, until 1992, personally, I never gave Vietnam much thought at all. I wasn't in denial or in any euphoric state; I was too engrossed in the military to give it much attention. I have never suffered flashbacks or post traumatic stress syndrome and felt completely justified in what my mates and I did there. It would have been nice, but I didn't need public support or approval to make me whole.

Wellington was always a favourite city of TeAo's and mine. We had family and many good friends living there, augmented by numerous memorable experiences as young adults in Newtown and the surrounding suburbs. The "Tramways" and "New Caledonian" pubs were favourite drinking holes for East Coast residents. The Wellington Train Station and Inter Island Ferry Terminal are almost as indelibly stamped into the brain cells of any Kiwi infantry soldier of the 60's and 70's, as is the dreaded train station at "Stalag Waiouru." Before air transport became affordable, these places were the focal point for all travel to and from the North and South Islands. In my mind, Wellington City was the only place capable of providing the atmosphere required to host the official Welcome Home Parade. New Zealand politicians need to be reminded of their country's involvement in the Vietnam War as well as their predecessor's decision to commit us to the conflict. We soldiers merely answered the call and volunteered for the scrap, the political leaders and politicians of that era decided on the N.Z. military involvement.

It was a hard sell to convince my brother-in-law and fellow vet, Mosey Rangiuiaia, to come along. Even in 1998 there were still mixed feelings about our involvement in this war thirty years earlier. As it turned out, it was well worth my effort particularly when I saw Mosey, arm in arm with old friends, with a smile on his dial that stretched from ear to ear.

The registering of the thousands of participants and their families was held down on the Wellington waterfront and the small pubs and restaurants were pumping. Every unit had a local bar designated as their host meeting area. It was a great afternoon and the evening was even better. It was extremely casual and deliberately low key. The conference hall was jam packed with veterans from all walks of life. With no big dramas or chest beating from the organizers, colonels to private soldiers, albeit for some, 30 odd years out of date, rubbed shoulders and caught up with their long lost comrades.

I was amazed over how many of the guys were no longer recognisable; without displaying their name tags it would have been a disaster. I recognised Bobby Upton, my platoon commander, straight away. He had retired from the military in the late 80's as an infantry colonel. His big grin and booming voice was hard to miss. As my boss, he had saved my bacon a few times during my infrequent, but significant, brushes with the military judicial system. In fact, it happened enough that I had picked up the title "Bobby's Boy" for a spell while in Malaysia.

During one mission, under the command of Lt. Bobby Upton, we were tasked to monitor local fishing vessels in the area and check them out for weapons and VC personnel. Befitting "McHale's Navy," there we were, resplendent in our newly acquired Australian military issue, flat-bottomed assault craft. The Aussies didn't trust us with their equipment, because they knew they would never see it again, so our "man o' war" came complete with a scruffy, conscripted Aussie boat handler. To our peril, we were about to find out that this "Ocker" was definitely not a member of the famous Bondi Surf Patrol rescue squadron. Befitting of his officer status, Bobby and his signaller sat near the coxswain. Ngatoko Kupe, the ambassador of Te Kuiti cradled the M60, Les Ngawhare and I made up the Taranaki contingent and, finally, Scrubber Ryalls signed on as "cabin boy." The patrol consisted of several other craft, and without much planning we started our voyage to hell. Throughout the day, we stopped and hassled a few of the numerous sampans and junks. The novelty wore off pretty quick and most of us got sick of the pounding boat ride and the incompetent Aussie boat handler. We finally stopped a suspicious vessel and its owner, and after securing it to our craft began towing the vessel back to the mainland. Our coxswain must have been from Tasmania, (they are rumoured to have only one branch on their family tree) because when it became obvious that our other friendlies were out of sight he decided to find the other craft as fast as possible. He obviously forgot that we were towing another vessel, and before long it had swung completely out of control. Panicking big time, the Aussie closed the throttle and stalled the boat. The resulting backwash swamped our flat bottomed Assault Craft and we began to go under. Les and I ripped the weighty M60 link from around Kupe's neck and chest as the boat capsized. Scrubber, Ngatoko, Les, Neville the Sig, Crocodile

Dundee from Tasmania, and I were able to grab hold of the gunnels, which were well below the surface of the South China Sea. Considering that we were a mile off a hostile shore and the area was now suddenly void of any fishing craft or friendly vessels, we had good reason to be concerned. On top of this small aquatic problem we had lost all our weapons, radio, and, upon further inspection, our platoon commander. We all new Bobby couldn't swim worth a damn, but right now we were trying to keep our own heads above water and anxiously scanning the empty ocean. Not a word was said about our missing platoon commander, and, besides, he was a big man and knew the score. In this case, it was women, children, and private soldiers first, then it was every man for himself. Eventually, he finally broke the surface, and with lots of thrashing, gagging, and sputtering was able to link up with the team again.

Thirty years later, the details of Bobby's deep-sea dive were finally revealed. When the craft flipped over, Bobby went gracefully with it and made an Olympic class clean entry into the briny deep. A large and solidly built individual, any buoyancy that he may have possessed was completely nullified by his impromptu swimming attire of combat webbing, clothing, and boots. If it had occurred to us to take bets, the odds on him resurfacing were only fifty-fifty in my humble estimate. To further complicate his matter of survival, not only were his feet entangled in loose fishing rope and old netting, but directly above him the two craft were wedged together and secured from moving apart by the taught tow rope. No thanks to us, he miraculously managed to find his way to the surface and live.

Over some beers, Bobby further related that he almost gave up and stopped struggling. However, it occurred to him that he was not going to become the first Kiwi to go down with his ship in Vietnam, and that embarrassing scenario spurred him on to rip free and claw his way towards daylight. Knowing Bobby as I do, once he unleashed his size and strength, the Aussie boat handler was lucky he went around the craft rather than torpedoing his way through it.

Mike "Crooked Neck" Morrison's name rekindled another hard luck story. Our platoon, supported by other elements of the company, had been dropped onto Long Son Island, just off the coast of South Vietnam. Our task was to provide security support for the combat engineers. They were carrying out a "hearts and minds" civic action project for the local villagers that had started months earlier. Mike, our company clerk, had decided to don the warriors garb and come out for a taste of combat. Sure as shit, a Vietcong soldier, pissed off with us trespassing on his turf, drilled our "combat clerk" through the neck with a well delivered thirty calibre round. Once it was all over and Mike realised that he had survived, he commented that the wound did not hurt as much as being monstered by two strapping

Maoris who dove into his one man shell scrape several seconds after he made the move.

Of my four former Nui Dat tent mates, only Ben Tenamu and his replacement, Wi (Jap) Taepa, were present. I hadn't seen Ben since Vietnam and his presence alone was worth the trip for me. We didn't get to say much to each other, but just being with him for a couple of days bought it all back.

Billy Kahaki's heart problems prevented him from attending and this is another obstacle he is currently surmounting. Fortunately, he lives not more than a couple of hours away from my home and I get to catch up with him from time to time. One of his sons is named after me and for that I'm deeply honored. Billy also managed to attend my daughter Paula's 21st birthday at Whareponga Marae and, in turn, TeAo was able to return the honor at one of his boy's celebrations sometime later in Te Kaha.

Rau Te Haara was the other missing mate and, hopefully, in time we will see him back in the fold. Wi Taepa is amazingly full of energy these days and his talent as an artist in Maori sculpting and clay work has gained world wide notoriety. His two sons are following in their father's artistic footsteps, and along with my son Bardo they all attend Massey University and are striving for a degree in Maori Visual Arts.

Peter Harris is currently the project manager for Thiess Contractors in West Australia and has undergone a remarkable transformation from the ratbag "Titty" Harris (the pale skinned Maori from Pleasant Point) who caused his cousin so much aggravation in South Vietnam. On one occasion, Titty and Scrubber Ryalls actually jumped a ride with an American resupply convoy during a platoon stint in a fire support base. They ended up AWOL for 24 hours and earned a wee stay in Sand Bag City, the military stockade in Vung Tau.

Unfortunately, Nev Carmichael is not enjoying the best of health, but like many others, takes it in stride.

Scrubber Ryalls has not changed much, and except for the loss of most of his teeth and acquiring a ponytail, he looks like he did when he was beating the bush with his SLR. However, he has fallen into a lifestyle most blokes would die for. Currently, he lives on his yacht on South Island's Milford Sound.

Gannet Mullins and George Nicholls, both inseparable mates since basic training, were bouncing off the walls by the end of the reunion, in the same manner as they had done in the houses of ill repute and dingy back street bars of yesteryear. Gannet runs a charter diving service and lives on his yacht with his great wife, Debbie. Not to be out done by her worldly husband, she performed an entertaining bar top dance during the celebrations, reminiscent of her days as a glamorous "Go Go" dancer from the

"Happen Inn" television program of the 1970's. Gannet's effort to do likewise was considerably less pleasing to the eye. He almost single handily succeeded in destroying half the surrounding tables of beer. Alas, some things will never change.

Ginge Phillips is living in Australia, but has been unable to abandon his South Island sheep shagger's accent. Graeme (Black Harry) Harris has had his share of dramas, but continued to remain in the military until his retirement as a warrant officer. The old square jaw was still there, but his body was now more suited for a front row prop rather than the dynamic loose forward that he had been when he tried out for the Maori All Blacks.

Graeme Edwards was also missing from the reunion, but he continued to serve in the army and retired as a major sometime during the 1990's. Graeme was our section 2IC in Vietnam, and because he was more refined and better educated, we made things a bit awkward for him at times. He also aspired to become an officer, but for whatever reason he became the fly in the ointment more often than not. Near the end of our tour, we "baggies" agreed that some sort of retribution was appropriate for this lance corporal lifer. True to script, old Duke drew the short straw for the punishment detail. To make matters worse, only a few days earlier, along with a handful of other reprobates, I had survived a severe bollocking from Major Torrance and CSM "Pinky" Macintosh after our AWOL visit to Vung Tau. Pinky had promised us a lengthy incarceration in the British Military Prison in Singapore for this latest misdemeanor. I sure as hell did not need this added section burden thrust upon me, but peer pressure has no mercy in the combat zone, and so the story of my life continued.

Finally that same afternoon, after revving up my courage with the lads in the Baggie's bar, it was decided that I had to carryout the disciplinary mission, right then and there. I staggered over to Graeme, who was also enjoying the surroundings, and commenced my battle plan with a stinging verbal attack. Graeme was quite up to it, and being over six feet tall, lean, and rangy, he definitely had the arms reach and height advantage. His most important advantage, however, was that he was sober and I was on the way to total inebriation. What I lacked in height and reach was more than equalized by One Sections honour lying heavily on my shoulders. Graeme didn't muck around, and with a disdainful look, he simply shifted drinking hands and threw a single, straight right hand. This punch rocketed through my non-existent guard and landed square on my chops. Even from the receiving end, I had to acknowledge that it was a nice shot. Observing the laws of Newtonian physics, I duly went down arse over kite and spat out a tooth. I lay there waiting for someone to administer the ten count and signal the end of the bout. No way, the boys had other plans. They hoisted me to my feet, poured a can of cold Budweiser over my head and threw me back into the fray. Graeme wasn't counting on this at all, and in the now extended melee I managed to topple him over onto the bar furniture. By now, I was feeling no pain and had gained my second wind. Later, when cooler heads prevailed and peace had been restored, the fight statistics were summed up as follows: Graeme had received a coupled of cracked or severely bruised ribs and I was minus a tooth with a split lip. The down side of our little fracas was that we were both booked in for a disciplinary meeting with Lieutenant Upton the next morning.

Years later, Graeme and I both served together at the Papakura Military Camp. By then he was a captain and I had reached the rank of Staff Sergeant. We saw each other frequently and chatted whenever time permitted. Our foolish occurrence has never been mentioned since that day and hopefully I will meet Graeme at the next annual reunion.

Snide Pagan, the gangly, crew cut white boy from way down South, is now Lewis Pagan, a respectable citizen and livestock supervisor for the Wrightson's empire in Cromwell. He too "killed" a few pints and told some even bigger stories.

Rex Ryan did not attend the reunion, and by all accounts he is living in Bluff. He is still a clean living son of a gun and was New Zealand's veteran single and double sculls rowing champion. I didn't ask, but wonder what happened to Charlie West...

Dick Schwas, Ngatoko Kupe, Nigel Clifford, Gordon Alex, Paul Moana, K.K. (Kahukiwa), Bobby "Nono boy" Newson, Vic Hill, and Tracker Wilson all made the reunion that weekend.

Gannet enlightened us all with the startling news that after a hard night on Bugis Street, (probably with the infamous "Lisa Lust," the Kiwi soldier's best friend), he consequently missed the 1971 "company freedom flight" from Singapore back to N.Z. We were a pretty lawless crew for sure, but, hell, it was all good clean fun.

The cabaret was a huge affair, and because of the thousand or so additional vets and families registering on the last day, it was vastly overbooked. As a result of the unexpected large crowd, a few of the paid up groups were unable to gain access to this function and it was the only sour note sounded during the reunion. I left TeAo with Faxy Metara and other friends and families that she hadn't seen for sometime listening to John Rowles and other Motown artists. I shot next door and grabbed a beer in another packed bar with Midge Marsden and his Blues Band, doing their best to keep us in the mood. Bill Lillicrap and his family, Len Constable, Danny Wilson and sons, Buster Nathan, Dicko Dickson, John "Fite" White, Bubs Holmes, and Andy "Petorei" Peters were all present and accounted for.

Organizers would have received some flack for what went wrong; however, these glitches were more than balanced by the incredible parade of veterans and families. Not withstanding the belated, but much-needed, welcome home for the warriors of Tu Ma Tauenga by the Kuia and Kaumatua of the Maori delegation. For many, the long-awaited traditional welcome from the Maori contingent was the main reason for the reunion, and the cultural significance of lifting the Tapu of War was finally achieved. The people of Wellington responded wonderfully, and sincerely embraced the opportunity of hosting the parade. I was literally bursting with national pride, and the parade will remain with me for as long as I draw breath. Once again, the politicians played it safe and were very conspicuous by their absence. The Prime Minister accepted the key appointment as the national reviewing official for the pass in review, but I was unimpressed when she departed immediately for Christchurch to watch a Canterbury rugby match.

The next day's church service was a sombre affair. It served as a final honor to those who served but were no longer with us. By far, the Australian MP who had served in the conflict as a Platoon Commander was the most well received speaker. Very appropriately, a couple of Huey helicopters flew overhead when he concluded his remarks. Flashbacks resounded around the pews and I could see eyes moisten and hear the clearing of throats from more than a few at this open-air service.

Vietnam has finally been recognised by the politicians and general public as part of New Zealand history.

To the surviving Vietnam Veterans and family members, this has been a fact of life since 1967.

Life with the Rich and Famous

Alan's Story

Global VIP Protection

My involvement in bodyguard and security work goes back to 1982. During that time, I was an assault trooper on the SAS Counter Terrorist Team. Our training was constant and intense and was conducted both internally and from external sources. On a routine basis we conducted exchanges with our brother SAS units world-wide. They would come to us for our jungle warfare expertise and we would seek their particular specialties. On one occasion, Mac, a member of the British SAS, arrived to assist us in forming our own bodyguard cell. Mac was a legend within his command, and through the ensuing years Duke and I would cross professional paths with him again and again. Fifteen years later, after being Mac's student, we worked the same protection detail in Italy as civilians. Since then, we have operated together in Germany, Norway, and Japan. He imparted a realistic approach to this difficult calling and gave me skills that have served my former unit and me well.

VIP protection is one of those vocations that you either love or hate. To many "Walter Mittys," it is definitely an ego trip and they derive vicarious status by being in the presence of important personalities and celebrities who are often in the lime light. However, real operators consider it a damn difficult job with 1,380 minutes of daily monotony and maybe 60 minutes of excitement. If I had to choose between participating in a SWAT operation that required a hostage rescue, or working a VIP detail for a famous person, I would choose the SWAT job in a heart beat. The former task might be more dangerous, but most are normally resolved in a short period of time. Conversely, security details can and have averaged eighteen hours a day for several weeks on end and it can become an exhausting grind. With the exception of motorized escorts, you are constantly on your feet, while maintaining extreme mental alertness, being diplomatic with assholes, and subject to habitual scrutiny. You are representing and become, therefore, an extension of the dignitary and his interests. Make the slightest mistake and cause him an iota of embarrassment and you will get fired. I have worked for clients who are all business and couldn't care less about the fact that you have three kids and a mortgage to pay. They will fire you on the spot just for picking up the wrong telephone line. I have had the opportunity to perform protection details at a government level and also for the entertainment industry. Without a doubt, members of the entertainment industry are the most difficult to work for. With government details, your job description is usually set and you know what to expect. You are assigned a dignitary that is experiencing a certain threat level against him. This will determine the size of the detail and the degree of close protection he will receive. His schedule and daily routine will be laid out in advance, your mission and responsibilities will be clearly defined. Weapons, equipment, and procedures will be codified in regulations and SOPs, so there will be no misunderstandings concerning your profile, reactions, and rules of engagement.

Celebrities, on the other hand, are totally unpredictable and you are purely a number who can be replaced at any time. Half of the time they are not sure if they want you to accompany them or not. They are very whimsical and their schedules can change hourly. At times you are expected to be clairvoyant and able to anticipate their intentions and, right or wrong, it is always your fault if things "go south." The best part of any detail is when your shift is over and you are driving out the gate. Phew, I survived another one, what is tomorrow going to bring? There can be very little job security in this work, but that is the way it is when you are working for the rich and famous. With over 1300 security companies in Los Angeles alone, there was never a shortage of people to replace you. I was fortunate during the mid 1980's to be tasked to oversee all VIP protection training and operations within the SAS. This job brought me in direct contact with the New Zealand Police Diplomatic Protection Squad. The officer in charge of the Auckland office was Detective Senior Sergeant Terry James.

Terry was a great guy and we became good friends. Elaine and I would often visit him and his wife Margie until I left the unit and moved overseas. He would constantly be inviting us to accompany his team "unofficially" on high profile operations and, in return, we would expose his team to some pretty high-speed training. I remember once when Phil and I were on a mission with Terry's team who was looking after the Prime Minister of India. A couple of weeks prior to the mission I approached our operations officer to get approval for Phil and me to accompany the Diplomatic Protection Squad on the mission. He gave us his blessing; however, I guess that he forgot about it two weeks later. When we showed up for the detail, one of the senior N.Z. Anti-Terrorist Squad officers who was also in charge of the Counter Assault Team, recognized us and about shit. Challenging us, he barked, "What the hell are you SAS guys doing on this job? You better not be fucking packing." With that warm reception, Phil and I conducted a hasty withdrawal. Rather than head back immediately to our base, we justifiably hit a local pub and sculled a few cold ones. What a wanker, we could not fathom why he made a big scene out of what probably was an innocent mistake. Well, that wasn't the end of it.

Instead of resolving it with us personally, he went off the deep end and called our boss, the Colonel. The boss categorically denied that we had any operators involved and as far as he knew, we didn't. The Colonel and the Ops Officer arrived at the compound all panicked to fuck and went directly to the duty NCO's room. It just so happened that my Duke was on duty that night and he knew exactly who was out there and why, but in no way was he going to get involved in this. He pretended to be busy and kept his mouth shut. He reckons that they were floundering around, going through rosters, cursing and swearing for hours. Once they figured it out, I was summoned to the CO's office bright and early the following morning for an ass reaming. Damn Ruperts, they never seem to have a sense of humor or appreciate initiative.

My first two years in the U.S. were spent working in the Beverly Hills as part of a 42-man protective detail. There were 22 permanently assigned personnel, most of whom had military and police backgrounds, and twenty adjuncts who worked special events. The latter group consisted of active duty law enforcement officers. Mark Lonsdale, my U.S. sponsor and boss, had secured this contract years ago and the detail had evolved into a well-structured and highly organized contingent. The VIP was an extremely wealthy movie producer and real estate tycoon. He owned homes in Beverly Hills, Malibu, Santa Barbara, and Aspen. Much of my time was spent travelling with the family throughout the world and a trip could last anywhere from a week to a month. His primary residence in Beverly Hills was simply unbelievable. When it went on the market in 1991 it was advertised as the most expensive private residence in the country. The asking price then was $52-million in cash. The forty-room mansion was laid out over seven acres and the two kids "doll houses" behind the main house, individually, were bigger than my apartment. The dogs even had air-conditioned kennels. Our client was extremely generous and supported a lot of good causes with huge fund-raisers at the house.

It was not unusual to have 1200 guests on the grounds being entertained by the likes of Sting, Paul Simon, Don Henley, Elton John, Bruce Springstein, Bono, Bonnie Rheitt, Axel Rose, Earth, Wind and Fire, and Rod Stewart, to name a few. During my tenure, we must have had every liberal, Democratic Party oriented movie star come to the house to support one leftist cause or another. Conspicuously missing were staunch Republicans like Arnold Swarzennegger, Sylvester Stallone, and Bruce Willis. The

family's close Hollywood friends included Goldie Hawn and Kurt Russell, Melanie and Don Griffith, and Lionel and Brenda Ritchie. They were good people who were easy to get along with and appeared to respect the job we had to do.

The glamorous side of VIP protection – luxury vehicles; luxury mansions, Beverly Hills, California; luxury yachts – The Catalina, South of France; luxury hotels – The Copocabana, Rio de Janiero; luxury private jets – worldwide.

While I was there, I worked the night shift. I preferred the after-hours duty because you did not have to interact with the secretaries, screen deliveries, and you didn't have to take the wife shopping or the kids to school. The boss and wife would go out every night to a movie, restaurant, or night-club, and that kind of routine made the job a little more bearable. They would hit the rack by 0100-0200 hours and the rest of the night was usually uneventful. Quite honestly, the less you saw of each other, the better.

It was during this job that I first met Max, my long time Senior Instructor at T.E.E.S. Max was fresh out of the Marine Corps, and, like his high and tight haircut, he was wired for action. There is something about Marines that perceptively stands out from all other servicemen. They are extremely disciplined and good at what they do, but there is the question of institutional brainwashing. Over a period of time, with my patient and understanding guidance, Max slowly de-programmed himself and finally realized that he was now a civilian and not a devil dog and hard-core killer anymore. Rather than growling in response to a question, he now spoke in single syllables. In 1992, the boss hosted another grand fund -raiser for the then Governor Bill Clinton, who was running against former President George Bush, Sr. in the general election. Every weenie from Hollywood attended, kissing Slick Willy's ass and poured thousands of dollars into his campaign fund.

Max and I were stationed in the VIP room and it was nauseating to see these fools fawning over him. An army of Secret Service agents shadowed Clinton and we augmented them with our full compliment of personnel. It was an incredible party and somehow, but certainly not by design on his part, Max ended up standing next to the man himself. He was not one of the President's biggest fans and it made him extremely uncomfortable. I could imagine him thinking to himself, "Shit, what would my Marine buddies say if they knew I was protecting this draft dodger." Far worse than the mental torture he was going through, I was concerned that his Marine training would take over and he would play the Corps hymn off Clinton's skull. It was a tense moment and I could see dollops of sweat were running down Max's brow. To this day, he has never had to exercise so much self-control and has not forgiven himself for being a member of a detail assisting in the safeguarding of someone that he despised. This incident serves as a good example of the discipline that a personal protection officer has to exercise. He must set aside his personal prejudices and concentrate on the job at hand.

In spite of his gung-ho approach to everything and insistence that his men spit shine their shoes and get hair cuts for every detail, we became great mates and have been working together ever since. He also developed his own firearms and tactics school and spends most of his professional time running his Southern California facility or working for me in either Memphis or Brazil. Max is indeed one of a kind. An excellent instructor and an accomplished beer drinker, who some how always answers the call to duty after a hard night of partying, but most of all he is a loyal friend who would not hesitate to risk everything for a mate. There were many other former Marines working the detail, including Jon Darrah, who went on to become one of Los Angeles Police Department's finest and graduated first in his recruit class. Another great mate was Robert Van Landingham, who was medically discharged from the Marine Corps after being wounded by a Cuban-fired Soviet RPG7 rocket while fighting in Grenada. I am also indebted to Troy Tolmack, a Marine Force Reconnaissance veteran who got me on the Mother of all VIP details that took me to about 15 different countries. Todd Parris was one of our members who had no military background, but was a former police officer. We became friends because he was an American who happened to be a big time rugby fan and had visited New Zealand in 1987 to observe the World Cup. In addition to that he was also a stalwart rum drinker and on that basis alone we naturally hit it off.

We shared several security assignments and one in particular stands out. The boss was divorcing his then wife, so she wanted to fly to Aspen, Colorado to claim "her" furniture from the old estate for the new, $27-million house that he had just bought for her and the kids. This was a "fastball" mission and she wanted two guards to accompany her and one of the secretaries. Todd and I volunteered and the next morning we departed on their private jet for what was to be a one-day trip. The plan was for her to identify what she wanted and the movers would pack it up and drive it to L.A. She proceeded to move through all three floors of the house and place a yellow sticky note on every item that was to go. Two hours and three pads later, she finally realized that it was going to take a tractor-trailer to haul it all back. She was not about to hang around for the details so, turning to us, she told both of us that we were to stay for as long as it took to supervise the packing and transfer. As she put on her designer coat, she further instructed that the house and cook were ours and we could have any bedroom except the master. Sensing the cold as she walked toward the Mercedes, she generously told us that if we needed more clothing to charge it to her former husband. After safely putting her on her jet, it was straight to the nearest sports bar for several rum and cokes to inaugurate seven days of sheer bliss. We had the keys to a mansion, a limo, and everything that went with it! We were snow bunny magnets.

As previously mentioned, the Secret Service periodically visited the main Los Angeles residence and the most famous dignitary they ever escorted to the house was former President Ronald Reagan. I was on duty twice when he arrived and it was an honor to meet him. He is truly a heroic president who believed in tough, straight talk followed by strong action. His way of getting the enemies attention was not politically correct as far as Democrats and liberals was concerned, but it was effective. Of the hundreds of sports and entertainment celebrities that we got to meet, there was only one other individual that I can say I was proud to shake hands with. I was working the wedding detail for Mark Hughes, the President of Herbalife International. He was getting married and the reception was held at his mansion in Beverly Hills.

During the dinner, he and his new bride were continuously being approached by well wishers. Consequently, they were not able to eat. Trip, another close comrade, and I closed in around their chairs and advised him that no one would be allowed to interrupt them until they had completed their meal. People kept pressing to see them and we politely, but firmly turned them away. A very attractive woman approached me and I respectfully informed her that the couple was not to be disturbed. However, she reacted by saying that she was most offended and embarrassed by my "Neanderthal attitude" and stormed away in a huff. It turned out the pissed off lady was Faye Renswick, one of Nicole Brown Simpson's closest friends and who was to become one of the prosecution's leading witness's during the OJ Simpson murder trial. Fatalistically, at least in hindsight it seems, the very next person attempting to run our gantlet was Robert Shapiro, the future lead defense attorney for Mr. Simpson. Neither of them knew each other and the chances of that happening must have been astronomical. Just before we were scheduled to drive the groom to church, a carefully packed gift arrived at the security office for him. We inspected it and it was a magnificent portrait of Buzz Aldrin standing on the Moon and signed by him. It was a great gift from a true American hero. Naturally, he was wearing his space suit and you could not see his face, so when the next person approached us we nearly made an exception to our blockade. He was a well-dressed elderly, but fit, individual who projected great bearing and air of confidence that you could not ignore. Both Trip and I apologized to him on behalf of Mr. Hughes. "Do you know who I am," he asked? "No sir," was our simple, but honest reply. With that he whipped a business card out of his suit pocket and handed it to us. The name on the card read, "Buzz Aldrin — Astronaut." I shook his hand admiringly and told him that it was an honor to meet him. We chatted informally for about thirty seconds, but regrettably had to reiterate that he still couldn't see the couple during dinner. He smiled, shook his head in acknowledgment and, like the true professional he was, quietly returned to his table. However, we informed the boss because we knew that he would want to personally speak to him after dinner and thank him for the unique gift.

As a young rugby-playing Kiwi, there was one other celebrity who had a similar impact on me. I was twelve when I represented my province in a major tournament. We did well and I was overwhelmed to be presented my winner's medal by Colin "Pinetree" Meads, New Zealand's greatest rugby player of the 20th century. Meads enjoyed rare and unprecedented fame. As an All Black rugby forward for fifteen years, he was feared by his opponents worldwide and was considered to be an extremely tough, no nonsense combatant. Meads, like Captain Charles Upham, recipient of two Victoria Cross's and New Zealand's most esteemed World War Two hero, would always lead from the front and defend his team mates under any circumstances. It is men like these that all young people should look up to and emulate as role models, instead of the small community of renegade, out of order, drug taking, immoral entertainers and arrogant multi-millionaire sports personalities.

Since my arrival in America and becoming a citizen, I have performed security details in over twenty countries. As I alluded to earlier, people in general, and in Hollywood specifically, get too hung up on the mostly fictionalized glamorous aspects of being a professional bodyguard. Yes, I have seen some glitter, ridden in expensive cars, flown first class, or in a private aircraft, and have eaten and partied in some of the world's finest homes, hotels, nightclubs, and restaurants, but I have yet to experience the run and gun, high speed combative and assassination attempts that usually form the plots of filmdom's depictions of this profession. To me, it's a job like any other that requires a great deal of focus, awareness, and dedication, but regardless of all the perks, at the end of the day exhaustion claims you as it does any person who gives his vocation a one-hundred percent effort.

My wife, Elaine, was to experience life as a "bodyguard," firsthand in Los Angeles in 1990. She knew nothing about this skill, but she was a competent shot and had a good head on her shoulders. Without a doubt, the ability to think was way more important than the ability to shoot. A Santa Monica police officer was looking for a female to assist him on a detail that involved Prince Badar and Princess Khalud from the Saudi Royal Family. It was to last for a month while they were vacationing in Beverly Hills. Elaine was responsible for accompanying the Princess wherever she ventured in L.A. Their daily routine appeared to follow a predictable pattern — do nothing till around 2:00 pm when the princess got up, then it was "shop till you drop" mode until she hit the rack. It got old quickly for Elaine, and the final straw came when the princess refused to call her by her given name, and instead referred to her as "Lionel." It appears that the name Elaine was prettier than Khalud and, of course, that was totally unacceptable in the eyes of royalty.

For a time, I also worked for the U.S. State Department as a foreign police instructor. As a result of this training interaction, I was able to develop a large number of international contacts and make many good foreign police friends. When on an overseas assignment, I often employed some of these former students as drivers and additional security. They were intimately familiar with the turf, knew what to avoid, kept us out of trouble, and packed all the heat necessary to discourage troublemakers. They really greased the skids for us and the client was duly impressed with our connections. Weapons for us were always an issue when travelling, but one thing we never did was try to buck the system of the country we were in. This means that you, as a bodyguard, better have something else going for you than relying solely on a 9mm pistol to get you and your client out of a shit sandwich. Be advised, certain countries are firearms phobic and you should not even think about carrying concealed or otherwise in those environs. Singapore, Japan, Mexico, England, Australia, and Canada are definite no-goes, whereas South America and parts of the Middle East and Eastern Europe are more accommodating. It mostly boils down to how much discretion the local authorities can exercise, along with how much you contribute to the police welfare fund.

Japan, which touts its low murder rate because it does not trust its "subjects" with firearms, yet exports many sporting arms from their factories, is one of the most fucked up places to visit or do business. Unfortunately, I had developed some negative preconceived notions regarding the land of the Rising Sun after meeting one of its more colorful citizens. In 1990, while residing in Los Angeles, Buzz, a former SAS buddy of mine, called me from Colorado after completing a bodyguard course in Aspen. He advised that I might be getting a call from a Tetsuhiro Nagahata, who was a course mate of his and would I mind taking him to the range for a shoot. "No worries Buzz," was my unthinking reply, without knowing what I had just gotten myself into. There was no immediate call from Tetsu; however, the following morning there was a knock on my door. Taking a quick look through the security view port, I couldn't see anyone. Grabbing my 1911 A1 Colt, I stepped back as I slowly opened the door. Before me was this bald headed, bowing, and mumbling little incarnation, at least in his mind, of a Samurai warrior in mufti. To this day (I hope you are reading this Tetsu), I have still not been able to shake this little Ninja. Since then, Tetsu has become our little adopted and inseparable Buddhist son. He and I have had some serious dust-ups over the years but, deep down, I can't help but love this arrogant, ignorant, pig headed, stubborn, obnoxious, argumentative, midget, four-eyed little bastard. Thanks Buzz, I owe you big time.

As a nation, the Japanese are the most conforming people in the world. It's either their way or no way. Flexibility, or the slightest deviation in the game plan, is not in their lexicon. In fact, this rigidity was a trait that made them vulnerable to defeat in small unit combat during WWII. You are slapped with it as soon as you get off the plane and enter the customs area. All customs and immigration officials are dressed in blue suits with white hats. As you proceed into their domain, you can see them scrutinizing you and imagine them thinking to themselves, "How can I fuck with this Fu Man Chu bearded, round-eyed American today?" This has to be part of their payback for what happened to them 55 years ago. Even our client, who generated millions of dollars worth of business annually for Japan, would have his luggage dumped out onto the counter for a "security check." I was in line behind a German on one occasion and the authorities found in his bag an extremely mild, soft porn magazine that showed pictures of scantily clad females. Whistles and sirens went off and it just about created an international incident. When I witnessed that reaction, I cringed at the prospects of what they were going to do to me when they discovered the latest issue of Penthouse secreted between my skivvies and my socks. What a bunch of hypocrites. Japanese society is well known for its eroticism and South East Asia remembers well the Imperial Army's practice of forcing captured civilian women into prostitution for their troop's benefit during WWII.

The questions were always the same and perfunctorily expressed in their best Pidgin English, and I always answered in the same manner. Going through my bags with white gloves, an official, without making any eye contact, would ask a bunch of absurd questions.

"Do you have any drugs on you?"

"No," was my honest reply.

"Are you sure?"

"Yes."

"Do you have any guns on you?"

"No."

"Are you sure?"

"Yes."

"What is this?"

"It is the latest issue of *Penthouse.*"

"What is it for?"

"It is for wanking, over."

"What is wanking?"

"It means to jerk off — you stupid ignorant little bastard."

"Crazy American — go!"

Although it was rare, we had our physical confrontations with some of their security types. On one occasion, a female employee at our corporate venue was being harassed by a slant-eyed, squatty-bodied security guard. She was very upset and complained to our team leader. Without warning or hesitation, Rusty grabbed the little prick by the throat, picked him up, and threatened to rip his balls off if he ever messed with the ladies again. The little bastard started groveling and spitting up apologies to such a degree that I thought he was going to commit Hari-Kari on the spot.

Other Asian countries and their officials were way easier to deal with. They seemed less hung up on the minutia of life and were more broadly focused. Taiwan expects that their Peoples Republic of China cousins were about to invade at any moment so they were wired a little tight. They liked having Americans around because it gives them a sense of psychological security. Traffic in Taipei is horrendous and was dominated by millions of little motor scooters and bikes. However, congestion in many of these countries means that civil infrastructure has been unable to keep up with its prosperity. Trip Wynn, handled venue security for us. Every time we left a venue, regardless of which country we were in, he would be out on the road blocking traffic to facilitate our convoy's smooth exit. The only exception was Taiwan. We were ready to leave this particular venue and he charged out into the middle of the street with his arms spread out to each side trying to stem the flow of mass motion. Slowing momentarily, you could see this disjointed hoard of mechanized, two-stroke cavalry trying to collectively figure out what the fuck this stupid round-eye prick is doing in the middle of their road? Their surprise did not last for long, and, belching clouds of acrid smoke, hundreds of bikes roared down at him. Looking in my rear view mirror, the last thing I remember seeing was Trip dodging and fending off these crazy bastards while scrambling to make his way back to the sidewalk. Chuck was his sidekick and both were super great guys.

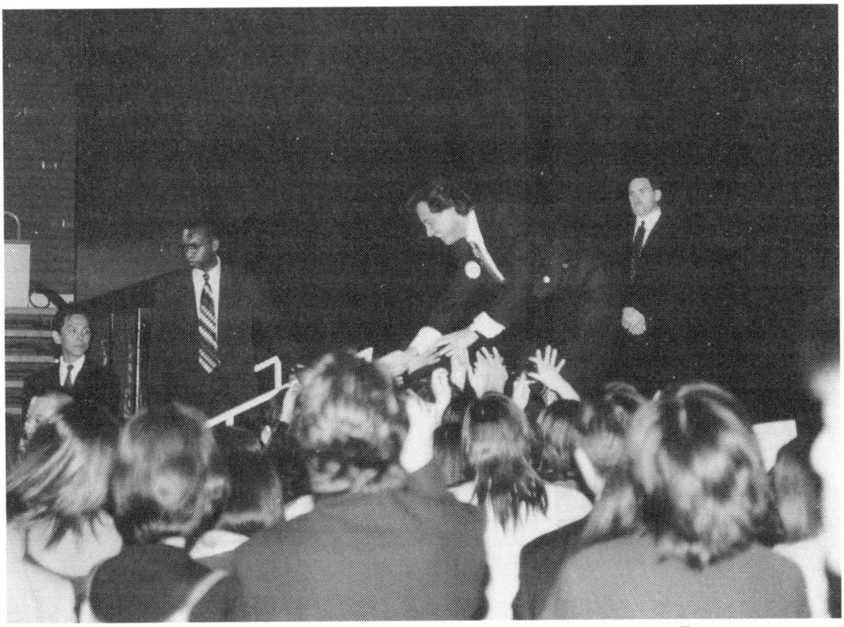

Alan and Chuck Maulden providing security for Herbalife Director, Mark Hughes – Taiwan, 1999

They were consummate professionals. Chuck is a six-foot, two-inch, bald-headed Black guy who always attracted weird looks and a lot of attention from Asians. Because of his size and ominous appearance, they never gave him any shit. Whenever Trip performed his daredevil road antics, he would stand there and shake his head in disbelief.

For this particular client, the entire team was composed of an exceptional group of guys. David Martin was the detail leader or personal protection officer (PPO). His side-kick, Barry Burtt, ran the Los Angeles security operation for the client and the rest of us augmented the detail only for trips outside California. Rusty, Mac, Playboy, and Snapper represented the Anglo aspect of the contingent, and being former 22 SAS operators, they were great at what they did. We invaded Hong Kong before and after the hand-over to the PRC, and, at least on the surface, it was business as usual. They still looked and acted like Chinese with capitalist cravings that are going to be difficult to suppress.

Thailand is a great place to be a man, and Bangkok, in particular, is known for its fun and games. There is very little that one is unable to see or obtain in that town because everything is for sale, and the Thais are usually easygoing people. However, on this trip, which was our first excursion to this country, we ran into some unusual staffing problems. On the last night of the business trip, we took our client to a party in a hotel. At this juncture, we had not established contacts among the police and had to hire drivers from a native limousine company. The food and entertainment were fabulous, everything was going smoothly, and we were looking forward to flying home the next day. Rusty, David, Barry, and I were upstairs with the client and it looked like he was getting ready to leave. I contacted Trip by radio and advised him to get the vehicles ready. Knowing how squared away he was, I expected to hear Trip to call back within a minute informing me that the vehicles were in position and ready to go. Instead, I heard his slightly raised voice informing me that he could not locate the drivers. We had no time to waste, so I didn't ask questions but told him, "Trip, the boss is getting his jacket on — sort it out." "Roger that — stand by."

"Alan, this is Trip — stall the boss, I can't find the drivers."

"Trip — he is shaking hands and heading towards the stairs."

"Roger that — stall him, tell him a vegemite joke or something."

"Trip — find the Goddamn drivers, we're on our way down."

Holding my breath in anticipation of a major fuck up, we arrived at the limos two minutes later. I was greatly relieved to see the drivers at attention behind their respective wheels, with Trip flagging down the traffic. Everything subsequently went as smooth as Thai silk.

The next morning, I bailed up Trip at breakfast and asked him what happened the previous evening. Speaking through a mouthful of eggs and bacon he exclaimed, "Kiwi, you won't believe this shit. You know, per SOP, I briefed the two drivers to stay with the vehicles constantly, but if they had to take a piss or anything like that to clear it with me first. I don't know whose Army these guys were in, but so much for orders. I looked in the bathroom, the lobby, the coffee shop, the restaurant, and couldn't find those little bastards anywhere. I ran my fucking ass off checking the parking lot and road and still nothing. I finally wandered down the sidewalk another 15 yards and I could hear this giggling and slurping noise in the bushes. I looked in there and about shit."

Getting interested now, I asked, "Well, what did you see?" He looked me in the eye, hesitated and blushed a bit and almost coughed out, "Both drivers were rolling around inside the hedgerow giving each other blow jobs." Upon hearing that excuse, I laughed so hard I barfed my breakfast clear across the table. Thank God no one was sitting opposite me and the client was in the main dinning room. Recovering somewhat, I was able to ask, "What did you do Trip?"

"What else could I do?" he stammered, "I kicked them up their bare brown asses and told them to get behind the fucking wheel." All is well that ends well, but next time we made sure we could use off-duty Thai police.

European cities are all much the same, except for Italy. It is unthinkable for Italians to forego their lunch or breaks and it was tough shit for us if we had to go somewhere when they were getting a coffee or taking a smoke. You can literally scream at them, but they don't give a damn. Mediterranean life has been this way for them for centuries and they aren't about to change for us. However, when they are passionate about something like their blood-red cars and women, get out of their way. The French, well, what can I say? While in Paris, our driver was a retired French Army colonel. He was a Parachute Regiment Lieutenant during the battle of Dien Bien Phu in Indo China and we spent many a good hour chatting away. He was a hard old kick-ass fuck, and after his release from a Viet Min prison, he turned right around and fought terrorists in Algeria. He related that many of the colonial conscripts from North African countries practiced homosexuality. However, they did not consider themselves gay, but were blessed with dual sexuality. If they were not buggering each other, they picked on the young boys in the nearby villages and were deeply hated by the Vietnamese for this perverse practice. I remember a federal agent friend of mine, who was a Marine advisor in Saigon, telling me about a liaison that he had with a young Vietnamese woman whose husband had been killed in battle against the Viet Cong. They were taking care of mutual and long unmet needs on her huge mosquito-netted bed at her flat in the heart of the Chinese section of Cholon, when he missed and plunged himself deep into her butt. She stifled her scream so she wouldn't wake her two children, and when she caught her breath she gasped, "Oh, you fuck like the French." She definitely gave him the impression that she, and Vietnamese in general, considered the practice abnormal and a "Phap" (French) abomination. The French officers however, tolerated it, as long as it kept the boys from the dark continent happy. Consequently, that is what they did during most of their war zone down time, when they weren't being over run by the Viet Minh. And, like Errol Flynn, they never went to bed alone.

Norway is one the most law-abiding and gentile places I have ever visited. It is hard to imagine that their roots sprang from the conquest and plunder-seeking Vikings centuries ago. It appeared that there was little or no crime and everyone seemed to trust each other. This was interesting to me because of their Quisling history of betrayal during WWII. Wherever we traveled, we stayed in the most elaborate hotels with our client usually occupying the Presidential Suite.

In Norway, we knew that we were in for a real treat when we checked into this particular hotel. The Presidential Suite turned out to be the size of a match-box, with two single beds. We had just flown in from Italy and Germany and everyone was wiped out so no one was about to complain. While not the Waldorf Astoria, the boss just laughed and hit the rack like the rest of us.

My friends, South America is the place to go. My affection for this part of the world does not stem from the facts that my training facility, Base Choque, is located in Brazil, or because I have trained numerous police personnel from many of the countries below the Tropic of Cancer for the U.S. State Department. It is derived from a whole host of intangibles. The people are great and know how to enjoy themselves, life is free and easy, the entertainment goes on forever, the women are the most beautiful in the world, and cops rule. The atmosphere is infectious and, fortunately, we have been accepted by the police as brothers, so everything else falls into place. My friends Rafael and Heidi always looked after us in Caracas, Venezuela, and since Rafael was a cop, we utilized him on our protective details. Obtaining weapons was never a problem. It seemed that regardless of where you were a cop in the world, the South Americans treated you as one of their own. American law enforcement, particularly street cops, are greatly respected by their Latin counterparts.

Driving in South America has been the worst I have yet to experience. The only rules are that there are no rules. Traffic lights, if they are working, mean nothing. If you ride a motorbike or are a pedestrian and venture forth into traffic, watch out, because you are a legitimate target. If you get hit, the police may find you at fault for unnecessarily placing yourself in jeopardy. It is a real free for all and it's every man for himself. If the freeway has three lanes, it will be transformed into a five-lane facility by rush hour. Turn signals are for pussies and horns are the primary means of communication.

Decio, my police contact, arranged for a couple of cops to assist us on a detail in Sao Paulo. Decio drove the lead car, carrying David, who was functioning as the personal protection officer, and the client. Officer George handled the chase vehicle, with Barry and I on board. George spoke English and was a very friendly guy, but one thing you cannot criticize Brazilians for is their driving. Every man considers himself the modern incarnation of Brazil's most famous Grand Prix driver, Ayrton Senna, and a powerful car automatically brings this latent alter ego to the surface. Trying to make suggestions regarding their driving would be like telling them how to play soccer. George habitually followed the VIP car too closely and at excessive speeds. True, you do not want other cars penetrating your convoy, but it meant that he was frequently slamming on his brakes to avoid rear-ending the client and then flooring it like a fool to close the gap again. Barry's nerves could only take a day of this jerking back and forth, so, consequently, I ended up in the front seat. I soon found out why he bailed out of the shotgun rider's seat. We hadn't gone more than two kilometers and my legs were literally worn out from trying to drive them through the floorboards every time he panic stopped. Finally I lost my patience and yelled, "For fuck's sake, George, slow down and smooth it out." Apparently taking my protest in stride he replied, "No problem Mr. Alan, I know how to drive in Brazil, leave it to me."

By the time we got to the venue, I was a nervous wreck. He had another bad habit of always putting the gear-shift stick into neutral when we stopped at lights. This was not a good practice, because when the light turned green, the VIP car was off and George was fucking around trying to get our car into gear. This meant that he would fall behind again and end up driving like a madman in order to catch up. I had had enough of this bullshit, so I reamed him out and told him not to take the car out of gear again. I could see him raise his eyebrows and heard him sigh as he probably said to himself, "You stupid foreigners, you don't have any idea how to drive here in my homeland. If you don't keep quiet you will get us all killed." We had to stop at the very next light and sure as shit, George took the transmission out of gear. By now, I was so pissed off I was perspiring with pure rage. On green, Decio gunned the client's car and we were left in the dust. When George finally slammed into first, the lead vehicle was 100 meters down the road and a big truck was masking it from us. With a screech of smoking Michelins, we were off, but there was only one little problem. It was in the wrong direction.

George had found reverse instead of first and I nearly got whiplash. All I was thinking about was the impending impact of ramming into the inevitable vehicle behind us. I guess that was our lucky day as all we hit was fresh air. That was the final straw and both Barry and I threatened him with death if he didn't get his shit together ASAP.

Most of the time, life on the road is damn dull. Living out of a suitcase, airports with their delays, hotels with inept service, and eating less-than-healthy restaurant food gets old pretty quick. The days are long, tiring, and tedious. One aspect of a protective detail that is usually more enjoyable than other tasks is the advance party. The advance party travels ahead of the main body, ensuring that all arrangements are properly made and meets the main body upon arrival. Normally two of us were assigned to this element and it was a relief to be separated from the client and his entourage and subject to your own time schedule. Rusty was an excellent advance man and had a reputation for being very methodical and meticulous. He had been to the Soviet Union and later Russia dozens of times.

Prior to one of these trips he had all his dress shirts cut and hemmed at the sides, so he could run his radio accessory wires through a slot rather than down his sleeve. He was extremely proud of his idea and was thinking of patenting the system. While in Moscow, he put all his shirts into the hotel laundry for the normal service. When the maid returned with his shirts, she was all excited and proud of the fact that she had spotted these "rips" in his shirts and sewn them up. She was anticipating a huge tip for her initiative, but all I think she left that room with was a good bollocking and a kick up the ass.

Speaking of advance work. On one particular trip to Orlando, we took Duke along to augment the escort section. David was sick, so Barry was running the detail. He told Duke and I to whip over and recon a hotel where our client was scheduled to give a speech the next morning to a large gathering of people. Duke and I checked out the theater, met with the organizers and scouted a secure route through back corridors and the kitchen. We planned to have the client enter the hotel premises through a rear service door, move through the nearly deserted corridors, and proceed straight to the stage. However, the morning of the speech we ended up short of personnel. Trip and Chuck had to secure a meeting room at another hotel; one operator was escorting the client's wife; and Barry, Duke, and I were with the VIP. It was fortunate that we did our advance because we did not have anyone to spare to move ahead and act as our advance reception contingent. This turned out to be a big mistake! We arrived and exited the vehicles. Duke led the way through the back corridors, Barry acted as the PPO, and I held the rear security slot. Just outside the door to the theater, we paused for a moment. The client straightened his jacket, did the usual hair thing, and took in a big breath in anticipation of his entrance to an enthusiastic and very receptive room full of people. "All right, Duke, let's do it," said the VIP. Duke hits the door and barrels into the room like a rugby forward. Strange! From my rear security position, I expected to hear thunderous applause and cheering, but instead there was stone cold silence. Christ, the theater was empty. "Holy shit, this is embarrassing," I thought to myself, but relived somewhat because I was not up front. Damn, I was positive this was the right door. I could see Barry and the VIP staring at Duke like he was a moron, but Duke, beaming with confidence and acting like "Joe Cool," didn't even bat an eyelid. Backtracking, Duke strode down the corridor another fifteen meters and stopped in front of a door that was identical to the first one.

"This is it sir," he announced with slight twang of hope in his voice. Again, the boss preps himself for the grand entrance and nods to Duke to open it and lead him in. I'll be damned if we didn't end up in a pitch black, empty room that was deathly silent.

What the hell was going on? A normal man would have dug a hole and put his head into it, but not Duke. He just looked at me with a blank expression and shrugged his shoulders as if to say, "Fuck it, let's just give it a miss and go home and have a few brews." The VIP had different ideas, and looking up to the heavens with his hands held out to his sides and pleaded, "Goddamn it, are we even in the right hotel?" With that exasperated blasphemy, he stormed off and headed toward the hotel lobby. Eventually, a successful entrance was made but with Duke acting as our "tail-end Charlie." The bloody organizers had moved the gathering to another location in the hotel complex and not bothered to contact us with the change. Lesson learned: Do not proceed without some type of Advance Team.

Fifteen of us deployed to Europe for a four-week job with the client, his wife and children, their nannies, and about twenty close friends. He not only brought all the amenities with him when he traveled, but occasionally took the neighbourhood along as well. Mike, an LAPD narcotics officer, and I flew to London as the advance and had everything squared away by the time the main body arrived. He was a big rough bastard who made me a little nervous because I had deeply offended him during our first meeting a couple of weeks earlier. The client was hosting a huge fundraiser at the mansion for the Brazilian Rain Forest. Since Sting was the organizer of this foundation, he and a number of his close friends from the entertainment industry gave a concert for 1200 invited guests. Mike and I were initially posted along the perimeter fence line behind the estate. It took me a good thirty minutes to elicit just a grunt out of Mike. He was definitely not a conversationalist. However, one thing that I did notice was that he was a heavy smoker and would light a fresh one up every 10 minutes. Even though we both spoke English, I was soon to find out that my version of the "Queens English" was a bit different than his version of American English. In New Zealand we referred to a cigarette as a "fag," whereas a homosexual was known as a "poofter." After I saw him light up his fifth "fag," I was desperate to break the ice and establish a rapport with this guy. The conversation went something like this:

"So, Mike, you enjoy the odd fag now and again do you?"

After nearly swallowing his cigarette, he replied, "What the fuck did you say?" Innocently I replied, "So you enjoy the odd fag now and again?" Instead of killing me, he cursed and stomped off and I didn't see him again for the event's duration. My gaff was further exacerbated when no one came to relieve me and I remained on the fence line for the next four hours. I finally called in and asked where my replacement was. "Come on back to the security hooch," was the immediately reply. Upon arrival, I was braced and immediately asked, "What the fuck did you say to Mike, he is really pissed off." That was the night that I found out what a "fag" meant in America. Eventually everything got straightened out and Mike and I became good mates.

Our client leased a Boeing 727 for the trip and we had the limousines and bus waiting for them at a private airport. He spent a week in London, where he rented a house for himself and the family, and the rest of the party and security contingent were accommodated at a nearby hotel.

The following week, we moved to a 2500-acre chateau, formerly owned by the King of Belgium, that was located just outside of Paris. This was a refreshing change from the hustle and bustle of London and our days were spent lounging around the grounds and either horseback riding or taking archery lessons. The rent for this extravagant estate was a mere USD$200,000 for the week.

This was also my first opportunity to work with and get to know Tom, who was a federal officer and good mate of Mark's. He was a big, impressive man and easy to get along with. From Paris, Mark and I flew to Naples to perform the next advance. At this Italian port we boarded the Katalina, a luxury yacht that our client had leased for a two week cruise through the Mediterranean. The vessel made port calls to all the hot spots like Rome, Portofino, Cannes, and Monaco. It was in Naples that I first met and worked with Bobby G. Reed, who not only became a great friend, but also exerted a huge influence on my decision to move from Los Angeles to Walls, Mississippi. Bobby is a little hard to describe because I had never met anyone quite like him before. He was born and raised in the Mississippi Delta and had been a Mississippi State Trooper since 1975. We were short on manpower, so a distress call went out. It was not feasible to pull one of the men from residence in Los Angeles, so Bobby was contacted. This was his first major overseas mission and his trip from Mississippi to Italy was not a positive one. All his baggage was lost and has never been found. I encountered him standing in his hotel room door in his underpants and all he would talk about was how much he missed shooting his guns — hell, he had only been gone a day. I guess the fact that he was a keen combat shooter and a member of the world champion Mississippi Highway Patrol shooting team explained his urgings. His first assignment was to accompany a truck driver from Naples to Cannes with a load of suitcases that the client's wife had filled with new fashions. He couldn't speak a word of Italian and the driver couldn't speak a word of Southern red-neck, so it turned out to be a long two days.

Bobby was very popular with the client's kids and six months later was brought on board to provide security at the Aspen, Colorado mansion. Being the festive season, the client's twelve year old daughter and two of her friends wanted to head down town for a couple of hours. She requested that Bobby accompany them, so being the man that he was, he disappeared in a flash. Ninety minutes later, the kids appeared at the security office, excited and ready to go. All hands were floored when Bobby, the trusty bodyguard, strolled up wearing a wig, dress, high heels, stockings, and handbag and made up with lipstick and rouge. No doubt, he must have worked undercover in drag and made a passable female. It was difficult to fathom his motivation for this far-out initiative, but I guess he felt the girls would be more comfortable shopping in the presence of a female rather than with a knuckle dragger. However, he paid for his good intentions when he returned two hours later, with feet aching and his make-up running down his face. Bobby was also not allowed to answer the house intercom phone because the client couldn't understand a word he said. Skiing was one of the main reasons the client and his family went to Aspen house and this trip was no exception. I had never skied, so I took a few lessons and stayed on the beginner's slopes. Bobby, however, was ready by the second day for the double black diamond runs. I still look, but I have yet to find any mountains, let alone snow, in the Mississippi Delta. Maybe water skiing helped, but it is still a mystery to me where Bobby learned to become an "expert" snow skier. Apparently things did not go quite as planned on one of his kamikaze runs. After ten smooth meters, the snow must have reached up and grabbed his skis and he completed the run tumbling and cartwheeling like a white ball of shit. The next time I saw him, he was lying in bed moaning and groaning and barely able to move. The rest of the detail spent a good half hour retrieving his equipment, which was splattered over

Mississippi State Trooper Bobby G. Reed with some petty cash during his attachment to our team on a four-week VIP detail in Europe – July, 1989

the side of the mountain. Humor aside, Bobby was a wonderful human being and would literally give you the shirt off his back, including his skivvies (or panties, depending on the moment), and has helped me out immensely in my transition to the Southern lifestyle.

There is no other place on Earth that has the concentration of wealth than there is in Beverly Hills. This opulent enclave within Los Angeles county is, however, divided into three tiers. There are definite areas assigned to the rich, super-rich, and ultra-rich. The luxurious shopping and business centers that serve as an outlet for all this green are located between Santa Monica and Wilshire Boulevards. Rodeo Drive is one of the most costly strips of business real estate any where in the universe. Within walking distance are the "low cost" mansions and homes owned by some of the most wealthy and influential businessmen in the county. These "shacks" terminate at Sunset Boulevard. From this foot-hill location, the land rises dramatically towards Mulholland Drive and it is from this dominating terrain that its occupants can stare down at the rest of us common folk. In this oasis of extravagance, the huge mansions and estates of the movie stars, entertainers, and mega-rich are located. Hidden behind seven-foot steel and concrete walls, electronic gates, barbed wire, and protected by armed guards and the latest electronic security measures, these people live in a fantasy world of their own: the luxurious manicured grounds, the children's Disneyland play areas, the costly art work, custom furniture, private movie theaters, gymnasiums with personal trainers, huge bedrooms, and the cavernous closets crammed with the latest of the latest. At our client's estate, two of the three vaults of conspicuous consumption were located underground and were larger than my apartment. The families live in a cloistered environment and those that were born wealthy have little idea of what life is all about in the real world. Since childhood, everything has been laid out on a gold platter for them, and our responsibility was to ensure that this routine went uninterrupted and their lives proceeded smoothly.

The VIP that I worked full-time for from 1989-1991 had divorced and, subsequently, adopted a less extravagant lifestyle. When he recognized that life could go on without a reinforced platoon of bodyguards, they were gone. Out of the original 42 stalwarts, he maintained a small group of heavies to cover his residence 24/7. The client bought a huge house that overlooked the city for his bachelor pad. It was a stunning modern design and featured a huge dance and party area with elevator access to all floors. It was perfect for a single man of extreme means and "Mike Tyson" seemed to share the same opinion. We had a Black gent on our original detail that had been a loyal and excellent employee for years. Klaus was a great guy and seriously into boxing. He was also a practical joker, as were most of the crew, and they were always taking the piss out of each other. Another officer named Alan was on duty one evening when a vehicle pulled up to the front gate. The security system was brand new and the camera image was somewhat fuzzy. Alan could make out a Black face, so he asked the individual to identify himself.

"Mike Tyson," was the instant reply. Slightly annoyed, Alan admonished, "Stop fucking around Klaus, you were supposed to be here thirty minutes ago." Alan then opened the gate and went out to the courtyard to meet his buddy. To his regretful surprise, a black Mercedes pulled into the courtyard, which was the first indication that something might be wrong. The door flew opened and out jumped one pissed off "Iron Mike." Looming over Alan, he growled, "I am here to check out my house."

"Sorry Sir, this house belongs to my boss, he bought it last week."

"Like fuck, this is my house and I am going in to check it out."

With the appearance of Tyson's 300-pound body-guard, Alan realized that this was getting serious. He then firmly placed his hand on his Colt .45 and advised in his strongest, but cracking, voice that under no circumstances could he allow him to enter the residence. With Tyson's veins popping and sweat pouring down his face, he unleashed a rash of abuse and threatened Alan within an inch of his young life before racing out the gate. Screaming in a very credible Schwzanneger imitation, "I'll be back," indicating that the heavy artillery was about to be deployed. Alan's little legs hardly made it back into the security room, where he collapsed into a chair and tried to figure out what the fuck had just occurred.

Sure enough, Tyson returned a few nights later with his heavies in tow. However, this time his pugilistic force didn't get past the gate because all hands were present, locked, and cocked. It appears that Tyson also had bid on the estate, but more money talks, and our client wasn't about to let this one slip by.

Many people often wonder why an individual needs bodyguards. In addition to their primary duty of establishing and maintaining the client's security, BG's ensure that the entire family's lives habitually proceed smoothly. Therefore, you have to be extremely serious about this profession, otherwise there is no way in hell you will make it at the corporate or entertainment industry level. The long hours, travel, boredom, grating personalities, and general bullshit associated with the job will always be present. Conversely, one can derive a great deal of personal satisfaction in knowing that you have contributed something to the safety and well being of an important individual and his family. However, never function under the illusion that you are something special to them. You are merely an employee and, contrary to Whitney Houston's movie experience, the BG usually does not marry the client. One client I worked for summed it up nicely. He said that if he stopped to say said "good morning" to everyone in his army of employees, from the time he got out of bed till the time he arrived at the office, he wouldn't get there till lunchtime. The client rarely thinks about anyone's welfare outside his immediate family because he is concentrating on the multi-million dollar deal of the day. In ten years of full- and part-time security work, Max's client had spoken to him about nine times. On one of these rare occasions, the client was going out on a hot date by himself and was running late. Max worked nights and had been at the range all day and was also running late, so was unable to go home and swap his grungy range truck for his city truck. Via security cameras, he observed the client rush down the stairs, get into his Rolls Royce Bentley, and roar off down the driveway. On cue, Max had the electronic gate opened, but the vehicle came to an abrupt halt. The client jumped out and was swearing at this $240,000 bullet-proof vehicle. Max, a closet car lover, went out to prevent unnecessary damage to such a fine car and to see if he could help. The culprit turned out to be a flat tire, and assuming the client had never changed one, Max offered to do it for him.

The boss glanced at his Rolex and immediately made a command decision. "I am extremely late, Max, your vehicle — right now, let's go."

"Oh shit," Max thought, this is not going to be good. Nevertheless, being the outstanding Marine that he was, Max charged across the parking area, cranked up his pick-up truck, and ground it into gear. In a cloud of blue smoke he pulled up next to the impatient VIP. The boss scratched his head, surveyed the mess in front of him, but thinking time and sex waits for no one, jumped in. A cloud of range dust came floating off his seat and impolitely settled on his $2000 suit. Kicking empty beer cans and ammunition boxes aside, he made room for his feet. The windshield was cracked and caked with dirt, so visibility was nil. Max gunned it and took the first corner, tires screeching in protest and the suspension begging for mercy. As the VIP grabbed for his seat belt, a half-full mug of ancient and cold black coffee spilled over his finely tailored trouser leg. Hitting a bump, the glove compartment door flew open and banged him on the knee as they sped down Sunset Boulevard. When they were forced to stop at a red light, the client slid down in the seat and shielded his face. God forbid if one of his contemporaries saw him now! The boss directed Max to stop short of the restaurant rendezvous so he could coolly traverse the last few meters on foot. Prior to the boss slamming the door shut, Max politely and dutifully (with a grin on his face) inquired of the client as to what time did he want to be picked up? With a relieved expression, he stammered, "It's okay Max, just arrange for a limo, if you wouldn't mind."

Hopefully, this was a beneficial as well as humbling experience for the client to see how the rest of us little folk live!

Bandit Country

Duke's Story

Mindanao — The Philippines

I settled down to relax on my large veranda and gazed across the Waiapu River. Mount Hikurangi, the first landmass in the World to see the morning sun, was unfortunately veiled from my sight thanks to the monstrous Gingko and English Oak trees that encompass my property. The settlers who planted these magnificent trees 100 years earlier would be suitably impressed with their size and stature today. The rich and fertile East Coast soil coupled with healthy rainfall and long periods of Summer Sun are a proven recipe for growth. According to the local tree hugger's society, we also had the largest known Mexican Golden Oak in the Southern Hemisphere on our property.

It's a great life if you don't weaken, and especially today, being Friday, the best day of the week. I had been home on and off for the last six months. During this latest interlude, I had worked for awhile in the U.S.A., with T.E.E.S., which included a brief body-guard detail in Florida. With this involuntary layoff, not much money was coming in so things were getting tight again. As far as I am concerned, being home and unemployed is no fun. TeAo and my two teenagers were not the problem. My son Bardo was attending college while my second daughter, Paula, worked with her mother in the cafe. Tanya, our eldest daughter, was in the rural housewife mode complete with two great kids. Other than for frequently mowing our spacious lawns, cutting endless chords of next winter's firewood, chasing wild pigs with the dogs and the odd tame one that ventured too close to my house, venturing forth in all sorts of weather and seas, while helping Ian and Stan with their cray fishing enterprise, and frequently doing my best to prop up the Ruatoria Pub's bar, I was not being very productive. In grunt rifleman terms, I was a complete waste of rations. I desperately needed to get my arse into gear and get back into the global security circuit and close protection work force.

Since Captain Cook's first keg of Navy rum was tapped at Young Nick's Head in nearby Gisborne, all New Zealanders have traditionally celebrated the Friday weeks end with a healthy drinking session. In my father's era, work ended at 5:00 pm and, strangely, the pubs closed one hour later. As a result, the infamous New Zealand six o'clock swill began out of necessity. Men folk, at least twenty-one years old at the time, would belly up to the bar and drink themselves senseless in the allotted 60-minute time frame. It's no wonder that the generations who remember this phenomenon, myself included, became staunch practitioners of binge drinking.

Dad did not drink and my grandparents only drank occasionally, if ever, and never to excess, so there goes alcohol gene theory. I was definitely a late bloomer, but thanks to good old infantry training, I made up with amazing capacity and a huge appetite. I started drinking around age 17 and never looked back. The military of the day was a huge influence on my drinking habit. Alcohol laws for the military were lax and sources were very convenient. The military recognized the value of social drinking sessions for building comradery, and they would rather have you drink on base than off. We had Sunday trading in the 1960's, which was years before the civilian pubs were granted seven days trading. Add happy hours every Friday, NAAFI and duty-free beer while overseas, and the cheapest beer prices in New Zealand to this encouraging atmosphere. Every battalion sports event or official occasion always ended up with a huge social piss up. Drinking and socialising was a significant part of the soldier's code and considered essential to team bonding. Conversely, non-drinkers were treated with some caution. Who can say it was wrong. In previous World Wars, New Zealanders soldiered as a nation all over the globe. Talk to the old veterans and listen to their stories, and after a few fascinating anecdotes about contacts and shots fired, these accounts will eventually include drinking adventures in the most unlikely places on Earth.

Stan Hovell and Hori Hearn were my good mates in Ruatoria, and between us we maintained the Friday night tradition with punctual dedication. In fact, it was not uncommon for us to enjoy several extended Fridays each week. Stan and Hori are both Maoris, but with significant European ancestry. Stan's grandfather was originally from the U.K., and like many of his era, retained links to the old country through the naming of his children and his strict, unforgiving Old England posture. Although 50 years of age, Stanly Strangeway Hovell is still a tall, raw-boned individual with a great sense of humour and an abiding love of country and western ballads. He was a rugged guy, but had a heart of gold and he seemed physically incapable of not spending everything in his pocket once on the turps. Stanly would buy anybody a beer and he often did. Thanks to him and Tiger John Pohatu, nips of Black Sambucca's became a common, but devastating beverage for our cadre of friends. Once the first round of Sambucca appeared, then all thoughts of an early night were destroyed.

Hori, the son of an English sailor and Maori Mum, was a fitting partner in crime for Stan and his ability to spin jokes and yarns only surpassed by his dart playing and capacity for Rhinebeck beer. His barrel chest and tree stump legs were complimented by a large, shaved head sporting a rakish goatee, with clear, twinkling, black eyes, and one-and-a-half ears. The missing portion had been bitten off in a brawl as a young soldier. Covering his massive forearms were a selection of ethnic Maori tattoos and, in fact, were the second layer, because the originals had been of lesser merit and self-applied by him many years earlier. Hori and I had been soldiers together in the late 70's, during which time he helped mentor a very young Alan Brosnan through his early years in the military. These two were great fun, along with Warren Richards, Ian Smith, Mohi Haenga, and others. They managed to fill the significant void left by my former military mates and were true East Coast companions. Hori and Stan both loved an audience and women were always part of their scene. They could both entertain and were gracious hosts. However, hunting, fishing, and socialising, in that order, were the priorities in their lives, with necessary employment representing an obstacle to these sacred activities.

My mind drifted along as I lounged on the porch. However, this did not last very long and my tranquil state was violently interrupted by the tumultuous sound of cattle dogs barking and bellowing livestock, interspersed by the loud swearing of horse-mounted stockmen. "Skip, get the fuck out of there, you bloody mongrel!" Shrill whistles and the sharp clatter of iron-shod horses on the highway temporarily shattered the prevailing peace and rural harmony of my home. With some detachment, I watched the daily battle between stockmen, horses, cattle, and dogs as they pushed and prodded the large mob past my property to the nearby stockyards. It had been a hard winter and the lack of an early rain had resulted in a stunted crop of grass. This had forced farmers to reduce their herds by prematurely selling off stock at lower prices. Local economic depression and its inevitable ripple effects were beginning to raise its ugly head.

Without a steady income, life can become very tedious and frustrating. My wife and I had received local approval to commercially develop our modest property. We were in the process of obtaining a refinancing package, but it required collateral in the form of a consistent income to satisfy the banking system. For me, this represented a formidable obstacle because, similar to many other rural areas in New Zealand, the East Coast was not considered to be a viable region to invest in.

The shrill ring of the telephone caused only minor interest. With a nineteen-year old daughter and sixteen-year old son at home, there was very little reason to expect that the call would be for TeAo or myself. How wrong I was. The call came from a long time acquaintance of both Alan and mine, who was currently the director of a security corporation based in the Philippines. He needed a man for a twelve-month stint in Mindanao. It didn't take much to convince me to volunteer, and without a hell of a lot of thought or preparation, I packed my war bags and, once more, I took off for distant shores.

Manila, the capitol of the Philippine archipelago, has one of the most disorganized international airports in the world. Although the overall service is satisfactory, it's passenger-processing system is bloody chaotic. And, it really becomes confusing when you encounter the taxi stands. Taxis vary in the degree of service and reliability in every country, and here it was no different. I had been briefed on which cab company to patronize and my contact quoted me the price to pay from the airport to my destination. The wrong taxi over here can cause problems well out of the ordinary.

The trip to Makati, a wealthy urban commercial area in central Manila, can take hours depending on the traffic. Much of Manila remains typically third world, violent, dirty, crowded and badly polluted. It was typical of the types of countries people like myself frequently work in. Although the police attempt to direct traffic, road rules are totally ignored. However, unlike Malayan drivers, they don't get into heated verbal battles with each other, but instead, slowly and deliberately creep across intersections, forcing other vehicles to swerve or stop to avoid collision. If their vehicle Hari-Kari act prevails, the traffic flow is forced to change until another suicidal driver can reverse the tide. Of course, if you're politically powerful enough, you can travel in any direction, at any time, on any side of the road courtesy of heavily armed and blaring police escorts. Pedestrians have no right of way, but an amazingly resilient population of road-side peddlers, from pre-schoolers to Grannies in their 80's, hustle a living on the main road systems with their trays of cigarettes, candy, newspapers, and carts of steamed peanuts. They just stand in the middle of three and four lane highways seemingly oblivious to the dangers of death and injury that have to be common experiences for these folks. Like in any other country, traffic wardens stand in small-elevated kiosks at the crossroads directing traffic, but for some reason they do this even though the traffic lights are fully functional.

The international security and special operations arena is a small one. Many operators in the South East Asian Theater know, or at least have heard of, each other. My new boss, John Wilson, director of the organisation in Manila, and I had first met in 1984 on a Royal New Zealand Air Force flight from hell. As part of a military exercise, we were packed into a lumbering C-130 that flew for eight crowded and miserable days from Auckland to the United Kingdom. The stopovers and the overnight stays were many and damned hectic. John, like a number of us, had become a casualty from some hard drinking and partying during a brief stop in Los Angeles and missed the next leg of the flight. Nevertheless, he measured up to the task, and after purchasing a commercial ticket, not only managed to catch up, but was waiting for us in Washington D.C. somewhat wiser and definitely somewhat poorer. However, his problems were far from over, and the liaison officer in charge waded in and gave him a severe verbal bollocking with a promise of further punishment upon our return to N.Z. in six months.

John was a slightly built, blonde and blue-eyed Kiwi. He had completed 20 years of service as a military policeman before retiring and striking out for security contract work in the U.K. Numerous years on the circuit accepting both the good and the bad jobs bestowed upon him sufficient credibility and contacts to acquire a management position in Manila. He had changed slightly, but haven't we all? He still appeared quite fit and healthy and was obviously enjoying his duties in this part of the World. He was performing well within the organization, which, among other activities, provided crisis management assistance to wealthy and high-level corporate clientele world-wide.

We chatted for a couple of hours at the company apartment in Makati, where he gave me a through briefing on the situation and my responsibilities. Divining that I was at least working for a reliable organization, my confidence was greatly enhanced. After a good nights sleep, I trotted down to the office and met the staff.

The offices were modern and tidy, complete with an attractive Filipina office staff and several resident male analysts. John explained my contract in more detail, including medical and life insurance coverage. Having browsed through the "Company's" promotional documents and literature back at the apartment I had a fairly good idea of the organization's global structure. So far, things were all measuring up and I was pleased with my new appointment.

My task was to provide a corporate client with the security expertise they required to maintain their operations as a mining exploration company on the Southern island of Mindanao. I would be the only company employee on the island, but an established network and liaison system enabled me to contact and discuss security issues with numerous indigenous organizations and individuals. The information gleaned would then be relayed back to Manila, Australia, and the United Kingdom, where it would be processed and eventually incorporated into regional security reports. The Manila based staff was an integral component of this informational chain where they constantly collated, analysed, and disseminated intelligence data on a daily basis to support both their field agents and clients.

This employment was somewhat different from my previous contracts where I worked one step closer to the threat, or threats, that prevailed in my area of responsibility. This job required more finesse and diplomacy, and the development of contacts and sources was critical. The international cross section of individuals this contract brought together was incredible and I developed a high regard for the Filipino's I came in contact with. The majority of them demonstrated a loyalty and work ethic sadly lacking in many parts of the world. However, the bad guys were just as dedicated to their various causes and ideologies, resulting in a lethal synergy that permeated the country.

The next morning, I flew down to General Santos City, the capitol of Mindanao and my home for the next 12 months.

Mindanao is the second largest island group in the Philippine Island Group, with a population of about 17 million. Ethnically, the dominant faith is Christianity (70-percent) and the Muslim community represents about one-fifth of the populace. The remainder consists of various indigenous tribes. The Christians are mainly settlers from the Visayas. Of the 24 island provinces, Christians dominate eighteen of them. In spite of a government peace accord, the island's most pressing problems were being violently hammered out between the various Libyan and al Quida sponsored Muslim factions rebelling for independence and the Philippine military and paramilitary police. Both of the latter organizations share responsibilities for peace keeping throughout the province and are configured and equipped like their American counterparts. I mainly became involved with the officers and men of the 25th Special Forces Group and the 601st infantry battalion. They were as loyal and professional as any military formation that I have had the privilege to work with. Many of them have trained with elite foreign units. They were combat hardened entities and thoroughly understood the situation and their responsibilities.

However, plain banditry, kidnapping for ransom, and other criminal activities were continuing to increase in spite of draconian measures.

To further exacerbate the problems, local politics is often a bellicose and highly personalized matter. The Philippine grass roots political situation has bred a hierarchy of political bosses from the towns on upward through the political chain to the national leaders. They are all tied to each other in some way and support each other in a complex web of favours granted and received. Many politicians maintain private armed groups and consider their constituents and provincial areas their personal property to be handed down as an inheritance to their offspring or close relatives. Shootings, kidnappings, and assassinations of political figures are common during and after election campaigns. A number of these activities were strongly related to the Moro independence and Lost Command" groups (disenchanted Muslims operating as independents from the main parties).

Understanding the Islamic conflict on Mindanao is difficult enough for people who have lived here all their lives, let alone for a foreigner to decipher. I had to digest the following background information fairly quickly:

The three main Muslim groups during my period of service were the Moro National Liberation Front (MNLF), The Moro Islamic Liberation Front (MILF), and the Abu Sayaff Group.

In the 1970's, the MNLF waged an insurgency campaign in Mindanao against the government. After years of fighting, where allegedly 50,000, civilians were killed, a peace accord was signed in 1994. However, not all of the local commanders recognized the peace agreement, and to this day continue to carry out armed actions independent of the MNLF leadership. The government estimates that the MNLF has a current strength of 16,000 heavily armed combatants.

The Moro Islamic Liberation Front (MILF) was an MNLF splinter group. They want to establish an independent Islamic state in Mindanao, and conservative estimates put the group's strength around 12,000. However, this group is considered the biggest threat to the security of Mindanao. They have gone toe to toe with the military on numerous occasions and continue to do so years after the peace accord.

Abu Sayaff and his band of radicals emerged in 1992 (also known as Al Harakat Al Islamiya. AHAID). They also desire to create an independent Muslim Mindanao. Reportedly, they have 800 members. They have been engaged in numerous terrorist attacks including bombings in the main cities of General Santos and Davao. In 1995 they mounted a full-scale attack on the town of Ipil and 53 people were killed. During my stint in Mindanao, they were fully involved in the kidnapping business and had abducted numerous locals and foreigners in Sulu and Basilan. Currently, they are being pursued with a vengeance by authorities with U.S. Special Forces assistance.

Mindanao's fundamentalist Muslim groups and the international terrorist Osama Bin Laden have close links. The participation of Filipino Mujahedin in the Afghanistan and internal Russian-Chechen wars is common knowledge. Bin Laden has a Filipina wife from Mindanao, as well as several other spouses around the world, and business interests in the region. His last known visit to the area was in 1993.

The Communist Party of the Philippines/New Peoples Army (CPP and NPA), are less active these days, but they continue to carry out extortions, ambushes, and assassinations when the mood or necessity strikes them.

Our client had two areas of concern. One resided in General Santos City, and the other in the rugged hill country of South Cotabato. While the Islamic threat could not be dismissed, the most important issues for me were the indigenous Filipinos from the hill country known as the B'laan. There is no official legal system in this part of the world. The tribal system is, as in other relatively primitive places, biblical in nature, and an eye-for-an-eye philosophy prevails. These bad boys all have one thing in common, they all respect the age-old payback system and retaliatory revenge is definitely a matter of honor and a natural attribute for these tribal societies. The clans settle conflicts between themselves and no questions are ever asked.

Once or twice a week my driver and I would travel the two hours from Gensen (General Santos City) to our hill country base camp at Tampakan and stay overnight. I would check up on the security force, catch up with the on-site company reps and attend to other routine matters. Although it was considered unwise to travel at night, there was little evidence to indicate that normal daytime travel was unsafe. The drive on the main highway from Gensen to the base camp is a decent one, and although traffic is somewhat hectic near the townships, once out in the rural areas it's not a bad ride. Filipinos drive with élan, and a lot of horn, but generally safely. Beautiful Dole pineapple plantations on leased land stretch for miles. In the background, the impressive Mount Matutum dominates everything. Local farmers and large landowners both till extensive land areas with the native "caribou" (water buffalo) that dot the horizon. Huge maize and cornfields are everywhere. I am amazed at how the caribou can walk and pull a singled-bladed plough through the young corn shoots without destroying the tightly arranged plantings. Rice, maize, papaya, bananas, coconuts, and many other varieties of fruits are also being cultivated and harvested, supporting Mindanao's claim as being the food bowl of the Philippines.

Members of the Philippine National Police (PNP) detachments could be spotted lazily lounging around the city and township areas during the day's heat. However, this posture of "relaxed readiness" did not personify the group as a whole. During my stint in the wilderness, I met and developed strong ties with several very professional and experienced law enforcement officials. The police carry small arms similar to the military, and the line between them, the Philippine Constabulary and the military, is often a blurred one. In the rural areas, small military outposts assume law and order responsibilities, to a degree, because the police seem somewhat reluctant to venture too far from their support bases in the city. Considering the furious and at times high-powered weapons contacts between militants and the military, this was a tactically sound decision. However, in B'laan country any allusion to law and order is strictly cosmetic, and above all else, tribal law prevails.

Continuing on our journey into the rural hinterlands, we exited the concrete highway and started our final forty-minute drive into the hills of the last B'Laan stronghold. The terrain began to dramatically change. Gone were the rolling farmlands, large towns, and settlements. Now we were plying a narrow dirt track more suitable for ponies and motor-bikes than for four-wheel drive vehicles. However, in this backcountry the preferred mode of transport was the numerous "Skylabs." These are motorcycles with extended seats that could accommodate several passengers. Some bikes were also modified to carry two huge woven baskets like gigantic saddlebags for goods and produce. Another very popular form of privately owned public transportation was the lavishly decorated "Jeepnies." These extended body, WWII jeep-like contraptions and their drivers would careen down the hills with reckless abandon in an attempt to gain precious momentum for the struggle up the next steep grade with their precarious loads of people, squawking chickens, and bags of maize. Loading was to the extreme and every vehicle's maximum gross weight was exceeded many times over. Every inch of space was occupied, and bodies and gear also hung from the roofs, taking advantage of any available handhold. Physical fitness and agility were definitely a requirement for all passengers, both inside and out.

Thatched huts and timber dwellings now dominated the rural village landscapes. The B'Laan villages were very simple and usually consisted of a cluster of several dwellings. Women toil long and hard to simply get the water required to do laundry and for other daily uses. Nevertheless, community cleanliness was scrupulously observed. Although they are a warrior society, the B'Laan toil on the mountainous slopes that surround them, and with basic methods cultivate crops of maize that mean survival to them. However, this idyllic lifestyle is often disturbed by armed clashes and tribal murders. Expressionless male faces gazed our way as we drove through the area, and the women shyly looked up from their daily tasks as we passed by, but also displayed no sign of recognition or emotion. Like kids the world over, the children had a different reaction to our presence and were extremely vocal and happy with any change in their daily routine. The B'laan are a small race of people with copper-toned skin and are fine-boned and lean in testimony to their diet and active lifestyle. Their traditional clothing is extremely colourful, but is reserved for important celebrations and activities. The men are fiercely protective of their women and families, and they very subtly, but unmistakably, project this. We would frequently drive past wiry B'Laan men, mounted on a their stunted native ponies, sitting like Apache warriors complete with rope bridle, home-made saddle, stoic expressions, razor sharp bolos, and WWII M1 .30-caliber carbines.

The company base camp was in a majestic setting surrounded by the mountain ranges of South Cotabato, with a grand view of the imposing Mount Matutum. The camp was a well-constructed facility and I was pleasantly surprised. Although small in number, the security force looked good and appeared to carry out their duties with diligence. The only downside was the never-ending struggle and balance required when initially forming a security force including local indigenous members. Loyalty to their clans is far stronger than it is to anything else, let alone to a foreign mining company. Most of the company employees were involved in community relations and were augmented by a handful of administration personnel. They were a dedicated group of Filipinos, and the company's considerable success was in large part attributable to this efficient group. The community relations staff lived with the locals and several were B'Laan tribal members. Their dedication was almost embarrassing and something that I have not often witnessed anywhere else. I was very impressed. The camp reflected company policy and was deliberately non-hostile in appearance. The company was definitely out to win the hearts and minds of the indigenous people. However, this openness presented me with difficult physical security conditions, but was understandable in light of company policy.

CAFGU troops, Davao-Mindanao. These detachments, consisting of four 10-man teams, guard their posts for months at a time with little to no backup.

The company set up tribal trusts and created the required infrastructure to ensure that the traditional B'Laan would survive and prosper into the new millennium. As far as the Philippine government is concerned, the B'Laan are a forgotten people. They have no government schools, hospitals, or public services that are common elsewhere in the country. However, in the government's defense, the B'Laan have rejected any proposed changes or reforms and desire to continue their traditional lifestyle. This tribal system definitely has its downside, and rapes, murders, wife stealing, and indiscriminate revenge killings are part of the fabric of this feudal society. However, for hundreds of years, land hungry settlers, much like any colonization process, have steadily eroded their land base. Furthermore, Filipinos from

Regular force troops, even though better equipped, still lack immediate backup from assisting forces – Mindanao

the Christian areas have intermarried with the B'laan, thus gaining land through dowry and slowly forcing indigenous people out.

Although the elders are mainly Animists, some members of the tribe have converted to Christianity. These conversions have provided mainly spiritual benefits for the B'Laan and the only visible material gains that I could see was the building of more churches in Mindanao than the Baptists had in America's deep South. In contrast, the mining company has provided educational grants and built the existing schools. Limited medical care is also available through infirmaries established by the company. The B'Laan have now been forced into their last bastion and the tribal councils have very difficult decisions to make regarding the future. My client and other non-governmental organizations are attempting to guide the B'Laan into the best outcome, as they perceive it. I have observed similar situations in a number of countries and I have, therefore, developed my own views on native displacement. In this case as in others, the ore deposits in the exploration area are significant and will be exploited by someone. Whether it is an international company that respects and abides by international law and is dedicated to ensuring the indigenous people are fairly compensated and cared for, or, in contrast, operations are conducted by a local mining company not as committed and without the resources or financial backing to properly look after the locals, this ore body will be mined. I don't want to portray the mining company as being completely altruistic, because this "attitude" toward indigenous peoples has, to a large degree, been forced on global mining corporations after strong governmental "recommendations" and global pressure in general, which resulted from the negligent practices and abuses by mining consortiums in the past.

A week prior to my arrival, a comely young B'laan women had been visiting relatives in another village. On her way home she caught the eye of an admirer from another opposing clan and he decided, married or not, he wanted her as his woman. She was not interested and told him so, but this only enhanced her desirability. No B'Laan warrior can tolerate rejection, so he grabbed one of her small children and forced her to accompany him to his village. The abduction completed, she was forced to become his mistress/wife. Other witness's versions allege that she went willingly and we are still not sure of what actually happened.

After a couple of weeks, the distraught husband of the victim confronted a woman from the transgressor's clan about his wife and then demanded her return or compensation for the original bride payment. Rather than showing some compassion, she laughed at him instead. This was a bad move on her part and the humiliated warrior rounded up his friends. At day-break they launched a retaliatory raid on the kidnappers village, blasting anything that moved. In the ensuring gun battle a women and her infant child were shot to death. This is an example of their "tit for tat" justice system and was considered appropriate under B'Laan law.

Both sides were now appeased and had drawn both real and symbolic blood. Now the two tribal councils met to begin the lengthy compensation process. The tribal elders amicably discussed the remunerations for a few days and a decision was finally agreed upon that all parties were obligated to live by. However, this did not necessarily mean the matter was closed, and like the Hatfield's and McCoy's, the deadly feud could reignite at any time in the future.

The B'Laan are a fine looking race, and when compared to their distant hill country cousins from Papua New Guinea's Western Highlands, they look like refined gentlemen. However, they both shared a mutual lethality and lust for revenge over any insult, no matter how slight.

Although most of the clans had leaders that were either elderly or wise men, in days gone by warriors also ruled groups. One of the clans located in close proximity to our site was lead by a strong and ruthless leader named "Goq." At the time, he was being processed by a government amnesty board and was hoping to receive a pardon for his previous sins of banditry and general mayhem. In B'Laan eyes he was not a brigand, but instead a warrior leader of considerable magnitude.

Goq was quite charismatic, and among his people he enjoyed a huge following. Our day-to-day functions relied on the peace and harmony that generally prevailed throughout the community. Leaders like Goq were instrumental to the law and order process in the high country. The lonely Special Forces military outposts were far and few, while the PNP kept well clear of these isolated areas. After attending the amnesty board's initial meeting, Goq was convinced that he had a reasonable chance of being pardoned. However, his violent bullying, extended wave of crime, and wild lifestyle was coming to an unanticipated, but abrupt, end. Riding a stolen horse along a mountainous trail, he too became a victim of B'laan justice. His ambushers took him down at close range with an assortment of shotguns, M1 Garands and M-16s. A ragged but effective fusillade connected and he pitched ass over kite from his saddle on to the narrow dirt track. Without achieving his destiny, a great warrior's death in battle, he simply gasped his last breath and bled his life away on the lonely jungle floor. Who killed old Goq would never be determined and the B'Laan did not appear to be overly concerned. The list of people who had good reasons to pull a trigger was extensive, but after checking out a few facts and theories, we came up with the following information:

Goq had been accused of passing information during his amnesty discussions to the military concerning a rival group of narco-bandits known as the "Fong Twins."

It was also alleged that he was the leader of the kidnapped woman's retaliatory raid that resulted in the death of a women and infant.

The owner of the stolen horse had been killed during the robbery. The murdered victim's survivors also were justified in seeking revenge.

So, a thuggish strongman and formidable local legend expired rather ignominiously, but there were many family members that lamented the reality that he was the last warrior leader of his clan.

I saw Goq in a slightly different light and believe that many will honour his demise as one of the B'Laan's last folk heroes, and, thus, he will live on forever in tale and myth. To me it seemed only fitting that he leave before he also became a "contemporary member of the human race," totally compromised by the politically correct, New World Order.

Whether Goq's alleged cooperation with authorities instigated a joint military and police operation, which uprooted a 420-million Peso, five-hectare marijuana plantation in a hinterland B'Laan community is neither here nor there. However, the Kiblawan and Davao del Sur areas were identified as one of the top marijuana producing areas in the country. During the raid, a thirty-minute running gun battle between the narcos and the strike team took place. A number of people were killed, and this action caused widely felt repercussions among the indigenous communities. This disruption of illegal activity also manifested itself by creating substantial civil unrest in an area of my client's interest.

Kidnapping statistics were on the rise, and crimes of this nature, and others, generally occurred more frequently just prior to the Christmas holidays. In addition, the MILF was negotiating another peace accord, but the word around the intel traps was that chances for diplomacy were not good. Predictably, once this became obvious to all sides, the abduction business would resume in earnest. Abu Sayaff, the culprit mainly responsible for these trends certainly hadn't slowed down and reportedly, was targeting people for future snatches. I was convinced that my expatriate manager of the exploration program was a potential target. An Australian television documentary crew managed to interview several of our employees without our knowledge. The documentary was extremely one sided and damaging. Ominously, Al Hajj Murad, vice chairman for the MILF, was also interviewed, and his comments were pointed and very disturbing. The MILF considered our company among the enemy and we could expect direct actions against us in the future. Our emergency alert status went up a couple notches, but there was little we could do to prevent an all-out assault except rely on the military to screen our installation. However, this additional external security would be temporary because they had other, more pressing priorities. My liaison with the military and police became even more critical, but our biggest threats still lurked in the cities.

One case that gained significant headlines was the kidnapping of Father Benedetti, a Catholic priest. He was held for 68 days by a ten-man "Lost Command" group of the MILF, led by a "Commander Dasdasan." After intense negotiations and extensive military operations in the area, he was uncharacteristically released unharmed. It seems another MILF Company surrounded the group's safe house and "encouraged" the splinter group to strongly consider releasing Father Benedetti and let him return to the pulpit. However, the seven million Pesos of ransom invariably ended up in the MILF's growing treasury. Reintroducing the death penalty was the government's simple answer to the rash of kidnappings, which appears to be an equal opportunity employer because among the latest defendants awaiting sentencing, three were women.

Again, prior to the Christmas holidays, major hostilities erupted between the MILF and the military on a ten-kilometre length of highway between General Santos and Cotabato City, about two hours from our office. In an unprecedented show of strength and daring, the guerrillas launched simultaneous attacks against seven army detachments in Maguindanao. The attacks came despite an existing cease-fire agreement between the rebels and the government. The MILF tightened its grip on the detachments and for the next three days the fighting continued to rage. MG 520 attack aircraft and helicopter gun-ships bombed, rocketed, and strafed the rebel concentrations in concert with armoured personnel carriers and heavy troop deployments.

Four soldiers, including an officer, were captured by the MILF on the first day of the offensive and their tortured, beheaded, and mutilated bodies were dragged out of the river several days later. No accurate body count was given and both sides claimed victory. Over fifty were killed, including civilians, and many more were wounded. However, the military insisted that many of the civilian casualties were, in fact, Muslim guerrillas. A large refugee crisis developed when thousands of civilians fled the area and descended upon the cities.

The Malacang Active Combat Force, complete with black uniforms, black and red headbands, and other vigilante groups, were making a significant comeback. This 150-man armed group claims legitimacy by falsely insisting that they have a government-sanctioned mission order enabling them to carry out their anti-crime and anti-Muslim activities.

Under the command of Sultan Kudarat, another self-styled militia group, the Pulahan Paramilitary Force, is seeking to establish an operational base from which to fight the various Muslim groups. Both these illegal organizations are based in South Cotabato, which is close to our area of interest. However these self-styled counter crime forces are only the tip of the iceberg.

To add to the volatile mix, a "Sparrow Team" (assassination squad) from the Communist NPA assassinated a Higaonon tribal leader in Agunan Del Norte. He was a former NPA member who had surrendered to the authorities. Following that was the successful shooting of a police major by three members of the NPA in Tagbilaran City. Dormant for quite awhile, the NPA hit teams decided to join the party and help stuff up the area even more.

Guerrilla actions also managed to shut down the critical Caltex oil depot in Zamboanga del Sur. Abu Sayaff's boys routinely fire-bombed the depot and attacked company executives and workers.

The situation was definitely reaching the boiling point and the season was capped off with rumours propagated by Manila newspapers that some retired generals were organizing a military coup against President Estrada. Life in Mindanao was becoming fairly interesting. I struggled at times to take in the magnitude of lawlessness that revolved around kidnap for ransom (KFR) actions and blatant extortion demands that all of the militia groups carried out with considerable enthusiasm.

During this period of seasonal unrest and good Christmas cheer, TeAo arrived for a two-week holiday. Since we had been married in Singapore, it was a pleasant and romantic flashback to the Asian food stalls and markets we explored as newlyweds and we thoroughly enjoyed ourselves. The hospitality we were shown was extraordinary. During this period, Mike Smith, a long time friend and former SF operator, came down from Manila. Mike had only recently arrived in the Philippines, but he was not shy when it came to entertaining. We started early with a great seafood feast and marched onward to the popular local drinking establishments. As we drank down the evening, our choice of bars deteriorated dramatically. Every military man knows that the sleaziest pubs with the worst reputations are the most fun. In the wee hours of the morning we finally ended up at seedy club surrounded by bar girls and singing our lungs out into the Karaoke microphone. TeAo is probably the only female Maori blues singer to have ever graced the Karaoke stage in the infamous seedy and downright dirty Kawaii Bar in General Santos City on the island of Mindanao. Mike kept the American flag flying and managed to take three young ladies back to his hotel. However, by that time, he was exhausted and, believe it or not, they dropped him off, tucked him into bed, and left. No funny business, they just made sure he was okay. Before they departed, Mike gave them a handful of money and mumbled something about food. Not typical Manila bar girl hustlers, the girls returned the next morning with breakfast. Still hung over, they propped him up in bed and hand fed him like a baby. As soon as he finished, one of them wiped his face with a hot towel and said they were off to church.

Fortunately, the Christmas holidays remained relatively calm and I started the New Year with renewed enthusiasm. My driver, Poppy, and I returned to the hill country exploration site to assess the current situation. Things appeared fairly quiet in the highlands; the local tribesman pointedly ignored us again as we passed through their land, although by now they sure as hell recognized the wagon, Poppy, and the White man.

This small clan was situated a couple of hundred yards from our base and well within visual range. An hour or so later, I happened to be observing the valley and general area while sipping a welcome cup of coffee, when suddenly I heard the loud report of a firearm. The round had been fired from the village of Datalmagisi. Women and kids were chaotically racing around, wailing, and screaming. A few more seconds expired and three more rounds cut through the air. Men could be heard yelling above the confusion and with considerable anger. We moved toward the main gate to assess the situation. By the time we arrived things had quieted down and we were apprised of the shootout by our shotgun-toting security force.

Several youths had been playing a game of basketball and one of the older players, Kuamin Puli Sucal, was accidentally hit in the face with the ball. He took offence and threatened the kid who hit him with a beating. An adult named Johnny Tilo intervened and told Kuamin that if he hit the child he would have to "fight him." This warning seemed to resolve the matter, but thirty minutes later Mr. Tilo was sprawled on the ground with his left buttock ripped apart by a close range load of buckshot. Getting shot in the backside usually generates a lot of laughs and snickering among those that were not on the receiving end of the blast. However, Kuamin was about to become a murderer; Johnny was shot when he was bending over picking up firewood. The nine .33 caliber, 12 gage lead pellets penetrated deeply, causing significant internal injuries. Johnny's assailant high tailed it out of the village chased by a fusillade of small arms fire and "blooper" 40mm M79 grenade launcher rounds.

Poppy and a member of the security team administered first aid and evacuated the victim to the hospital. I remained on site so two of Johnny's relatives could accompany the patient in the vehicle. Unfortunately, Johnny succumbed to his mangled intestinal wounds and died some twenty minutes later while still some distance from the hospital. Without much prompting, our guard force prepared for the inevitable. We didn't have to wait long, and 48 hours later eleven raiders hit Kuamin's village with the usual assortment of weaponry. An M79 grenade launcher initiated the assault as they prepped the camp with their 40mm artillery. With all that fragmentation and generous small arms fire whizzing around, only one villager was wounded before the raiders retreated. Two of the raiding party were members of our security team. Simply fitting a guy up with a uniform and giving him a monthly salary cannot nullify tribal loyalties.

B'Laan group, ten minutes after a shooting incident over a basketball game. The individual with the grenade launcher and shotgun led a raid in retaliation a few days later – Mindanao, Phillipines

General Santos, and Mindanao in general, is loaded with expatriate characters and I met with several of them every few weeks. Chris, an Englishman, owned the Cambridge Farm, which was a large and sprawling restaurant with a bar, swimming pool, and accommodations. This basic, but comfortable, establishment had become their weekly meeting place where we discussed numerous issues, drank copious amounts of alcohol, and retold many a tall tale. Chris was a big old boy, former British military, and upon retirement became an engineer or drilling foreman. The others were Rolf the Aussie, a mining surveyor; skinny Brian, a former coal miner from the U.K.; Marty, the tough old New Yorker who had retired from the Alaskan oil production scene and wanted to be warm again; Oscar, the eccentric African American Vietnam veteran chopper pilot turned journalist; Ted M., another Australian, who held a "doctorate in Asian pub crawling." and a man with a hell of a thirst for the amber fluid; and, finally, Stewart, the small Scot from Glasgow. Stew was a quiet spoken but tough little guy and worked the offshore oil rigs on the Australian coastline. During field breaks he spent time with his wife and children in General Santos.

Stew's brother-in-law was a firearms enthusiast, as are many male Filipinos. On this particular morning, he decided to shoot a chicken for midday BBQ. Filipinos have an unrivalled passion for cock fighting, and birds that win not only become pampered pets, but feathered stars that garner tremendous status for their owners. Stew and his brother-in-law's wife pushed her husband into the backyard in his wheel chair. He signals them to stop and then holds out his hand for his 9mm Beretta. The good woman, acting like a faithful gun bearer, removed the pistol from its case and hands it to her husband. He slaps in a full magazine of ball ammo, aims in, and strokes one off. It was great fun and he was doing the manly thing by bagging tonight's dinner. Turning to Stew, he chortles, "Here, Stew, have a go." Knowing nothing about firearms, he wisely declines. The brother-in-law ejects the magazine and gives the weapon to his wife who returns the weapon to its case, places it on a table, and puts the magazine in a side pouch. The brother-in-law wheels himself back inside and his wife picks up the perforated chicken's body.

Stew is now sitting on the porch benignly sucking on a bottle of San Miguel Light. However, curiosity gets the better of him, and looking at the pistol case he decides to take it out and have a hold. Bad move. Assuming that the Beretta had been cleared and made safe because he had witnessed the removal of its magazine, but not knowing any better, Stew picks up the weapon and starts practising his sight picture. Proudly perched on his commanding bamboo stand near the end of the property is the number-one fighting cock. Stew, totally focused on the gun and oblivious to the downrange background, finds the trigger, and without much thought, gives it a tug. A 115-grain missile races across the lush yard at 1200 feet per second, and without the slightest protest the head-shot rooster flips backwards and is history. Stew's mouth flops open and he is in total shock. Suddenly the neighbour's twelve-year-old son races across and grabs the bird by the feet and is sprayed all over his chest with blood. At the sound of the shot and resulting drama, both families charge into the yard. The boy's panicked father takes one look at his blood-soaked son and tries to choke Stew into the next world. Eventually, the father's death grip is broken and the situation subsides to a relative degree of normalcy. Stew's introduction to shooting was a real bummer, and as soon as his pulse got back to normal he swore he would never touch a gun again.

Alan offered me a sweet deal in Brazil and it was almost too good to be true. It was a chance to help under his T.E.E.S. banner in training of police and military teams. This was right up my alley.

I thoroughly enjoyed my time in Mindanao, and especially the people, who are among the easiest to work with anywhere.

What is in store for the island of Mindanao is a question few can answer with any certainty. However, the militant Muslims minority will not ultimately achieve their goals through the power of the gun, nor will the Christian vigilantes and death squads now back in force. The "salvaging" (murder by death squads) of the criminal elements and Muslims has re-commenced and these extra legal groups are, in many instances, strongly supported by local governments and the people who have reached the saturation point with anarchy and lawlessness. Where a vacuum of security has been created by federal incompetence or neglect, free people will eventually step forward and fill it.

A strong president and competent military and police forces with ingrained integrity are the primary ingredients for peace and posterity in the Philippines, not vigilantes or paramilitary extremists.

The Shock Base

Alan's Story

The Mean Streets of Brazil

The sounds of sirens blaring and lights flashing enveloped us as we raced at near warp, and, therefore, recklessly dangerous speeds through the seedy and filthy streets of Sao Paulo. I was literally hanging on for my life as the SWAT Sports Utility Vehicle wove in and out of vehicles and pedestrian traffic at freeway velocities. However, this was Brazil, and Sao Paulo alone is home to some 16 million inhabitants, so at any time, day or night, there is no such thing as an empty road. We had received a call that "shots had been fired and police officers were down." As we skidded to a halt, a large crowd of officers, some in uniform, some dressed as civilians, and all heavily armed with sub-machine guns and shotguns, had gathered at the crime scene. Immediately, I noticed that weapons discipline was non-existent as gun muzzles with their owner's fingers on triggers, continuously swept my colleagues and me. Nevertheless, I debussed, took up a covering position with my 9mm Taurus pistol, and faced outboard. I scanned to my left and I could see that my T.E.E.S. Brazil partner, Kevan, had done the same. As usual, there was a great deal of confusion, and everyone, it seemed, was trying to assume command. I was called in by my good friend Junior and informed of the situation. Lying before us were the broken bodies of two drug dealers. Both had been shot and one had also been knifed in the back. They were still alive but bleeding profusely and in great pain. No one paid much attention to their agony, or the fact that their lives were ebbing from their bodies. The array of officers stood over them while casually smoking and formulating a plan to enter the "Favela" (slum) to arrest or kill the people responsible. This area was literally an armed shanty-town, and a gun battle was likely to erupt with someone, and not necessarily the targets of this raid. It was obvious that no one really wanted to execute the plan because doing so could reduce your life expectancy drastically. Eventually the task was assigned to the special operations personnel of the elite Civil Police Special Operation Group (GOE). Under Junior's care, we entered the festering slum, which was one of the hundreds spread throughout the city. The only formation that we could adopt was a single file because the alleyways were extremely narrow. No vehicles could pass through, so we had to go in on foot. Apparently, six drug dealers had ambushed the two victims after they had been sent in by narcotics officers to set up a buy-bust caper. This was an indication that the trafficker's intelligence was good, as well as timely, and the police probably had a leak.

The situation seemed far worse than any previous combat patrol that I had been on in Brazil. There was absolutely no place to maneuver unless you kicked in a door and took cover in someone's shack. A plethora of potential ambush sites existed at every turn and while crossing alleys. We were canalized and vulnerable from almost every possible direction and dimension. We not only had to scan our 360, but overhead as well. Nerves, expectedly, were taut and everyone's senses were in hyper-drive and working overtime. It was almost a relief when two rapidly fired shots passed over our heads, but instead of aggressively closing with the location, we slowed down and became more cautious. Junior gave me a nod and wink of reassurance as we pushed on deeper into this shit hole.

At the next bend we bumped into a team from the military police who had been patrolling in from the opposite direction. This scared me more than anything and I thanked God that we did not have a blue-on-blue tragedy. Again, their weapons handling was atrocious and endangered us as well as their own teammates. Fuck this. I thought — if we are going to die, at least let it be at the hands of a worthy adversary rather than from a negligent discharge by a fellow officer. After about 30 minutes of tension-filled but fruitless patrolling that involved sporadic gunfire, followed by the scuttling of feet and slamming of doors, Junior gave the signal to withdraw. No one was about to argue with this order.

The two victims were still flopping around when we arrived back at our start point. This was good because their vital signs were still detectable. Of course, no one had bothered to call an ambulance. These were simply the bad guys and they deserved to die. They would just have to fend for themselves, just as the police do when they are caught and assassinated in the slums. However, a credible rumor was circulating that fingered the police as the shooters, who subsequently fled after initiating an officer down call to cover their tracks. The bad guys would never claim that this was the case, because doing so would surely mean death. Either way, they were fucked. Welcome to Brazil, a land of ruthlessness, extreme brutality, and corruption — a country that I dearly love.

My first contact with Brazilian police officers occurred when I was working for the U.S. State Department engaged in training foreign officers. However, it was not until June 1997 that a unique opportunity presented itself. Two Brazilian military policemen had enrolled in my explosive entry course in Memphis, and accompanying them was Kevan Gillies, acting as their interpreter. The structure of Brazilian law enforcement is similar to the U.S. model. They have Federal, State, and Highway Police. However, the Civil and Military Police dominate the overall scene. The Civil Police wear civilian clothing and conduct investigations, high-risk patrolling, and special operations. The military police retained its name from the days of the military dictatorship, but are civilians now. They wear uniforms and patrol the streets and slums of the country. One of the Brazilians attending was Lieutenant Pericles DeMatos, who was the commander of the Curitiba-based C.O.E. (Special Operation Commando Group). "Slim" is one of the most professional and dedicated officers I have worked alongside. A leader and a fighter, he has proven himself on many operations. In the eyes of some of the corrupt commanders that are members of his organization, Slim has one irredeemable fault. He is too honest and will not bend the rules or jeopardize the career of a subordinate to further his own. The same can be said for my mates Major Bittencourt and Lieutenant Cesar from Belem, which is North of Sao Paulo. Both are excellent operators who expect only the best from their men regardless of the situation. Pericles, who is now a captain, has been recently re-assigned as commander of a small town on the outskirts of Curitiba. This town had been in the news after nineteen of its young women were murdered. In the end, it was not surprising that investigation determined that it was a rogue group of police officers that were responsible for the brutal murders. It appeared that they knew too much about the officer's illegal drug operations.

Indirectly, Pericles is responsible for the establishment of my international school, "Base Choque," in Brazil. Halfway through the course that he and his subordinate were attending, I had to hand over the reigns to Senior Instructor Max Joseph and Bill Yaegle because I had to leave and handle a VIP protection detail in Rio de Janeiro.

Two weeks after my return stateside, I received a call from Brazil. It was Kevan and he asked if he could accompany a second, but larger, team of officers to T.E.E.S. in August. It was during that time, that Kevan and I had the opportunity to sit down and talk in-depth about the dire need for police training in Brazil. When he departed he promised that he would get us down there in November to conduct a course at the police academy. True to his word, Max and I traveled to the Guatupe Police Academy and taught a hostage rescue course to a class of thirty that included two colonels, one lieutenant colonel, and several majors. As they say, the rest is history and we were back for numerous repeat performances after that.

Kevan is a wiry, tough, no nonsense little Brit who has been living in Brazil since 1977. As a black belt in Karate who owned his own academy, he was hired by the police to assist them in developing a suitable martial arts and defensive tactics program. Upon meeting Kevan, it is immediately evident that as a lad, he had been through the Brazilian trenches. However, his humble demeanor should not deceive one, because he is an absolute genius when it comes to business and marketing. On his third trip to the States, Duke and I sat down with him and offered him the job of creating a T.E.E.S. Brazil in his home city of Curitiba. Up until this time we had been using the police department's facilities and to say that it cost us a small fortune in potential profits would be an understatement. By the time we paid this colonel and that colonel, our remuneration was considerably reduced. Kevan was tasked with locating a piece of land where we could construct our own facility and become an independent entity. "Base Choque," which translates to the "Shock Base," was named after the fine military police officers of the Curitiba based, Choque Battalion. Under the command of Major Sarmento, an extremely hard nosed and professional officer, these men would hit the slums and aggressively enforce the law on a nightly basis. The respect that they received from good and bad guys alike was evident, and whenever anyone saw their vehicles barreling down the road, they immediately sought the quickest escape route.

Our Curitiba facility was officially opened in May 1999 and in the next 30 months, some 2000 Brazilian police officers passed through its gates. Assisting Kevan and the American instructors were some of Brazil's finest. Pericles was always there to augment tactical classes. Gerson is our lead instructor in all aspects of defensive driving and has developed into an excellent all-round teacher. Paulo, from the GOE group in São Paulo, has made several trips to T.E.E.S. U.S.A. and has been a staunch ally since day one. Caca, from the Civil Police in Rio, is the latest addition to our team. A graduate of every T.E.E.S. course, we quickly identified him as an excellent prospect. Along with his winning personality, he has proven his worth and ability to work with all the branches of the police and also possesses an incredible ability with firearms. Without doubt, he is the best Brazilian shooter we have had come through our school. Kevan's wife, Linda, handled the administration and is assisted by Fabio and Kelly. Our Portuguese translation team consists of Kevan, his father, Ian, and step-mother, Anna.

This venture would never have been possible without the assistance of Pericles and Sandra Garcia, another great friend from Curitiba. Pericles's police contacts smoothed the way through their various chains of command, but it was Sandra's help with obtaining various government licenses that really saved the day. There is no such thing as an easy way in Brazil. You simply have to know the right people, and I will always be indebted to these two people for their assistance.

As the fifth largest country in the world, with a population of 165 million, Brazil has its fair share of crime. This point was hammered home to

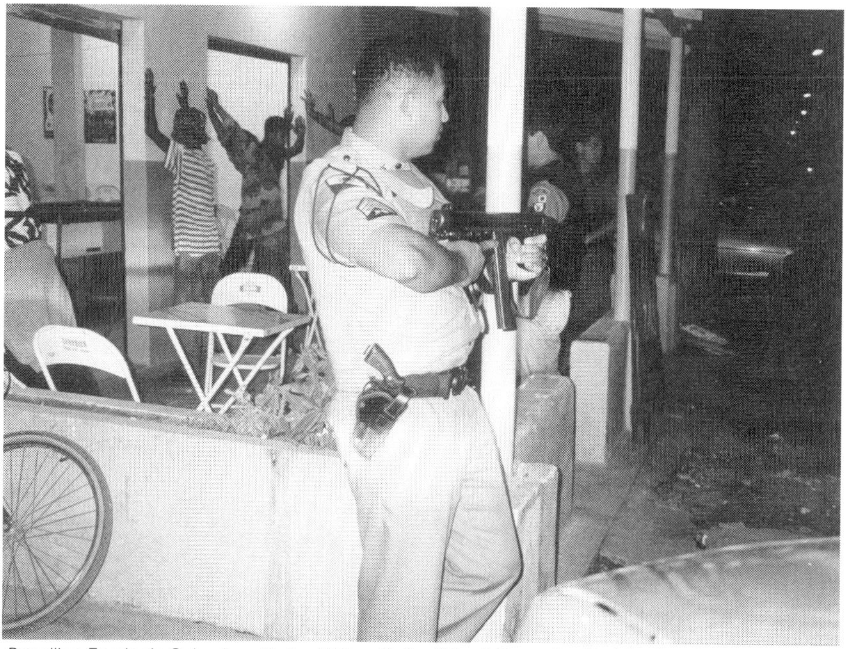

Patrolling Favela de Colombo with the Military Police "Shock Troops" – Curitiba, Brazil, 1998

Routine shakedown for guns and drugs, Favela da Capanema – Curitiba, Brazil, 1999

the citizens of New Zealand in November 2001 when their most famous yachtsman, Sir Peter Blakc, winner of the America's Cup, was murdered while conducting an environmental survey on the Amazon River. Reputa-

High Risk Patrolling with the troopers from Shock Battalion RONE, Favela da Trindade – Curitiba, Brazil, 1999

tions and status mean nothing here, and, reportedly, the bandits who took his life just wanted the party's money and watches. The law enforcement community loses between 750 and 1000 officers a year. However, the kill ratio, as you can imagine, is decidedly in the cop's favor. So many people are on the wrong end of a policeman's gun that they have almost stopped counting.

Lack of training is the main reason why so many cops are killed. The old saying "as you train, so shall you fight" is 100-percent true. With zero training you have no acquired skills, so your chances of survival are extremely low. You can usually gauge an officer's competence level as soon as he puts a weapon in his hands. It is extremely rare that we do not have at least a couple of "soup sandwiches" on every course. As they attempt to load their weapons, Kevan and I just look at each other and shake our heads in disbelief. On one course in Rio, we had 18 semi-auto shooters and two officers armed with revolvers. After I thoroughly demonstrated our loading techniques, I stood off to the flank beside the guys with wheel guns watching them perform the drill. I could tell that number 19 was totally confused, especially when I ordered the other shooters to "press check" their weapons to ensure that a round was in the chamber. After glancing to his left numerous times to observe the other shooters perform the drill, he still hadn't figured out they had a different weapons system than him. No worries mate — if they were checking their chambers, then, by God, he was going to check his. Without hesitation, he rotated his muzzle and held it between his eyes and conscientiously counted the rounds in the cylinder. Hey, what the hell, at least his finger was straight.

Kevan and I with the infamous British "Great Train Robber" Ronnie Biggs at his home in Rio de Janeiro, 2001

Brazil now rates second behind Colombia for the number of murders per annum. That fact, coupled with serious conflicts between the civil and military police, makes for an extremely volatile situation. In general, the civilian population is extremely fearful of the police, and it is understandable because the police are responsible for much of the crime and engage in shoot-outs with each other on a regular basis. Police corruption and brutalization of the citizens they are supposed to serve is a way of life and is frequently overlooked by administrators. Many of the officers are also from the slums and receive a mere USD$250 per month. Therefore, corruption and crime makes ends meet. However, not all police crimes are overlooked, and this is evident from the number of "police prisons" located throughout the large cities. They are separated from mainstream prisons because the prisoners would rape and murder them as soon as the gates were closed. Driving through Sao Paulo, you can readily see the huge structures that house either the military or civil police offenders. They, too, are always segregated because it would be like putting two rival gangs in the same cellblock. I was working in Rio once and happened to be at a military police prison. It was extremely sad to see the young wives and kids visiting their husbands and dads who had been incarcerated for crimes like theft, assault, extortion, and murder.

One of the main problems encountered by the Civil Police are prison uprisings. Each city is divided into districts and each district has its own jail. It is hard to describe these filthy dungeons, but I guess the easiest thing to compare them with would be the movie, "Midnight Express," which is about a young American incarcerated in a Turkish prison. In Sao Paulo alone, there are some 100 districts, which means 100 jails. Each jail will house several hundred inmates, mainly for petty crimes. However, a dangerous mix of murderers and armed robbers is not uncommon. A number of these jails are located underground, but that makes little difference because the inmates will not generally leave their cells or see daylight for the duration of their sentence. You might be housed in a cell built for eight, but it has twenty inmates crammed into its confines, or housed in a large room built for 100, with 175 unsavory neighbors. You only have the clothes that you are wearing and one blanket that also acts as your mattress. Once a week, a hose is pushed through the bars and if you want a shower you make use of this opportunity. Food is delivered through cell bars because any contact with prison guards is forbidden. On a recent visit to a Sao Paulo jail, I was informed that there were only three guards for the 183 inmates. One hundred and seventy five inmates were in one cell and the other eight, who happened to be gays, were housed in a small barred cell that measured five by two yards. They were literally sleeping on top of each other. There are no recreation yards or private areas, but once a week, after a complete body search, private, one-hour conjugal visits are permitted. One look inside these cells and you can sense the hate and disrespect that these inmates have for the police. You would have to be crazy to even poke your nose inside a cell, let alone enter it. Doing so would cause an immediate riot and end in the violent and slow death of the offending officer. It is amazing just how many of these riots involve the criminal use of firearms. Consequently, when the special operations teams move in, they are fully kitted up and ready to use deadly force against the participants. On one hostage-barricade situation that took place in a Sao Paulo prison, a 42-man team assaulted, and once it was all over, 114 inmates were laid out in the courtyard. The officers had shot every one of them.

The use of non-lethal weaponry by law enforcement is still in its infancy in Brazil and is not yet considered to be a viable option. When inmates rebel, they are in effect signing their death warrants, but when you appreciate the conditions they are incarcerated under, you can understand their desperation. On a recent Sao Paulo operation, one of our team members completely severed a prisoner's arm after shooting him several times with a .223 caliber weapon. In the States, a shotgun, loaded with rubber ball shot, or perhaps a bean-bag round, would have been considered reasonable force in this case. I guess that he was lucky it was only his arm and not his body that was exposed.

It's an undeniable fact that the inmates run the larger prisons. The guards have no control over the day-to-day activities, other than for delivering food. However, the guards often aid and abet this situation by providing goods and services for a fee to the prisoners. There are two main prison entities. The Political Prisoner Group (PPG) and the Satanic Cult Worshippers (SCW). The former organize and control the internal system and dictate the rules. They orchestrate many of the prison rebellions that frequent-

My Brazilian buddy, Paulo, inspecting a recently filled in tunnel at a Sao Paulo Prison. With 22 confirmed and justified kills under his belt in just nine years, Paulo epitomizes the professional Brazilian officer.

ly occur all over the country. At times these rebellions are coordinated incidents in an effort to deplete the police resources. Inter-prison communications are very contemporary and simple. The inmates purchase cell phones from the guards for $100. If it comes with a charger the cost will be doubled. For some guards it represents almost a months pay, so these transactions are very popular with them. Ironically, this instrument could contribute to the guard's eventual death or injury. PPG leaders will call other leaders throughout the country and plan a date and time when all hell will break loose. This becomes a nightmare for responding special operation teams, who are already stretched thin by external counter-criminal missions.

Inmates were able to "buy" explosives through the prison network to bust out of this Sao Paulo Prison in 2001.

The SCW is a scary and much feared terrorist group of ruthless and crazed killers. Generally, their administration of justice involves a hideous death followed by decapitation. Various satanic paraphernalia is placed on the remains as a graphic warning to non-believers and those that might oppose them. Cannibalism is not uncommon and the victim's blood or body parts will be ingested, allegedly to give cult members inner-strength.

The violence is not only restricted to adult facilities. At a boy's reformatory, three young offenders were caught informing to the guards. Punishment involved torture and their subsequent murders were ruthless and designed to send a message to the institute's population. After sodomizing them with broom-sticks, their executioners stabbed, beheaded, and burned the teenagers. They were left for all to see and reflect upon in the prison yard. Where was Amnesty International?

Early on, it was of critical importance for my American instructors and I to be exposed to the Brazilian ways of policing. The curriculum that we initially taught was based on tactics adapted from more conventional forms of special operations, where human-rights is an important and Constitutional consideration. Military Police Colonel Iranil and his brother, Lieutenant Colonel Itamar, in Curitiba, approved this essential hands-on experience. They arranged for Kevan, Max, and me to accompany troops from the elite RONE unit of the Choque Battalion on a night operation in the slums. We were issued uniforms, vests, and weapons and attended the brief given by, at that time, Lieutenant Pericles. It was during this brief that I determined that these guys were professionals and serious about their task. Moving out to the tactical vehicle parking area, I experienced flashbacks to my days in the military. What an impressive sight. Fifteen of their gold painted troop vehicles were lined up with their five man crews standing at parade rest in front of them. Five yards to their front stood the detachment commanders, and facing the parade was Major Sarmento, the special operations commander. Once the formalities of the formation were over, Major Sarmento assembled the company around him and gave the men what amounted to be a father-to-son talk concerning the importance of taking care of each other on tonight's mission. Once the members of the force gave their roar of approval, everyone mounted up, and with flashing lights and sirens blaring, charged out of the compound. The convoy sped through the city towards its target 25 minutes away, and cars frantically maneuvered to get out of the way. Three warriors sitting in the sport utility's rear seats were armed with pump-action 12 gage shotguns and handguns held in a ready position. The front-seated team leader had either a Brazilian Taurus 9mm pistol or an Italian Berretta sub-machinegun. Each vehicle also contained a gun rack situated between the front seats that held additional shotguns and a lever-action .357 Magnum caliber carbine.

Suddenly, we were enveloped in darkness and a nauseating stench which signaled that we had reached the first slum's outskirts. These slums are the size of small towns and the almost feral inhabitants controlled everything inside this urban jungle of shacks. On command, the convoy split and teams headed in several pre-designated directions. In a couple of minutes we hit our first street corner and Pericles gave the word to deploy. Our two vehicles screeched to a halt and ten of us were out and covering our arcs of responsibility. Engines still idling, both drivers positioned themselves close to their doors for cover and also in case we needed to make a hasty withdrawal. The plan was to have both team leaders (TL) with two cover men, approach any suspects, interview, and search them. The remaining four members would face outboard and form a defensive perimeter around the vehicles and target area. It was imperative that each team member watched his area of responsibility and did not become distracted by what was happening around him. On Pericles's nod, our drivers jumped back into the vehicles and were immediately followed by the TLs and personal cover men. Once they were seated, the perimeter team collapsed on the SUVs and we were off as quick as we had arrived. The most dangerous part of these operations was when you were stationary, whether it was in a vehicle or on foot. A moving and evasive target is always more difficult to hit, but a static one was a gift to even the most inept sniper. Two minutes later, we found ourselves rolling on a "shots fired" call. However, two other units beat us to it so we pushed on. The next stop involved detaining a group of youths milling around on a street corner. We hadn't deployed for more than ten seconds when three rounds sang by us. I nervously glanced at Max and he seemed to be reading my mind. We found suitable cover and continued to maintain security over our respective areas. As the night expired, it was obvious to us that Pericles and his men were quite used to the random shot being sent their way, or ricocheting off one of their vehicles, and were not too ruffled by it. All we had to do was follow their lead, as they were, without a doubt, the experts when it came to operating in this environment. Kevan, Max, and I all agreed on one thing at the end of the night — these guys were good at what they did and our initial concern over watching each other's backs was greatly allayed because the men of Choque Battalion, RONE were doing it for us.

Base Choque is a facility that we are extremely proud of. It is nestled in the midst of a beautiful primary jungle with a large quarry rock face as a backdrop. If there is one disadvantage, it is our necessitated 25-minute drive down "the highway to hell," to reach the city of Curitiba. It gave a new definition to "road warrior." Pitch black after sundown and full of gaping pot holes that look like artillery shell holes, the road is inundated with people on horseback, cars, and motor bikes minus lights, scrawny, flea-infested dogs, the occasional cow, and an endless stream of drunk locals. Mixed in with these formidable obstacles are the detested "Lombadas" (speed bumps). Unless you intimately knew the road, you would not spot these obstacles until it was too late and then all you had time to do was brace for impact. Garages specializing in wheel alignments made a fortune, and some I am convinced belonged to the cops. We had a special SOP at Base Choque and that was you had to consume at least two stiff rum and cokes prior to departure. Many of us followed the double, with a large third shot, or the proverbial one for the road, to calm our nerves en-route. What an unbelievable experience.

The "highway to hell" was one of the main reasons that prompted me to construct on-site housing for instructors and visitors. Now many a good night is spent on the porch sipping a cold one among these beautiful surroundings and listening to yarns being seriously stretched as the night flows on. Several American police officers have traveled south to experience Brazilian policing and the social life that this country is famous throughout the world for. Ben Stradford and Jeff Scoggins from Memphis SWAT; Jeff Winn and Cris Mandry from New Orleans SWAT; Ron Yanor from Sangamon County, Illinois Sheriff's Department; Curt Hagman from San Bernardino, California, Sheriff's Department; Devin Crinklaw from Omaha, Nebraska Police Department; former FBI Hostage Rescue Team commander, Woody Johnson; FBI HRT negotiator, Dee Risario; and Mike Odle and Rick Massa from LAPD SWAT have all enjoyed the facility and Curitiba's hospitality.

The carefully selected location of our numerous shooting ranges, shoot houses, classroom and slum area mockup, and explosives and sniper ranges permit us to conduct two courses simultaneously. To facilitate the whole operation we had to have a sound maintenance and logistic system. Our trusty caretaker, Carlos, quickly filled this void. Carlos was part of a package deal that came with the purchase of the land. Initially, when we were renting the land, Carlos and his family lived just outside the facility's main gate. Carlos and his wife, both in their mid-thirties, had seven kids, two dogs, cats here and there, and a bunch of roosters. How they got by in their small two-room shack that had no electricity, running water, shower, or toilet amazed me. It didn't seem to faze them as they had lived like this for years. The land owner paid Carlos $50 per month to work in the quarry, and work he did. It bothered me to see his little kids, who ranged in ages from two to fifteen, sitting around all day with snotty noses, dirty faces, and torn clothes. Kevan and I would frequently drop off supplies for them and gifts for the kids. When we saw their faces light up with joy it gave us a great feeling. It is no secret that whenever I am in town those kids will get spoiled rotten. Many children in Brazil never have a childhood because of the abject poverty, so my heart went out to these kids, especially when I thought about SeanBenet, my own daughter. I only hope I am not expected to pay their dentist bills when they get older. Once the land purchase was sealed, we built Carlos and his family a "mansion" inside the compound. Now they had a civilized residence, consisting of three bedrooms, a toilet, shower, kitchen, and furniture that included a small television. They must have felt like Hillbilly Jed Clampett and family, when they moved to Beverly Hills. In addition to the new house, his pay was raised to $150 per month and I have never seen a man work so hard in my whole life. By himself, he chopped down trees, dragged them up hills, dug the holes, and with barbed wire, fenced in the property's entire 42,000 square meters. However, upon completion of the protective perimeter, Kevan informed him that a portion of the fence was in the wrong spot. Without raising an eyebrow, Carlos relocated it 20 meters further out. Shortly after moving into his new digs, Carlos became a grandfather when his sixteen-year-old daughter gave birth to a beautiful boy. We were really amazed and shocked when Carlos and his wife had their eighth child in 2001. Unbelievable, now he had a grandson older than his own son! Carlos is a man of few words, but we did manage to get a grin from him when I presented him with a cold beer and a packet of condoms on the day number eight was born. Of course, Kevan got the dubious job of showing Carlos how the "rubbers" were applied.

Rio de Janiero is considered by many to be the epitome of tourist destinations in Brazil. However, I must take issue with that assessment. To many believers, the statue of the Jesus Christ overlooking Rio means it is blessed, sacred, and safe for one and all. Try telling those who have been victims of random and targeted acts of violence that include assault, rape, kidnapping, hostage situations, and gratuitous murder, or the police who have fought countless gun battles in its environs. Rio is a cesspool of crime and filth and has to be considered one of the most dangerous cities on the planet. I have had the opportunity to perform several VIP protection details for American clients and also to conduct numerous courses for the police and military in that fabled, but fucked up city.

During one visit, Kevan and I had a day off, so we arranged to meet with England's most famous fugitive, train robber, Ronnie Biggs. We got the introduction through Kevan's dad, Ian, who had known Ronnie for years. Ronnie was a member of the gang that pulled off the U.K.'s biggest heist in 1963, when they took down a train and netted several million pounds in cash. After his capture and trial, Ronnie was sentenced to 30 years in the slammer, but he would have none of that. In 1965, he broke out of prison and hit the road. After fleeing to Australia, Venezuela, Bolivia, and Argentina, he eventually settled in Brazil where he fathered a young boy named Michael. Because he could not legally work in Brazil, he made his living from hosting thousands of tourists at his house where he would flip burgers on his BBQ, sell Ronnie Biggs T-shirts, and tell stories about his past. Ronnie survived many extradition and kidnapping attempts to get him back to the U.K. Where they failed, his poor health eventually prompted him to return to his homeland and face the music.

Kevan and I were in Rio to conduct a Close Quarters Battle Rifle course for the elite troops of the BOPE, the Military Police Special Operations Battalion. For their entire careers, these men patrol the perpetually multiplying and horribly congested slums. These are Brazil's powder kegs and it takes skill, guts, and nerves of steel to survive each operation. Captain Pedro, a 30-year veteran of the slums, is one of a kind. He is lucky to be a few inches over five feet tall and looks like a stiff wind will whisk him away, but he possesses balls of steel and I cannot begin to imagine what he has experienced during his 30-plus years of active service with the battalion. He lives for the job and relishes passing on his knowledge to the young men coming up through the ranks. It will be a sad day when he has to retire. Captain Pedro has seen them come and go, fight and die, but one incident in particular deeply hurt him. In September 2001, three of his young officers attended our explosive entry course and brought with them his best wishes. The men selected to make the trip were outstanding and had a burning desire to learn and be the best. They passionately wanted to emulate Pedro, their mentor and personal hero. Two days after returning to Rio, they were again occupied in patrolling the slums and applying their newly acquired skills. Majors Panheiro and Silva and Captain Rene were with us at T.E.E.S. at the time and received some bad news on morning two of their course. Young Lieutenant Luiz took an AK47 round the night before and had his arm severed at the elbow. Only twenty-three years old, he was now a cripple and without a job. In an instant, he joined the ranks of the maimed or killed in the name of justice. And now he would have to struggle to survive not only the loss of his livelihood, but also the respect, dignity, and authority his position bestowed upon him. Such is life in the slums of Rio.

I first trained Major Silva when he attended a U.S. State Department course, and he is one of the most capable training officers in his unit. Major Paneiro and Captain Rene possessed immense knowledge, but were quite humble and just wanted to see things done right. I remember standing on the fourth-floor balcony of their castle-like headquarters and being briefed by the unit's commanding officer and Major Paneiro. They were pointing out a huge slum on a mountain side immediately to our front and then another adjacent to it. They told me about the numerous fire-fights that periodically occur between rival gangs from one mountain to the other, while middle class citizens living in the valley between the mountains huddled on their floors and prayed for it to end. From a distance, the green and red tracers, indicating former Communist Bloc and Western ammunition, ergo weapons, were being employed, were quite colorful and might even be considered to be entertaining, if you were not on the receiving end.

However, the next day, when the police could move in, the evidence of carnage was everywhere. A cardboard or plywood shack does not give you much protection from incoming, so every shanty had trenches near them. In spite of the many dangers of living in such a hellhole, people continue to flock to them.

Their issue weapons consisted of the excellent, but dated 5.56 x 45 MM Fabrique National (FN) folding stock rifle and Brazil's version of the Berretta, the Taurus 9mm pistol. In one respect, the Taurus is preferred over its Italian cousin by veteran police officers because it is capable of being carried in condition one, "cocked and locked," or in its single-action mode. This is similar to the highly acclaimed Czech CZ-75 and Colt Model 1911 A1 pistols. However, it became apparent during training that these rifles were old and no longer operationally effective. The number of stoppages and malfunctions that occurred during our course were unacceptable. In the end, I gathered the twenty operators around and asked one simple question: "How many of you men have experienced a malfunction or stoppage during a fire-fight?" I expected to see only a couple of hands appear, but to my amazement, every individual in the class put his hand up. I could not believe that at least some of them would not have been killed or at least wounded and told them they were living on borrowed time. All I could imagine was that their transition skills from long gun to short gun must have saved a lot of them.

By now, Kevan and I had been on numerous operations in the slums of Sao Paulo and Curitiba, but we were yet to experience the unique and extremely difficult operational environment presented by Rio's over 500 Favelas. Hanging precariously on the sides of surrounding mountains and containing up to quarter of a million inhabitants, they presented huge problems for the police. Unlike most urban areas, which are flat and open to vehicular traffic, the majority of these teeming hovels only host foot travel. This magnifies officer vulnerability, and once they enter into the depths of the slums, they are entirely on their own and cannot rely on receiving reinforcement or support of any kind.

Our opportunity to accompany the BOPE arrived and we readied ourselves to go on a mission into Favela, Dono Marta. We assembled at their headquarters and lined up with the men to draw weapons and equipment. One of the officers asked what rifle I would prefer to carry. Having experienced first hand the problems encountered with the FN's, I asked if they had anything else. An M-16 that was recently taken from a dead drug dealer was thrust into my thankful hands. I immediately noted that it was stamped "Property of U.S. Government" and briefly wondered about this black rifles history. Kevan opted for a 12 gage shotgun and we also packed Taurus nines in our leg drop tactical holsters.

Like Afghanistan, the best way to assault these mountain redoubts was from the top down, if you could get the high ground. Transporting thirty of us to the top of the mountain was slow and tedious, but I was glad that we would have the tactical advantage of fighting downhill. Reaching our drop-off point, we broke down into five six-man patrols and departed, carefully maintaining regular intervals between each man, along a small dirt track. Rio was a beautiful sight from our vantage point, as, like stars, its millions of lights were brilliant against the blackness below us. When we reached the edge of the slum, we employed bounding over-watches and we covered the open ground as quickly as possible. Sure as shit, we came under immediate fire from sentries patrolling the entrance to the slum. Suddenly, an eerie silence prevailed and the place looked deserted, but there were thousands of hidden eyes watching us. We were now on their turf, and thirty men against potentially thousands did not bode well for this Kiwi and I mentally kicked myself in the butt for getting involved in such a hairy undertaking. However, if you want to gain the respect of these men, you have to show them that you are not just all talk and they appreciate your willingness to share their hardships. I settled down and got back to business.

Navigation was not a problem and we simply let gravity take us through and down. Eventually, we would hit bottom and exit onto the streets leading up to the slum. Being locked inside this massive labyrinth of shacks, huts, and narrow, thirty-six-inch-wide, stench and filth laden alleyways did not make for a happy camper. Little Pedro was our point man and a marvel to watch. He and his bandy, but muscular, little legs would move with ease across the uneven ground that without warning would frequently drop away from you. My biggest concern was the threat from above. The roofs on the more substantial shacks were flat. The owner would then sell his rooftop to a friend, who would build his shack on it. In turn, the second tenant would do the same and a multi-storied shack would take form. Small, wooden single-rung ladders would be employed to access the elevated Flintstonian apartments. Furthermore, if a resident decided to snipe at us from above, we were trapped and he could escape jumping from roof to roof. Helicopters were available, but the police were reluctant to use them in this environment. Gang members, just prior to our operation, had shot down a police helicopter in São Paulo. As in Mogadishu, the downed, but alive, pilot was executed with a gun shot to the head.

Random firing occurred throughout the night, which helped everyone to stay hyper-alert and focused. The living conditions there are hard to depict. Only when you have experienced it first-hand can you begin to understand how these gangs can intimidate the slum's inhabitants and defy the police. However, this is not unusual in the world's ghettos and ethnic neighborhoods. This includes some inner-city areas in the U.S. where police are hated and it is ill advised to enter without sufficient back up. Like the drug war, you make a dent, but overall you have little lasting effect on the criminal situation in Brazil.

Police power is something that is generally feared in third world and countries emerging from that degrading designation. The man with the gun and badge has the authority to make your life miserable, and in many cases, end it. The cop is always right and you are always wrong and regardless of the circumstances — you will pay the price. In one particular country that I visit regularly, two of my police friends responded to a bank robbery in progress. Two of the perpetrators were killed outright and the third ran for his life. Pursued by these officers, they shot him several times with their handguns. Coughing and choking, this hard case was struggling to live to fight another day. Forget the ambulance and police first aid. In this draconian "democracy" criminals forfeit any rights, so out comes the handy plastic bag and over the head it goes — end of story. The next casualty was the bank security camera taping this example of swift street justice. And security personnel saw nothing and knew nothing. They completely appreciated the fact that their family's lives were worth more than the suffocating scumbag rolling around in the alley.

In this part of the world, discretion is always better than valor, unless you want to become a ten-cent martyr. Just take your whipping and get on with life. The best thing to do is to join a police department and become a thumper rather than a thumpee.

Certain countries, particularly in South America, appreciate the problems with police power, its corruption and abuse. In many cases, the military, which is the true power behind most of these governments, has been given the responsibility to "oversee" the police and ensures that they do not get too much training, weapons, equipment, and advanced technology. The police must be kept in their place so they do not become a rival to the Army. Hence the military is often tasked to approve all ranges, training courses involving tactics, and the distribution and storage of all weapons, ammunition, and explosive materials. This professional rivalry also carries over to other branches of the military and the fear of their gaining too much power and the possibilities of a coup are very real.

With all the political interference, inter-agency police and military problems, lack of training, and corruption, there are still, however, some extremely fine officers out there carrying the load. Although they are in the minority, professionalism, dedication, integrity, and honor are words that they understand and try to apply daily in order to make the streets safer for their citizens. It is tough for them to resist the temptations that others succumb to and often advance by.

Doctor Sergio leads the Special Operations Group of the Sao Paulo Civil Police. The term "Doctor" preceding their name indicates that they received a law degree prior to becoming a civil police officer. This term also denotes their rank and status within the organization. He succeeded Doctor Luciano, another friend, who was sadly killed in a gun battle. While driving home one evening, Luciano made a carload of wanted suspects when they stopped next to him. He ordered them to surrender, but in return he was shot seventeen times in the head and shoulders with an AK47. I remember him well. At the range I was always shaking my head and correcting his techniques. He was not a primary operator, but that was not his job. However, prior to his attending my course, he miraculously survived a gunfight involving three bandits. He even had the presence of mind and control to perform a combat reload while under substantial fire. In the end, his mind and tactics dominated the situation and the score was three dead suspects and one relieved police officer.

Doctor Alexandre is one of Sergio's GOE street commanders. Quiet and unassuming, he has earned the respect of his men by leading from the front. Operators like Chumbino, nicknamed "Little Lead Balls," after he was shot with a 12 gage shotgun in the face and Xandon, Marquinhos, Chris, Ninja, Cobra, Collor, Kangaroo, Clovis, and particularly, good friends Junior and Paulo, who I consider my brothers-in-arms and true professionals.

If they have any spare time or money, both are spent at schools trying to improve themselves so they can be the best at what they do. Whether they are at work or at home, you will never see Paulo or Junior without their body armor on. It doesn't make any difference if they go for a jog, to a wedding, the drug store, or just checking the mailbox. They know they are marked men and nothing would please the bandits more, or give them tremendous status, than offing a couple of GOE commandos. They have both survived dozens of firefights and Paulo, after only ten years as an officer, has been credited with 22 kills. They used to call him "Dr. Death," but now his nickname is "HIV." He doesn't have the disease, but he just seems to kill more people that it does!

After completing a training stint at Base Choque in March, 2001, Kevan and I decided to visit the Sao Paulo GOE for a couple of nights of patrolling before returning to Memphis. Things were getting interesting, and on a previous GOE operation, Kevan had been shotgunned in his bullet-proof vest and wounded in the hand. He and Chris had rounded a corner in a narrow slum alleyway and were basically ambushed by a scumbag. Shots were returned but, of course, the suspect was up, up, and away before the smoke had even cleared.

We were met at the airport by Paulo and after dumping our excess gear and changing clothes, we were taken to their headquarters to rendezvous with the other patrol members. After a quick brief by Dr. Alexandre, we mounted up and headed into Indian country. The night was unexpectedly quiet until we re-grouped at a district jail and were informed that a gang of gun-runners from Rio were staging in an apartment complex and if we were going to hit them, it had to be now. In my experience, Brazilians lack the ability to plan under ideal conditions, let alone when time is against them. Regardless, I had full faith in Paulo and Dr. Alexndre's ability to take care of business. Life in Brazil is hazardous even at the best of times, but nothing rivals a high-speed car chase, or a Code-3 response, through its cluttered and dingy streets. The most accurate way to describe such a scene is to visualize a high-speed chase in a big-budget Hollywood movie, like the French Connection. The only difference being, of course, this is real. Seatbelts rarely exist, and when they do, it's considered wussy to wear one. All hands just hang on for dear life. The roads are jam-packed, but citizens understand the rules. If you notice a GOE vehicle with flashing lights and siren blaring getting larger in your rear-view mirror, slow down, maintain a

Kevan and Alan after another interesting night with two men who understand the dangers of the fearsome Favelas of Sao Paulo – Chumbino (little lead balls) and Paulo. Chumbino got his name after getting shot in the face with a 12 gage birdshot round.

Duke and Alan with a true leader – Major Sarmento, commander of the Curitiba Military Police Shock Battalion Troops. Every night he could be found up the sharp end with his troops, leading from the front.

straight heading, and do not attempt to change lanes until it is well past you. If you panic, it will probably be the last thing you ever do. In all my years of convoy driving during executive protection details, the GOE guys have to be the most competent high-speed drivers I have ever encountered. They routinely weave in and out of rush hour traffic at high speeds, knocking wing mirrors off vehicles without touching their brakes. Regardless of their competency behind the wheel, I always shit myself and just pray that I will not die before we get to the target. En-route to the apartment complex, we were joined by several other GOE vehicles. We were greeted by mass confusion when we pulled up and, sure enough, confusion often leads to failure. As a result, we hit the wrong building complex and managed to scare the shit out of a bunch of law-abiding citizens.

The next day saw us at one of the city's ten prisons. It was capable of holding around 4800 inmates, broken down into several 300-man pods. One of the original 1200 man units was destroyed by a recent riot, so those inmates were redistributed among the other nine institutions. Aping their success, another group of inmates hoped that their riot would get them transferred as well. Armed with 12 gage shotguns and Taurus handguns, we were led into the complex by one of the five prison guards on duty. We were in a column formation with Kevan as our unit's point and me in the second slot. Paulo followed me and Doctor Alexandre was rear security. When the guard turned the corner, he presented his shotgun and her let rip. "What the fuck?" I thought as Kevan and I scrambled to take up covering positions to support him. By the time we aimed in at the gate, the offending inmates had disappeared and retreated into the yard. "Damn," I thought to myself. Back home, we would have simply ordered them to get back inside.

The guard disappeared, and Paulo took over as point. The hundreds of inmates in the yard started chanting and building themselves up into an uncontrollable frenzy. Holy shit, the last thing we needed was a full-scale riot. Suddenly, everything went stone cold silent. A moment later, the stillness was interrupted by a dull thud and tapping noise coming from the gate. Mutually confused, Kevan and I moved cautiously forward, weapons at the ready. Both of us were jolted and repulsed by what we saw. Lying before us was the half naked, quivering, and dying body of an inmate. He had been stabbed repeatedly in the chest and neck and the tapping noise that we heard was a metal bar being forced into his skull. His brains were literally oozing out of his crushed skull and mixing in the ever-widening pool of blood around his head. Reflexively, I snapped my gun into a firing position, but here we were, five of us, separated by a set of questionable bars, facing at least 300 crazed inmates who had just been whipped into a murdering frenzy by their leader. This was a very delicate situation and the wrong move on our part could trigger a blood bath — ours included. We knew that we could take out the first few rows of these savages, but once we ran dry, it would turn into an emergency evacuation because it would only be a matter of time before they tore the bars down. Dr. Alexandre recognized the gang leader from a previous incident, so he stepped forward and initiated a dialog in a calm and professional manner. The dead inmate was guilty of whistling at a fellow inmate's wife as she was leaving the pod after a conjugal visit. Naturally, his sentence was death. He was sitting on a bench in the yard when a group moved on him. After slicing and dicing him, they dragged his wounded body over to the gate we were covering. From there, various inmates took turns driving the bar into his brain. It was customary to drag the body to the gate so the guards would not have to physically enter the yard — something they would never consider doing. Instead, the inmates would be ordered back, and once the gate was open, the guards would grab the feet of the deceased, along with any body parts, and drag him out. However, prior to this final act a certain ritual had to be performed. All offending inmates are routinely decapitated to complete the terror. The prisoner "honored" by being chosen to perform this grizzly task could claim the kill. In reality, probably a couple of dozen inmates had been involved in the physical aspects of the murder. Rules are rules, and we had to pull back so they could perform this final postmortem act. We withdrew, but were able to access the roof via a ladder and acquired an elevated view of the proceedings. A huge blade had materialized and now it was just a matter of time. The rooftop between the pods was littered with dozens of small packets of drugs and money that fell short of their intended target — the opposite Pod. The inmates would either wrap up the stash and tape it to a rock or imbed it into a bar of soap for weight. Looking down, I speculated on whether it was worse being separated from these barbarians by a rusty single gate, or on top of the roof where there was absolutely no escape route should they manage to get out. That wasn't a pleasant thought, considering what we had just witnessed.

Paulo explained later that it was an established unit SOP that if, during a physical confrontation with the inmates, one of the GOE officers were captured, his fellow officers would immediately attempt to fire a fatal shot to his head in order to spare him the torture and slow death that would inevitably follow.

Many American officers often incredulously ask why the GOE just doesn't go in there and kick ass. Without knowing the conditions and layout of these prisons, it is hard to explain, but the main factor is the opposition. These bastards are absolutely ruthless and with the weaponry they have access to, the police would just not have the numbers to overcome the situation. It would be a more suitable job for the Army.

On the way back from the prison, Kevan and I sat in the back of Paulo's vehicle and said nothing. There was no joking or even small talk. The blatant savagery we had just witnessed was an everyday occurrence in every Brazilian prison and jail. It was nothing new or special to the inmates, it was simply just survival. If you weren't an animal prior to entering the penal system, then you sure as shit would be one if and when you came out.

I looked Kevan squarely in the eyes and said. "Kevan, if I ever break the law in this country and the judge sentences me to jail time, it will be your duty to put one in my head before leaving the courthouse. There is no way I could survive inside that environment."

His reply will be with me for as long as I live: "Kiwi, you idiot, you don't have to break the law to end up in jail in Brazil, you just have to piss the wrong cop off."

However, what I intentionally seek to experience in Brazil is definitely not the norm. The sole reason I go to these shit holes and participate in these raids is because I need the experience to become a more responsible and professional instructor for these men. It is also the nature of this line of work and the life that guys like Duke and myself have chosen. We do it so the world's soccer moms don't have to worry about it and also so most of the critics can sleep peacefully in their beds at night. We deal with the horrors of society so some of you readers don't have to. Altruism aside, we also do it because of the adrenalin rush that comes when one's life is dangling on the edge. We are action-oriented individuals, and if we were not, most of us would never become warrior police officers in the first place.

What country in the world does not have contested areas that are characterized by serious crime and anti-law-enforcement mentalities? Back home, I would never even consider letting Elaine or my five-year-old, Sean-Benet, venture into North or South Memphis without being tooled up and wearing body armor. However, twice they have accompanied me to Brazil to experience the wonders of this great country. Although there is a tremendous undercurrent of crime and violence, for most tourists this place still remains as one of the finest vacation spots in the world. From the Amazon's tropical rain forests in the North, to the German-influenced areas in the country's South, Brazilians are some of the most hospitable and friendly that you will find anywhere on the globe. Forget about coming here for business during the month of February, because that is when Carnival is in full swing. Tradition is tradition, and Brazilians, short of World War III, will bend for no one or anything once the drums start beating, the parades start moving, and the booze begins flowing. The same can be said when the national soccer team is beating up on us poor foreigners. Soccer to Brazil is like rugby to New Zealand, and the country literally shuts down during World Cup finals. This was particularly true in 2002 when the boys dealt the Germans a severe blow. Forget it if you intended to fly during those two hours. Ticket counters were closed, baggage handlers were sitting on the suitcases peering at portable TV sets, and the Varig pilots were locked in their preparation rooms hollering as loud as the janitors were.

The food here is not only unique, it is also abundant, particularly the Chuhascaria restaurants that will feed you till you drop. Every type of meat imaginable is grilled on open spits and carved off huge skewers, straight onto your plate. No sooner has that waiter gone and the next one arrives with a different carnivore's delight. And on it goes until you summon a wheel chair to roll you out of there and to your car. All this for USD$5 and even Jack Benny would have agreed that eating out here is a good deal.

The beaches up and down the Eastern seaboard need little introduction and I would be doing the country an injustice if I did not add my accolades to Brazil's most precious natural resource, the most beautiful women on the planet! Fitness and pride in ones personal appearance means a great deal to the young ladies. Couple that admirable and alluring trait with their man-oriented personalities and ability to dress to the ninety-nines, and they are among the most desirable women anywhere. There was many a night that my U.S. students and I sat in a mall restaurant, scarfing it up, trying to look disinterested, while "Bonita mulheres" paraded around half naked in front of us. Most of us got indigestion, but it was not from the delicious food on our plates. After World War II, the influx of Europeans, particularly Germans, made for some interesting mixtures. Forget about the stereotypical Latin look. Here you will not only see the darker native color, but also Latino redheads, brunettes, and stunning true blondes.

If you get bored with life in Brazil, which is unlikely, you can visit any of the ten countries that share its border: Argentina, Paraguay, Uruguay, Bolivia, Peru, Colombia, Venezuela, Guyana, Suriname, or French Guiana, and they all have their unique attractions.

Brazilians are a great people who know how to socialize and live for the moment. All you have to remember is: enjoy yourself, but do not be disrespectful to the boys in blue.

Solomon Sortie

Duke's Story

Guadalcanal — Evicted Again

The "Blue Boar Tavern" was finally operating at a satisfying tempo and money was coming in and satisfied customers were staggering out. I was pretty damn impressed with the finished results of the tavern's new lounge. The lumber had been felled and milled by local contractors and the building was designed and constructed by my good mate, Henry Hitchener. All interior walls and the ceiling were lined with natural timber, complete with seven-meter exposed beams running across the ceiling as bearers. The bar top itself was made out of recycled native rimu flooring jousts. The bar leaners and drinking surfaces were also made of recycled timber and adroitly decorated with hot poker etchings of hunting scenes by the tattooed and talented Hori Hern. The décor was extremely rustic and sturdy, and it needed to be because our stalwart patrons gave it a good workout. Stan, Hori, and I decided to decorate the place with the appropriate accoutrements befitting the bar's name.

Stan was the first to front up, and he donated a fearsome looking wild boar's head. It had been quite an impressive animal until Stan and his pig dogs put an end to his free-roaming days. One of the requirements for obtaining the best possible trophy mount is to skin out a good portion of the forequarters or shoulders, as well as the head. This gives the taxidermist sufficient material to work with. When fully stuffed, this accurately portrays the animal's size and features. Stan is a keen hunter and a great lover of wild pork. Because of his appetite for pork chops and puha this trophy was lucky to have its ears attached let alone any neck or shoulder meat. Nevertheless, this was the first donation, and although overshadowed in the presence of some of our more recent acquisitions, it remains in a special place on the tavern's wall. Still missing was a truly impressive specimen that would adequately celebrate the breed and epitomize the tavern's name — we needed a Blue Boar to adorn the trophy wall.

One hundred years earlier, the original pigs were liberated by Captain James Cook, the British explorer, and had evolved into "Captain Cookers."

Today's feral specimens are mean, long snouted, predominately blue-black animals with powerful barrel chests and forequarters. In contrast to these colour characteristics, today's generous wild pig population has resulted from the cross breading of feral and domestic animals. As a result, these pigs are not as pure as their predecessors and brown, black, and blue-grey varieties are not uncommon.

Nestled in the rugged backcountry and pine forests of Ruatoria is Waingakea Station. Chalky White was the original owner, and in his day was a tough old boy.

During the Second World War, his aircraft was shot down over Germany and Chalky basically walked back to England and eventual safety. His two sons, Les and James, along with their parents and respective families, have farmed this area since the 1940's. For many years, the surrounding natural bush and farmland has been the haven of a strain of wild, blue-grey pigs. This would be our hunting ground and our pig assault plans were discussed for many months over numerous jugs and handles of beer. At this juncture, the ultimate Blue Boar remains on our most wanted list.

Two weeks before we actually opened the tavern, Roger Lockley, a local farmer, called and mentioned that he had a four-year-old blue boar that he had captured as a piglet in the bush. Noticing that we had a good deer fence around the establishment, he thought it would be nice to have "Boris," the tame "wild" pig, as an attraction. Boris had his nuts cut off as a youngster to quieten him down somewhat, and this worked to perfection. However, even without his jewels, he is still a fine looking fellow and quite capable of fooling the average, uninformed tourist. Although a bit rotund from pampering, his hooks and size indicate he has the makings of a good trophy in the future. One day Boris will become a permanent fixture on the inside of the tavern with pride of place on the wall.

Once again, reality reared its ugly head in the form of required cash for my favourite watering hole. As a result of this financial boot in the backside, I started talking to my contacts around the globe for possible work opportunities. I was fortunate to secure a six-month contract with a London-based company, and within a couple of weeks I was bound for the sunny South Sea islands of the Solomon Group, situated just off the coast of Australia and Papua New Guinea.

The Solomon's Islands are probably best known for the heavy sea and land battles that occurred there during the Second World War. Mention Guadalcanal, Bloody Ridge, or Iron Bottom Sound, and any U.S. Marine worth his salt will get an instant erection. My new client was head of a large international Palm Oil company that required a security manager for their Honiara-based office. Honiara is the capital city of the Solomon Islands and situated on the South West coast of Guadalcanal, which is the main island. For the previous six months they had experienced severe problems because of increased tension created by militant factions on the main island. Current trends and local intelligence indicated that this was not a temporary situation, but was in fact, the pre game warm up for full-scale anarchy.

Information is a vital key in the asset security game so I checked my "old boy" network and sought out several individuals in the know. All this would ensure I had a basic plan of action on day one of my new employment.

Civilian security training contracts do not resemble military or Government sponsored training teams. As a contractor, you are usually on your own and must rely on yourself to set up a program. Often this is without adequate funding and it is extremely difficult, if not impossible, to obtain simple things that we take for granted in the Western World. Fortunately in this case, this was not a shoe-string operation and I was moving into a well set up and administered organisation. Ken, one of the former unit lads and a good friend, had returned from the U.K. several years earlier and established a creditable security company based in Auckland, New Zealand. Ken, assisted by Spence and Shane, had completed a training gig six months earlier for the same client in the area that I was about to venture into. I managed to spend a morning with these guys at their Auckland office and received a thorough brief on what had been in place earlier. Upon arriving at their office I was surprised to see Dirty Dave, another friend of mine, and Shane and Spence, all decked out in clean and pressed slacks, white shirts, and ties, and all working quietly and efficiently in their office spaces. Shane, was, as always, meticulous in his appearance, but Dave and Spence had definitely elevated their game plan. Looking at Spence with his hair gel, fragrant after-shave, and nifty civilian attire, I couldn't help reminiscing about days gone by. As part of the early transition of the NZSAS to the counter-terrorism role in the late 70's, it was decided by the powers to be that bodyguard training was a required skill for the unit. In the early 80's "John the Jock" came across from the U.K. on attachment for 6 months, and conducted several bodyguard modules for us. This was the beginning of a strong personal friendship between John, Alan, and I, and he introduced a necessary skill into our special force capabilities.

Spence, Alan, and I were all on the initial course. In those days, Spence was extremely rudimentary in his civilian attire and more at home in his rural East Coast uniform of gumboots, rugby shorts, and swandri (N.Z. bushman's poncho-style woollen shirt). His prowess as a tracker and reputation as a gifted rural operator was well deserved, but take him out of the jungle and he was a total disaster. Upon completion of the first week's classroom training, John in his unintelligible Scottish accent, gave us a verbal brief on dress, etiquette, and the requirements for the next weeks training. We all sat there like totally stunned mullets, mesmerized by John's accent, which even today requires careful attention to fully grasp his intended meaning. We all went home that evening and prepared for the next stage of the course. We now required suits and all the civvy kit for our first VIP protection exercise in the nearby city of Auckland.

Spence is of Maori-European extraction. Stocky in build, he would be lucky to reach 5 foot, 6 inches in height. However, according to his measurements, he was just below six feet in stature. This understandable exaggeration was put in cold perspective when the unit lined up for the annual ANZAC Parade. On RSM Whee's command, "SHORTEST ON THE LEFT, TALLEST ON THE RIGHT," there was always a frantic and occasionally violent scuffle between Spence, Boydie, and Little Mac for the dubious honour of being the Squadron's dwarf. Spence is known for his penetrating glare which he can turn on and off at will. Many a candidate on SAS selection has experienced that chilling look and decided to chuck it in right then and there and go home early. It's even been known to melt the odd scrubber's knickers in the infamous Forge night-club in downtown Papakura, but that's another story.

Fronting up the next morning, we loosely paraded in our best civilian threads. John gave us a quick once over, and initially appeared suitably impressed. Other than for "Grecos the Viking" wearing a pair of Nike running shoes with his conservative two—piece suit, the boys had accomplished their mission, or so John thought. Those of us in the rear of the group, a position of strategic importance, could observe Grecos more clearly. True to form and in keeping with his inability to wear any military or civilian clothing without showing a little butt crease, the tail of his shirt was hanging down just below his suit coat. Today Grecos is a veteran member of the West Australian Police Force and I hope his personal dress code has improved. John conducted a more detailed inspection and suddenly, came to an abrupt halt in front of a very uncomfortable looking Spence. He was wearing his black army service shoes, a pair of decade old, completely out of fashion flared trousers, and to top it off, his sports coat had been liberated from a dummy target in the "killing house." When John realized where this ensemble had come from he muttered something in Scottish about, "Fooken Antipodeans" (Australians or New Zealanders), shook his shaggy head, and then proceeded with the day's training. Amazingly, Ken had achieved something no one else thought possible. Spence had been transformed visually into a normal middle-aged, well dressed member of the civilian society.

I flew to the Solomon's via Australia and landed at Henderson International airport in Honiara. Security and customs processing was fairly straightforward and I breezed through without a problem. Before I was able to take much stock of my new surroundings, I was bouncing along the highway in a security wagon while getting my in-country brief on the move. Jack Hoft, the security manager, was a large former Aussie Army major. He appeared to be a good guy, but definitely in need of a break after nine months in-country. Nevertheless, Jack had set up a thorough and much appreciated security package for me. I learned that while in the "badlands," Jack had been shot at by criminals and militants, successfully foiled an attempted car jacking on his Hi Lux, and received numerous death threats from local thugs. I was well aware that threats are part of Melanesian life and to be expected. I was banking on my past experience in the Pacific Region with similar militants to pull me through. However, when you are surrounded by angry, machete-wielding boys from the back blocks, twenty miles from any safe haven, and out numbered by fifty-to-one, it suddenly becomes an unwelcome reality. Jack, for understandable reasons, had taken a promotion in Australia and was moving on. I was his replacement and I could sense his relief when I finally arrived. My basic responsibility would be to administer the security program already in place. Our area of concern was a series of large well-matured and productive Palm Oil plantations, the down side was that the GRA rebels had taken control of the whole Guadalcanal island, except the capital city Honiara. You guessed it, the plantations were well and truly in the badlands.

Honiara is a pleasant city and typical of the Pacific Islands. It is still very colonial in appearance, but gradually shedding its pre-war trappings as the older ex-patriate community passes on. Situated right on the coast, it has a good port facility. With the exception of one main street of shops, the city appears to be devoid of any urban planning. Houses are situated randomly located and it could be any small city in the numerous archipelagos in this region. Few road signs were evident and there was no such thing as numbers on the houses. The postman must have had one hell of job delivering mail. The population is composed of the typical Melanesian-Polynesian mix of peoples from other Pacific Island communities, with fair amounts of Mainland Chinese, Taiwanese, Australians, New Zealanders, and British ex-patriates thrown in.

When the island was first colonized, the European settlers favoured the Malaitans (ethnic group from the nearby island of Malaita)) as the preferred work force. As a result of this preference, the Malaitans, over the years, have acquired positions of power within local and provincial governments, including the national police force. However, since the original inhabitants from the island of Guadalcanal were Guales and not Malaitans, resentment grew until in the late 90's a violent confrontation took place.

The IFF (Isatabu Freedom Fighters) and GRA (Guale Revolutionary

Army) were interfering with our client's operation. Both these Guale militant groups had focused their attentions on traditional enemies from Malaita. Through intimidation and armed violence, the Guales had managed to force twenty-odd thousand Malaitans back to their neighbouring island homeland. Many of our palm oil plantation's original work-force of 2000 had left after numerous murders and ambushes by the Guale militants. Guadalcanal Island, except for the capital city of Honiara was totally under control of the Guale forces. The only reason that Honiara remained under their control was that the National Police Force consisted primarily of this ethnic group.

The situation was further aggravated by the resurgence of the MEF (Malaitan Eagle Force). This group of cut-throats appeared to be supported by the police, politicians, and businessmen. When I arrived, the battles were mainly between the opposing militant factions and the national police. This violence has had a considerable impact on the island and the statistics are alarming. The GRA militant's weapons were predominately home-made and, therefore, are as much a danger to the firer as the intended victim. However, their .50-caliber pipe guns loaded with ammunition cached from WWII had to be pretty damaging to whoever they hit and would easily defeat the set of body armor that my predecessor handed over to me. The similarities between the various other violent confrontations that have plagued the South Pacific for the last ten years were alarming. Papua New Guinea, Bougainville, Indonesia, East Timor, Mindanao, and the Philippines are among the plethora of countries and former colonies in this area that have exploded into racial conflicts, or wars of independence.

PNG had only recently survived a horrendous civil war with Bougainville, which resulted with international condemnation of the "Sandline affair." This British run mercenary force composed mainly of veterans from the South African and Angolan guerrilla conflicts, was contracted by the government of Papua New Guinea to suppress the rebels of the Bouganville Revolutionary Army (BRA). The repercussions are still ricocheting around this part of the world, and any reference to training teams or security programs immediately sends alarm bells ringing in interested embassies and high commissions. Sandline tried to establish a mercenary force on the island of Bougainville. This included sufficient military hardware and air support to suppress and force the BRA to cease operating and sign a peace accord. The current PNG prime minister and several of his cronies supported this political-military settlement. Sandline, reportedly received USD$36-million for their promised, but undelivered, results. The Australian and New Zealand governments gave the impression of being completely unaware of the mercenary force. However, I can't help but feel that Mr. Chan, PNG's premier, was slipped a fast one. The operation was compromised and exposed by General Jerry Siringok, PNG's military commander, which resulted in massive public demonstrations against these actions by outsiders. Subsequently, members of the Sandline contingent were apprehended and expelled from the country. The idea of contracting a mercenary force to handle matters of security within the region was repugnant not only to the citizens of PNG, but to other sovereign island countries as well. I have my doubts as to the rationale of this holier-than-thou attitude. True peace, whether by conventional means or mercenary force, is all that matters. Ask the citizens of Sierra Leone who they would rather have providing law and order in their war-torn domain — Executive Outcome, Sandline, or ECOMOG and the UN peace-keeping forces.

Pound for pound, the BRA, in this rugged terrain, would give any conventional force that tried to take them on a bloody nose. In my opinion, had Sandline's forces succeeded in getting to the war zone, I am reasonably convinced that in a protracted engagement they would have had their asses severely kicked all the way back to the PNG mainland. I was not in favor of Sandline's involvement or ultimate intentions in PNG. Their head shed was seemingly more interested in the financial potential of the Panguna Gold Mine and not the cessation of hostilities for humanitarian or other noble reasons.

The Australian government transferred military helicopters to PNG forces during the civil war period, supposedly for medevac and humanitarian missions. However, both civilians and militants alike were justifiably concerned when they were "brassed up" by these "slicks" that had, on occasion, been converted into gun ships. The questions of "how did this happen" and "who flew these choppers" was rife for a significant period throughout the Pacific. A common rumour was that some of the pilots were Aussies or Kiwis. Who knows or even really cares, but democratic governments should not get too sanctimonious about foreign mercenaries serving in Bougainville, or anywhere else for that matter.

The police of Guadalcanal were tasked with providing law enforcement for the entire country. This would be an incredible task for any modern police agency, but nigh on impossible for the poorly trained and financed Royal Solomon Island Police Force. In addition, they had no military forces to establish a defensive posture for the islands. With the increased tensions emanating from militant groups, plus the added displacement of all expatriate and Malaitans from the rural areas into Honiara, things had become increasingly difficult. Furthermore, the large number of displaced Malaitans had seriously eroded the customer base for the Honaira businessman. Many of the large commercial agricultural industries were also no longer in operation because in addition to reverse migration of the Malaitans, workers could not venture safely beyond the city's limits.

The tribal chiefs have lost much of their control over the young people who often constitute the rank and file of these militant groups. The relatively new Chinese community from Taiwan and Hong Kong were settling in and establishing themselves but do not appear to venerate to the senior Chinese families who have been part of Honiara since colonial times. An extremely high percentage of island inhabitants are under 21 years of age with few opportunities for employment or advancement, and the option to join criminal gangs under the guise of militancy is, therefore, an attractive one. Organized crime was a significant problem within the city, with larger numbers becoming involved and more violent criminal acts were occurring.

In spite of its precarious position in the middle of the IFF's stronghold, the rural based "Gold Ridge" gold mine was still operating. But, this was very much a day-by-day situation. No other corporation or company of significant size was generating any substantial income from the hinterlands. During the Bougainville war, the BRA funded much of their war effort with raw gold from the rich Panguna mine. During hostilities and post-war, many BRA militants harbored up in the Solomon Islands. Some married local women and now reside here, and a strong relationship exists between the former BRA members and the IFF. This warrior caste is capable of providing military expertise and knowledge to assist the militants now and in the future.

The Chinese-Taiwanese trading and fishing community have the necessary infra-structure that can handle the illegal importation and distribution of weapons and military equipment. In West Africa, rebel funding is derived from diamonds and here, as in Bougainville, it could just as easily be from gold. An example of the attempted liberation of gold for unsavoury purposes was the ill-fated Port Moresby robbery in 1999. A "Raskol" gang with militant connections hijacked a Kiwi pilot and his helicopter to carry out their audacious heist. Fortunately, the Papua New Guinea Constabulary took more positive actions than the authorities did at the Munich Olympics in the 1972. Alerted to their intentions, they riddled the helo when it inserted and killed most of the robbers. Amazingly, the pilot survived. Capers like this one were unheard of in the mid-nineties when I first worked the mines in the Western Highlands. Prior to gold shipments by chopper from Porgera to Moresby, our "actions on" contingency plans always addressed this possibility, and we were well prepared for any Raskol ground attacks at the airport transfers, both in Port Moresby and Mount Hagen.

The militants from the MEF, GRU, and IFF factions were fully capable of planning significant robberies and raids. If they ever got around to merging, the island would experience complete lawlessness and bloody confrontations.

The ex-patriate community and staff from the various embassies were all very knowledgeable, but appeared to be in complete denial regarding the similarities between the events that had transpired and the previous Bougainville crisis. Perhaps I am too paranoid, but one of my first priorities was to check out escape and evasion routes and identify people who would assist me in this endeavor, should it become necessary. The Honiara Yacht Club seemed like a good place to start and this visit led me to the incorrigible Lenny Palmer. Lenny was a fourth generation Solomon Islander, still a European but very much a Melanesian and Polynesian in his style, nature, and temperament. A retired merchant seaman between 40 and 50 years of age, he spent most of his free time drinking beer at the yacht club and offering any female within range the privilege of having a blue-eyed child with him. He was an incredible bull-shitter and his tales were hard to beat. For local entertainment and a source of information, there would be none better than this old salt of the Islands. His Island networks were extraordinary, and in very short time he became a good friend and number one asset in my "E and E" plan.

I met several other great and interesting people at the Yacht Club's bar. Geoff Mitchell and his son, Steve, were also long-time residents and about as straight and honest a breed as can be found. More importantly, Steve had his helicopter pilot's license and Geoff had an escape boat. Geoff had worked in the Solomon's for over 30 years, and initially had been an integral part of the development of the Plain's area and rice program. His prawn farms, with Steve's help, became an extremely viable local enterprise. Unfortunately, this was all binned when the militants evicted them from their farm and other assets. Geoff's main vocation, in the months that I knew him, was to be the perfect host at the club's bar. He confessed to being around 48, but his son confided that Geoff has been the same age for the last ten years. His popularity was not just confined to his drinking mates. The island ladies loved old Geoff, big time. Aussie Greg was another character and possibly the first accountant I have ever chanced upon who could actually find his wallet when it was his turn to shout for a round of beer. Married to a local woman, he and his good wife had adopted several local kids, and as a harmonious couple they are an example of the many positive aspects of life in the Solomon Islands. Hopefully, through this turbulent period, people of good-will will somehow remain in the islands and be part of its eventual reconstruction.

One night down at the club, I noticed Lenny in animated discussion with two elderly, but worldly looking American gentlemen concerning the current militant problems fouling this small island paradise. From their comments, I discerned that both had served during the Second World War as part of the U.S. Marine Corps forces on Guadalcanal. They were genuinely concerned about the area and made a pilgrimage back to the South Pacific every couple of years to catch up with old comrades and provide assistance wherever possible. Even though they weren't Solomon Islanders, by having fought and bled on this tiny piece of contested turf fifty years earlier, they definitely had the right, as far as I was concerned, to pass judgment on the current issues. They had a couple more beers, shook hands all around, and then politely excused themselves and quietly returned to their hotel. It turned out that these humble and courteous men were retired Marine Colonel Jefferson De Blanc and Major Ashley Bill Fisher, both of whom won Medals of Honor not far from where we drank. They also headed up a foundation dedicated to the collection of memorabilia and the preservation of famous World War Two battle sites in the South Pacific.

In the short period of a few months, several policemen had been killed or wounded in confrontations with the militants. Those statistics might be insignificant in larger countries, but to the small Solomon Islands Police Force, it was devastating. Considering the police armouries were the only source of factory-made weapons within the whole Solomon Island Group, the next step was inevitable.

Similar to PNG, the Melanesian tradition of an eye pay back is custom and cannot be ignored. It may take several generations to change, but a death of a clan member can only be appeased or made whole through retribution followed by compensation. A prime example of how a simple incident can escalate in a relatively short time to a major drama was an American inner-city-style drive-by shooting by the MEF.

Nobody was injured, but the action caused the local GRA to set up a roadblock to the village area. That same day, a local contractor's vehicle was hijacked by the GRA. Four-wheel-drive Hi Lux vehicles were worth their weight in gold and became popular targets for both militant groups. Our Palm Oil company alone had lost 15 vehicles in the previous ten months through car-jacking and thefts. A retaliation raid took place two days later when fifteen armed MEF members left their encampment alongside the Henderson International Airfield and covertly made their way through the jungle and attacked the GRA roadblock. Apparently there was no attack plan and it degenerated into a free-for-all shooting spree. The group charged through the Foxwood/Red Beach areas completely out of control. A local store was robbed of several thousand dollars and the packed market area was wasted by small arms fire creating general chaos. Guale men, women, and children were attempting to escape in all directions, and confusion and panic was rampant in both camps. The MEF withdrawal plan was probably formulated on the run. An unlucky police vehicle happened to be passing through the area and was accosted by the MEF. Suddenly, the poor old coppers were looking into the nasty ends of the barrels of the militant's weapons. The police did what they do best, changed down a gear, and bolted along the narrow, pot-holed road to safety. The vehicle took numerous shotgun blasts and, fortunately, only one policeman was wounded. Once they finally figured out what to do next, the MEF managed to scuttle back to their lair in relative safety.

However, the incident was far from over. In turn, this action garnered an immediate counter-response from the IFF/GRA and they constructed a steel gated roadblock on the only road out of town the very same day. Twenty minutes from the city, the barricade was manned by 60 or more militants, some decked out in full, traditional regalia and others in the more favored military-civilian mix of clothing. Weapons ranged from the homespun .50 caliber pipe guns, to factory made shotguns and .22's. Although not Kalashnikovs, the eclectically armed lads could still do a lot of damage if provoked. Reserves for the hasty fortification consisted of two to three hundred more rebels who established a shanty-town encampment alongside the road. All hands had rallied to the call to arms and were straggling in from even the distant Weathercoast areas. For an area that has very poor mobile phone service outside the city and dependant on mobile generators for power, information gets around the island pretty damn quickly. Since this roadblock stood between my workplace and our city office, I acquired a deeply personal interest in the situation.

On the morning of the third day of the Tenaru road-block, the body of a middle-aged male dressed in traditional kapilito dress was dumped in the market place on the main street of Honiara. It was widely circulated at the time that this was the body of a teenage Weathercoast lad that had been snatched by MEF several weeks earlier. In reality, the corpse was identified as a Guale security guard who had worked for an overseas company in Honiara. Since head hunting still persisted as a common practice, it was no real surprise that this man had also been decapitated and, incidentally, his head has never been recovered. This killing was unusual in that the murder and decapitation was committed elsewhere. The dumping of the body at the market place was an attempt at terrorism and a warning to all Guales to steer clear of Honiara City. I travelled up-country every day and along with the Gold Ridge Security team the only ex-pats with any need to go through this volatile region. The down side of course were the suffering civilians, minimal aid or medical supplies were scarcely available in the best of times, now with the rebel roadblocks in full force. Nothing was coming through, rice, salt, and all other staple products were non-existent. Malaria and other treatable problems were at danger high and doctors or emergency services non-existent.

Of considerable interest to me was the location of the large MEF camp only a couple of hundred meters past the Henderson airfield. Egress from the airport was a prominent part of my E&E plan, but now serious consideration had to be given to other alternatives. I grabbed my trusty number-two, and with considerable visible apprehension on his part, we took off in the four-wheeler for the plantation process plant, 20 miles in Indian Country. I had been given the go-ahead from our up-country security team and assured that they would assist us with our potentially precarious passage. These boys had been trained several months earlier by Ken and his team to protect the process plant and company assets, all Guales to a man. Had they not been they would have been slaughtered pretty damn quickly. In the initial ethnic cleansing by the Guales weeks earlier, several of our Malaitan plantation workers had simply disappeared and rightly presumed murdered. The complete security team changed status to GRA as soon as the MEF put in their counter road block at the airport. My security team was still driving company vehicles and performing security procedures at our area of concern, but all were now serving under the GRA militant's flag. I hadn't told my 2IC and he was feeling the pinch big time. We wound our way out of town and after passing the airfield, the road becomes a real driving challenge. Left or right hand lanes did not exist, and you had to use all of the road to negotiate the deep and lengthy corrugations and water-filled pot-holes. Vehicle speed is determined by the driver's ability or naked fear level, and because of the ethnic violence, people tried to motor as fast as possible to negate any .50-caliber snipers. On we slogged, and rather sedately crossed the Alligator Creek Bridge and gave the RSIP outpost a lofty wave. Now we were in the badlands and around the forested curve, another 100 yards or so, was our gate to freedom, Heaven or Hell. Tensing up for the fusillade of buckshot, .22 hollow points, or, God forbid, the elephant gun, we gingerly approached the guerrilla's gate.

Resembling a Tarzan movie, the GRA lads were dressed to kill and looked extremely capable of doing so. The huge .50 cal pipe guns looked fucken dangerous although they were amazingly simple in construction. However, just looking at them intimidated the hell out of me. God help us if they ever perfected a good sighting system. Apparently, four of the five policemen that were murdered were shot with these cannons and exhibited entry but no exit wounds. One unfortunate chap stuffed up the statistics by getting his jaw shot completely off by a similarly armed militant. Numerous warriors surrounded us with factory made .22s and 12 gage shotguns. However, out of the corner of my eye I spotted a trusty SLR or FN .30 in the hands of a dread-locked and evil-looking character. It looked like the baddies were upgrading their weaponry. It would be a race for the police armouries once the balloon went up. We stopped at the makeshift steel gate at the mercy of the hundreds of rebels sitting on the roadside and jungle's fringes. I was tremendously relieved to spot some of our security lads in among the crowd, and although it was hard to tell who was who, it was obvious that we would be okay. They came up to our human cordon and after much shaking of hands and an exchange of red-mouthed, betel-nut smiles, we were waved through the gap. Once the Guale's gates were opened, a young one-eyed, but serious looking, bloke sprang into the vehicle's back seat. He was festooned with shotgun and traditional accoutrements. Obviously eager to get out of there, and wanting to break up the monotony of guard duty, he was reinforced by half a dozen more armed militants who leapt up onto the vehicle's tray. With minimal chatter, we preceded on to our next destination a damn site safer than before.

Six weeks earlier, I had re-commenced security team training, and impressive progress had been realized. Every day we performed physical training along the roads and plantation tracks of Tetere and the lads sang their hearts out while I puffed and sweated alongside them. For me, it was a welcome break from the tedium of the city and always a satisfying couple of hours. After the physical exercise, we would carry out an audit of our buildings and area of concern. We would often meet with the local elders and tribal leaders and discuss the significance of protecting company assets and matters of local interest.

One morning an MEF raiding party of between 15 and 20 hit to the rear of the roadblock from behind the Catholic school. When the gun-smoke cleared, two Guales were dead and the MEF had suffered four KIA, but the barrier remained.

Severed heads and headless bodies again appeared at roadsides as a warning to MEF aggressors. I have nothing but respect for the Guale security crew and good friends that I made in the short time that I was there. Because of increasing violence and murders that were committed proximate to the roadblock, eventually I was unable to continue with my daily trips up-country.

It was becoming obvious that the situation had escalated far too dramatically for our law enforcement authorities to handle. The Gold Ridge Mine had become a focus of militant aggression. One of their police security teams was mauled and a manager's vehicle was car-jacked at the roadblock. These incidents forced the up-country staff to adapt a siege mentality and they bunkered up at the mine site for several days to reassess the situation. A helicopter finally flew in from PNG and evacuated most of the foreign and ex-patriate staff and the mine had to close down production. This drama was no sooner squared away through productive dialogue and negotiations between the mine site and the GRA leaders when suddenly the MEF decided to shake things up a bit and get some combat time in. The GRA lads had stolen several SLR's and other weapons from police stations, and thereby acquired increased confidence from their augmented and superior firepower. Boldly, a platoon-sized MEF force launched a hostile mid day visit to the Alligator Creek police checkpoint and at the end of the day they were the proud new owners of a GPMG (General Purpose Machine Gun), three more SLRs, numerous police uniforms, body armor, a police radio, and sufficient 7.62x51 MM NATO ammo to defend the Alamo. The police (Malaitan sympathisers) at the roadblock simply walked from the outpost without firing a shot in anger. This police out-post was approximately half a kilometer from the GRA roadblock and only a couple of hundred meters from the end of Henderson International Airfield and, accordingly, generated a significant threat to its safe operation. The MEF had also taken complete control over all vehicles attempting to enter or leave Honiara. Thorough vehicle searches were now part of the drill, and anyone transporting items of food, fuel, or anything else that could be deemed to be contraband for the GRA cause, would be in trouble. Several Chinese workers from the Malaysian Timber Company found out the hard way and suffered the consequences of a good thrashing and a couple of hours of mental torture. They finished up by wearing blindfolds and becoming the main actors in a mock execution. After much begging and pleading with their captors for clemency and mercy, they were released, but minus their four-wheel-drive vehicle. The next day they were the first to line up with their suitcases and personal belongings at the airport's departure lounge. Another Chinese businessman coming to Honiara from Foxwood was relieved of a significant sum of cash by the MEF. Fuel tankers critical to the gold mine's daily production were also targeted and the mine was forced to pay SI$10,000 for the release of each vehicle and driver. The MEF roadblock had become an excellent source of revenue for the war chests of the rebels.

After eleven months of non-production, my client and the board of directors in London decided to cease working and negate the 30-year-old joint venture operation with the landowners and Solomon Government. The company and its staff would vacate the islands until peace was achieved, or at least law and order was restored. However, we still had an obligation to make final payment of wages and stipends to the guard force and landowners. My young security manager and I, with one "Brother Willy," of the Melanesian Christian Brothers and armed with his "magic staff," flew over the roadblocks in a helicopter, piloted by Kiwi, Brent Parkinson, to the Gold Ridge mining site. Native superstition believed that to be touched by this magic staff would cause one to lose his soul and, in turn, face real problems with the gods. As a result, none of the indigenous islanders would confront the brothers in any way. They have been a tremendous resource for peace and have had a beneficial effect on the islands. After taking off, we were able to observe the two rival roadblocks with all their militant and ruffian crews crowded around the jungle edges about 500 meters from the end of the airfield runway's perimeter fence. Shortly thereafter, we passed over the rather insignificant looking, but infamous, "Bloody Ridge" of WWII. Fifty years before, the Imperial Japanese Army and U.S. Marines slaughtered each other for this now seemingly inconsequential piece of real estate.

We flew above 3000 feet so the militants wouldn't be tempted to bring their eclectic armoury to bear and try to bring us down. Furthermore, we had nearly SI$200,000 with us, which for these parts would be a bloody substantial windfall and well worth any effort to perforate us. We arrived without any real fuss, and proceeded by vehicle down to the armed security post. Our Guale security, now GRA rebels, were all there and greeted us like the long-lost brothers. Days earlier, our company trucks had been featured on a television documentary overloaded with cheering and armed GRA/IFM militants rushing to the former police checkpoint at Alligator Creek. One of those company trucks commandeered as a troop carrier was here, but at least the boys were being discreet and all weapons were concealed. However, their efforts were somewhat marred by the odd steel helmet and camouflaged face mixed in with the throng of employees. Like a traditional military payday, wages were paid to the boys as they trooped in and signed on the dotted line. There were no incidents and finally, after a marathon hand-shaking session, it was time to go. It was a sad moment for me; because once again I found myself leaving the security teams I was responsible for, knowing full well that the days ahead were going to be fraught with danger for them and their families. I wondered who would survive from my security crew to see peace once again on the plains. With reluctance, I re-boarded the chopper and flew back out of the danger zone to the so-called reality of Honiara.

This contract was almost over and my British manager was going through the diplomatic procedures of winding down the Joint Venture project with the island's government. As the finishing touches were being hammered out between the bureaucrats and our head shed, the MEF and rebel elements of the National Police Force took armed control of Honiara. I rolled out of bed early that morning aware that I and another consultant were trapped on the wrong side of the coup's forces, whose road-blocks were located outside the main police barracks. The hotel owners and staff had gone underground and the only other occupant was an extremely nervous young Scotsman who had recently been appointed as the Solomon Island's national soccer coach. Unlike Sierra Leone, this time I was responsible for two other foreigners, so a solo sprint for the jungle was not an option. Escape by sea had been made untenable by the deployment of two naval patrol craft by coup members. These craft not only patrolled the coastline, but also strafed the Alligator GRA roadblock from the sea with its machineguns. After making a number of frenetic phone calls and confirmations, we were able to come up with alternative plans. I desperately needed to get to the main hotel in Honiara and contact my two other comrades, but, more importantly, ensure the safety of the company's chief operating officer.

During the afternoon, a local Malaitan "heavy" arrived at our location, well under the influence and bragging about his actions over the previous couple of hours. He was a tough-looking individual and fairly wealthy,

Duke's security team prior to coup – Solomon Islands

judging by his clothing and choice of vehicle. He was not a nice guy. He had been ordered by Malaitan leaders to find the young soccer coach and get him to the safety of the international hotel. Soccer is a big thing throughout the Pacific Rim and the wealthy fans were very keen on getting the youth and senior national teams onto the South East Asian circuit. After stroking his ego, he finally agreed to escort the three of us to the safety of the hotel in Honiara. This stroke of luck enabled me to link up with the CEO and our two employees, which enabled me to arrange for their safety.

We remained at the hotel for a week, and although foreigners had not been targeted or terrorized, the Australian and New Zealand High Commissions evacuated my client and 400 other ex-patriates via the Aussie frigate, Tobruk. It took us five days to reach Cairns, Australia and although I am grateful for the Navy's assistance, this was a journey that I would rather not repeat due to the crowded and rough sea-going conditions.

The Solomon Island's ethnic issues continue to boil and the country is not only bankrupt, but no one seems even faintly interested in helping, other than for a few token gestures from its Pacific Rim neighbours. Without any exportable natural resources, the future looks extremely bleak. Unlike Timor, which has enjoyed substantial amounts of assistance from the global community and the United Nations, the Solomon Islands have been left to its own diplomatic devices. Their only hope at this juncture appears to be Australia and New Zealand.

The Foreign Connection

Alan's Story

Maintaining International Relations

July 7, 2002 found Bob Taubert, Steve Mattoon, and myself suited up and sitting in one of the palace's ornate waiting rooms just outside the office of His Majesty King Abdullah II of Jordan. Accompanied by Captain Ghazi Daghistani, a cousin of the king, we were ushered into the king's office by a member of his large security detail for what turned out to be a 55-minute meeting. The French Foreign Minister, who proceeded us, got only fifteen minutes and our lengthy audience was unheard of for a busy head of state's schedule.

Captain Daghistani, a member of His Majesty's Special Forces, had organized our visit. Its purpose was for us to assist His Majesty in a special project that involved units of his security forces. It was a thrill and a dis-

Meeting with His Majesty, King Abdullah II – Amman, Jordan, July, 2002

tinct honor to be able to meet a man that is so admired and respected throughout both the Middle East and Western World. King Abdullah II was the eldest son of King Hussein, who tragically and prematurely passed away during January 2000 after a long battle with cancer. It was no secret that His Majesty King Hussein, a warrior turned diplomat, was a great friend of the United States. He was one of the world's most charismatic, effective, and honored leaders, particularly for his tireless efforts in the pursuit of peace in the one of the globe's most volatile regions.

Abdullah II had no aspirations to be king and was not directly in line to be his Father's successor. Jordan's expansion into the role of Mid East peace broker presented the monarchy with a huge and frustrating mission and to follow in his father's footsteps would be no mean feat. In February 2001, the young monarch took the helm and is well on the way toward establishing himself as one of the region's great leaders. Like his father, younger brothers, and sister, he is a graduate of Great Britain's elite Sandhurst Military Academy. He rose to the rank of general in his Father's Army, where he also acquired his helicopter pilot and Special Forces credentials. He is definitely a warrior, and after becoming fully commando qualified, became the commander of the realm's first counter-terrorist battalion. However, in spite of his lofty position, the king is an extremely cordial and down to earth individual who is also a firearms and Harley Davidson enthusiast.

Events such as this do not come too often for a grunt like me. I feel extremely fortunate to have had the opportunity to travel the world working and meeting people from all walks of life. My big break came in January, 1993. Mike Smith, a former Delta Force operator who was working for an American company, contracted by the U.S. Department of State contacted me. Although I did not personally know Mike, he had worked with my former unit in New Zealand. He asked me if I would be interested in joining a team of instructors that would be tasked to train foreign police officers in skills associated with counter-terrorism. I jumped at the chance and what followed was six years of contract work for the State Department's Anti Terrorism Assistance Program. I have many fond memories of those years, especially those that relate to the friendships formed between my fellow instructors. Mike, Kit, and Matt, also former Delta operators, are great friends as is Geoff, an ex-member of the British SAS who can best be described as a nuggety little Brit who understood the meaning of "work hard, play hard." Bill Yaegle, Todd Taylor, Bob Taubert, Ron Brady, Ver Dayrit, "Gunny" Hank, Paul Robert, Kenny Beaudoin, and lead instructor Bob Walters completed the "core" instructor team for these six-week courses. The initial aim of the program was to support the democratic efforts of the former Soviet Union after it was dissolved during President Reagan's tenure as head of state. Working with the Polish, Bulgarians, Hungarians, and Lithuanians was an experience. All former henchmen for the disintegrated Soviet Union, they performed their fair share of evil deeds against

U.S. State Department Anti Terrorism Assistance Program training team. Alan is kneeling in front of Lead Instructor Bob Walters (white shirt). Mike Smith is standing to Walters' left; Bill Yaegle is on Walters' right. Bob Taubert is standing far right in the photo.

Des Moines, Iowa SWAT Officer and T.E.E.S. instructor, Todd Taylor, and I with Tunisian Camel Corps Officer Zarfhori during counter terrorist training — 1996

the West and anti-communist regimes.

Whether it was in the form of providing arms and explosives, training terrorist groups, providing passive support or safe havens for terrorist organizations, or plotting and supporting the overthrow of a democratically-elected government, they were, nevertheless, soldiers. And, like us, simply followed orders under the direction of ambitious politicians. These guys, a number of whom were former Spetsnatz, were young, hard men who one-on-one would give any American a run for his money. The Lithuanian operators were all studs and kicked the instructor's butts during a building and obstacle course competition. Victor G. was and is their "Eagle Force" team leader and they all were extremely serious about the training. Since the fall of communism, most of these former East Bloc countries have experienced serious crime waves. Citizens, who in the past expected to be executed or sent to the salt mines for their misdeeds, now realized that they had a chance to survive even if caught. Bargaining tools such as legal representation and limited rights were suddenly available. Welcome to the "free world" of the West, where criminals and lawyers dominate the legal system.

The program shifted to South American countries that were known to have a "Narco terrorist" problem. Colombia, Peru, Ecuador, Bolivia, and Venezuela were the initial recipients followed by Paraguay, Argentina and Brazil.

Following the bombings of the United States embassies in Kenya and Nigeria, certain allied African countries were also trained and, eventually, they were succeeded by members of the Baltic region.

Several Arab countries spent 42 days in the U.S. and the Jordanians led the way as far as skill levels, professionalism and general attitudes were concerned. Voluminous contacts were made and great friendships were established among all these countries, but one man always sticks in my mind. Zahfori was a member of a 24-man contingent from the Tunisian National Police who was eager and ready to be transformed into one of his country's finest. There was however, one major problem — Zahfori could not hit the proverbial broad side of a barn even if he was only ten meters from it. This may have stemmed from the fact that he was a former member of the Camel Corps and was armed with a WWII Enfield .303 caliber rifle while patrolling some remote border post. Pistols were alien to him, but his difficulties might have been less complex and could have simply been attributed to his lack of trainability. Regardless, he was a great little guy and one that Todd and I befriended from day one. It became a ritual that when Zhafori was about to move up on the firing line, all other personnel with half a brain would check their body armor, helmets, and their defensive location in relation to Zharfori's muzzle. We had a phrase that we would shout to the shooters as they were about to fire their weapons — "pick-up your front sight." In other words, focus on it prior to pressing the trigger. Old Zahfori would take this admonition literally and would physically pick-up (elevate) his front sight and immediately slap that trigger like a wild man. This usually resulted in the nine-millimeter projectile being launched over the high protective range berm and screaming its way towards the nearby town. After frequent kicks up the ass, he would just smile with that big old toothless grin but remained none the wiser from our individual instruction.

Coming from more developed, wealthy, and organized countries, we tend not to appreciate how the rest of the world lives and gets by day-to-day. Traveling the globe has allowed me to realize one thing — I am extremely fortunate to be living in America and even though we all bitch and moan, 75-percent of the world survives under conditions that we would consider sub-standard and unacceptable.

Suriname is a third world country that truly fits that classification. The people are wonderful, but it's one of those places of poverty that has you always looking over your shoulder as you barrel down the pot holed dirt roads on the way to town. Road rules are non-existent and on-coming traffic can come from either side of the road. It was a strange experience hearing natives speak Dutch in a predominantly Black country. Amado Gayol, Bob Taubert, and I were conducting a firearms and VIP protection course for the Minister of Defense's personal security detail. He was on the hit list of the local Cuban-trained Communist party and we felt uneasy when we did a security survey of his residence under the watchful and wary eye of his AK47-toting military guard. During one training day, a motorcycle courier showed up at the range and delivered a large envelope to the students. In it was the opposition's poster for a political rally and its subtle meaning was that they knew what we were up to and that they were watching us. At the end of training that day, we returned to our quarters with all pistol magazines and pistol fully loaded and an enhanced sense of awareness. The students were a challenge, and with their mix of questionable weaponry ,were still using one-handed, bladed techniques to engage hostile targets at all distances. We began introducing them to more contemporary techniques and they expressed amazement of over how shooting had progressed.

Regardless of what the government says, Peru continues to have a credible terrorist threat from the severely injured, but surviving, Shinning Path and Tupac Amura factions. In December, 1996, we were hosting a team of Peruvian police officers and an interesting thing happened. It was week six of the course and we invited the delegation leader to give us a presentation on any interesting operations they had been involved in. The major quickly accepted and the next day he took control of the classroom. For an hour, he gave us an excellent overview of a notable operation they had successfully conducted against the notorious Tupac Amura Revolutionary Movement (MRTA). He explained how they had wiped the organization off the face of the planet by killing some and imprisoning 400 others. His officers were cheering and encouraging him as he described in detail how the mission was accomplished. It was your typical emotionally filled South American tale of balls and bravery. By the time the presentation had concluded, they had worked themselves up into frenzy and we complimented them on their achievement.

I remember the following work day morning Matt yelling to me as I dragged myself out of bed, "Hey Kiwi — check this out quick." Holy shit! I couldn't believe what I was seeing. A band of Tupac Amuro terrorists (that no longer existed because they had been "annihilated") had seized the Japanese ambassador's embassy-residence in Lima and were holding approximately 600 hostages. At 0800 hours when we walked into the classroom, the Peruvians were sitting there with their heads hanging low. Our boss, Bob, walked in and spoke to the delegation leader. "Major, it appears that there has been a minor uprising in Lima. I will make immediate arrangements for you and your men to fly out today and join your countrymen in resolving this incident."

"Oh, please, no, Bob," was his immediate reply. I believe the Major knew something we didn't and that this was not a minor incident, but rather a major terrorist attack that would test his country's counter terrorist capabilities to the limit. As far as he was concerned, he would rather remain safely ensconced in the United States, and, hopefully, by the time he got back the problem would be over. Unfortunately for him, the incident lasted for over four months and the day after the class's graduation the boys reported to the embassy perimeter for duty.

In 2001 I was working with Fujimorie's successor, President Toledo, and his security detail during the general election. It is interesting to see how resources and manpower are utilized in this and similar countries. It is usually a family affair with a relative acting as head of security and he, in turn, hiring other family members and close friends to form the protective detail. Fronting up in front of the president's residence was an instructor's nightmare. What I saw was an eclectic array of clothing, footwear, weapons, and holsters that left me shaking my head and wondering how these guys functioned as a team protecting a head of state. And their weapons discipline and skill were as bad as they looked. However, they were willing to learn, and learn they did.

During one of my trips to Venezuela, two federal officers and I were tasked to fly into a cross border area near Columbia to conduct a reconnaissance in preparation for an impending operation. I was about to conduct in country training for the officers that revolved around jungle operations. This would be done in a series of phases, starting with a course in a secure location in central Venezuela. Next we would deploy to a staging camp on the Venezuelan side of the border to acclimate ourselves and conduct patrolling and reconnaissance missions. The final phase would involve linking up with an army group to locate Colombian narco-terrorists who were penetrating into Venezuelan territory to establish safe-haven base camps. From these camps they would distribute their drugs and also perform direct action hit-and-run missions against Colombian soldiers who were searching for them. They would then be seen scuttling back across into Venezuelan territory where they considered themselves safe and sound.

Our small aircraft was held under armed military guard twice during re-fueling stops somewhere in the middle of the country. The soldiers did not give a shit about who we were or what we were doing. We were immediately disarmed, silenced, aggressively searched, and had our aircraft torn apart for contraband. What the hell, I thought. If these are the good guys, I sure didn't want to meet the bad bastards. We finally made it to our destination and picked up a local informant on the border who guided us into the vicinity of terrorist locations. I don't know which was worse, flying evasive maneuvers at 100 feet above the ground to avoid enemy fire or being held at the mercy of a 19-year-old Venezuelan soldier nervously covering you with his finger on the trigger of his .308 rifle. No one trusts anyone in these countries, and a lot of innocent people have paid the ultimate price because of police and military incompetency.

For many reasons other than being an expatriate, one of my favorite countries to conduct training in has to be New Zealand. In 1995, I had the very good fortune and honor to be asked to work with the New Zealand National Police Special Tactics Group (STG) and my excellent working relationship with them has continued to this day. Additionally, I am now working with Prestige Personnel, Ltd. This is a top-notch security company in Auckland, run by former STG operators Andre Chatfield and Darren (Tex) Morton. My initial association with the STG occurred in 1981 when, as a member of the SAS counter-terrorist team, we periodically cross-trained with them. It was very gratifying to see the professional progress they have made since those early days. Under the leadership of Chief Inspector Neville Mathews, the team's operators have developed into an extremely competent unit through sheer dedication, pride, and commitment.

My good friend, Peter McCarthy, from the Christchurch police STG has been extremely instrumental in his team's training and development over the years. Pete's motivation and drive and professional approach rivals, and may exceed, that of any dedicated American special operations officer.

Each time I have journeyed to New Zealand to train, our Aussie comrades have flown across the Tasman Sea to participate. Under the initial leadership of Victoria's Special Operations Group Sergeant, Marty Keogh, and subsequently, Darren Harris, their operational capabilities have progressed by leaps and bounds — fair dinkum, mates!

If you asked me which country I enjoyed working in the most, I could not begin to decide. Each one has its own unique appeal, and depending on what type of job I was involved in performing, my experiences differed. I am not much of a tourist, so that aspect of traveling has never been a consideration. Working in Sudan at the outset of their conflict was exciting and I enjoyed it, but so was staying in the presidential suite of Rome's most famous hotel. Each experience was just that — an individual opportunity to expand one's horizons and sample this great world of ours on someone else's dime.

A famous author of military sagas once said that to know your enemy, "You had to read his books, eat his food, and sleep with his women." This absorption and appreciation of culture applies to understanding foreign societies in general, and as a professional I pursued two elements of this sage advice with gusto.

Countries that Duke and Alan have operated with or in:

Afghanistan
Argentina
Australia
Austria
Azerbaijan
Belgium
Bolivia
Brazil
Bulgaria
Canada
Colombia
Costa Rica
Dominican Republic
Ecuador
Fiji
Finland
France
Germany
Guam
Guinea
Hungary
Israel
Italy
Jamaica
Japan
Jordan
Lithuania
Macedonia
Malaysia
Mexico
Namibia
New Zealand
Norway
Papua New Guinea
Paraguay
Peru
Poland
Puerto Rico
Singapore
Taiwan
Thailand
The Netherlands
The Philippines
Republic of China
Sierra Leone
Solomon Islands
South Africa
Sudan
Suriname
Sweden
Switzerland
Tunisia
United Kingdom
United States
Uruguay
Venezuela
Vietnam

Last Hurrah

Duke's Story

Body Guarding in the Philippines — 2002-2003

After the Solomon Island's fiasco, which barely caused a ripple in the New Zealand media, let alone the South Pacific Region, I returned home totally pissed off with the third world scenarios that seemed to dominate my source of employment. Once again, for obvious reasons (military style coup) my contract had been negated well before its scheduled completion date. In the international security business, binding contracts that guarantee remuneration for the full term of proposed employment simply don't exist. If it's cancelled prematurely, there are no pro-rated payments or severance checks. If you were real lucky you might get a pat on the back and a handshake from the boss, but either way it was straight back into the unemployment line. However, with disappointment there are always positives, and in my case this was the first time since 1980 that TeAo and I would live together continuously under the same roof for more than a 12 month duration.

Back on New Zealand's East Coast, my new job description was as follows: "All-round handyman, roustabout, bar manager, and bouncer." Hours of employment were 40 to 80 per week with limited time off and no holidays or vacations included. This assumed contract for employment was at a significantly reduced salary and I was totally under female supervision. My compensation was so reduced that I virtually worked only for my board and lodging and a few perks on the side. TeAo was the boss and my daughter Paula, with Rio, my sister-in-law, were the other full-time employees. Without a doubt, they all worked a damn sight harder than I did. I very quickly came to the conclusion that it isn't easy being self-employed. Those of you out there who rave on about the benefits of this life make damn sure that you go into a venture with both eyes open. For the family it was old hat because they had been toughing it out for the last four years, but for me it was a brand new road and it became quite daunting at times. It was a harsh but necessary apprenticeship and I hoped it would prove to be worthwhile in the not too distant future. We were operating on a strict margin and did not have much time to start realizing a profit.

My usual reactions to bothersome issues were definitely mellowing and I was slowly acquiring some business acumen. Now, I was able to engage in a calming dialogue with unruly patrons and the outcome was much more positive than my earlier responses to deviations in behaviour. The only two occasions that I had reverted to "attacking the attacker" while working in the bar convinced me that it was time to consider changing my tactics. Young studs full of "beer and bullshit," but seriously toughened by working the mountainous forestry land tracts and man-handling large chainsaws and kit while negotiating this torturous terrain, are by no means pushovers. I finally employed a long time friend and relation, "Tiger John" Pohatu ("Puss Puss" to his mates), to straight-arm the occasional problem lad out the front door. He had only one weakness. He preferred to take his pay in drink, but he usually drank a hell of a lot more than his daily rate. Nevertheless, the odd altercation occasionally bubbles to the surface, but this is all part and parcel of traditional East Coast socializing. On one particular evening at the Blue Boar, I observed with a practised degree of detachment, Dick "the Bear" Carlson apply a murderous choke-hold on his top honcho and right-hand man, Charles Collier. Dick was a huge guy, and, for my money, would easily have had an edge on old "Butterbean" in a four-round boxing match. Now in his mid-forties, he lacked the mobility he once possessed as a front row forward for the city's rugby club, but once he got his huge mitts on his intended victim it was usually lights out and an early shower for the unfortunate recipient. Luckily for young Charles, Dick's level of Steinlager consumption had impaired his physical capabilities and the choke-hold was not as efficient as it could have been. Charley was a good guy and a big, rugged individual in his own right, but sometime during the night he apparently had transgressed the Steiny barrier of sensible behaviour and was about to pay the price. Although he was able to deflect Dick's initial lunge, Charles was desperately trying to break free of the huge hand around his throat, while at the same time avoiding Dick's poised, sledgehammer-like fist. He looked like the Christmas turkey dangling from the cook's grip seconds before decapitation. Dick's drinking crew of Hone Collier, Steven Rangiwai, and Thunder Mackie looked on for a few minutes with mild interest while sipping away rather nonchalantly on their handles of Steinlager. This establishment of dominance and display of force between two good friends had to run its necessary course, and if broken up too quickly would rage on through the evening until an all-out and bloody brawl evolved. Eventually and without any obvious signal, the boys casually moved forward and surrounded the belligerents. Displaying considerable expertise in physical arbitration, suggesting this was a frequently practised activity, they pried Dick's pit-bull like grip from Charles's throat and slowly and calmly separated the two battle-weary combatants. A gasping Charles reflexively continued his somewhat unfocused counter-attack and began circling Dick like a sheep-worrying pig dog. Sucking air back into his starving lungs he began to regain his second wind, but some small flicker of sanity prevailed. Gary Walsh, my forestry boss, lumberjack, and brother-in-law, successfully ended the confrontation with a couple of free jugs for the lads and a boost in the jukebox volume of a soothing Al Green melody.

The New Zealand media frequently focuses on the alleged lawlessness of the East Coast region of the North Island. Long time residents find such opinions rather amusing. It is a fact that on the East Coast, men are men, unabashedly macho, and chauvinistic to boot. It is also well known that our hospitality is legendary and those that come as friends are treated accordingly. Nevertheless, many a fool has come from the city and tried to project the, "big deal" impression. If you want to get a good ass whipping or, in Kiwi terms, a good old fashioned hiding, then just start playing it up and big timing it amongst East Coast locals. Your chances of getting through the night unscathed are pretty damn slim as any number of so-called tough guys can attest. TeAo, Paulam and our female Samurim Big Lana Takarangim were well capable of handling the at times boisterous crowds of customers in the Blue Boar. When the odd hassle got past their level of control, Chris Lowe and his 6-foot offsider, Tamahou, were more than happy to assist the cause.

Like golf, bowls, or tennis, in mainstream New Zealand weekend relaxation for many East Coast locals consists of hunting and fishing, or diving along the ocean shoreline for bountiful seafood. This is complemented by traditional Friday and Saturday night socializing at the local drinking establishments. The Blue Boar Tavern and the Ruatoria Hotel, formerly known as the Manutahi, are the only venues open after 7:00 pm, so the pubs are our only source of late night amusement. Joe Parata and his good wife, Aroha, have given the Ruatoria Hotel a sound revamp in both drinking style and hospitality since purchasing the establishment several years earlier. They have helped TeAo and I in many ways with our transition into the Tavern trade and in fact donated and paid for the first Keg of Steinlager to go through the beer taps at the Blue Boar. Such actions are seldom experienced in the modern world and probably unique to the East Coast these days? Patrons from 18 to 80 mingle in the public bars and this is what makes the rural areas of New Zealand so special. Young and old can still have a good time together without any age barrier conflicts. The only time patrons date themselves is when they protest Englebert Humperdink's displacement of Wyclef Jean's sound tracks on the massive and ornate Jukebox.

To make our Blue Boar tourism venture fully operational we needed a few more improvements and, as always, cash flow was the essential ingredient. As a result of this reality, in late December, 2001, once again I strapped on my work kit and for the next seven weeks travelled sixty odd thousand miles around the globe as team leader for an American security detail. In light of the tragic events that occurred several months earlier, air travel wasn't considered the most relaxing mode of transport, and I must confess I had a few anxious moments while personally profiling suspicious-looking fellow travellers on the numerous, but necessary flights.

2002 has started well, and fortunately continued in this vein. Back home for just two weeks, I barely had time to change laundry and recharge the old batteries and I was off again. This time I returned to my old stomping grounds, the Philippines, for another one-year contract. I was pretty chuffed about it and it came at a good time. The deal was sound and my clients were probably the best I have ever worked for. My task was to select, train, and develop several close personal protection teams for three different venues within the archipelago. To initiate a selection process, conduct the training, and then progress to operational tasking is every security team leader's dream. The operational performance and capabilities of these teams would reflect upon my reputation as a trainer / operator. One true test of leadership is how such Teams perform when their mentor or leader is not available. The 3 groups were operational and within 6 months the second phase of continuation training had begun. Close Protection work in the Philippines is no place for dreamers or wannabe's. At some stage the BG teams or individuals will be tested. In most cases, it will not be the Hollywood gun battle or the Ninja punch up, but it will be hair raising and pulse popping and you better be ready to deal with it with as little as drama as possible. My selection process is simple and direct. First and foremost, I needed men with uncompromising attitudes and unswerving loyalty. The other determining factors, besides the obvious weapon and physical attributes, is the ability to think on your feet and react or anticipate problems prior to them eventuating, thus avoiding confrontation and danger for the VIP's.

The impact of Islamic terrorism in the United States has made the personal security aspects of life very real to all Americans. However, in the Philippines and elsewhere this has been a reality of life for many years. Osama Bin Laden's lethal influence and the long-standing problems with the Abu Sayyaff group have made Mindanao a focal point for the war on terrorism. Operational demands ensured that the focus and threat level remain at a high standard, the threat of failure or injury, possibly death, was a constant reminder to the BG teams. Motivation in this contract was not something we had to forcibly endorse or reinforce. My contract called for three months on a 24/7 basis, with two weeks of R&R back in N.Z.

This rotation would continue for the balance of the year and was well within my tolerance level, so I was more than happy with this arrangement.

Ironically, I had been offered a contract in Mindanao some months earlier, but had immediately passed on it. At the time, the thought of doing another year on that wild island was too harsh a mouthful to swallow. Instead, I re-established contact with Phil Cairns and he gladly accepted the contract. Phil had been in-country for three months before I got to my area of operations on a neighbouring island.

In typical Phil Cairns fashion, he loved every minute of his assignment and was attacking every issue that arose at his normal cruising speed of at least 100 miles per hour. When you enter into these overseas contracts and have no home or family to relax with at the end of the day, the job becomes your total focus. Working until the job is done and mission single-mindedness occupy all your waking hours. In my case, I was alcohol-free and diet coke a constant companion; it was strange indeed after years of thrashing the party animal activities whenever the chance made available, to suddenly switch tactics. Many an evening I sat in the infamous "Kiwi Lodge" in Cebu City with the proprietor, Dick, his son, Ken, and good wife. I can tell you now diet coke tastes like shit without any Tanduay rum in it. Nonetheless, as team leader it was my call and all the boys followed this simple rule. For them they could get a few beers in on their day off each week, in my case I could get a few ales down during my three month break at home.

In this new millennium, the Philippines finds itself in the midst of an extremely dangerous and awkward predicament. U.S. Special Forces "advisory contingents" are working out of Mindanao and are sending a clear message to the indigenous Islamic terrorists of the region, and the world at large, that terrorism is a no-win proposition. However, even though the government enjoys numerical superiority, technology, and advanced weaponry on their side, it's proving to be a tough assignment to eliminate the terrorist threat. The country's tough Margaret Thatcher-like, no-nonsense female president has recently included the Kidnap for Ransom Gangs as part of her national cleanup. She identified 21 major KFR groups as priorities that, hopefully, will cease to exist in the near future. With the continued existence of the Communist New Peoples Army, Muslim independence forces, and numerous other illegal terrorist and revolutionary factions, the Philippine military and police have their work cut out for them. The jungle and, somewhat less, the cities (excepting crime ridden Manila), are the bad guy's turf and they have been waging their style of low intensity conflict for decades, and, like crime, will never completely be eradicated.

During my first six months in this troubled theatre, the militants have hammered the neighbouring island of Mindanao and General Santos City repeatedly. The two main shopping malls have been burned to the ground leaving only one of any significance for the already hard pressed local population. Subsequently, Muslim fanatics, allegedly led by one Basid Usman, an Indonesian trained explosives expert from the ASG, bombed a group of innocent civilians. Purposely avoiding a military, or "hard" target, Usman instead planted an improvised explosive device in a trishaw. It riddled the area, killing 15 and injuring 50, most of them women and children. Revenge was certain, and days later government forces caught and shot four so-called ASG fanatics in the coastal area of Gensen. These periodic flare-ups of the island's smouldering conflicts serve as a grim reminder to me that little had changed during my three-year absence. Months later a motorcycle blew up outside a small food outlet in Zamboanga. The home-made bomb (explosives packed with nails etc) killed several locals including a member of the US Special Forces and wounded many more. The question we were all asking ourselves uppermost in our minds. Was this the desperate act of a suicide bomber or simply a case of a terrorist with bad explosive handling techniques? Either option indicated times were changing fast.

The U.S. Embassy announced that the government was offering a reward of up to USD$5-million to anyone who could provide information leading to the arrest or conviction of Abu Sayyaf and his leaders that were responsible for kidnapping an American missionary couple. Originally, three Americans had been kidnapped, but, subsequently, the Muslim abductors had decapitated one. Considering that the original Sayyaf bounty was for USD$1-million, it was difficult to gauge the effect this monetary escalation would have on military and police activity in the region. We are talking about 250 million pesos, and I imagine that a race has commenced and military commanders are out in the bush in force trying to claim all or at least a share of the booty. Weeks later, the bounty paid off. The military located and attacked the kidnappers in their jungle hide-out, and the ensuring battle resulted in one of the Burnhams being killed and the other suffering gunshot wounds to her leg during the rescue. It's amazing what a significant wad of cash can do in this land of contradictions.

Corruption is and always has been epidemic in the Philippines. Across the economic spectrum, confidence in the government, particularly the police and military, have been deeply eroded by the blatant abuse of power. In most countries corruption exists, but usually the bribe or sweetener will enable the deal to go ahead. Over here, the corruption system is corrupted. You pay the bribe, and then one week later you have to pay someone else for the very same service. There is no honour among thieves in these parts.

Civilian confidence in the police is sadly lacking throughout much of the Philippines. For example, a young child was snatched up and held hostage by an obviously spaced out individual in central Manila during the morning rush hour. For several hours, this extremely agitated man, allegedly under the influence of "shabu," the local drug of choice, frantically wandered among the large crowd of gawkers and voyeurs with the poor kid dangling from his arms. The local SWAT team leadership claimed that they could not initiate a rescue without authority from higher headquarters and insisted they had to wait for the green light from above. The only dialogue between the captor and the rest of the world occurred through a reporter and his cameraman who were more interested in making the event the story of the day rather than resolving the situation with minimum violence. The results were predictable and the crack head finally snapped, and in a frenetic frenzy stabbed the boy multiple times with his ice pick. This was all the cops needed and a fusillade of shots followed. The ensuring post-mortem revealed that the seven year old hostage had been shot five times, which included a fatal chest wound. From the dramatic footage shown on live television, it appeared that even the most hesitant could have easily overwhelmed the assailant who was no more than ten feet away from the crowd of spectators. He carried the small child close to his chest and clearly exposed his upper torso and head to the authorities. At seven to ten meters, it was an easy shot, and it would have been swift and clean — right between his glazed running lights.

Subsequently, a shoot out, again in central Manila, went horribly wrong. Two policemen shot it out with several armed payroll robbers, and the end result speaks for itself: one policeman killed, one policeman wounded, no robbers arrested, but ten passing bus passengers suffered gun shot wounds. This is not a blanket indictment of all who loyally serve in this untamed country. I have worked with many Filipinos, both in the law enforcement and military sectors, that I have profound respect for.

In Cebu, the commanders of the Philippine National Police were extremely professional and efficient, which in turn gravitated to the officer on the beat. Good leadership will promote a sound foundation, and as the old saying goes, "You can't push string, you must pull it," or, in other words, you have to lead by example. Of course, this is much easier said than done.

As a result of all this chaos, murder, and mayhem, the rich and famous no longer have the time or inclination to gamble with these safety issues and have opted for private security. The business and commerce leaders of the ASEAN region should emulate their South American counterparts and generate the necessary funds at the corporate level to ensure that military and law enforcement personnel receive proper guidance, equipment, and training from established private companies and contractors. Without competent police and military forces, this country will never see peace and ultimately prosperity. Conversely, all this turmoil and paranoia creates employment for guys like me, and many others involved in the security industry. Since September 11, security is no longer a dirty word, but embraced with open arms by those with too much to lose.

Although I frequently tire of this nomadic lifestyle, it is probably going to be difficult to eventually give it up. Then again, I have made serious decisions before on my pathway through life with surprising ease. So perhaps it will be no big thing when it happens.

Timing is always critical, and our East Coast "Plan B" is nearing fruition.

"Duke and TeAo, host and hostess of the Blue Boar Outfitters and Guides For The Ultimate Kiwi Outback Adventure."

Yeah, I like the sound of that.

Soldiering On

Alan's Story

Afghanistan — 2002

I had operated in a number of third-world countries before, but this one topped them all. There was stunned silence among our team as we departed the airport and wove our way through filthy streets littered with garbage and crowded with desperate looking people. Seeing it on television from the comfort of our living rooms fails to do it justice — it is a thousand times worse. We had just arrived in Kabul, Afghanistan, a country and capital with no infrastructure and nothing to offer its citizens but vague hope. If there is a hell on Earth, we had just landed in it.

Alan next to captured Soviet tank – East Kabul, 2002

I was part of an American security team charged with selecting and training indigenous personnel to protect President Karzai, the country's new head of state. Working with foreigners was not new to us and we fully appreciated potential operator limitations and could predict the standard that they would probably achieve after an intense training period. However, our most difficult task would be inculcating the intangible attributes of trust, honor, and loyalty. Those vital traits are readily grasped by first-world operators, but try instilling them into people who have not only been fighting foreign invaders but each other as well for centuries.

In mid-2002 I received a call from my buddy, Mike, who had initially hooked me up with the U.S. State Department in the early 90's. Mike had progressed up the bureaucratic ladder and was now in charge of making this extremely challenging and difficult task happen. I couldn't think of a better guy to do this because Mike had the intelligence, determination, and experience to pull it off. When he informed me that Matt, our other former state department running mate, had already opted for the deal, I signed on immediately. As far as I am concerned, there are no two more competent guys to have around in a country that had a well-earned reputation for danger. The remainder of our team was also made up of highly experienced professionals. The majority of them were former military Special Forces veterans who had been on the circuit for years. Among them, I don't believe that a world hot spot existed in the last decade that they had not worked in either as military operators or civilian "contractors."

After a brief stay in Tashkent, Uzbekistan we boarded our C-130 and headed south over snowy peaks toward Kabul. As we descended, Matt and I could easily spot the odd bomb crater and ruins among the scattered villages that occasionally dotted this barren, mountainous region. Most served as remnants of the recent U.S. led invasion to oust the Taliban from power, but the most stark reminders dated back to the Soviet invasion. The U.S. campaign was nothing compared to the rubble we saw that was left by the Soviets after their unsuccessful 1980's war against the Islamic and American-backed Mujahaden. Bombed out villages were in evidence around our camp and vast graveyards of Soviet tanks, artillery pieces, Mig fighter jets, and armored personnel carriers dominated the landscape in places. It was incredible to see and nothing had been rebuilt from those days. People were scratching out a living in the midst of this bombed out carnage as if nothing had occur-red. One such area behind our camp resembled "Stalingrad" as it appeared in the movie, "Enemy at the Gates."

A shot-down Mig – a remnant of the Soviet conflict – lying in front of a bombed out Taliban base – a remnant of the U.S. campaign of 2001.

A Soviet tank graveyard just outside our camp – East Kabul

Driving through Kabul was a singular experience. Road rules are non-existent as you weaved your way in and out of broken down or slow vehicles, donkey carts, push carts, one-legged war veterans, and a hoard of kids giving you the thumbs up sign. The winter air was heavy with smoke and smog and stunk like hell. We habitually coughed up shit from our lungs, and, just like the locals, deposited it with interest onto the dusty roads. The only thing that gave us some degree of comfort was that we were heavily armed and locked inside our armored Humvees as we squeezed through the crowded streets bumping the less formidable out of the way.

Luckily, Mike had selected a great spot for our command post, located about twenty minutes east of downtown Kabul on the road to Jalamabad, Pakistan. Not only were we distanced from the filth of the inner city, but we were also nestled among thousands of troops from the UN-led International Security Assistance Force (ISAF). Our compound was constructed in the middle of a former Taliban camp that was quite active until American aircraft visited it. However, they were careful to bomb only the officer's quarters, headquarters, command centers, and logistical areas, but left the barrack blocks still standing for the ISAF and troops of the new Afghan Army to occupy.

Our humvees following a truck load of local Militia gunmen – downtown Kabul

The downside of being settled amongst the ISAF troops was that we were also considered a target for the nightly rocket attacks that were directed towards the troops. As the holy month of Ramadan (November) came to a close, the intensity of the attacks grew and sporadic hits of between 1-7 rockets were normal. The ISAF troops would respond by firing flares and dispatching aggressive patrols to search the area for the attackers. Nightly patrols were increased around our base, and major vehicle checkpoints were established on the main road from Jalalabad to Kabul. Last night, President Karzai's palace received a near hit but luckily there were no injuries reported. I am sure the President understands that he is not allowed to die until our mission is complete and our bank accounts have been credited with that good government money! Everything here seems to revolve around luck, so let's see if my luck can hold out for two more weeks.

As we settled into our preparation routine, the advanced party which preceded us continued the candidate selection process. Personnel selection in itself was a daunting task. At least 90-percent of them were either illiterate, or from the "wrong" tribe, mentally unsound, missing limbs, or suffered from poor health. In addition, we had to guard against attempts to infiltrate the camp security force by al Quida or the Taliban for obvious reasons. President Karsai had narrowly missed being assassinated by one of his personal protection officers a few weeks prior to our arrival. Out of one hundred applicants, five to ten might be deemed suitable candidates.

There were many issues to contend with once training commenced. We had to teach them to safely handle and shoot a variety of small arms and heavy weapons not usually found in VIP protection amories, driving safely as part of an armored motorcade, and to operate as an organized and coherent team. When instructing students engaged in VIP protection, hygiene is usually a given. You may have to sharpen their dress code, but normally you don't have to tell them to brush their teeth and comb their hair... However, in this situation, we had to take these men from the cities and mountains and teach them all aspects of personal hygiene and we weren't looking forward to it. If they were to carry out their tasks in extremely close proximity to the president and other VIP's, they had to be clean and presentable. Again, that might seem relatively simple to achieve for a Westerner, but we do not dress in robes and blankets, wear sandals everywhere — even in bitter winter — lack bathing water to use on a regular basis, and clean our butts with our left hands. I was relieved that I was on the weapons team and not a member of the medical and health cadre!

It is universally considered to be a social norm that first impressions are lasting ones. I was scheduled to spend the next 30 days with these people, while the remainder of the team was here for another six months. I felt the country was somewhat divided about the U.S.-led war and occupation of their country. Talking to the younger guys (you never spoke to or even had access to the females) was always interesting as they were totally against the backward, fundamental ways of the Taliban. They wanted nothing more than for the U.S. to lead their country toward democracy and development. The older men were a different kettle of fish, however. The evil looks that we got from them as we drove through the streets were frightening, to say the least. It did nothing to enhance the relationship that we were trying to foster, but rather just made us tighten our grip on our carbines and prepare for the worst.

The Afghan "warrior," with his British .303 Enfield rifle followed by his AK47 in modern times, developed a reputation as a legendary and fierce fighter. This may be true but I have trained enough of these types of people to state that they will never be able to muscle it man-on-man with the western world military powers of today. The Russians were beaten because they made the mistake of leaving their occupied Afghan cities and chasing the Mujahadeen into their territory — the mountains. Third-world countries such as Afghanistan have neither the technology, training, nor sophistication to be a formidable foe. I guess that for young soldiers of today, if there was to be a war then let it be against people like this rather than militarily-developed and more advanced countries.

Kids fighting for our .50 caliber brass after a range practice.

Since the Taliban were ousted, the women are enjoying an unprecedented degree of liberation. Many of them are walking around without the traditional and oppressive blue Berka completely covering their bodies, but it continues to be a slow process. The tempo of transition still depends on the husband's attitude regarding how he will allow his wife or daughters present themselves in public. It is not uncommon to see the men sitting around chatting as the women and girls slave away in the fields. Obviously, some of the men are still living in the Stone Age and attitudinal changes will not occur during their lifetime.

People outside of our community often look at guys like Duke and me sideways and wonder what the hell we are doing and why on earth would we want to subject ourselves to these primitive conditions and dangers. I cannot speak for Duke, but I am sure that his reasons are similar to mine. At the age of 21 I joined the SAS and that was when my life dramatically changed. I was now working alongside some of the most competent men in the world. They were supremely motivated and more loyal to each other than they were to their families. We were entrusted with our country's greatest responsibilities and challenges and it was up to us to achieve these goals no matter what obstacles we encountered. The quality of the man is always paramount and what is ultimately important to me. The technological advancements that we have witnessed since the Gulf War are critical and that is why there is not a country in the world today that could successfully challenge the might of the United States in a conventional conflict. For me, when my butt is on the line, it is the men like the ones that I operated with in the SAS and other Special Forces units worldwide, as well as the young police officers on my SWAT team in Mississippi, the slum patrollers in Brazil, and the professionals I am sharing this current hellhole with that make the ultimate difference — the sacred fraternity of men that you can depend on and entrust your life to. There is no greater feeling among men who pursue the warrior tradition than that.

Soldiering On

Duke's Story

From the Philippines, 2003

2002 has seen the Western World reeling once again from fanatical and suicidal terrorism. The Bali bombing was a tragic wake up call for the Pacific Rim countries and confirmation that they, too, are in the extremist's gunsights. For many third-world countries this is business as usual, and particularly in the Philippines events like this have been all too frequent for the last decade. Long before September 11 and Bali, Philippine government forces were regularly engaged in contacts and running gun battles with a plethora of religious extremists, communist forces, and common bandits that rarely receive global media attention. However, after Bali, terrorism in the Pacific can no longer be ignored.

With the exception of the Olympics, this part of the world has, in my opinion, been guilty of ignoring the al Quieda and Bin Laden phenomenon. Indonesia has always been a concern of the Australian and New Zealand intelligence organizations. With the recent Bali incident, international terrorism, the like of which we have not experienced before, is here, right now, on our respective doorsteps. New Zealand, for obvious reasons, is particularly vulnerable and all of us from "down under" may yet pay a heavy price for this previous disassociation from regional security. Let us not get caught with our guard down. Unless we, as a nation, change our traditional religious affiliations and convert to Islam, then we must ally ourselves with a world power much like Australia has done with America and the United Kingdom.

For those of you who can remember, think back to the Battle of Midway during the South Pacific Campaign of World War II. The American Fleet took on and destroyed Japan's invasion capabilities in one decisive engagement. The Americans didn't start that war, but they sure as hell saved New Zealand and Australia from the probability of hosting Japanese occupation forces. ANZAC's fought bravely along side American GI's in the vicious and no-quarter ground battles in Papua New Guinea, The Philippines, Guadalcanal, and many other bloody Pacific Rim campaigns.

It's a well-established military tenet that it is always better to fight on the other guy's turf, so let's keep it that way.

As a result of Bali and other attacks in our area of responsibility, my bodyguard teams in the Philippines had approached the training with a renewed new sense of urgency. The pucker factor had ratcheted up and the weekly range practices became a priority that no one missed. Weapons retention, CQB drills, and protective formations were no longer treated in a light-hearted or cavalier manner. Several of the operators had already been blooded in this demanding job; it's interesting to observe what a taste of fear and the resulting adrenaline rush can do to a security unit.

I remain a fiercely independent and extremely proud member of the nation of New Zealand, but like my forefathers before me, I fully realize that we need allies in the emerging global struggle. "No Nukes and Clean, Green, New Zealand" are fantastic ideals, but hardly realistic in the current environment. Although important to us, the hardships being experienced in Papua New Guinea, the Solomon Islands, and East Timor, when placed among pressing global issues, are almost irrelevant. Australia and New Zealand valiantly attempt to help, but our limited resources and military capabilities severely curtail our effectiveness.

Unless in the near future we acknowledge that we represent only a tiny place in the antipodes and are rather insignificant without a big brother to align ourselves with, then, in my opinion, we are doomed. This national demise may not occur in my time, but the fact remains that New Zealand and Australia have huge tracts of unpopulated territory and increasingly are becoming an attractive solution for the teeming over-population problems plaguing our Asian neighbors.

We Kiwi's have to take an active and pro-active role in the ongoing struggle against this new breed of terrorism and indiscriminate attacks against our civilization both at home and abroad. Our young men must continue to step forward and answer the call to bear arms if required.

The BG contract was coming to an end for me and, as always, I was not sure where I would go from here. Corwin Noble, a good friend from the U.S.A., advised me of a contract currently running in Haiti; the money was sound and the CP Team of good caliber.

Will Scully, my running partner from Sierra Leone, contacted me and advised me he was working out of Northern Iraq, so once again the opportunities where still coming in. I would catch up with Alan Brosnan early next year, and with a bit of luck we will get a few beers in before we split up and move on once more.

Has my turbulent but adventurous lifestyle been worthwhile? Is my friendship with Alan still as strong as ever, and was writing this story worth the effort?

Without hesitation, the answer to these three questions is, quite simply, "yes."

When I left the SAS in November 1992, TeAo and I had a great send off. In my farewell speech I mentioned there were only three things that meant anything to me as an SAS soldier:

Loyal companions, campaign medals, and the generous Military Superannuating fund.

As a security operator in the big wide world, life is bloody marvelous. I have a wonderful wife and family on the East Coast of New Zealand, four pig dogs, a rat catching cat, an unbroken Pinto filly, Boris the Blue Boar, and three Emus. To top things off, I can get a beer any time of the day or night at the Blue Boar Tavern.

It doesn't get much better than that, and as Alan's brother, Mike Brosnan, the proud owner and publican of Dunedin's Valley Lodge Hotel, would say: "Good on yer, Mate."

Glossary of Terms

22SAS	British Special Air Service Regiment
All Blacks	New Zealand national rugby team
ANZAC	Australian and New Zealand Army Corp. term created after Gallipoli campaign during WWI
AO	Area of operations
Aussie	Australian
Basic All Arms	Every basic recruit had to complete and qualify on this course. From there he would go to his chosen Corps and begin that unit's training cycle.
BRA	Bougainvillea Revolutionary Army
Back squaded	Soldier fails a module of training and has to repeat it
Baggies	New Zealand private soldier, the lowest rank.
Belt Order Pouches	Worn by soldier around waist containing vital survival equipment (ammo, water, grenades, etc.)
Bergen	Rucksack carried by field soldiers.
Boonies	Deep jungle.
Bunker	Below ground fortifications or trenches often linked by tunnels.
"CLAYTONS"	A non-alcoholic drink of the 80's, but promoted as a bar drink. Clayton's signifies something that's not the "real McCoy."
CO	Commanding Officer
CSM	Company Sergeant Major (non commissioned officer rank)
Clubby	N.Z. Regular Force Cadet. Cadets were stationed at Waiouru Military Camp and lived and trained as 16-17 year-old regular force soldiers. Invariably, these cadets advanced through the military system and were for many years the backbone of the professional armed forces.
Corp Training	Advance infantry training after recruit course (following Basic All Arms).
E and E	Escape and evasion
East Coast	New Zealand province where Ruatoria is located.
Delta Force	1st Special Force Operational Detachment (Delta). American equivalent of the SAS, considered by many to be the elite unit of the American Forces.
Digger	Australian soldier.
Dinks	Slang for Vietnamese.
Finder	Pig dog that searches for and locates the pig by scent or sight.

Fire & Movement	One element moves while another element provides an over-watch, or covering fire.
Flying Nines	New Zealand Infantry Battalion transport section in Terendak, Malaysia.
Geylang	The slum and red light area of Singapore in the 70's.
GPM	Garrison Military Policeman or General Purpose Machinegun (7.62mm x 51)
GR	Gold Ridge gold mine located east of Honiara City.
GRA	Guadalcanal Revolutionary Army
Greenpeace	Worldwide environmental protection organization.
Haka	Traditional Maori war dance
Hard bailer	Pig dog that corners a pig until the holders or hunter can move in
Hard Routine	The patrol commander's option of no cooking, smoking or any activity that would alert the enemy.
HiLux	Four-wheel-drive flat deck, single or double cab vehicle.
Hong Kong Bibles	Hard porn written literature printed and purchased in South East Asia.
Holder	Pig dog that secures the pig by the ears or scrotum
IFM	Isatabu Freedom Movement — Guale or Guadalcanal Militant Group
JNCO	Junior non-commissioned officer (lance corporal, corporal)
JTF2	Joint Task Force 2, Canadian Army elite counter-terrorist unit.
KIA	Killed in action
Kina	Sea Urchin — seafood
Kiwi	New Zealander
Koura	Crayfish (called Lobster in the United States) — seafood
LZ	Landing zone (for helicopters)
MEF	Malaitan Eagle Force — militant group
MP	Military policeman
MPAG	Multi-National Police Assistance Group
Maori Battalion	Maoris who volunteered for WWII were assigned to the famous 28th Maori Battalion.
Battle of Midway	Significant American victory over the Japanese Fleet in the South Pacific during WWII.
Marae	Maori tribal meeting house
Mutton	Slaughtered and dressed sheep carcass
NAAFI	Soldier's shopping center and duty free bar in garrison.
National Service	Civilian's called up for military service under ballot system.
Native Schools	First schools for Maoris, started in the late 1800's.

Ngati Porou	Maori tribe originating from New Zealand's East Coast
Nga Puhi	Warring tribe from New Zealand's Northland Province during Maori wars.
Nui Dat	Base camp in South Vietnam for Australian and New Zealand service personnel.
NZSAS	New Zealand Special Air Service
ONCO	Orderly non-commissioned officer — duty NCO
OO	Orderly officer — duty officer
Orderly Room	Where the presiding officer, or the area referring to the "orderly room," heard charge reports.
OSGT	Orderly sergeant — duty sergeant
Otago	Second-most southern province of New Zealand
PNG	Papua New Guinea
PTI	Physical training instructor
Pakeha	European or stranger.
Paua	Abalone — seafood
Pipe Gun	Home-made firearm designed to fire cached WWII ammunition — normally .50 caliber.
Poverty Bay	Province on N.Z. East Coast
Regular Force	Fulltime volunteer soldiers.
RP	Infantry Corps regimental policeman
RSM	Regimental Sergeant Major (senior non-commissioned officer rank)
RNZAF	Royal New Zealand Air Force
RNZN	Royal New Zealand Navy
RSA	New Zealand Returned Servicemen Association — location for veterans to socialize; originally formed as a service club for ex-serviceman from the Navy, but now includes the Army and Air Force.
RSIP	Royal Solomon Island Police
Ruatoria	Township in N.Z. East Coast province
Rugby	New Zealand's national sport.
Rupert	British term for commissioned officer — upper class name
SAS	Special Air Service (United Kingdom, Australia, New Zealand) army special forces and counter terrorist unit.
SAS Wings	Uniform insignia indicating current or former member of SAS.
SEAL	U.S. Navy commando unit — sea, air, and land operators.
SNCO	Senior non-commissioned officer (sergeant, staff sergeant, CSM, RSM)

Stand To	Australians and New Zealanders have adopted this practice from the early Malaysian Confrontation days. Prior to last and first light, all hands sit or lie in their defensive positions, with all equipment on or packed away. This has been determined to be the patrol's most vulnerable time for attack.
SOP	Standard or standing operating procedure
SVN	South Vietnam
Sheila	Australian term for woman
SLR	Self Loading Rifle — 7.62 x 51 MM
Shearer	Man who shears the wool or fleece of a sheep.
Stoush	Punch up or fist fight.
Tabbing	Tactical approach to battle — soldiers term for walking.
TOD	Tour of duty
UD	Unintentional discharge of firearm.
UN	United Nations
USMC RECON	United States Marine Corp's Force Reconnaissance Unit, or Reconnaissance Battalion — elite troops of Marine Corps.
Urupa	Family cemetery.
Ute	New Zealand term to describe a utility vehicle.
Vung Tau	Rest and recreation city for ANZAC personnel in South Vietnam; also hosted the medical teams and hospital, plus numerous aid agencies.
Waiouru Command	Waiouru Military Camp Headquarters
WIA	Wounded in action
Whiskey Company,	W3 COY. Whiskey and Victor were the N.Z. infantry companies assigned to Vietnam who served in SVN, W1 to W3 and V1 to V6.
Whanau	Family
Whareponga	Name given to the original tribal marae of TeAo's family.

NEW ZEALAND

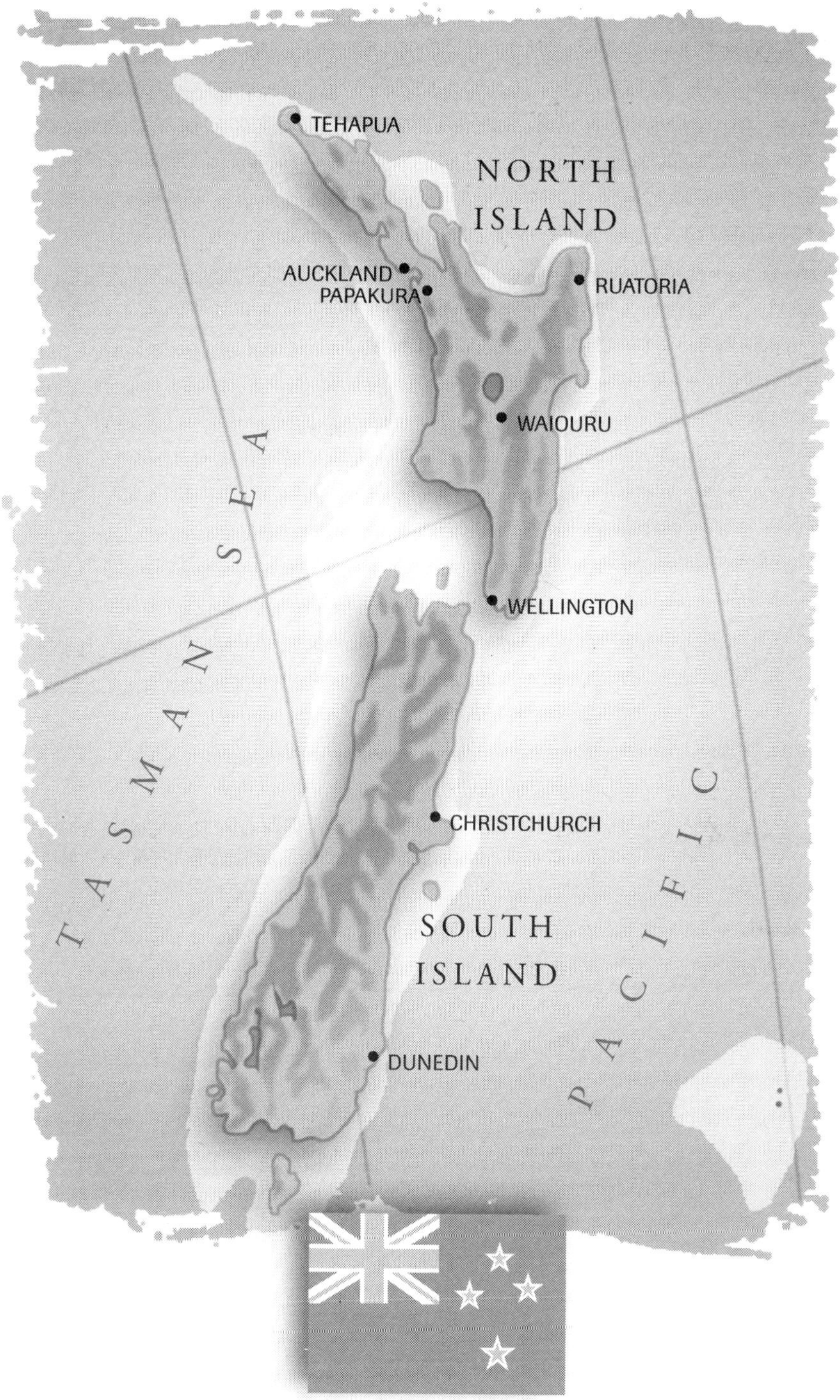
TEHAPUA
NORTH ISLAND
AUCKLAND
PAPAKURA
RUATORIA
WAIOURU
TASMAN SEA
WELLINGTON
CHRISTCHURCH
PACIFIC
SOUTH ISLAND
DUNEDIN

About the Author
Robert Taubert

Bob Taubert

When most men his age are weeding their gardens and watching their grandchildren grow, Bob still seeks the "rattle of musketry."

A two-tour Vietnam veteran as a Marine infantry officer, he followed that with 24 years as a special agent of the FBI. His career with the Bureau revolved around special operations and counter-terrorism and he was one of the early founders of the FBI's Hostage Rescue Team. He specialized in Maritime terrorism and piracy and assisted what was to become the U.S. Navy's Development Group in gaining official recognition as a national counter-terrorism asset by the military.

Through his security company, he continues to impart his skills around the world to police and military special operations entities and predicts that one day we will find him belly up, on the ten-yard line.

He has written hundreds of articles for various firearms and tactical periodicals and this is his first venture into the challenges of a book-length project.